Whitman's Manuscripts

Leaves of Grass

(1860)

Whitman's Manuscripts

Leaves of Grass

(1860)

A PARALLEL TEXT

Edited with Notes and Introduction

By

Fredson Bowers

THE UNIVERSITY OF CHICAGO PRESS

CHICAGO & LONDON

Library of Congress Catalog Card Number: 55-7313

THE UNIVERSITY OF CHICAGO PRESS, CHICAGO & LONDON
The University of Toronto Press, Toronto 5, Canada

To
JAMES SOUTHALL WILSON

From the Barrett Collection

I do not discredit old times

I ~~remember~~ ~~ancient things~~ forget

I returned, to

I ~~have listened to~~ the past — I ~~have~~

    heard the great masters, sat among

    and listened to them

Now if it be eligible let them

    return ~~with the rest~~ and

    listen to me.

~~Antiques of men,~~

~~Ancient of men~~ + Antiques of men,

Ancestors ~~of men~~

~~Antiques of men~~ (16)

Dead ~~po~~ philosophs and priests,

Captains, ~~mothers~~ Martyrs artists,

    inventors, language = ~~makers~~ 'shapers'

    governments long since,

Nations once powerful, now ~~reduced~~,

    withdrawn, or desolate,

      dare

I ~~dare~~ not proceed till I respect=

    fully ~~turn my eyes upon~~ credit

    what you have left,

I own how admirable ~~how is~~

    ~~credible~~ it is — I think none

    can ever deserve more than

    it deserves — I regard it

    fixedly a long while,

Then I take my place for good

    ~~on my own day,~~ ~~in my own days,~~

    ~~on my own ground,~~ with

    my own ~~race it today~~ —

        my own day here.

From "Premonition" [p. 6]; a typical pink-paper leaf

passed through a

remained awhile

Once I pass'd passed through a

celebrated city full of shows, customs,

with wealth, architecture, and

traditions

But now I remember all that

for city city has — now I

remember nothing of all

that city I remember

nothing except that

I wandered day by day, with

one who loved me, love of me,

All else has long been forgotten

by me — But I remember

one rude and ignorant

man who, when I

departed, held me long by the

hand, with silent lip, pale

and tremulous. —

From "Enfans d'Adam" [p. 64]; in the 1860 edition the
sex is changed from 'man' to 'woman'

#14 Calamus=Leaves.
p 360 Live Oak, with Moss.

II.

Not the heat flames up and con=
sumes,
Not the sea=waves hurry in and
out,
Not the air, delicious and dry, the
air of the ripe summer, bears
lightly along white down=balls
of myriads of seeds, wafted,
sailing gracefully, to drop
where they may,
Not these — O none of these, more
than the flames of me, con=
suming, burning for his love
whom I love — O none more
than I hurrying in and out;
Does the tide hurry, seeking some=
thing, and never give up? — O
I, the same, to seek my life=long
lover;
O nor down=balls, nor perfumes, nor
the high rain=emitting clouds,
are borne through the open air,
more than my copious soul is
borne through the open air, wafted
in all directions, for friendship, for
love. —

From "Calamus" [p. 92]; the first leaf of the private notebook containing the original cycle of twelve poems

Foreword

This edition offers a parallel text for a large group of previously un-published Whitman holograph manuscripts with the first printed appear-ance of these texts in the 1860, or third, edition of *Leaves of Grass*. In-deed, these manuscripts represent the final written-out form of the ma-jority of the new poems added to the 1860 *Leaves*. The parallel text in both its parts is a diplomatic reprint, an exact and unemended reproduc-tion of the original documents in all respects save for those differences in type, size, spacing, lining, and paging which result when in non-facsimile manner a printed or manuscript document is given new clothes. However, because of the occasional usefulness for the reader to visualize the physical form of the manuscripts, the line-endings in the manuscript texts are marked by a vertical stroke |.

The manuscripts have been transcribed in the final, revised form that Whitman gave them. Thereupon, by a series of notes I have attempted in a partly narrative manner to reconstruct in these manuscripts the revisory progress from first inscription to the finally achieved version. I do not provide notes to indicate the differences between the manuscript and printed texts in parallel: the reader may see these subsequent revisions with ease by comparing both facing pages. Moreover, since this does not purport to be a variorum edition of the poems in question, I have not collated the variants introduced by Whitman in later editions. Hence the reprinted third-edition text, although it bears the closest relation of any to the manuscripts concerned, does not always represent the poems in the last form Whitman chose to give them.

The order in which the manuscripts are printed is that found in the present arrangement of the papers in the Valentine-Barrett collection. The decision to follow this arbitrary order was not an easy one, for the arrangement does not correspond either to that in the 1860 edition or to Whitman's earlier plans as indicated by the numbers he attached to the manuscripts and by his partially preserved list. For the first, the conven-ience of being able to refer to the folders in consecutive order weighed heavily. For the second, all poems cannot be identified by number or in the list; and thus an attempt to reproduce the complete order he proposed before the proof stage would fail in some details. Moreover, there is some shadow of evidence that Whitman may have abandoned, at least in part, his originally conceived order before he sent the papers off to Rome

Brothers to be set in type for his further consideration. Since the Introduction contains a reconstruction of what can be determined about his early plans for the sequence of the poems, and since the order of the folders falls into the 'cluster' arrangement of the 1860 edition, though not the precise relationship of the 'clusters,' it seemed most convenient for the reader and for scholars consulting this collection to retain the collection arrangement, arbitrary and unauthoritative as it is.

With the exception of the interesting notebook containing earlier drafts of lines for "Premonition" (i.e., "Proto-Leaf" in 1860, and later "Starting from Paumanok"), owned by Mr. Charles E. Feinberg of Detroit, Michigan, the so-called 'Valentine Manuscripts' printed here come from the Library of Clifton Waller Barrett. Prefixed to the general introduction is a listing and short-hand analysis of these to serve as a reference. The folders in which the various manuscripts are now laid, and their arrangement in the 1860 order, were made up previous to Mr. Barrett's purchase of the collection, and of course bear no relation to the order in which the poems were sent to Rome Brothers for typesetting.

In the general Introduction I have described the manuscripts and analyzed to the best of my ability the circumstances of composition and their dates. Here the study and argument has been chiefly 'bibliographical,' with only occasional notice of literary and critical matters outside of textual considerations. The prime purpose of this volume, indeed, has been only to offer full texts for this unique collection of manuscripts, in combination with an analytical study of the history of the documents in which these texts have been preserved. In my own view, the critical possibilities which these manuscripts open up for the study of Whitman as a conscious artist and of his methods of composition and revision are so remarkable that for an editor in his necessarily brief space to attempt any summary evaluation would be an act of supererogation.

My principal debt of gratitude, and it is a large one, is to Mr. Clifton Waller Barrett, who in September of 1951 introduced me to these manuscripts in his collection and subsequently encouraged me to undertake the editing by generously lending them for my convenience to the University of Virginia Library. Mr. Charles E. Feinberg not only called my attention to the Whitman notebook in his collection and the Thayer and Eldridge letter but also generously sent me photostats and gave me his permission to print the material. Mr. John Cook Wyllie, curator of Rare Books at the Alderman Library, University of Virginia, very kindly rechecked for me in my absence from Charlottesville in 1952–53 numerous questions of readings and of paper study. I am especially grateful to him in this as in many other matters. Mr. Michael Papantonio of New York City kindly answered queries about the past history of the manuscripts. I am indebted to the New York Public Library for permission to consult a "Calamus" manuscript in the Berg Collection, and to reprint the Rome Brothers sales list of manuscripts. The Research Committee of the University of Virginia has supported the expenses of the research.

It was my good fortune to find that Professor Gay W. Allen of New York University was writing a new biography of Whitman at the time I was transcribing the manuscripts and attempting to analyze their physical characteristics. Since some of these manuscripts offered fresh biographical clues, with especial reference to the dating by means of a paper study combined with the cross-references that could be established from rejected drafts, I was concerned to offer the transcripts to him; and in return he generously made available to me his private investigations, and the results of the new research to which the manuscripts stimulated him, biographical and factual material of great value to the development of my theories. I am happy to acknowledge his most helpful correspondence with me on various points of interest concerning Whitman, the more especially since my previous experience had not prepared me for the close investigation of the work of a nineteenth-century American poet.

When this Foreword was in page proof the Valentine-Barrett manuscripts, together with much other Whitman material, were presented by Mr. Barrett to the University of Virginia Library, where they have been added to the American literary manuscripts already the gift of this distinguished collector.

CHARLOTTESVILLE, VIRGINIA   F. B.
15 October 1954

Contents

The Valentine-Barrett Manuscripts

Folder	No. of leaves	Whitman's ms. series no. & title	1860 ed. no. & title	"Camden" ed. vol., page	Paper	Footnote Comment
			PREMONITION			
1	33	Premonition	Proto-Leaf	[I, 16–32]	p1 (a, b), tax bl., blue wove, white wove	1
			ENFANS D'ADAM			
2	1	Leaves-Droppings	1	[I, 110]	w2	2
3	3	85/84 You and I	7	[I, 132]	p3	
4	2	82 (pencil)	8	[I, 133–4]	w	
5	1	[none]	9	[I, 134]	w3	3
6	1	80/79 Hindustan, from the Western Sea	10	[I, 135]	p1(c)	
			CALAMUS			
7	1	[none]	1	[I, 137]	w2	
7	7	81 (pencil)	2	[I, 138–9]	w	4
8	4	[none]	4	[I, 142–4]	w2	
9	2	[none]	7	[I, 145–6]	tax bl.	
10	3	V	8	[III, 298–9]	w1(a)	
11	2	VIII/IX	9	[III, 299]	w1(b)	5

1 For full details see the special chart for "Premonition" appended.
2 For an early draft, see folder 20.
3 On the verso of this leaf is a draft for sec. 23 of "Premonition"; there is also a line from "Chanting the Square Deific".
4 The first two leaves are a conjugate fold of smaller white wove paper. The remaining leaves are larger and of a different stock. On the back of these is a draft for an editorial on the Brooklyn Waterworks.
5 The two pieces making up this leaf are pasted together in the back by a strip of the pink paper.

Folder	No. of leaves	Whitman's ms. series no. & title	1860 ed. no. & title	"Camden" ed. vol., page	Paper	Footnote Comment
12	2	VII	10	[I, 147–8]	w1(a, b)	
13	2	III	11	[I, 148–9]	w1(a)	6
14	2	To a New Personal Admirer	12	[I, 149]	w	
15	1	52/51 Buds	13	[I, 149–50]	p2(a)	
16	1	I Calamus-Leaves/ Live Oak, with Moss	14	[I, 150]	w1(a)	
17	1	Confession Drops	15	[I, 151]	tax bl.	
18	2	43 Leaf/Leaflet	16	[III, 300]	p4(b)	
19	2	79/78 Poemet/Leaf	17	[II, 225–6]	p3	7
20	1	[none]	18	[I, 151–2]	w3	8
21	2	II	20	[I, 152–3]	w1(a)	
22	2	34 As of Eternity	21	[II, 228–9]	p3	
23	2	95/94 To a Stranger	22	[I, 153]	p1(e)	
24	1	IV	23	[I, 154]	w1(a)	
25	1	54/53 Prairie-Grass	25	[I, 155]	p1(c)	
26	1	84/83 Razzia	26	[I, 156]	p2(a)	
27	1	44 Leaf	27	[II, 230]	tax bl.	
28	1	71/70 Leaf/Leaflet	30	[I, 156]	p1(f)	
29	1	69/68 Leaf/Leaflet	31	[I, 14]	p2(c)	
30+37	1	[none]	44, 38	[I, 156, 160]	w1(b)	
31	1	[none]	37	[I, 157–8]	w	
32	1	XI	36	[I, 158]	w1(b)	
33	1	IX	34	[I, 158]	w1(b)	
34	1	VI	32	[I, 159]	w1(a)	
35	1	[none]	39	[I, 160]	w1(b)	
36	1	XII	42	[I, 160]	w1(b)	
38	1	?100/101/100 To One Who Will Understand	41	[I, 161]	p4(a)	
39	1	X	43	[I, 161]	w1(b)	

6 For an earlier draft of this, numbered V, see verso of leaf 15 of "Premonition" in folder 1.
7 On the verso is a draft of "Enfans d'Adam" no. 1, folder 2.
8 Bucke, *Notes and Fragments*, p. 51, reprints the verses found on the first leaf from a paper found among Whitman's effects.

TABLE OF MANUSCRIPTS

Folder	No. of leaves	Whitman's ms. series no. & title	1860 ed. no. & title	"Camden" ed. vol., page	Paper	Footnote Comment
40	1	[none]	40	[I, 161]	blue wove	
41	1	?101/102/101	45	[I, 162]	p1(f)	
		CHANTS DEMOCRATIC				
42	16	90/89 Feuillage	4	[I, 206–12]	P5, p2 (c)	
43	6	41 Evolutions/Poemet	7	[I, 292–4]	p1(d, a)	
44	6	A Sunset Carol	8	[II, 278–80]	p1(e)	
45	2	Thought 2d piece in Book	9	[II, 275–6]	p1(e)	9
46	2	Thought	11	[II, 276–7]	p1(c)	10
47	1	To a Historian	10	[I, 4]	white laid	11
48	5	68/67 Orators	12	[II, 157–9]	p1(e)	
49	3	American Laws	13	[II, 160–1]	p2(a)	
50	2	To Poets to Come	14	[I, 15]	w2	
51	2	48 Mediums	16	[II, 262–3]	p1(e)	
52	2	51/50 Wander-Teachers	17	[I, 11]	p2(b)	
53	1	74/73 Leaf	18	[I, 12]	p2(a)	
54	1	76/75 Leaf/Leaflet	19	[II, 162]	p1(c)	
55	2	55/54 Mouth Songs/Songs— always wanted/Leaf	20	[I, 13–4]	p4(a)	
		LEAVES OF GRASS				
56	3	42 Confession and Warning	13	[II, 160]	tax bl.	
57	3	73/72 Night on the Prairies/Leaf	15	[II, 231–2]	p1(c)	
58	2	72/71 Leaf	16	[II, 21]	p1(f)	
59	2	78/77 Leaf	17	[II, 34]	p1(f)	
60	4	35 As of the Truth	18	[II, 257–8]	p2(b, c)	
61	1	As of Origins	19	[II, 31]	p1(c)	

9 On the verso is a draft of verses 53-55 of "So Long" (folder 80).
10 On the verso is a draft of sec. 65 of "Premonition" (folder 1, leaf 33), also containing a line later found in "Enfans d'Adam" in 1860 edition.
11 This was originally conjugate with the leaf in folder 68; on the verso of both are unidentified prose lines.

Folder	No. of leaves	Whitman's ms. series no. & title	1860 ed. no. & title	"Camden" ed. vol., page	Paper	Footnote Comment
62	2	47 Voices		[II, 158–9]	p1(d)	
63	1	70/69 Leaf		[II, 166–7]	p1(c)	12

MESSENGER LEAVES

Folder	No. of leaves	Whitman's ms. series no. & title	1860 ed. no. & title	"Camden" ed. vol., page	Paper	Footnote Comment
64	2	96/95 To One Shortly To Die	21 To One Shortly to Die	[II, 230–1]	p3	
65	1	99/98 To Rich Givers	22 To Rich Givers	[II, 34–5]	p1(d)	
66	1	To a Pupil	To a Pupil	[II, 165]	tax bl.	
67	2	40 A Past Presidentiad	To the States	[II, 39]	p1(c)	
68	1	To a Cantatrice	To a Cantatrice	[I, 11–12]	white laid	13
69+70+72	1	To You secs. 1 & 2	To You / To You	[I, 15; III, 300]	p1(f)	

[SEPARATE POEMS]

Folder	No. of leaves	Whitman's ms. series no. & title	1860 ed. no. & title	"Camden" ed. vol., page	Paper	Footnote Comment
69+70+72	5	57/56 Mannahatta	Mannahatta	[I, 256–7]	p1(d)	
71	20	36 Poem of Joys/ Contact	Poem of Joys	[I, 213–22]	p, w	14
73	5	87/86 France	France	[I, 287–8]	p6	
74	5	82/81 Unnamed Lands	Unnamed Lands	[II, 144–6]	p1(c)	
75	2	56/55 Kosmos	Kosmos	[II, 167]	p1(e)	
76	1	83/82 Hand Mirror	Hand Mirror	[II, 30]	p3	
77	1	53/52 Savantism	Savantism	[I, 12–13]	p2(a)	
78	2	86/85 Says	Says	[III, 301]	p1(c)	
78	1	87/86 Say	—	[III, 301–2]	p2(b)	
78	1	88/87	—	[III, 302]	p1(e)	
78	1	89/88 Say	—	[III, 302]	p1(f)	
79	1	Nearing Departure	To My Soul	[II, 271]	w	
80	7	103 So Long	So Long	[II, 286–90]	blue laid and w1(b)	15

12 On the verso are deleted unidentified verses.
13 The leaf was once conjugate with that in folder 47 and has unidentified prose on the verso.
14 Leaves 1–3, 5–6, 9–10, 13–20 are p1(b); leaves 7–8 are p1(a): leaf 4 is p2(a); leaves 11–12 are white wove.
15 A draft of verses 53·55 is in folder 45. The white wove paper is a paste-over.

[1870–71 Edition]

Folder	No. of leaves	Whitman's ms. series no. & title	1860 ed. no. & title	"Camden" ed. vol., page	Paper	Footnote Comment
8_1	2	Sparkles from the Wheel	Sparkles from the Wheel	[II, 164–5]	white laid	
8_2	1	Fables	Passage to India, sec. 2	[II, 186–7]	white laid	16

Barrett Manuscripts

Folder	No. of leaves	Whitman's ms. series no. & title	1860 ed. no. & title	"Camden" ed. vol., page	Paper	Footnote Comment
(separate)	1	As of Forms	not printed	[III, 266]	$p^1(f)$	
(separate)	1	To an Exclusive	not printed	[III, 267]	p	
100	1		not printed	[III, 267]	p	17

16 For details about the use of this manuscript in its subsequent proof-sheet form, see my "The Manuscript of Whitman's 'Passage to India'," *Modern Philology*, LI (1953), 102–17.

17 This poem is apparently distinct from that entitled "To an Exclusive." On the verso appears the beginning of the numbered list of titles in the order Whitman proposed for his third edition before he evolved the "cluster" principle.

PREMONITION

Leaf	1860 sec.	Paper	Comment
1	1	tax form	Revision of sec. 1 on leaf 2
2	1 (deleted fragment) / 2	$p^1(a)$	
3	3, 4, 13	$p^1(a)$	
4	14	tax form	Revision of sec. 14 on leaf 5
5	14 (deleted) / 16	$p^1(a)$	
6	17, 18, 19	$p^1(a)$	
7	20	$p^1(a)$	
8	23 (deleted)	blue,	Sec. 21 is lower part of leaf 7 pasted at foot of leaf 8. Earlier draft for sec. 23 on verso of Enfans d'Adam no. 9.
	21	$p^1(a)$	
9	21 (concluded)	$p^1(a)$	
10	22	blue	
11	22 (concluded)	blue	

Leaf	1860 sec.	Paper	Comment
12	23, 24	white	Sec. 23 revises leaf 8. Poems transposed by cutting apart the leaf. Drafts for secs. on leaf 13 on verso.
13	25, 27, 28, 35	white	
14	35 (concluded)	white	
	36		
15	rejected	white	Verso contains draft for Calamus no. 11
16	38, 39, 40	white	
	41, 42	p1(a)	Sec. 41 is lower part of leaf 15 pasted at head
17	43, 44	p1(a)	This leaf is the lower part of pink leaf 9
18	45	p1(a)	
19	46, 47	p1(a)	
20	48, 49, 50	p1(a)	
21	51, 52, 53, 54	p1(a)	
22-25	55	p1(a)	
26	55 (concluded)		
	56, 57		
26½, 27	58,	p1(a)	Sec. 58, on the original upper part of leaf 30, is pasted at the head and numbered 26½
28	59	tax form	Deleted title "Aborigines"
29	60	p2(b)	
30	61, 62	tax form	
31	63	p1(a)	The lower part of leaf from which the pink section 26½ on leaf 27 was cut
32	63 (cont.)	p1(a)	
33	63 (concluded)	p1(b)	
	64, 65	tax form	Draft for sec. 65 appears on verso of Chants Democratic no. 11

[The following leaf, printed on one side of the paper, is found among the material pertaining to Whitman in a bound volume containing an early manuscript of "Passage to India" deposited in the New York Public Library by Mr. Oscar Lion in 1954. It appears to be a list offering the manuscripts for sale; but unfortunately it is not dated.]

WALT WHITMAN MANUSCRIPTS

IN POSSESSION OF T. H. ROME, 513 LAFAYETTE AVENUE, BROOKLYN, N. Y.

1 Passage to India.
2 Ethiopia Saluting the Colors.
3 The Singer in the Prison.
4 To Him that was Crucified.
5 To a Common Prostitute.
6 To a Cantatrice.
7 To the Future.
8 To a Pupil.
9 To a New Personal Admirer.
10 To Other Lands.
11 To One a Century Hence, or | any number of centuries hence.
12 To Rich Givers.
13 To You.
14 To One Shortly to Die.
15 To One Who Will Understand.
16 Poem of Joys.
17 Feuillage.
18 Sparkles from the Wheel.
19 A Past Presidentiad and One to Come also
20 Says.
21 That Shadow, my Likeness.
22 Mouth-Song.
23 American Laws.
24 Unnamed Lands.
25 Prairie Grass
26 City of my Walks and Joys.
27 Premonitions.

35 Savantism.
36 So Long.
37 Leaf.
38 Mannahatta.
39 Thought.
40 As to the Truth.
41 Thoughts.
42 To Rich Givers.
43 O Male and Female.
44 A Sunset Carol.
45 Night on the Prairie.
46 Buds.
47 Wander-Teacher.
48 Tests.
49 Voices.
50 Beginners.
51 Paumanok.
52 Hindustan from the Western Sea.
53 Longing for Home.
54 You and I.
55 Poets to Come.
56 A Hand-Mirror.
57 Beginners.
58 Kosmos.
59 As of Origins.
60 As of the Visages of Things.
61 As of Eternity.
62 Leaves-Droppings.
63 Razzia.

28 Confession Drops.

29 Confession, etc.

30 Leaf.

31 Walt Whitman's Caution.

32 France, the 18th Year of These States.

33 One Fleeting Glimpse.

34 Of the Doubts.

64 Fables.

65 Leaf.

66 ,,

68 Calamus Leaves.

Proud Music of the Sea Storm. (Dr. I. H. Platt.)

Thou Vast Rondure Swimming in Space. (U. S. Scollay.)

[short rule]

The manuscript of the first edition (1855) was accidentally destroyed in 1858.

Introduction

I. *The Valentine-Barrett Manuscripts*

The Walt Whitman poetical manuscripts in the Library of Clifton Waller Barrett represent the largest single accumulation in existence of Whitman's holograph verse. In this collection the previously uninvestigated and unpublished[1] Valentine manuscripts are of singular importance since they comprise the holograph for the majority of the new poems first appearing in the third edition of *Leaves of Grass* printed in Boston by Thayer and Eldridge in 1860. It is this third edition and, specifically, its added poems which have attracted the especial attention of recent Whitman scholarship as representing the *Leaves* in perhaps their most dynamic and personal form.

This particular group of manuscripts has been handed down with the tradition that it had been preserved by Rome Brothers, Whitman's Brooklyn printers and friends.[2] At some unknown date the manuscripts were sold by them to the New York autograph dealer W. R. Benjamin, who in turn disposed of them to Patrick Valentine. In 1929 or 1930 the collection was purchased by Gabriel Wells, and from him by Barnet J. Beyer. On Mr. Beyer's death the manuscripts came to Clifton Waller Barrett through the Seven Gables Bookshop.

The manuscripts are at present inclosed in green cardboard folders, the collection containing 79 separate folders in all, numbered 1–82. (One folder has a double number, and another a triple designation.) It is known that Mr. Beyer made up the present folders. Very probably he also wrote in the pencil annotations now found on most of the manuscripts which identify them with the appropriate poems in the 1860 edition. An earlier set of folders containing the separate manuscripts before Mr. Beyer's purchase arrange the poems roughly in their 1860 order. The present folders ordinarily follow the sequence of the poems within the sections of the 1860 edition but alter the order of the sections to "Premonition," "Enfans d'Adam," "Calamus," "Chants Democratic," "Leaves of Grass,"

---

1 At some date before 1921 Professor Emory Holloway had limited access to the Valentine collection and from it reprinted (although without record of the revisions) the important short poem found in the 1860 edition of *Leaves of Grass* as "Enfans d'Adam" no. 9: see his *Uncollected Poetry and Prose of Walt Whitman* (1921), II, 102.

2 Fortunately, the tradition can be proved. What appears to be a Rome Brothers printed sale list has been preserved, for which see below.

"Messenger Leaves," and finally those separate poems under no specific heading.[3] There seems to be no special significance to this arrangement, although within the "Calamus" section there is a slight dislocation of the 1860 order of the poems, apparently due to following the order of the "Camden" edition. In the 1860 edition the general arrangement was "Proto-Leaf" (the "Premonition" of the manuscripts), "Chants Democratic," "Leaves of Grass," "Enfans d'Adam," "Calamus," "Messenger Leaves," and the separates, these groupings being interspersed with poems taken from the second edition of 1856. From the history of their preservation nothing can be determined, therefore, about the arrangement in which the manuscripts were received by Rome Brothers; and from what seems to be the Rome Brothers sales list it is clear that the printer did not preserve the initial arrangement. The list mixes poems of different dates and editions, duplicates one, and in general has no rationale for the order of its items. We shall be dependent, therefore, on internal evidence for a further inquiry. The chief value of the printed sales list is that it establishes the ownership of most of these manuscripts by Rome Brothers.

A question of very considerable importance is the relation of these manuscripts to the 1860 Boston edition, for since they came from the shop of Rome Brothers in Brooklyn they could not have served as printer's copy for Thayer and Eldridge. At the time Emory Holloway saw the Valentine manuscripts, he found among them a "letter from T. H. Rome to Walter R. Benjamin, in which he states that from 1858 to 1872 'we set up and struck off proofs of a large collection of Whitman's poems, which, after correction and revision by the author, were printed in future editions of his works.'"[4]

Unfortunately this letter is not now preserved in the Valentine papers; but the account of it by Holloway not only helps to establish the history of these manuscripts but also suggests their relation to the 1860 edition. From another source comes confirmation of Whitman's practice in these years. Preserved in the Houghton Library of Harvard University is a manuscript of "A Passage to India" with an accompanying letter dated 15 March 1870 from Whitman, written on stationery from the Attorney General's Office in Washington, D. C. Addressing his 'dear friends' Andrew and Thomas Rome, he encloses a postal order for ten dollars and

---

3 The last two poems in the collection, folders 81 and 82, were first printed in 1871. It would seem that they were composed later, not that they were withheld from the 1860 edition.

4 Holloway, *I Sit and Look Out* (1932), pp.

19–20. To this Holloway adds the footnote: "The letter and a list of the poems I have examined in the Valentine Collection. Many of the poems listed were later included in the 1860 edition."

requests that the manuscript be set up in type, proofread, and proof returned. Also in the Houghton Library are two large sheets containing the poem set up in three columns of galley proof, presumably an extra pull from the typesetting though in a corrected state.[5]

There is an added interest in this manuscript at Harvard (as also in the earlier version deposited in the New York Public Library), for Whitman pasted in it, in lieu of writing out, a printed version of part of section 2 of "A Passage to India" which was formed from the poem "Fables" in the Valentine collection (folder 82), one of the two manuscripts in the collection which postdate the 1860 edition. The typesetting for this fragment of printed text does not correspond to that in any edition (and indeed the poem was never independently printed); moreover, its text is that as found in the Valentine manuscript form, which was altered in the Harvard manuscript in a few respects to that printed in the Harvard proof sheets and later in the first edition of 1871. It seems clear, therefore, that this piece of printed copy pasted to the Harvard manuscript is another example of Rome Brothers proof, in this case of the poem "Fables" in the Valentine collection. The proofs for another poem, manuscript unidentified, were similarly used in "Passage to India."

Thus it would seem that at an advanced stage of Whitman's preparation of his third edition of *Leaves of Grass* he ordered printed copies in proof form of the Valentine manuscripts from Rome Brothers, who retained the manuscripts. When the subsequent unexpected invitation came from Thayer and Eldridge, therefore, it was substantially the revised proofs which served as printer's copy for the added poems in so far as these are preserved in the Valentine collection.[6]

Whitman's purpose in having his poems set up in type by his friends

---

5 For an account of this manuscript and its proofs, together with a reprint of the text, see my "The Manuscript of Whitman's 'Passage to India'," *Modern Philology,* LI (1953), 102–17. An earlier manuscript of the same poem, also with some proof clippings as text, is deposited in the New York Public Library.

6 The alternatives are not easy to accept. The connection of these manuscripts with Rome Brothers is too well established for us to believe that they served as actual printer's copy for Thayer and Eldridge; moreover, the wide variance sometimes found between the holograph and the printed text goes farther than could reasonably be expected from normal proof alterations. It is true that the manuscripts exhibit no traces of handling by the printer, but neither does the Harvard manuscript of "A Passage to India" which was certainly that set up by Rome Brothers. Hence we must suppose that the Valentine papers were actually typeset for proofs, since the alternative—that Whitman made fair copies of them for Thayer and Eldridge—is fantastic. As contributing evidence in favor of this position we have the letter of T. H. Rome to Benjamin, the Rome printed list, and Whitman's 1870 letter to Rome Brothers. The copy finally submitted to Thayer and Eldridge must have resembled closely that part of the Harvard manuscript of "Passage to India" which employs segments of proof sheets.

is somewhat obscure. To some extent, perhaps, he was using them as a modern author would employ a typist, although on the evidence of the price ($10) he paid for "A Passage to India" the cost was materially heavier even in those days of cheap printing. It would seem that the ex-printer Whitman had some concern for the visual appearance of his verses on the printed page and therefore wished to make his final revisions in typeset copy.[7] Since Rome Brothers had been his earliest printers, it is just barely possible that in his original plans for the third edition, when it appeared that he might be forced to put it out himself, Whitman had in mind that to save expense the standing type of his proof sheets might perhaps be utilized in the final printing.[8] However, when Thayer and Eldridge offered to publish the next edition, Whitman went to Boston in March, 1860, to prepare and see the edition through the press. The Rome Brothers typesetting was of no use for the Boston edition, but the proofs, revised, would have been the logical printer's copy to offer his new publishers.

The Valentine manuscripts, therefore, represent Whitman's last holograph copy for most of the poems added in 1860. But these papers did not serve as actual printer's copy. Instead, proofs—now lost—pulled from the typesetting made by Rome Brothers from these manuscripts were revised, sometimes very heavily, and these proofs plus new manuscript served as printer's copy for the Thayer and Eldridge edition. Critical estimates of Whitman's alterations between manuscript and the 1860 printed text must take into account this intermediate stage; but since the proofs are not preserved, one cannot tell precisely which alterations were made before turning the copy over to Thayer and Eldridge, and which in the Thayer and Eldridge proof. One would suppose, of course, that most of the revision was accomplished during the interval between the delivery of the proofs and their use as printer's copy. There is nothing in Whitman's letters from Boston to indicate more than mechanical proofreading there.

The date at which these manuscripts were turned over to Rome Brothers for typesetting, and the allied question whether they were sent to the printer in one batch or at several times, are matters of some interest. That

7 It is worthy of note that many of the alterations of poems in successive editions of *Leaves of Grass* consisted in the rearrangement of lines to form new verses.

8 The evidence to be presented later suggests that the manuscripts were sent to Rome Brothers only when Whitman was preparing to move in the matter of a third edition. Thus the interval in which the type would be standing need not have been very long, according to his original plans. However, there is no evidence to support this guess about the possible plans to use standing type, and we know from the Harvard "Passage to India" that Whitman was prepared to order this preliminary proof even though the volume was to be printed elsewhere.

the entire group of manuscripts (less the final two poems first printed in 1871) was given to Rome Brothers at a single time seems most probable from the evidence of the revisions found in the papers. Whitman went over the majority of these poems on a number of occasions. One or two revising inks cannot be identified with certainty, but at a minimum four respective stages can be traced: revisions in pencil, in a dark ink with a fine pen, in pencil again, and finally in a thin light-brown ink. It is possible that a further round of revision in pencil (perhaps even in ink) followed on the thin light ink. Although not all of these stages are present in every poem, they are scattered throughout the manuscripts with such relative evenness that no group of poems or batch of paper can be isolated as not having undergone in part some revision or addition (or even inscription in some cases) in the light revising ink that represents the final or near-to-final stage. Moreover, it is a most significant fact that the long poem "Premonition" contains all these stages of revision as well as the three major kinds of paper used at various intervals in the expansion of the original group of poems. Thus there is no evidence that some poems were sent off before the final stages of revision, and considerable evidence (including the holes made from pinning them together) that the manuscripts as a whole were kept together for a lengthy period and then released at the same time for setting up into proof.

The exact date is another matter, however. From evidence that will be detailed below in the section on the growth of Whitman's plans for the third edition, we know that on 20 July 1857 Whitman had in mind a particular scheme for the contents and arrangement of the third edition. This plan can be traced in some detail in the Valentine manuscripts. Whitman at this date proposed to use the plates of the 1856, or second, edition for the first thirty-two poems and to add enough new poems to make a total of one hundred. Evidence exists in the Valentine manuscripts to indicate that when the tentative plan to produce an edition in 1857 fell through, the revision of the existing poems and the number of fresh additions caused Whitman after a time to put aside the fixed order of the hundred poems which he had already established. But very late indeed he must still have envisaged some such plan for a long series of ungrouped poems, for two of the poems on the final white wove paper were assigned the numbers 81 and 82 in pencil.[9] The poem numbered 81, the heavily revised draft of what was to become part of "Calamus" no. 2 (folder 7),

9 Original pink-paper No. 81 has not been preserved, but pencilled No. 82 for the early part of "Calamus" no. 2 conflicts with pink-paper no. 82 (earlier revised from no. 81), "Unnamed Lands" in folder 74.

was written on the back of paper which had previously been used to rough out in pencil the draft for what seems to be a proposed editorial on the Brooklyn Waterworks for the Brooklyn *Daily Times,* of which Whitman was then editor. The draft is entitled "Important Questions in Brooklyn" and reads as follows (revisions not being noted):

The most prominent public question in Brooklyn, just now, (co-incident with the April charter election, and of far more permanent importance than that event as to which party succeeds) is one which includes the perfect completion of the Water Works, the mode of their future control and management, and also the inauguration of a grand system of Sewerage.—These involve the welfare, the very lives of many future generations.—The Brooklyn Water Works in all the essentials of their conception and execution, have already taken their place among the first-class achievements of modern science, with the single exception, that of the thirteen miles of aqueduct between Hempstead Reservoir to the great Well Pump only five miles were (by a provision in the original plans) made a permanent closed brick conduit, and the remaining eight miles were to be left a temporary open ditch, an earthen canal of the same general nature as many parts of the old Erie canal of thirty years ago,—which some of our readers probably recollect.—The unanimous opinion of the Board of Water Commissioners, at the instance of all the Engineers from whom they have required opinions,—indeed the common sense of the case, as can be understood by every man of thought and foresight—makes it imperative that this provision should be abandoned, and that this *whole line* should be a continuous brick conduit,—and to make this change the Commissioners and Brooklyn public are now determined—asking legislative authority to that purport.

As to the relative merits of placing the onus of finishing the Works and the future control of them directly in the hands of the Common Council, or in a Board like the present, it is certain that the former would be merging the whole affair in the selfish struggle of politics, to be made spoils of by party victors,—while real specific public interests would be left unattended to and indeed probably violated.—Had the Water Works been from the beginning managed by the contentious Common Council of Brooklyn, instead of such a compact Board as at present, they would be before completion costing the city from ten to twenty millions of dollars, instead of four millions,—would be lagging far behind their present advanced stage—and half the essential work would be ruined by wretched contracts, instead of the job over the whole line being executed under the severest tests and inspectorship. Yet there should be stringent checks, especially financial ones, over the Board of Control; the Common Council should have the Holding of the purse-strings.—

Professor Gay W. Allen has very kindly searched the files of the Brooklyn *Times* for the years 1857, 1858, and 1859 but has not discovered that this editorial was ever printed. In his opinion Whitman discarded the draft in favor of amplifying his remarks, and Professor Allen points to the *Times* editorial of 16 March 1859, as an example. In an editorial on 15 March entitled "Our Brooklyn Water Works—The Two or Three Final Facts, After All," Whitman praises the Water Works and the sweetness of the water, and on the 16th, continuing, he takes up several matters mentioned in the manuscript draft. The low cost is spoken of and the Commissioners are defended from extravagance in making certain alterations. Bickering between the Common Council and the Commissioners is touched on and the Commissioners praised. Whitman then writes: "We had intended to say something also on the subject of the change, recommended by the Commissioners, of the canal between Hempstead and Jamaica into a brick conduit. We will only briefly remark that our emphatic opinion expressed last summer[10] is more than confirmed by all our examinations since. The open earthen canal must be decided to give place to a permanent conduit—it is astonishing to us how there can be a moment's hesitation about it." Finally, Whitman writes of the current dispute whether the Common Council or the Commissioners should be in charge of the operations, and he mentions the Water and Sewerage Bills pending at Albany in his argument that the Commissioners must retain control lest the Council throw the Water Works "into the vortex of selfish politics, little narrow election interests, ward contracts, and all the low and mean turmoil of back room caucuses and struggling for the fat, regardless of the people or of the Works."

This editorial in the issues touched on coincides so closely with the draft editorial in the Valentine papers as to make it almost certain that the draft must have been written very shortly before 16 March 1859. Charter elections were municipal elections, so called from the charter providing for such elections originally granted by the state legislature. On 4 March 1859 the *Times* ran an editorial, "The Spring Election," about the contests for the municipal offices to be held on 5 April. At this time, as mentioned in the draft, there was a bill pending in Albany regarding the duties of the Water Commissioners; moreover, there was local agitation, led by Alderman Backhouse, to strip the Water Commissioners of their powers and transfer these to the Common Council. On 15 April, however, the state legislature passed the Water and Sewerage Bills substantially as recommended by Chief Engineer Kirkwood, whose views Whitman had been advocating.

There seems little doubt, therefore, that the unpublished editorial must be dated shortly before 16 March 1859, that the paper was then

10 See the editorial for 5 June 1858, "Progress of the Brooklyn Reservoir."

torn up and at some subsequent date, probably not too far removed, used for drafting the original part of "Calamus" no. 2. This is the only sure date we have to work with. However, these particular leaves form part of a chain of evidence connected with the poems on white wove paper which shows that the poem in question cannot be isolated as material sent to Rome Brothers at a later date than the body of the Valentine manuscripts. As will be worked out more fully in the section on "Calamus," the inscription of these leaves must have preceded that of other poems on the white wove paper which exhibit one or more of the revisory stages found in "Premonition."

The second piece of evidence is not so exact as one would wish, but in combination with the known facts about the use of the white paper it carries considerable weight. From a Whitman notebook containing other material dated 26 June 1859, Holloway reprinted an unpublished poem (*Uncollected Poetry and Prose*, II, 91). I quote the opening lines:

> Comrades! I am the bard of Democracy
> Others are more correct and elegant than I, and more at home in
>   the parlors and schools than I,
> But I alone advance among the people en-masse, coarse and strong
> I am he standing first there, solitary chanting the true America. . . .

The first, third, and fourth verses are manifestly early versions of the much revised lines finally printed as section 23 of "Proto-Leaf" in 1860. In the Valentine manuscripts a later draft of this section is found on the verso of white wove paper "Enfans d'Adam" no. 5, in folder 5. This draft was thereupon revised and transferred to blue wove paper on added leaf 8 in "Premonition," where it was subsequently deleted, to appear finally in further revised form on added leaf 12, white wove paper. The private notebook in which these lines first appear also contains the following note to himself by Whitman, dated 26 June 1859: "It is now time to *stir* first for *Money* enough, *to live and provide for M——. To stir*—first write stories and get out of this Slough."[11] The notebook from which Holloway reprinted these two extracts being among those stolen from the Library of Congress collection, we do not know whether the verses preceded the dated note, in which case they would be earlier, or whether they followed it as later jottings. In any event there is no cause to suppose that the time relation exceeded the span of more than a few months; and since the use of this stock of white wove paper seems firmly

11 Holloway, *Uncollected Poetry and Prose*, II, 91 n. 1.

to be placed in 1859, though perhaps beginning in late 1858, it would seem that T. H. Rome's memory betrayed him when in his letter to Benjamin he assigned 1858 as the first year that Whitman had sent him manuscripts from a large collection to be set up into proof.

There is every reason, then, to place this event after the middle of March, 1859, on the basis of the editorial used as scrap paper. Because of the uncertainty of date of the notebook verses later introduced into "Premonition," we cannot be positive that Whitman sent off the manuscripts until July or later; and it may be arguable that the dated note to himself does not sound very much as though he had proof in hand and plans in a forward stage for the third edition of *Leaves*. It is necessary to repeat, however, that the expansion of "Premonition," part of which must have succeeded the jotted verses in the notebook, contains the latest identifiable material in the Valentine papers and that earlier identifiable material elsewhere exhibits the same stages of revision as are found in "Premonition." With some reasonable confidence, therefore, we may assign April–August 1859, as very probably the approximate date that Whitman relinquished his manuscripts to Rome Brothers. And in view of the time necessary to set them into proof, and then the very extensive revision found in many poems, which must have taken place in proof before submitting printer's copy in March, 1860, to Thayer and Eldridge, this plus the addition of a fair body of new work, it is likely that the actual date was not very much later than August and it may well have been earlier.[12] In this matter, however, an exact date cannot be fixed even by conjecture.

Much hinges on whether the Thayer and Eldridge invitation came to Whitman after he had independently started the process of preparing a

---

12 The only other evidence has little application. We know that Whitman made certain revisions in the Rome Brothers proof at some date after 31 May 1859 but before 1 January 1860. In poem "?101 To One a Century Hence" (folder 41), verse 3, Whitman wrote of himself in the manuscript version as "thirty-eight years old the eighty-first year of The States" in what is perhaps a birthday poem on 31 May 1857 (see below). In the 1860 edition this is altered to forty years old and the eighty-third year, i.e., on or after 31 May 1859 but before 1 January 1860. That the change was made in proof is evident from the manuscript reading, but nothing more is certain. It is of interest that Whitman rewrote and expanded the poem in manuscript (including the lines in question, which appear in both holograph versions) in the final light revising ink which can be dated in 1859. Since he did not at that time, although the revision was made about two years after original inscription, update the poem, nor did he update the 1856 date for "Feuillage" until proof, it is clear that in his manuscript revisions Whitman had not concerned himself with altering such dates. Hence this evidence cannot be used to assign the delivery of the manuscripts to Rome Brothers as necessarily before 31 May 1859. All that we can be positive of is that Whitman changed the dates in proof at some unknown date after 31 May 1859 but before 1860.

third edition by sending his poems to Rome Brothers, or whether their inquiries spurred him to secure proofs for final revision of his papers. The following letter, printed for the first time by permission of its owner, Mr. Charles E. Feinberg, assists in clarifying the problem. This letter is contained in its original envelope addressed to Whitman at Fowler and Wells and postmarked Boston, February 10. On the face of the envelope Whitman wrote, "first proposition | of Thayer & Eldridge | Feb 10 '60".

Boston Feb 10/60

Walt Whitman

Dr Sir.   We want to be the publishers of Walt. Whitman's poems—Leaves of Grass.—When the book was first issued we were clerks in the establishment we now own. We read the book with profit and pleasure. It is a true poem and writ by a *true* man.

When a man dares to speak his thought in this day of refinement—so called —it is difficult to find his mates to act amen to it. Now *we* want to be known as the publishers of Walt. Whitman's books, and put our name as such under his, on title-pages.—If you will allow it we can and will put your books into good form, and style attractive to the eye; we can and will sell a large number of copies; we have great facilities by and through numberless Agents in selling. We can dispose of more books than most publishing houses (we do not "puff" here [here *interlined above a caret*] but speak *truth*).

We are young men. We "celebrate" ourselves by acts. Try us. You can do us good. We can do you good—pecuniarily.

Now Sir, if you wish to make acquaintance with us, and accept us as your publishers, we will offer to either buy the stereo type plates [plates *interlined above a caret*] of Leaves of Grass, or pay you for the use of them, in addition to regular copy right.

Are you writing other poems? Are they ready for the press? Will you let us read them? Will you write us? Please give us your residence

Yours Fraternally

Thayer & Eldridge.

Whitman's notation "first proposition" implies that there were further letters before an agreement was reached, as would, of course, be necessary.[13] Thus since Whitman went to Boston to supervise the printing in the next month, March, it is most unlikely (even if on the receipt of this first letter

---

13 In fact, various of these letters are in the Charles E. Feinberg Collection. On 27 February the publishers write, "We are ready to commence on your work at once." On 2 March they ask Whitman to defer his coming to Boston for a week; on 7 March they agree to pay Whitman "the amount you wish per week for four or five weeks, and shall expect to see you at our place . . . next week." See *An Exhibition of the Works of Walt Whitman* (Detroit Public Library, 1955), p. 49.

he had sent his poems to Rome Brothers) that there would have been time for the typesetting to be made and the numerous revisions incorporated before actual printer's copy was submitted to Thayer and Eldridge. In this connection, we must also consider that since there is every reason from the Rome sales list to believe that the Valentine-Barrett manuscripts are substantially complete, some number of the poems first printed in 1860 but not represented in the collection or in Whitman's or Rome's list may reasonably be taken as composed after the collection poems were delivered to Rome Brothers. If this is so, it would seem that there would scarcely be time for Whitman to write perhaps as many as twenty of these extra poems, revise them to his satisfaction, and also to handle the extensive revision of the Rome Brothers proof in the short interval between 10 February and his departure for Boston. When we further take into account the other evidence already adduced, and especially the evidence that the dating of "To One a Century Hence" was altered in proof before 1 January 1860, it would seem clear that Whitman had already embarked on plans for his third edition before the arrival of the first Thayer and Eldridge letter of 10 February 1860, and hence that a date of about August, 1859, for the typesetting of the manuscripts is as close as one can come in the present state of our information. To associate the first definite step toward putting his third edition into print nearer to the time that Whitman gave up his editorship of the Brooklyn *Times* may not seem unreasonable; but the only definite evidence we have is for the interval April–December 1859.

II. *The Growth of the Third Edition*

That the third edition was forming in Whitman's mind as early as 1856, the year which saw the appearance of the second edition, and that some of its poems were begun as early as this year may be demonstrated by two references. The first, in verse 5 of the manuscript "Feuillage," to the eightieth year of the states, i.e., 1856, has already been mentioned. The second is more interesting and perhaps more important, for it seems to set the date when Whitman began the surge of poetic activity which was to find its culmination in the vastly expanded third edition of *Leaves of Grass*. As printed in 1860, section 11 of "Proto-Leaf" serves for the climax to a proposed program of varied chants that will be found in the ensuing "Leaves," and, appropriately, it turns autobiographical:

> 11. In the Year 80 of The States,
>   My tongue, every atom of my blood, formed from this soil, this air,
>   Born here of parents born here,
>   From parents the same, and their parents' parents the same,
>   I, now thirty-six years old, in perfect health, begin,
>   Hoping to cease not till death.

This is a dedication to a lifework, the construction of a great series of poems of which the 1855 and 1856 *Leaves of Grass* had been but faint adumbrations. It is the language of the dedication to constructing the 'New Bible.'

What is of especial interest, however, is that it appears in a group of sections (5–12) which are not present in the manuscript of "Premonition" (titled "Proto-Leaf" in 1860, and thereafter "Starting from Paumanok") and therefore must have been written after about July–August, 1859, when it seems probable that Whitman turned over his manuscripts to Rome Brothers for setting into proof.[1] The mention of the eightieth year of the states establishes the year as 1856; but in 1856 Whitman was aged thirty-six only between 1 January and 30 May. We seem to have here, therefore, a conscious 'historical' reference to the start of the 'New Bible' of the third edition between January and May of 1856 and presumably also to the first drafting of verses for some of its poems. Here a notebook owned by Mr. Charles E. Feinberg assumes a considerable importance, for in it are contained very early draftings of lines for "Premonition" (and possibly for "Feuillage") together with starts on several other poems. On the last page is found the date 16 September, on the next to last 4 October, and on the first page a copied-out extract from a newspaper dated 21 October. None of these dates is on a page containing verse, but I am inclined to speculate that they give us something very close[2] to the actual

---

1 As will be shown later in the analysis of "Premonition" and its manuscript, the leaves are consecutively foliated, many of them exhibit revisions in the very late revising light ink, and the pink-paper sections on the earliest inscribed leaves have been expanded by additions on the late white wove paper. Thus it is impossible to believe that Whitman wrote these added sections 5–12 before giving the manuscripts to Rome Brothers; and the dating reference therefore is not contemporary. It is most improbable that this section 11 represents an early composed scrap rejected when "Premonition" was first completed but subsequently inserted.

2 The following reconstruction is mere guesswork but may seem plausible. Whitman began the verses on the recto of the second leaf (p. 3) and wrote about halfway through the book before he reversed it and began writing forward. It would seem that the 16 September date, followed by a list of books and of names, with the 4

period of composition. We cannot be sure, of course, that the notebook represents the very first writing-out of any of the lines, for Whitman may earlier have made jottings on scraps of paper now lost. The evidence suggests, however, that between January and May of 1856 Whitman began plans for the 'New Bible' and very likely started to jot down lines for the 'Proem' that was forming in his mind. This 'Proem' began to take shape in October, as attested by the notebook; and "Feuillage" could not have been long behind, for the themes of both poems are in many respects similar. Thus it is evident that Whitman was looking far ahead and already beginning to rough-out plans for a third edition even before the publication of his second edition in September, and that at least one ambitious poem to begin the new edition had been started by October, if not earlier. This situation is reflected in a letter of 21 June 1856 in which he writes of his determination to concentrate on the *Leaves* and on no other book (Camden ed., IX, 69).

Two later references by Whitman to the plans for his third edition deserve notice. The first was found among his papers by Bucke, who assigned it the date of June, 1857, on unrecorded evidence:

The Great Construction of the New Bible. Not to be diverted from the principal object—the main life work—the three hundred and sixty-five.—It ought to be ready in 1859.

(Notes and Fragments [1899], p. 57; see Camden ed., IX, 6)

Secondly, on 20 July 1857 Whitman wrote as follows to an unknown correspondent:

Fowler & Wells are bad persons for me—They retard my book very much.—it is worse than ever.—I wish now to bring out a third edition—I have now *a hundred* poems ready (the last edition had thirty-two.)—and shall endeavor to make an arrangement with some publisher here to take the plates from F. & W. and make the additions needed, and so bring out the third edition.—F. & W. are very willing to give up the plates—they want the whole thing off their hands.—In the forthcoming Vol. I shall have, as I said, a hundred poems, and no other matter but poems—(no letter to or from Emerson—no Notices or any

October date on the next leaf forward, was the original start of the notebook and that Whitman began his verses at the other end, preceding them on the first leaf by the following quotation which reflected the geographical interests in the verses: "N. Y. Express. Oct. 21. 1856 | 'But for the American party, | the Northern, sectional, geographical | party of Wm. H. Seward & Co. | would, under Fremont, have | swept the whole Northern | country.' (editorial.)". If this preceded the verses on the next leaf, we have a firm anterior date. If Whitman left the first leaf blank, and only later filled it by the quotation, we are forced back to 4 October as the nearest date, but it is most probable that when he first reversed the notebook he began with its first page, and that the verses were not written before 21 October.

thing of that sort.)—It is, I know Well enough, that *that* must be the *true Leaves of Grass*—and I think it has an aspect of completeness, and makes its case clearer.—The old poems are all retained.—The difference is in the new character given to the mass, by the additions.—3

There is some disparity between these two accounts of his plans written within a month of each other,4 but the more specific of the two—that in July, 1857—can be confirmed by the evidence of the Valentine-Barrett manuscripts. The purport of the letter is clear. Whitman has completed sixty-eight poems, which he plans to add in a new typesetting to the plates of the thirty-two poems of the 1856 second edition to create a third edition consisting of one hundred poems. He believes that the volume will have an aspect of completeness, largely owing to the new character given to the whole by the additions. It is evident that when this was written no idea had formed in his mind of the final arrangement by 'clusters' such as "Chants Democratic" or "Calamus" as is found in the 1860 printed edition, since it was the 'mass' which was to be given a new character by the additions. Moreover, as will be explained later, no 'cluster' can be traced in the Valentine manuscripts before the early "Live Oak with Moss" —the first and limited form of "Calamus"—the inscription of which in the present manuscripts can be dated in 1859.

In the Barrett Collection, separate from the Valentine manuscripts, are two pieces of pink paper containing a poem which Whitman never printed and which was found by Bucke among his papers.5 The first leaf

---

3 Rollo Silver, "Seven Letters of Walt Whitman," *American Literature*, VII (1935), 76–78.

4 In the June note Whitman is thinking of publication two years hence; in July, seemingly of an edition to be brought out in the very near future, since it does not propose the addition of more poems than he has in hand. Speculation here is perhaps idle, and it may be no more than that Whitman abruptly changed his mind. Yet the difference between an immediate edition and one two years off is a serious one and argues that his hundred poems of July, 1857, did not comprehend a much larger plan for the 'New Bible' which he had in mind. I find the June note difficult to interpret. Obviously his work— he was newly editor of the Brooklyn *Times* —he is saying must not be allowed to interfere with the principal object of his life, the construction of the 'New Bible.' But what is the three hundred and sixty-

five? Grammatically, these days of the year are in apposition to 'principal object' or 'main life work.' They cannot refer simply to the art of living each day and year fully, for then the 'New Bible' would be diverting him from that. It seems to me not beyond all possibility that the 'New Bible' was to consist of three hundred and sixty-five poems in its fullest form planned for 1859. If so, then his decision a month later to publish only a hundred poems immediately, becomes more explicable. The complete 'New Bible' would, then, require a fourth edition for fruition. On the other hand, of course, the object of the main life work may be the application of 365 days each year, these to be devoted to the New Bible.

5 *Notes and Fragments*, p. 26, where it is reprinted without mention of the list of poems on the verso of the second leaf. The complete text, with revisions, is given in the present volume.

contains verses entitled "To an Exclusive," which may be independent but which could have been prefixed to expand an earlier poem on the second leaf which is untitled but is numbered 100, revised from original 99.[6] On the verso of this second leaf in Whitman's hand is a list of poems with numbers and titles from 33 to 72. Unfortunately, what must probably have been another leaf continuing this list has not been preserved so far as I know, but a large part of the lost continuation can be reconstructed from the Valentine manuscripts. With only a few gaps, all of the poems in Whitman's list from 33 to 72 are found with the same numbers (in the revised series) and titles in the Valentine collection. Between 48 and 51, however, the poems numbered 49 and 50 in the list are not present in the collection; and beginning with 51 each numbered poem in the manuscripts has been upped one in a revised numbering, thus indicating that either 49 or 50 was an insertion made after the original series had been numbered but before the writing-out of the list. With some gaps this list can be continued to 100, and slightly beyond, from the manuscripts.

Whitman's list is as follows, with supplementary annotation,[7] and a continuation from the Valentine manuscripts:

33 A Handful of Air | As of Origins p1(c) L19 f61
34 As of Eternity | 34 As of Eternity p3 C21 f22
34 As of the Truth | 35 As of Truth p2(b, c) L18 f60
36 Poem of Joys | 36 Poem of Joys/Contact p1(a,b), p2(a),w L f71
37 Walt Whitman's Illustration |
38 Walt Whitman's Laws | American Laws p2(a) CD13 f49
39 Walt Whitman's Caution | [1860, p. 401]. See no. 31 in Rome list.

6 The two leaves have been trimmed for inlaying and thus there is little left of their original contours. What evidence there is suggests that the leaves are of different batches of the pink paper and that the left margin of the second leaf may have been torn rather than scissored. There is now no chance of fitting them in with other lots of similar paper. However, the pin-hole pattern of the two leaves is substantially the same and indicates that they were associated for some time.

7 The number and title to the left of the vertical stroke | is that of Whitman's list. To the right of the stroke is given the number and title of the respective poems as they appear in the Valentine papers. When a slant / separates two titles or two numbers, that to the left is a revision and that to the right is the original. The next item is a coded identification of the paper (full analysis is provided later), in which *p* stands for pink paper, *w* for white wove, *tax form* for the Williamsburgh tax blanks. Following this is the section and numbering of the poem in the 1860 edition, C standing for "Calamus," CD for "Chants Democratic," EA for "Enfans d'Adam," L for "Leaves," and ML for "Messenger Leaves." For convenience the various separates are coded as L with their 1860 titles but, of course, no section numbers. The final item *f* plus a number refers to the folders in which the poems are now preserved. Poems in the list not present in the Valentine collection but identifiable in the 1860 edition are provided with the 1860 page number within square brackets. A blank after a listed poem indicates that it has not been identified in manuscript or in the 1860 edition.

84/83 Razzia p2(a) C26 f26
85/84 You and I p3 EA7 f3
86/85 Says p1(c) L f78
87/86 Say p2(b) L f78
88/87 p1(e) L f78
89/88 Say p1(f) L f78
87/86 France, the 18th Year of These States p6 L f73
90/89 Feuillage p5, p2(c) CD4 f42
95/94 To a Stranger p1(e) C22 f23
96/95 To One Shortly to Die p3 ML f64
99/98 To Rich Givers p1(d) ML f65
100/99 To an Exclusive p (not in Valentine coll.)
?100/101/100 To One Who Will Understand p4(a) C41 f38
?101/102/101 p1(f) C45 f41
103 So Long blue laid L f80

This list must represent substantially the plan for the third edition
found in the Whitman letter of 20 July 1857 quoted above, although it
is clear that in the Valentine poems there has been some readjustment.
The poems are numbered in an ink which is not that of the text ink, indicating that they were composed without numbers and later put into a
series. At some time subsequent to this numbering, but before the making
up of the list, either poem 49 or 50 was inserted, and this necessitated
a complete renumbering from that point on. Before this revision the
series had progressed to 101 poems; hence, the addition of poem 49 or 50
inforced a revision of the last pink-paper poem to 102. It would seem
also that before further alterations were made in the series, "So Long"
was copied out on the blue laid paper and numbered 103 in its text ink.
The subsequent reduction of poems 101 and 102 (in revised numbering)
to 100 and 101 respectively, each with a prefixed query, was almost certainly consequent upon the withdrawal of poem 100/99 "To an Exclusive"
from the proposed edition, the question mark before the next poem number perhaps marking either some doubt about the permanency of the withdrawal or else other abstractions earlier in the list as well. Since the list
is written on the verso of the leaf containing the poem numbered 100/99,
it is probable that Whitman made this unofficial table of contents for
the added poems (the first thirty-two were to be printed from the plates
of the 1856 edition, and therefore their order was fixed) after he had withdrawn the poem from the manuscripts for the proposed edition.[8] Moreover, since this list reflects the revised numbering which resulted from

8 Since the list begins on the original leaf
of the poem, one might speculate that the
initial leaf containing the verses headed
by "To an Exclusive" was added after
the removal of the poem.

the addition of no. 49 or no. 50, it certainly postdates the revised numbering of the manuscripts.

From the numbering of the manuscripts it is evident that poem ?100 originally concluded an even hundred poems before the addition of no. 49 or no. 50; and its content suggests a conclusion to the edition. I am indebted to Professor Gay W. Allen for the ingenious suggestion that the content of ?101 is also peculiarly applicable to a concluding poem and that it has much the same effect as "So Long," which was the final choice. Moreover, he suggests that as Whitman was fond of writing a preface or a poem on his birthday, no. ?101 (printed as "Calamus" no. 45 in 1860 where it ends that sequence) sounds very much like a birthday poem, which could then be dated in its original form as composed on 31 May 1857 when Whitman was thirty-eight years old in the "eighty-first year of These States." If this is so, and it seems very plausible, we may conjecture that Whitman had the manuscripts for his third edition planned and numbered to 101 shortly after 31 May 1857 (the original plan and perhaps ordering to end with no. 100 preceding this date). The addition of no. 49 or no. 50, therefore, which caused added 101 to be renumbered as 102 must have come after this date. "So Long," thereupon, ought to have been added still later, after the revised numbering but before the withdrawal of 100/99 and the consequent tentative renumbering of 101 and 102. It would be tempting to endeavor to continue this line of conjecture and to assign "So Long" as another birthday poem, in May, 1858, but the evidence that its verses 53–55 were drafted before "Chants Democratic" no. 9 was inscribed on the verso (folder 45) does not encourage further speculation. Hence the date for the addition of no. 49 or no. 50, and thereafter of "So Long," is uncertain, and even less certain is the date for the withdrawal of no. 100/99, and the revision of the numbering of no. 101 and no. 102. All that can be conjectured is that when Whitman wrote his letter of 20 July 1857 his manuscripts were in approximately the state revealed by his list and by the pink-paper poems in the Valentine collection.[9]

The evidence, therefore, may be summarized as follows. Before 31 May 1857 (and certainly before 20 July) Whitman had a period of intense poetic activity extending back at least as far as October, 1856, and doubtless earlier. During this period of less than a year he composed a series of

---

9 Although Whitman is emphatic in his 20 July 1857 letter that he has a hundred poems, it is probable that in fact he was giving a round number and that this letter is of little use in dating the course of events. If the figure is to be taken exactly, then ?101 was not a birthday poem on 31 May 1857 and must have been written later. Moreover, either 49 or 50 could not have been added at the time the letter was written.

sixty-eight to seventy poems, more than trebling the content of the 1856 second edition. He conceived of these poems as lending a new character to the *Leaves* and, together with the thirty-two poems from 1856, as forming a unit sufficiently expressing his purposes. He had gone so far in his plans for publication of a third edition as to feel that work on it was completed; and hence he had arranged and numbered the new poems in a fixed order.[10] At some subsequent date, perhaps not far removed, he withdrew at least one poem no. 100/99, and on the verso wrote out the first part of a table of contents:[11] the second leaf completing the list is not recorded as preserved. This is the situation, then, in the summer of 1857.

When we isolate in the Valentine manuscripts those poems which by their numbering demonstrate that they once formed part of this original plan, we see that with the exception of two white-paper insertions added much later and pencil-numbered 81 and 82, all the preserved numbered poems are written either on the pink paper or on the backs of Williamsburgh tax collection blanks which were customarily used for fair copies of revised pink-paper poems.[12] The pink-paper leaves were scissored, six to a sheet, from what is customarily taken as a remainder stock of wrappers from the first edition of *Leaves of Grass*.[13] Whitman seems to have used this paper with some consistency for an extended period in 1856 and 1857. For example, of the five manuscripts on this paper in the Trent Collection at Duke University which can be dated, one reads January 1856—22 February, another early in 1857, a third 9 February 1857, a fourth 25 February 1857, and the last 1 March 1857.[14] In the Valentine poems the start of "Feuillage" and of the earliest form of "Premonition" may be dated in 1856, although the present inscription doubtless is later.[15]

10 The evidence of the paper, as will be shown, demonstrates that the order of numbering bears no relation to the order of composition or inscription.

11 Since the list reflects the revised numbering, which continues through number 103, it is impossible to conjecture that poem 100/99 was written on the back of a leaf already containing a partial contents list. The back of the already inscribed and numbered poem must have been used for the list.

12 The single exception is "So Long," added to the series with the number 103 and inscribed on blue laid paper.

13 Although I have seen remnants of the display title on yellow and green leaves from wrapper stock, no leaf on pink paper in the Barrett Collection shows any trace of printing.

14 *Catalogue of the Whitman Collection in the Duke University Library* (1945), Part III, Nos. 17, 26, 10, 5; Part IV, No. 18.

15 The Feinberg notebook, and the notes printed in Bucke's *Notes and Fragments* indicate, as we should expect, that the pink-paper leaves for both poems do not represent the first stage of composition. Thus it is not demonstrable that 1856 was in fact the date of inscription of "Feuillage" in its present form, for the reference to the eightieth year of the states could readily have been taken over in the pink-paper form at a later date from earlier drafted lines, or else the reference may be 'historical,' as the added lines in the 1860 "Proto-Leaf" seem to be.

On the whole, there can be little question that those poems written on pink paper are the earliest inscribed among the Valentine manuscripts. Moreover, it seems almost certain that no other paper than the pink was represented in the manuscripts in the form they possessed at the time of the 20 July 1857 letter.[16]

The date when Whitman began to use the backs of the Williamsburgh tax forms is not quite certain but can be estimated within limits. These blue bill heads have printed on their face the heading, "Collector's Office, City Hall, corner of South 2d and Fourth Streets," and underneath, "To City of Williamsburgh, Dr, To City and County Tax for the year 185 on the following Lot." The city of Williamsburgh was incorporated with Brooklyn by vote of the New York State Legislature on 17 April 1854, the act to take effect on 1 January 1855. All local distinctions were abolished except for the fire department.[17] Hence it seems clear that after 1 January 1855 such tax blanks would not be printed for Williamsburgh as a separate corporation under its old name, and that the blanks were remainders when Whitman used them. Although there is no evidence where these tax forms were printed, it is reasonable to conjecture that the Brooklyn *Daily Times,* which advertised for job printing, had run them off and that Whitman found odd lots of these about the plant when he became editor. This event took place, according to G. W. Allen's reconstruction of the available evidence, about the middle of February, 1857, a date coinciding very closely with the probable completion of the hundred poems for the third edition. The earliest dated use of these forms so far as I am aware was on 17 June 1857 when Oliver Dyer, lawyer for James Parton, gave Whitman a receipt on the back of one of these

16 This statement needs some qualification since one cannot deny the possibility that a small amount of revision might have been carried out by that time on the tax blanks. But certainly this can have been much less than is represented by the poems on this paper in the present collection; and it is almost certain that no poem which is not numbered could have been in the manuscripts in July, 1857.

In folder 67, poem number 40 in Whitman's original list and so numbered in manuscript, a pink-paper poem, has the date 1858 added by Whitman in blue pencil and then deleted. Blue-pencil alterations seem to come quite late in the process of revision. But the fact that this poem appears in Whitman's 1857 list and

by its paper and numbering was therefore written before 20 July 1857 (and probably well before 31 May) establishes that the 1858 added date has nothing to do with the date of composition or inscription. Incidentally, the 1857 dating, and the original title "A Past Presidentiad, and one to come also," show that the poem was not originally written about Fillmore, Pierce, and Buchanan as given by the 1860 printed title, "To the States, to Identify the 16th, 17th, or 18th Presidentiad." All that the blue-pencil date shows is that the manuscripts were in Whitman's hands sometime in 1858.

17 Stephen M. Ostrander, *A History of the City of Brooklyn* (1894), II, 105–8.

blanks for part payment of a debt, the transaction taking place at Whitman's home on Classon Avenue.[18] Although it is not impossible that Whitman had picked up these tax forms for scrap paper at Rome Brothers at some unknown date in 1854 or early 1855, or later, the date of the Parton receipt and the fact that Whitman seems to have used the blanks, at least in the Valentine manuscripts, to make fair copies of revised pink-paper poems indicates the greater probability that he secured them only when he came to edit the Brooklyn *Daily Times*. If so, we may assign those poems copied on the backs of tax forms as part of a revision of the original group of manuscripts which had consisted exclusively of poems written on leaves of the pink paper.[19]

We arrive, then, at a reconstruction of Whitman's manuscripts for a third edition in the spring of 1857 as consisting solely of numbered poems written on the pink paper. Some of these seem to be copies of earlier drafts; some may represent original composition. But since it is usually impossible to determine the exact stage in the construction of a poem which each reflects, whatever may be found by a study of the paper on which the poems are written can apply not to their order of composition but instead only to their inscription on the present leaves in the Valentine-Barrett collection.

By far the largest number of poems is found on six batches of p1 pink paper which can be fitted together to form one whole sheet. The greatest number of leaves in any one batch is 20, found in p1(a) and p1(e), with 19 in p1(c). It is a not unreasonable assumption, therefore, that Whitman took 20 sheets of the whole paper and scissored it at one time into six different lots, the total, therefore, comprising 120 leaves, of which only 97 are preserved here: p1(a)–20, p1(b)–16, p1(c)–19, p1(d)–13, p1(e)–20, and p1(f)–9.

If one imagines this lot of 20 sheets set vertically on its short end, the

---

18 *With Walt Whitman in Camden* (1938), III, 237.

19 Perhaps the most obvious case of the use of the tax blanks to revise poems on pink paper occurs in the first leaf of "Premonition" for which part of the original pink leaf has been preserved. Although this particular revision comes almost certainly in 1859, the numbering of the poems and the comparative lack of revision of their lines indicates that in this class we may very likely include tax-blanks poems 44 and 42 (folders 27, 56). There is no physical evidence preserved to indicate that Whitman copied revised forms of pink-paper poems on the white wove paper. However, there is some evidence that the use of the tax blanks was sporadic and covered a considerable period. Thus it is impossible to say on the basis of the paper alone, without other evidence, that a poem inscribed on a tax form is necessarily earlier, or later, than a poem on white wove paper. Professor G. W. Allen informs me that he has seen material in the Library of Congress collection written on the bill heads as late as 1860.

sheets can be reconstructed as follows. In the lower left corner p1(a) consisting of 17 leaves from "Premonition" (folder 1); leaf 6 of CD 7, no. 41 "Evolutions (folder 43); and leaves 7–8 of no. 36 "Poem of Joys" (folder 71). In the lower right corner, its left margin fitting the contours of the right margin of p1(a) is the p1(b) paper consisting of leaf 32 of "Premonition" (folder 1), and leaves 1–3, 5–6, 9–10, 13–20 of no. 36 "Poem of Joys" (folder 71). In the mid-section of the sheet, to the left, its foot fitting into the head of p1(a) paper, is p1(c) consisting of EA10, no. 80 "Hindustan" (folder 6); C25, no. 54 "Prairie Grass" (folder 25); CD11, "Thought" (folder 46); CD19, no. 76 "Leaf" (folder 54); L15, no. 73 "Night on the Prairies" (folder 57); L19, no. 33 "As of Origins" (folder 61); L22, no. 70 "Leaf" (folder 63); ML no. 40 "A Past Presidentiad" (folder 67); no. 82 "Unnamed Lands" (folder 74); no. 86 "Says" (folder 78). In the mid-section, to the right, is p1(d): leaves 1–5 of CD7, no. 41 "Evolutions" (folder 43); L21, no. 47 "Voices" (folder 62); ML no. 99 "To Rich Givers" (folder 65); no. 57 "Mannahatta" (folder 72). In the upper left corner, directly above p1(c), is p1(e): C22, no. 95 "To a Stranger" (folder 23); CD8, "A Sunset Carol" (folder 44); CD9, "Thought" (folder 45); CD12, no. 68 "Orators" (folder 48); CD16, no. 48 "Mediums" (folder 51); no. 56 "Kosmos" (folder 75); and no. 88 ["Say"] (folder 78). In the upper right corner is p1(f): C30, no. 71 "Leaf" (folder 28); C45, ?101 (folder 41); L16, no. 72 "Leaf" (folder 58); L17, no. 78 "Leaf" (folder 59); ML "To You" sec. 2 (folder 70); no. 89 "Say" (folder 78). Also written on p1(f) paper is the independent poem "As of Forms" found by Bucke among Whitman's papers and preserved elsewhere in the Barrett Collection.

From such an example as "Premonition" written straight through to the penultimate leaf on p1(a) paper (except for inserted leaf 28 on p2(b) paper), it seems reasonable to suppose that when Whitman cut up the batch of full sheets, each separate pack of individual leaves was added as a unit to the pile. If this is so, all the foregoing poems were probably inscribed on this p1 paper as a continuous operation without the intervention of paper from another batch of sheets. Moreover, it is probable that the pile was so arranged that poems would normally be inscribed continuously on each pack of leaves before paper from another scissored pack would become available. If this is so, p1(a) leaves must have preceded p1(b) leaves, since the penultimate leaf 32 (the last of the pink-paper leaves) of "Premonition" switches from p1(a) to p1(b). If the tax-form leaf 33 is a revision of an original pink-paper leaf, then p1(c) leaves must have been later than p1(a, b), since a draft for sec. 65 on leaf 33 is found on the verso of "Thought" on p1(c) paper (folder 46). Finally, if poem ?101 (folder 41) is indeed a birthday poem written on 31 May 1857 and added to the original sequence, then the p1(f) leaves must have been the last inscribed. This last may be partly buttressed by the evidence in favor of no. 86, the first of the "Says," being the initial one composed. Since this is on p1(c) paper, and no. 89 "Say" is on p1(f), it would seem that we could draw the sequence p1(a), p1(b), p1(c), and p1(f). Finally, on the evidence that the first five leaves of "Evolutions" (folder 43) were written on p1(d) paper, and the sixth was added on p1(a) paper, it would seem possible that the p1(d) leaves preceded p1(a). If so, only the position of p1(e) is unknown. However, since ["Say"] no. 88 is written on p1(e) paper, it is not likely that it preceded no. 86, with its head-title, on p1(c) leaves. Hence a possible sequence is p1(d), p1(a), p1(b), p1(c), p1(e), and p1(f). The evidence in favor of this is rather slim, and it must be admitted that it is difficult to see how Whitman could cut up a stack of paper and have the six batches of leaves fall in such an order. It may be, therefore, that p1(d), in fact, somehow belongs after p1(a, b), which would restore an order in the cutting up that can be visualized.

No other full sheet can be reconstructed in all its six sets of leaves. Three, possibly four, sets of leaves can be established as part of a p2 sheet. In the lower left corner comes p2(a): C13, no. 52 "Buds" (folder 15); C26, no. 84 "Razzia" (folder 26); CD13, no. 38 "American Laws" (folder 49); CD18, no. 74 "Leaf" (folder 53); leaf 4 only of no. 36 "Poem of Joys" (folder 71); no. 53 "Savantism" (folder 77). In the lower right corner, p2(b): leaf 28 of "Premonition" (folder 1), originally an independent poem entitled "Aborigines"; CD17, no. 51 "Wander-Teachers" (folder 52); leaf 1 only of L18, no. 35 "As of the Truth" (folder 60); and no 87 "Say" (folder 78). In the mid-section above p2(a) are placed the p2(c) leaves: C31, no. 69 "Leaf" (folder 29); leaves 12–15 of CD4, no. 90 "Feuillage" (folder 42); leaves 2–4 of L18, no. 35 "As of the Truth."

No other leaves of pink paper appear to fit in this p2 sheet, but since the upper right corner p2(f) is vacant and has no adjacent leaves against which to match its contours, on the evidence that leaves 1–11 of CD4 no. 90 "Feuillage" come on paper I have called p5, the final leaves 12–15 being p2(c), possibly this p5 paper is p2(f), as indicated by its proper straight edges. Since the p2 sheet can be recovered only in a fragment, no inference can be made about the number of leaves that were cut from a batch of sheets at this time. The known leaves total only 21, with 8 each of p2(a) and p2(c) paper being the largest number, although p5 (p2(f)?) has 11.

One set of leaves from an unknown sheet p3 match together. These 10 leaves consist of EA7, no. 85 "You and I" (folder 3); C17, no. 79 "Poemet" (folder 19); C21, no. 34 "As of Eternity" (folder 22); ML no. 96 "To One Shortly to Die" (folder 64); and no. 83 "Hand Mirror" (folder 76).

Two sets of p4 leaves match sideways by their long margin. To the left is p4(a): C41, no. ?100 "To One Who Will Understand" (folder 38); and CD20, no. 55 "Mouth Songs" (folder 55), totalling 3 leaves. To the right is CD 16, no. 43 "Leaf" (folder 18), totalling 2 leaves. Finally, there are the 5 leaves of p6 paper represented by no. 87 "France" (folder 73), paper which has been torn instead of scissored. If no. 86 "Says" was indeed the first inscribed, then it would seem that its p1(c) paper preceded the p2(b) paper of "Say" no. 87. Possibly this view may be buttressed by the reasonable inference that p2(a) leaf 4 in "Poem of Joys" is an insertion among p1(a, b) paper of an independent poem.

This is as far, seemingly, as a paper analysis of the pink leaves will take us. What it demonstrates is generally seriatim inscription of some quantity of poems on leaves from the same scissored batches, with—at least for the p1 paper—some grounds for placing leaves from the same whole sheet in an approximate order of inscription. The association of poems by order of inscription may be a far cry, for all we know, from their order of composition. However, there is some reason to speculate that in fact the order of composition is approximated. When one surveys the probable order of inscription, it is clear that no relation exists between this and the order of Whitman's numbered list or the numbered poems after the list stops. Thus it may be that a large group of drafts was not copied out according to a preconceived plan, but that instead the inscription in each individual case followed shortly on the achievement of what Whitman considered to be a reasonably final form for the poem concerned. If this is so, the literary critic may have to hand new and unsuspected evidence bearing on the order and growth of the original seventy poems which Whitman in 1857 planned to add to the plated thirty-two poems of the 1856 edition.

There are a few odd points worth comment in connection with the state of this group of pink-paper manuscripts in the spring and summer of 1857. The few unnumbered poems in which the lack of numbering cannot be laid to revision of the heading do not group themselves apart, but were composed always on batches of leaves used for numbered poems. This is what we should expect, since the poems were completely rearranged and the numbering added pretty much at one time after inscription of the whole lot was complete. When, therefore, we find such a poem as "As of Forms" to be unnumbered and rejected from the 1857 plan, though composed at the same time as the other poems, we are justified in assuming that Whitman removed it from the collection before numbering;[20] and for the rejection of poems we have the analogy of the removal of numbered "To an Exclusive." However, it must be remembered that even such an apparently clear-cut case as the insertion of unnumbered "Aborigines" as leaf 28 of "Premonition" (and possibly of "Contact" as leaf 4 of "Poem of Joys") is not demonstrably one made before the numbered list was formulated. The odds are certainly in favor of both these sections being added before the achievement of the final form of the list and the numbering of the finally chosen poems; but one can never be sure that rejects were not brought out at some considerably later date and added to the longer poems, perhaps at the same time as other revision on different paper.

A particular oddity exists in Whitman's list, which could hypothetically have some connection, but about which one may only speculate. In this written-out list nine poems between nos. 58 and 66 are given as "Thought(s)"; and seven "Thoughts" are printed in 1860 although, curiously, the manuscript for none of these is preserved in the Valentine collection. Two poems in folders 45–46 are not numbered but are titled "Thought" (the first with a curious note "2nd piece in book"). These two became "Chants Democratic" nos. 9 and 11 in the 1860 edition, but plus the seven "Thoughts" also printed there they make up exactly the nine given in the list. Why they were not numbered is odd, for their paper almost certainly precludes their being later revisions of numbered pink-paper poems. It is possible, of course, that Whitman, in spite of his list, did not invariably number the manuscripts for members of a series like "Thoughts" when he was still uncertain about the final order and even about addition to or subtraction from such a grouping. We should have more grounds for conjecture if the latter part of the list had been

---

20 "As of Forms" was clearly rejected, since it was discovered by Bucke among Whitman's papers after his death and printed in *Notes and Fragments*, p. 26. This poem has commonly been assigned as an early draft of "Germs," i.e., no. 19 of "Leaves" in 1860. But the resemblance is very general, and since the pink-paper manuscript for no. 19 has been preserved (folder 61, entitled "As of Origins," almost certainly corresponding to number 33 in Whitman's list, "A Handful of Air"), it is more than doubtful whether such an identification should be attempted. There is no indication, moreover, that pink-paper "As of Origins" is a revised working-over of pink-paper "As of Forms."

preserved, since there is a curious dislocation in this part which might have a bearing. It is odd to find that various "Says" were originally numbered in manuscript as 85, 86, 87, and 88, revised to 86, 87, 88, and 89, although "France, the 18th Year of These States" was also numbered 86, revised to 87, and that this duplication was allowed to stand even when the numbering was revised.[21]

On a few of the pink-paper poems exist remnants of foliation. Thus the three leaves of no. 73 "Night on the Prairies" revised from "Leaf" (L15, p1(c)) are numbered 1–3 over deleted 16–18, and the four of no. 35 "As of the Truth" (L18, p2(b, c)) are numbered 35–38. The first two leaves of no. 87 "France" (L, p6) are foliated 1–2 over deleted 6–7. Finally, the leaves of no. 103 "So Long" are very curiously numbered 75–81. The revision in some cases to an independent unit numbering from what must have been some sort of series foliation is impossible, on the slight evidence, to equate with any known arrangement either original according to the list or later according to the 1860 printed order. The foliation of "So Long" is particularly ambiguous since there is every indication that, no matter what the preceding order, this poem was always intended to conclude the volume once it had displaced no. ?101 for that purpose. It is unlikely that the fragmentary series numbering had anything to do with the order of the 1860 edition, in view of the alterations away from a sequential foliation. Thus we have only unintelligible evidence for some early plan of indeterminate date, certainly in a state of incompleteness.

We may conjecture that Whitman's apparent failure to find a publisher for the third edition, prepared in the spring of 1857,[22] combined with the pressure of his new duties as editor of the Brooklyn *Daily Times* to enforce a slackening off in his poetic composition. No poem on the pink paper can be dated after this time, and the evidence of the poems' number-

---

21 Of course, if Whitman had numbered only the first "Say" (the third, which follows, is untitled and its numbering may be an afterthought), then "France" would have followed without a break. On the evidence of the paper, the various "Says" were written at different times, yet presumably before the manuscripts for the long series were numbered. We can only suppose that Whitman had reserved one number for this grouping in his list, but on both occasions continued to number the parts in sequence, since the duplication would be more apparent than real. Nevertheless, the example is unusual.

22 Unquestionably the difficulty of finding a publisher held up the early printing of the third edition once it had been prepared in its pink-paper form. An editorial in the Brooklyn *Times* for 5 October 1857 is concerned with the hard times (Holloway, *I Sit and Look Out*, pp. 169–70), and there was a depression in the winter of 1857–58. According to an entry in his private notebook, as late as 26 June 1859 Whitman was still in financial difficulties (*ibid.*, p. 15).

ing combined with that for the order of inscription by packs of leaves cut from whole sheets suggests very strongly that, the plan being completed, the inscription of new poems stopped except in the draft stage. Hence when Whitman came to revise and to add to the collection subsequently, he abandoned the pink paper in favor of other less porous sources which had become available to him.[23]

If we except the white wove paper, which there is every reason to believe was not utilized before the first month or two of 1859, the only variants from the pink paper and from "So Long" in the Valentine manuscripts consist of one poem ("Calamus" no. 40, folder 40) on a ruled blue wove paper,[24] two on pieces of white laid paper which can be demonstrated as torn apart from a single large piece ("Chants Democratic" no. 10, folder 47, and "Messenger Leaves" entitled "To a Cantatrice," folder 68), and five on Williamsburgh tax blanks. Of these, two firmly associate themselves with the revision of poems in the original plan since they are both numbered in the long series and correspond to the numbers and titles of Whitman's list: these are "Leaves" no. 13 (no. 42 "Confession and Warning," folder 56) and "Calamus" no. 27 (no. 44 "Leaf," folder 27). Unless Whitman's list was made up considerably later than there is any reason to suppose, the two poems in question must be taken as fair copies of revised poems originally written on pink paper and similarly titled and numbered. Two of the remaining three poems are titled but not numbered: "Calamus" no. 17 ("Confession Drops," folder 17) and "Messenger Leaves" ("To a Pupil," folder 66). No inferences can seemingly be made about these. On the one hand, "Confession-Drops" seems to link itself with no. 42 "Confession and Warning"; but on the other it may have some relation to the late white wove paper poem with its head-title "Leaves—Droppings," ("Enfans d'Adam" no. 1, folder 2). The untitled and unnumbered "Calamus" no. 7 (folder 9) may perhaps be relatively late when titles for poems were largely dropped. On the evidence that inscription on the tax blanks could have come any time between March, 1857, and 1860, there is little ground for speculation; nor can anything be

23 There seems to be every evidence of such a relatively sharp break, at least for the inscription of finished poems. That he did not turn to other paper because the pink sheets were exhausted is indicated by the preservation of some quantity of the sheets and its sale in six lots in the auction on 15–16 April 1936 of the collection of Dr. Jacob Schwartz held at the Anderson Galleries. Still earlier manuscripts which lie behind the 1856 edition show that Whitman apparently used up the lighter-colored yellow and green wrappers before turning to the pink sheets.

24 This paper differs from the unruled blue wove leaves used to expand "Premonition."

said with confidence about the date of the poems on ruled blue wove and on white laid paper.

As already indicated, we reach firm ground only with the advent of the white wove paper, chiefly used for poems later to be printed as part of "Calamus" and for the inscription of the nugget of that sequence, the twelve poems of "Live Oak with Moss." This paper can be dated as in use in early to mid-1859, and the inscription of some poems on its leaves must have preceded rather closely the sending off of the manuscripts to Rome Brothers. What we seem to have, therefore, between the pink-paper poems before June or July of 1857 and the white-paper poems of 1859 are perhaps five poems on tax blanks, one on blue paper, and two on white laid. This is strikingly little for an interval of at least a year and a half, but we need not suppose that Whitman was entirely idle in this time. We have no information about the actual dates of drafting for most of the white-paper poems and it is possible that some, if not all, were composed at a date considerably earlier than their inscription on the leaves of the preserved manuscripts. Certainly to this period we may assign a considerable amount of the revision of the pink-paper poems as shown in the Valentine papers. But with all allowances, there appears to have been a striking lapse in poetic effort. When we compare the great surge which in less than a year produced the approximately seventy accepted poems for the 1857 plan of the third edition with this lacuna, and then in 1859 another outpouring, it is not difficult to believe that the first was brought to an end by the pressure of Whitman's editorial duties starting in February–March, 1857, and that his release from this burden between 1 June and 15 June of 1859, with some anticipation, produced the second group which went into the 1860 edition.

This later production will be surveyed in the section on "Calamus" and other 1860 groupings. Here it seems necessary only to point out that on the evidence of the two white-paper poems pencil-numbered 81 and 82, one of which must be after mid-March of 1859, at least in certain respects Whitman still had in mind at that time a plan for a long series of undifferentiated poems. Secondly, it is a reasonable inference that many if not most of the poems first printed in 1860 but not found in manuscript in the Valentine collection, or mentioned in Whitman's list or the Rome sales list, represent fresh composition between the time that the manuscripts were sent off to be typeset (perhaps about August, 1859) and the journey to Boston in March, 1860.

Excluding the poems taken over in 1860 from 1856, and the titles in

Whitman's or the Rome list that can be identified, the following twenty-seven 1860 poems must represent in some part composition subsequent to the delivery of the Valentine manuscripts to Rome Brothers: "Chants Democratic" no. 21; "A Word Out of the Sea"; "Enfans d'Adam" nos. 2, 6, 12, 13, 14, 15; "Leaves of Grass" nos. 1, 6, 10, 20, 23, 24; "Calamus" nos. 3, 5, 6, 19, 24, 28, 29, 33, 35; "To a President"; "To Old Age"; and "Debris" together with "Perfections" and alterations in "Says."

With the exception of various "Thought(s)" there are only three poems in Whitman's incomplete list which are not present either in the Valentine manuscripts or (identifiably) in the Rome sales list: no. 37 "Walt Whitman's Illustration," no. 45 "Poemet," and no. 67 "Song of Things." When Whitman's list stops and the manuscripts alone provide evidence, we have between nine and eleven missing numbers, some three of which may be represented by the three unnumbered poems revised on tax blanks. A few of these might perhaps be accounted for by unassigned titles in the Rome list; a few, also, may represent poems held back for further revision and therefore never sent to Rome Brothers.[25] But it is not impossible for as many as twenty or so poems from those first known in the 1860 edition to have been completed between the dispatch of the Valentine manuscripts to Rome brothers in August (?), 1859, and the work on the edition in Boston in March, 1860. These may eventually be identified if further evidence can be discovered.[26] In the meantime, the twenty-eight poems first heard of in the 1860 edition invite critical attention for the late date at which many must have been inscribed.

III. *Premonition*

The long manuscript poem "Premonition" was first printed in expanded and considerably revised form in the 1860 *Leaves of Grass*, where it was entitled "Proto-Leaf." In the 1865 *Leaves* further major revision was given it and the title was changed to the final one, "Starting from

25 For example, lines from the pink-paper period of 1857 that were later to go into "Enfans d'Adam" no. 6, for which no manuscript is found in the Valentine collection, are present on the verso of "Thought" in folder 46 and must therefore have been copied fair from that draft. But whether this poem was ever numbered or else remained in draft form to be completed later cannot be known. Doubtless other poems first known from the 1860 edition had a similar history.

26 However, attention should be drawn to three poems, nos. 37, 45, and 67 in Whitman's list, that cannot be positively identified among the 1860 printed poems.

Paumanok." It is almost certain that in its pink-paper form this poem was originally a part of Whitman's numbered series, one of the sixty-eight composed and written down before 31 May 1857, the assigned number before the title having been removed subsequently in the revision of the first leaf. If so, however, it must necessarily have come in the latter part of the sequence after Whitman's list breaks off, since none of the unidentified titles in the list fits the subject of "Premonition." This may seem rather odd, for the poem serves as a natural introduction to the *Leaves*, but Whitman's list offers no alternative.[1] If we may trust Whitman's dating of its inception when he added section 11 with others in his revision and expansion of the Rome Brothers proofs, the subject of the poem was conceived sometime between 1 January and 31 May 1856. From the notebook drafts owned by Mr. Charles Feinberg (the text of which is printed in this volume as Appendix II to the poem), we know that Whitman was working on a very early stage of the opening lines probably in October of 1856. It is unlikely that the whole poem had been sufficiently well worked out in an early form for copying in the present manuscript until some time in 1857: all we know is that the poem seems to have been among the first to form in Whitman's mind and that its p1(a, b) paper indicates that he must have written it out in the Valentine manuscript among the first of the poems inscribed on identifiable packs of pink-paper leaves.

The Valentine manuscript consists of thirty-three leaves numbered consecutively in pencil by Whitman in the lower left corners, and stabbed in the left margin with black thread. An annotator, probably Barnet Beyer, has added in pencil the section numbers according to the system of the 1860 edition. Although Whitman did not himself indicate the sections except by spacing or the start on a fresh leaf, in the following account the 1860 numbers will be used for convenience of reference. Four kinds of paper appear: pink, blue wove, white wove, and blue Williamsburgh tax forms. Although revision in some unidentifiable dark inks is probable, at least four definite stages are in evidence, made respectively with pencil, a dark ink with a fine pen, pencil again, and finally with a thin light-brown ink.

The different varieties of paper reflect the growth and revision of the

---

1 According to the plan as preserved in the list, "Premonition" could not have begun the volume since for reasons of economy Whitman was proposing to utilize the paged plates of the 1856 edition at the start. Hence there was no virtue to placing it as soon as possible in the added poems, and Whitman's reasons for the ordering of the poems in the proposed third edition may have dictated a position later in the volume.

poem. There can be little doubt that the pink paper, generally thought to be cut from unused sheets of wrappers for the 1855 *Leaves of Grass*, composed the original leaves as now preserved. All of the pink paper is from one identical scissored pack, coded as p1(a), except for two leaves. Leaf 32 is on paper, coded as p1(b), which represents the sideways conjugate portion of a fold with p1(a) before further scissoring apart. Since in the Valentine collection the only other appearance of p1(a) paper is the sixth leaf of "Evolutions" (folder 43) and leaves 7–8 of "Poem of Joys" (folder 71), there may be significance to the fact that the paper changes with the penultimate leaf 32 (the final leaf 33 is a tax form), perhaps indicating the exhaustion of the pile of p1(a) leaves. Secondly, leaf 28 containing sec. 60 is on p2(b) paper, and on the further evidence of its deleted title "Aborigines" was originally inscribed as a separate poem without relation to "Premonition" until it was inserted subsequent to the completion of the first set of leaves but before foliation.[2] Thus the continuity of the paper establishes that Whitman wrote out the pink-paper leaves as a fairly continuous operation. But unless we are to suppose that he uncharacteristically took a single batch of this pink paper and wrote some of the sections off seriatim in first-draft form, we may more probably take it that though a few may represent initial composition, many—if not most—were copies of poems already roughed out in whole or in part in manuscripts not now generally preserved.[3] The heavy revision given to some sections in contrast to others could be taken as bearing on the question of first drafts. But it is perhaps significant that several versions deleted in favor of a fresh copy were extra heavily revised beforehand, and we cannot know whether, in fact, heavy revision was not a general characteristic of poems still in an earlier stage of drafting than others.[4] All that can be stated with confidence is that these pink leaves offer the earliest known states of the poems in any complete stage. The numerous pinholes in the centers of the leaves testify to the fact that before stabbing the leaves were pinned together in batches and frequently unpinned for survey, revision, or supplement.

2 On the uncertain evidence that "Aborigines" has no long-series number, it might be possible to conjecture that the insertion took place before Whitman numbered his manuscript poems from 33 to 100, that is, prior to 31 May 1857. Much depends, however, on the association of this leaf with surrounding tax-blank leaves, for which see below.

3 In the Trent Collection at Duke University are two manuscripts containing phrases and ideas subsequently used in "Premonition" (*Catalogue*, I, Nos. 17, 18), and Bucke in *Notes and Fragments* preserves a few early drafted lines. See also the early drafts in the Feinberg notebook reproduced here.

4 However, the paper from the same scissored pack indicates that the less heavily revised sections are not fair copies of original pink-paper leaves.

The blue wove paper is shown to be later than the pink by the fact that when sec. 23 in intermediate draft form (subsequently deleted) was written on blue leaf 8, the leaf was inserted between sec. 20 on the upper part of pink leaf 7 and the start of sec. 21, originally following on the lower part of leaf 7, by cutting off the start of sec. 21 from the foot and pasting it on the added blue leaf below sec. 23. Again, when additions were made on both blue and white paper following pink leaf 9, further intercalation was managed by cutting off the lower part of leaf 9, a piece containing secs. 43, 44 (originally written below sec. 21 on leaf 9), and placing this cut-off as a separate leaf after the additions, numbering it as 17.

That the Williamsburgh tax blanks are later than the pink leaves is effectively demonstrated by the revision on bill-head leaf 1 of sec. 1 originally written on pink paper now foliated as leaf 2, and of sec. 14 on leaf 4 originally written on pink leaf 5. The relation of the white to the pink paper is shown not only by the evidence presented elsewhere for dating the white in 1859 but also by the insertion of a white-paper sequence between the pink part-leaves 9 and 17, which have been cut apart from one leaf.

The real problem, therefore, is to attempt to relate the order of revision and expansion between the tax blanks, the white paper, and the blue leaves. The evidence of placement in the series and of similarity of ink suggests strongly that leaves 8, 10, and 11, which constitute the whole of the blue wove paper in this poem, were written and inserted on one occasion. On the other hand, it is clear that not all of the tax blanks or of the white leaves were introduced at the same time, and thus that there is the possibility at least for these to be chronologically mixed in relation to each other and to the blue paper. Therefore one must first survey the evidence within the paper groupings before attempting to relate these groups, or their parts, to one another.

The tax blanks are not very informative. It is obvious that leaves 1 and 4 are revisions of preserved pink-paper sections, and that leaf 33—for part of which a pink-paper draft is known—may have been copied in whole or in part on a pink leaf 33 before final revision on a tax blank. This use of tax blanks for revised fair copies of poems on pink paper is what we have, in general, found elsewhere in the Valentine manuscripts, perhaps because the size of the two was very similar. Whether leaves 27 and 29, the only other tax blanks, are revisions from earlier pink paper, revisions of drafts from other paper, or new compositions is doubtful. The fact that they surround the inserted pink leaf 28, "Aborigines," which was not originally written as part of "Premonition," is suspicious as associating the sections on these tax forms with the introduction of leaf 28; and it is clear that this whole group secs. 59–61 has been placed between pink-paper secs. 58 and 63, which originally were continuous on the same leaf but have been cut apart to admit the additions. When the texts are examined, one sees that sec. 59 on leaf 27 must have been written to introduce the subject of sec. 60 ("Aborigines") on leaf 28 and is therefore consequent upon the importation of "Aborigines" into "Premonition." Similarly, secs. 61 and 62 lead out of "Aborigines" and must have resulted from it, although the fact that sec. 62 differs in its ink from sec. 61 shows that it was an afterthought. Thus tax-blank leaves 27 and 29 may be associated with each other as added at about the same time,[5] subject to the qualification to be made presently. However, there is no way of knowing whether these leaves are unusual in containing newly written sections, or whether lines already tried out on pieces of other paper were copied on the tax blanks to secure uniform size of leaf.

The black ink on leaves 1 and 4 and that on 27 and 29 looks much the same, but there is some evidence that these two groups were not added at quite the same time. Leaf 1 revises the opening section, in part preserved on pink leaf 2, but the figure 2 on this second leaf has been written over an original 1. It is just possible, but not quite certain, that the folio number for leaf 3 has been altered from 2. Leaf 4—tax blank—has its number undisturbed, as we should expect. The figure on pink leaf 5 shows no apparent sign of interference, but folio 6 has been altered from

---

5 An interesting question thereupon arises whether the writing of tax blank leaf 27 (and 29?) was simultaneous with the introduction of leaf 28, "Aborigines," or came later as a part of the general revision. On the one hand, it is true that "Aborigines" comes in lacking much reason or sense without the accompanying new sections. On the other hand, if the absence of numbering of "Aborigines" is significant as indicating that it was inserted before the long series was numbered, then the simultaneous use of tax blanks, though not impossible, would represent their earliest appearance in the Valentine manuscripts, perhaps rather too early. On such evidence we might conjecture that "Aborigines" was first added by itself; but the position is not secure since we do not know whether its wanting a number is not, instead, due to

Whitman having withheld it from the numbered series.

The odd numbering of 26½ (sec. 58) at the head of a paste-on of pink paper above Williamsburgh leaf 27 (sec. 59) may be conjecturally explained without assisting in the problem. After the leaves were numbered, Whitman saw that the addition of secs. 59–61, and perhaps sec. 62 by this time, placed sec. 58 after 51 (or 62), whereas he preferred it to follow sec. 57 on leaf 26. He therefore cut off sec. 58 from the top of leaf 30 and placed it between already numbered leaves 26 and 27, perforce foliating it 26½. Later, seeing that such a small piece of paper might easily drop out of the batch since it would not be caught by the central pinning, he cut off the lower blank part of added leaf 27 in order to secure uniform size for the leaf, and pasted 26½ above it.

5. The exact interpretation of this evidence is not wholly clear, but at least it is certain that tax-blank leaf 1 was added after present leaf 2, and perhaps leaves 2–4 (original leaf 4 on pink paper?) had been foliated but before the numbering had progressed through the subsequent leaves. It is possible, therefore, that tax-blank leaves 1 and 4 are connected and that this revision was made at the time Whitman started to number the leaves of what he had considered to be his complete poem. If this is so, the addition of leaves 1 and 4 would precede that of any other which disturbed the foliation of the later leaves. It is of interest, therefore, to find that leaf 31 has been altered from 30. Leaves 30 and 32, on either side, show no alteration, but both leaves have been cut off at the bottom, and it is possible that this has removed an earlier foliation. Leaf 33 is a tax blank, inscribed very late, and hence shows no change.

The evidence is perhaps too slight to carry very far, but if the original foliation of leaf 31 were not a case of simple error, the alteration must have been made as a consequence of the insertion of some part of the preceding grouping of "Aborigines" leaf 28 or its associates, tax-blank leaves 27 or 29. The pink-leaf sequence folios 17–26 has not been tampered with. If leaves 27–29 had all been added after "Premonition" had been foliated, present leaf 30 would have been 27, and 31 would have been 28. Thus—again if the original figure on 31 were not an error—it would seem that only tax blank 29 could have caused the disruption. If this had not been present when the leaves were foliated, present 30 would have been numbered 29, and present 31 numbered 30.

There is so much of conjecture in this reconstruction, however, that it can be suggested only as a possibility. It is true that sec. 61 is not so essential to the "Aborigines" theme as is prefixed sec. 59, and it is also true that 61 could have been an afterthought, since sec. 62, in the light revising ink, was manifestly itself an afterthought to 61. The possibilities seem to add up to this. If leaf 29 were indeed an addition made after the numbering of the whole poem, it must have been inserted later than leaves 1 and 4; but since leaves 27 and 28 are foliated regularly, there is no evidence whether they were added earlier or else simultaneously with leaves 1 and 4. If the original foliation as 30 of present leaf 31 were merely an inadvertent slip, then we have a complete standoff. In either case, however, the insertion of leaves 27 and 28 (and possibly 29) may have been earlier but could not have been materially later than that of leaves 1 and 4, since we may suppose that following the introduction of folios 1 and 4 Whitman would have continued the numbering of the leaves. The use of the tax

blanks, and the similarity of the ink for all four leaves, suggests the probability that leaf 27 was prefixed to leaf 28, and then leaf 29 suffixed if not
at the same time then very shortly after, at a point in time not far removed
from the revisions now found on tax leaves 1 and 4. It may seem more
probable to place the insertion of leaf 27 simultaneously with that of pink
leaf 28 ("Aborigines" having been a poem left unnumbered for some
reason); but no positive evidence can be adduced, and leaf 28 may have
been brought in at any time after the inscription of the original pink
leaves. Leaf 29, containing sec. 61, to which was added sec. 62 at a later
time, may have been inserted along with leaf 27, but there is some chance
that it was a later addition. Finally, on the evidence of the thin light revising ink, we may place the revision of secs. 64 and 65 on tax-blank leaf 33
(probably at the same time as the addition of 62) as among the final
touches given the manuscript before it was included in the whole batch
sent to Rome Brothers.

The use of the white wove paper in "Premonition" is confined to one
continuous inserted sequence comprising leaves 12–16 (various sections
between 23 and 42). The foliation is regular. However, the five white
leaves do not seem to have been added at the same time. On the verso of
leaf 12 are found drafts for sections inscribed on leaf 13; and since it is
reasonable to assume that these were copied on leaf 13 (secs. 25, 27, 28, and
start of 35) before leaf 12 was reversed and secs. 24 and 23 written on it,
we may infer that leaf 13 was added before leaf 12, an inference supported
by the fact that the ink on the two leaves differs. Furthermore, since sec.
35 starting on leaf 13 is concluded on leaf 14 in the same ink, and sec.
36 added below it also in the same ink, leaves 13–14 as a unit are established as inscribed before leaf 12. No positive assumptions can be made
about leaf 15. For what it is worth, the ink of leaves 13–14 differs from
the ink(s) of leaves 12 and 15; but the positive identity of that on leaves
12 and 15 cannot be established, although it looks very similar. However,
leaf 15—like leaf 12—contains deleted lines on its verso (though of an
early draft of "Calamus" no. 11 in folder 13, one of the numbered "Live
Oak" poems), and thus is distinguished from leaves 13–14 and 16, and perhaps associated with leaf 12 as scrap paper. Moreover, the fact that the
lower section 41 has been cut from the foot of leaf 15 and pasted at the
head of leaf 16, where it manifestly substitutes for some excised and cut-
away lines, may lead to the hypothesis that among the white-paper leaves
in "Premonition" folios 13, 14, and 16 were introduced earlier than 12
and 15.

On the evidence of the foliation of the whole poem, it is obvious that all the white paper was added before the revision of leaf 1, and probably of 4, but earlier than that of leaf 33. There is no physical evidence whatever, on the other hand, to indicate whether the white-paper leaves were inserted before or after pink-paper leaf 28 or Williamsburgh leaf 27. If tax-blank leaf 29 were in fact introduced after the foliation, it would, naturally, be later than the white paper.

The relation of the blue wove paper is also obscure. In regard to the tax-blank leaves, it stands on the same footing as does the white paper. However, there is a connection between the blue and the white paper that is worth investigation. The most obvious is that sec. 23 was written in draft form on the white-paper leaf later used for "Enfans d'Adam" no. 9 (folder 5) and was then revised and brought into "Premonition" on blue leaf 8, which was inserted between sec. 20 on the upper part of pink leaf 7 and the start of sec. 21 from the foot of the pink leaf, by cutting off the start of sec. 21 from the bottom of leaf 7 and pasting it on the added blue leaf 8 below written-out sec. 23. Subsequently, sec. 23 on the blue paper was deleted and further revised, finally being assigned its place on the white paper of leaf 12. Some irregularity is present with leaf 12 in that sec. 24 was originally written at the head of the leaf, followed by 23 at the foot; but the positions have been reversed by cutting the leaf apart and pasting sec. 23 at the top above 24. So far as can be determined, sec. 23 need not have been added below 24 in a blank space at a later time: the two seem to be written in the same ink and with the same pen, and thus to be inscribed one after the other. However, the cutting apart is suspicious and may well afford grounds for speculation that the sec. 23 lines were indeed written-in after leaf 12 had been added to the poem.

A second connection exists between the blue and the white paper. Section 22 was written on blue leaves 10 and 11 in the same ink and presumably at the same time as the first inscription of sec. 23 on blue leaf 8. Originally, secs. 43, 44 had followed sec. 21 on pink leaf 9; but these two sections have been cut off and the lower part of leaf 9 now takes its place as leaf 17, with sec. 22 on the blue paper and then the white-paper series intervening. This part-leaf 17 is backed for stiffening by a piece of pasted-on blue paper over its entire verso.

White leaf 12, and probably 15, has been shown to be inscribed later than white leaves 13–14, and probably 16. If sec. 23 has been added to white leaf 12 immediately after sec. 24, then leaf 12 must be later than blue leaf 8; but if, instead, sec. 23 has merely been copied in a blank space below sec. 24 at some indeterminate time after the inscription of 24, no inferences can be drawn that leaf 8, and doubtless leaves 10–11, were earlier than leaf 12.

The strict evidence of the paper, therefore, leads to no certain conclusions; but there still remain grounds for inference. Leaf 9 on pink paper has obviously been cut apart between secs. 21 and 43 to admit insertions. These insertions could be blue leaves 10–11, or white leaves 13–16 (or separate leaves from this last sequence), or both—although this latter is less likely on the evidence of the variant inks between the blue and white paper. Since blue leaves 10–11 seem to be firmly associated with blue leaf 8, and the insertion of blue leaf 8 has caused pink leaf 7 to be cut apart to admit the blue-leaf version of sec. 23, it seems plausible to infer that the dividing of pink leaves 7 and 9 to admit blue-paper additions was made at the same time; and if this is so we must take it that blue leaves 8, 10, and 11 preceded the insertion of any of the white leaves. That this is very likely true may perhaps be supported by the strengthening of pink leaf 17 (the lower part of original pink leaf 9) by a backing of blue paper.[6]

Literary evidence may offer some further substantiation. After remarking in sec. 16, on pink leaf 5, of his respect for the past but his determination to write for and of the present, Whitman on pink leaf 6 in secs. 17 and 18 introduces a discussion of the soul, and in sec. 19 concludes that in writing of materials and the body he will be writing most spiritually. In sec. 20 on pink leaf 7 he thereupon launches forth on the subject of the song he will make for The States; and in sec. 21, which originally succeeded on leaf 9, he announces his determination to be a global poet of the future, and to celebrate sexuality. Then sec. 43, which originally followed after 21 on leaf 9, asserts, "I will make the songs of passions. . . ." It is evident that the addition of sec. 23 on blue leaf 8 between secs. 20 and 21 is appropriate, for the assertion that he will sing of democracy follows naturally after sec. 20 and acts as a bridge between the songs for The States and those for the world. Thereupon, if sec. 22 on blue leaves 10–11 were added and inserted between secs. 21 and 43, we should have a series of verses continuing the statement of themes for his songs. The announcement of sexual themes in sec. 21 would be followed by the assertion of the theme of 'companionship' in sec. 22, succeeded by the further announcement of themes in sec. 43. But if white leaves 13–14 had first

6 Otherwise we should need to suppose that leaf 9 was cut apart to admit leaves 12–16 (or parts) and that only when blue leaves 10–11 were inserted before this sequence was leaf 17 strengthened. However, this is not impossible, and we may recall the white-paper leaf in folder 11 held together by a strip of the much earlier pink paper.

intervened, we should have the abrupt announcement "I dart forth Religion" followed by some autobiographical material on the loved young man before returning to sec. 43. All in all, it seems most probable that blue leaves 8, 10, and 11 represent the initial stage of revision or expansion of "Premonition" on paper other than the pink leaves.

On the basis of the evidence and the inferences one may reasonably draw from it, the following conjectural account may be given of the growth of "Premonition." If we may take literally the dating statement made in sec. 11, added in late 1859 or early 1860 as part of the expansion of the poem in the Rome Brothers proof, the inception of "Premonition" goes back to the first half of 1856. Except for a few brief records of ideas, the original drafts for lines have not been recorded as preserved save for the Feinberg notebook versions in October of 1856. At some time, probably in early 1857, Whitman brought together by copying, revision, and new composition the earliest known organized form[7] on a single batch of pink paper as follows, the leaf numbers listed being his final ones and the section numbers those of the 1860 edition:

Leaf	Section
2	1, 2
3	3, 4, 13
5	14, 16
6	17, 18, 19
7	20, 21 (start)
9+17	21 (concl.), 43, 44
18	45
19	46, 47
20	48, 49, 50
21	51, 52, 53, 54
22–26	55, 56, 57
30	58, 63 (start)
31–32	63 (concl.)

The status of secs. 64 and 65 on leaf 33 is uncertain. A draft for a few verses in what was later to be separated as sec. 65 is found on the verso of "Chants Democratic" no. 11 (folder 46), written on p1(c) paper. If the tax-blank leaf 33 were used to copy out a revision of these lines from a lost earlier pink leaf 33, as is possible, then secs. 64, 65 could be added to the

---

7 Since all the paper except leaf 32 is from the same pack, although the ink used varies somewhat, it is reasonable to assume that the copying-out was roughly seriatim; but except when sections are found on the same leaf, or continued on another, we cannot be positive that the order of inscription was that found at present. The earliest order of composition of the sections is, of course, quite lost.

foregoing list. But these sections would very likely not have been present in the original copying-out, since it is probable that p1(c) paper was used somewhat later than the p1(a, b) employed for the earliest "Premonition" inscription.

This list represents the earliest recoverable state of the poem, but a few speculations may be admitted about some sections which may represent later rather than earlier composition. When these original pink-paper sections are surveyed, it immediately becomes apparent that the universal and patriotic note struck in most of the sections, which are concerned with the announcement of themes and attitudes, is curiously broken in sections 56, 57, very likely 58, and also 64+65, which, figuratively speaking, introduce the scent of the calamus. Moreover, it seems reasonably evident that these sections constitute a unit, and that they immediately precede the lengthy sec. 63 and follow it. It also seems evident that this sec. 63 is directly concerned with the patriotic and universal announcements theme, in which it may connect with such sections as 55, and that its conclusion is a natural ending to the whole poem. It is possible to guess, therefore, that the only sections which insinuate anything of the calamus theme were not in the earliest form a part of the poem and that they have been added in the last stage of the copying-out. If this is so, we cannot tell whether there was or was not an early pink leaf 33 since the subject of its verses is similar to that of secs. 56, 57, and 58; and leaf 33 on pink paper, if it ever existed, would have been a revised ending on a different lot of paper from the p1 (a,b) found otherwise in "Premonition."

It is noteworthy that the majority of the subsequent additions to the pink-paper form of the poem concern themselves with the latent or explicit theme of 'manly love,' a subject already begun, apparently, in the last stage of the present inscription and one which differs markedly from what seem to be the earlier parts of "Premonition," or its earliest concept. This theme had been broached in a few of the poems on pink paper in Whitman's early list of a hundred; but it was to become the almost invariable preoccupation of the added poems on white paper in the Valentine collection.

The exact stages of expansion in "Premonition" cannot always be clearly marked. If we were to work with the evidence of themes alone, it would be tempting to place first the insertion of pink leaf 28 containing sec. 60 "Aborigines." This may well be so, since this poem strengthens and supplements the American note struck so firmly in the earliest parts; but in fact there is no evidence for the time at which this leaf was added, or whether one or both of its accompanying tax-form leaves accompanied it if the insertion were early. Among the first of the insertions we may certainly place sec. 23 in its intermediate form on blue leaf 8 and the 'companionship' section 22 on blue leaves 10–11, these inserts necessitating the cutting apart of pink leaf 7 to admit sec. 23 between secs. 20 and 21, and of pink leaf 9 to admit sec. 22 between 21 and 43. Since sec. 23 had first been drafted in a notebook containing elsewhere an entry dated 26 June 1859, and then on white wove paper subsequently used for "Enfans d'Adam" no. 9 (folder 5), there is every reason to place this addition of the blue leaves in mid-1859, at least two years after the inscription of the pink-paper form of the poem.[8]

Following this I should assign the insertion of white wove leaves 13, 14, and 16 (secs. 25, 27, 28, 35, 36, 42), and very shortly of white wove leaves 12 (revised sec. 23, and sec. 24 originally inscribed in reverse order) and 15 (an unpublished section, and secs. 38, 39, 40, and also 41 a paste-on from leaf 15 subsequently attached to leaf 16 perhaps as a revision of verses heading that leaf). Leaf 15 was written on paper previously used to rough out "Calamus" no. 11 (folder 13), one of the original group of "Live Oak with Moss" roman-numbered poems. If we make the tempting but dangerous conjecture that the fair copies of these twelve poems preceded the calamus-laden original sheets of "Calamus" no. 2, which can be dated after 16 March 1859, then these insertions on blue and on white wove paper may have preceded mid-March of 1859. However, the odds are that the insertions are later than 26 June.

At some indeterminate time after the insertion of white leaves 12–16, I conjecture that Whitman began to foliate the poem in the expectation that it was completed. During the process of numbering the first few leaves he read over the opening verses and decided to revise sec. 1 (original leaf 1, later renumbered 2) and sec. 14 (originally heading pink leaf 5). He rewrote these sections in a black ink on Williamsburgh tax blanks, and—revising his foliation for the early leaves—continued with his numbering, perhaps making pencil revisions in the text as he went along. I conjecture that either shortly before this revision producing Williamsburgh leaves 1 and 4 or else immediately after as he continued to foliate the poem, Whitman prefixed tax-blank leaf 27 containing sec. 59 to inserted pink leaf 28

8 The note book not now being available, I do not know whether the earliest draft of section 23 preceded or succeeded Whitman's dated note. In the present state of our knowledge, then, whether the blue leaves were added before or after 26 June cannot be determined. The subsequent draft on white wove paper, however, indicates fairly strongly that the date must have been in 1859.

(sec. 60 "Aborigines"),[9] this sec. 59 perhaps written in the same ink as leaves 1 and 4. Then, I take it, he continued to foliate the rest of the leaves, but very shortly felt the need to follow sec. 60 by bridging verses and so composed sec. 61 on tax blank leaf 29, inserting it with consequent alteration of the foliation of leaf 31 (and of 30 and 32, cut off). If, instead, the original numbering of leaf 31 as 30 were only a slip, we should need to assign the addition of leaf 29 at the same time as that of leaf 27.

The final group of additions or revisions was made in the thin light revising ink, doubtless not long before the delivery of the manuscripts to Rome Brothers, conjecturally in the late summer of 1859. Various sections were finally revised in this ink, and at roughly the same time, also, sec. 62 was inscribed on tax blank leaf 29 beneath sec. 61; and secs. 64–65 written on tax blank leaf 33, possibly—though not certainly—substituting for an earlier version on pink paper other than p1(a,b).

In this form the leaves, together with the other poems represented in the Valentine-Barrett collection, were sent to Rome Brothers for type-setting and pulling of proofs. Since Whitman's foliation, and the stabbing of the leaves, precludes the possibility that some of the sections have strayed, we may infer with confidence that the sections which appeared in the 1860 edition but are not found in manuscript are additions subsequently composed in late 1859 or early 1860. In the 1860 edition's numbering these are secs. 5, 6, 7, 8, 9, 10, 11, 12, 15, 26, 29, 30, 31, 32, 33, 34, and 37. Whitman rejected in proof parts of the manuscript version and very considerably rewrote some sections before submitting his mixed printer's copy to Thayer and Eldridge, the publishers of the 1860 edition.

IV. Calamus and Enfans d'Adam

The 'cluster'—to use Whitman's own word—which was to grow into the forty-five poems comprising the "Calamus" section in the 1860 *Leaves of Grass* began with a much smaller concept and with a different symbolic nexus. One of the most interesting facts revealed by the Valentine-Barrett manuscripts is that for the major period during the growth of Whitman's plans for the expanded third edition he seems not to have formulated the eventual cluster organization until a very considerable body of miscellaneous poems (at least seventy odd) had already been composed and numbered in order with the new edition in view.

From the analysis of the growth of "Premonition" it has been seen that

9 Provided always leaf 28 was not brought over at the same time instead of earlier.

the pink-paper leaves represent the poems of earliest inscription and that the white wove-paper leaves were a subsequent addition and expansion. Correspondingly, both pink paper and white wove paper from the same stock (as well as one leaf of a blue wove ruled paper and four of Williamsburgh blanks) appear in "Calamus" in circumstances which demonstrate that the white wove paper was employed later than the pink.

The list of poems between no. 33 and no. 72 found on the verso of the second pink-paper leaf of "To an Exclusive" numbered 100 (originally 99) checks with similar, revised numbering of numerous poems in the Valentine collection—including extension to no. 101 (originally 102) in folder 41—to show that beginning with no. 33 and extending through no. 101 a considerable proportion of the poems found collected in the 1860 edition under the sequence-headings "Chants Democratic," "Enfans d'Adam," "Calamus," "Leaves," and "Messenger Leaves" were earlier planned and written in an arrangement which had no relation whatever to these 'clusters.' Thus when the cluster idea was evolved as the major organization for the 1860 edition, the earlier conceived order was completely revised, and numerous poems already composed and numbered according to this earliest order were redistributed for inclusion in the clusters, although originally no such connection between them had existed.

In attempting to determine which poems among the Valentine manuscripts were composed from the start as "Calamus" cluster-poems, therefore, we may throw out all "Calamus" poems in the 1860 edition which are found in the Valentine manuscripts written on pink paper. The remainder are chiefly written on white wove paper, with one on blue wove ruled paper and four on tax blanks. Of those poems inscribed on the white paper, twelve fall readily into a connected roman-numbered series:

MS Poem Number	Foliation	1860 Poem Number	Folder	Paper	Ink
I "Calamus-Leaves" *	1	14	16	w1(a)	black
II	2–3	20	21	w1(a)	"
III†	4–5	11	13	w1(a)	"
IV	6	23	24	w1(a)	"
V	7, 8, 8½	8	10	w1(a)	"
VI	9	32	34	w1(a)	"
VII	9½, 10‡	10	12	w1(a, b)	"
VIII§	11–12‖	9	11	w1(b)	"
IX	13#	34	33	w1(b)	"
X	14	43	39	w1(b)	"
XI	15	36	32	w1(b)	"
XII	16	42	36	w1(b)	"

It is clear that these leaves originally formed part of a notebook in which the poems were written on the rectos continuously in the order indicated by their roman numbers. The normal vertical measurement of a full leaf is about $5\frac{3}{4}$ inches. The part leaves can be fitted together by their contours to reconstruct the notebook as follows:

Notebook Leaf	Poem Number	MS Foliation
1	I	1
2–3	II	2–3
4–5	III	4–5
6	IV	6
7–8	V	7–8
9	V (concluded)	$8\frac{1}{2}$
	VI (upper half of MS leaf 9 made from two pasted together pieces)	
10	VI (lower half of MS leaf 9)	9
	VII (half-leaf)	$9\frac{1}{2}$
11	VII	10
12	VII (concluded: pasted below full leaf above to make up complete MS leaf 10)	
	VIII (half-leaf)	11
13	VIII	12
14	VIII (concluded: pasted below full leaf above to make up complete MS leaf 12)	
	IX (half-leaf)	13
15	X	14
16	XI	15
17	XII	16

By their left margins, furthermore, these leaves can be fitted together to show that the notebook was originally of 20 leaves, made up of 10 conjugate quired folds. The original conjugacy of notebook full leaves 4+17, 5+16, 6+15, 7+14, 8+13, 9+12, and 10+11 can be established by the contours left by their having been torn apart. Thus leaves 1–3, at

---

* The original head-title, written in the text ink, was "Live Oak with Moss." The alteration to "Calamus-Leaves" was made in the light ink used for later poems to be described.

† This no. III is a revised version of verses earlier drafted under the heading V on what is now the verso of "Premonition" leaf 15.

‡ This foliation is written over other numbers each beginning with the digit '1' and probably representing 10 and 11.

§ This no. VIII was originally numbered as IX, the VIII being added in what may doubtfully be a somewhat finer pen. Since the tip of the number IX of the following poem is visible at the foot of the last leaf of revised VIII, it is probable that the original numbering as IX was merely a slip. The paper demonstrates, as will be shown, that VIII followed VII and preceded IX in the little notebook containing these poems.

‖ This foliation was written over two now illegible numbers.

The second digit of this foliation was written over some other number, now illegible.

present disjunct (w1a), as will be shown later, fitted together with three final blank leaves 18–20 (w1b) to form the complete notebook. A few of the leaves have some signs of paste in the left margin. Moreover, a few small holes in the left margins of the leaves as at present cut up, and a small piece of white thread still drawn through one of these holes on two leaves, indicate that after the notebook was torn apart the leaves were attached to each other by a form of stabbing.

The alterations in the numbering of MS leaves 9½–13 are not easy to explain. It seems clear that the notebook leaves were not foliated until they were sected in their present form and hence that the altered foliation does not represent an attempt to combine two systems. Leaf 5, for example, has a revising paste-over on its lower half which seems to have been added after the leaf was removed from the notebook, but the foliation is on the paste-over and not on the original leaf beneath. Moreover, when the foot of an original notebook leaf does not correspond to the foot of a MS leaf, no sign of numbering is present. Finally, the folio number 16 is added on a disturbed part of the paper and manifestly after the leaf had been torn out of the book. Thus it would seem that Whitman either inadvertently made some mistake which he repaired, or, more likely, that one of the reasons for cutting apart the notebook may have been a plan to rearrange the order, which was subsequently abandoned.[7]

It seems reasonably clear that in these twelve poems we have the start of the later greatly expanded "Calamus" cluster. In connection with this little series three points may be mentioned.

1. The poems appear to be highly unified and to make up an artistically complete story of attachment, crisis, and renunciation.

2. They are manifestly fair copies, as indicated by the comparative lack of revision which they have undergone as well as by the fact that a draft for number III (then headed V) is preserved on the verso of one of the white-paper additions to "Premonition." The pen and ink of all twelve poems appears to be the same, and there seems every reason to believe that they were copied out fair from lost drafts at substantially the same time.[8]

7 In view of the fact that part-leaf 13 (poem IX) was originally numbered something else, it is hard to see where a slip could have come unless it was recognized before leaf 14 was foliated. However, folios 11 and 12 seem to be written over some one-digit number now undecipherable but faintly resembling 7–8.

8 G. W. Allen has conjectured that the reference in no. III to "praised in the Capitol" goes back to a long review of *Leaves of Grass* printed in the *National Intelligencer* on 18 February 1856. The review was on the whole favorable, and in early 1856 one can imagine that Whitman was impressed by it. The event recorded in this poem, then, may precede even the second edition of *Leaves;* but its early date obviously has no relation to the date of composition, which must have been

3. The calamus symbol is nowhere mentioned in these poems, which instead, in no. I but especially in no. II, refer to the live oak. It is significant in the extreme that the early heading for the series was "Live Oak with Moss" and that "Calamus-Leaves" was substituted at a later date.

Among the "Calamus" poems as printed in 1860 there are eight additional in the Valentine manuscripts which are inscribed on white wove paper of the same stock as that utilized for the twelve in the roman-numbered series. Of these, no. 39 (folder 35) represents the conjugate half of leaf 2 of the notebook and thus must have been blank leaf 19; and nos. 44 and 38 (folder 30 + 37) were written on the conjugate half of leaf 3 and represent notebook leaf 18. The poems on both of these leaves are written in a light to medium brown ink. Because of the same general size of leaf, it would be tempting to assign no. 37 (folder 31) as perhaps the missing leaf 20 of the notebook though its torn margin forbids demonstration; however, the fact that paste-over slip no. 8 attached to "So Long" as one of its final revisions is made up from the top of a piece of w1(b) paper and is written in the same ink as the poems on notebook leaves 18 and 19 makes it certain that no. 37 is, instead, from some unidentified pack of paper. No. 37 is written in a black ink.

Of the remaining five poems, two and a portion of a third are inscribed on pieces of the white wove paper (w2) measuring approximately $6\frac{1}{4}$ inches vertically. These are written in the light to medium brown ink and comprise no. 1 (folder 7), the first two leaves of no. 2 (folder 7), and the four

much later. At any rate, there is no reason not to suppose that lost drafts underlie the draft found on the back of the "Premonition" leaf.

That these twelve poems had a special significance for Whitman seems clear from the form he gave them in the little notebook. The verses contained only on leaf 2 of the series (that is, the first leaf of no. II) were reprinted by Bucke in *Notes and Fragments*, p. 51, as no. 183. This text, found among Whitman's papers, has only one slight variant from the Valentine manuscript form. The Berg Collection in the New York Public Library also has a manuscript of this poem copied out on good paper and then cancelled by a diagonal line. This seems to represent a slightly earlier version. The special nature of the poem (and its series) can be evaluated by a note found on the back of the Berg manuscript:

"Poems

A Cluster of Poems, Sonnets expressing the thoughts, pictures, aspirations &c
Fit to be perused during the days of the approach of Death.
(that I have prepared myself for that purpose.—
(Remember now—
Remember then"

If this note refers to the "Live Oak" sequence, as seems possible, then the reference to Whitman having himself prepared the cluster is very likely to his having assembled and copied out the poems in a form to be kept by him. This would presumably refer to a still earlier notebook or collection than that preserved in the Valentine papers. The form of the preserved notebook suggests that for some time Whitman may not have intended to print these poems.

leaves in quired folds of no. 4 (folder 8). Of these, the two leaves begin-ning no. 2 cannot be identified as connected with any other of the white paper in the Valentine manuscripts, but no. 1 and 4, totaling five leaves, come from one large sheet of white wove paper measuring $15\frac{3}{4} \times 12\frac{1}{2}$ inches which had been folded and torn to make eight leaves in all. If we reconstruct this sheet by imagining it placed with its longest edge of $15\frac{3}{4}$ inches horizontally, the leaves will be in vertical position, the upper row reading from left to right (1) leaf 1 of "Chants Democratic" no. 14 "To Poets to Come" (folder 50); (2) leaf 2, conjugate with leaf 1; (3) "Enfans d'Adam" no. 1 "Leaves-Droppings" (folder 2); (4) "Calamus" no. 1 (folder 7); and in the bottom row (5) through (8) leaves 4, 1, 3, 2 of "Calamus" no. 4 (folder 8). These are all written in the same ink and apparently with the same pen except for "Leaves-Droppings" which seems to be written with a slightly thicker pen. Moreover, this ink seems to be identical with that used to inscribe the white-paper leaves of "Calamus" no. 2 (first two leaves), the small paste-on of no. 18 (folder 20) and the w1(b) leaves taken from leaves 18–19 of the "Calamus" notebook (nos. 44, 38 and 39). In addition, this same pen and ink seems to have inscribed the two white leaves of "Nearing Departure" entitled in 1860 "To My Soul" (folder 79), although this paper cannot be connected with other pieces of the white wove stock. Because these last leaves also measure $6\frac{1}{4}$ inches vertically, it seems possible to infer that they were part of another sheet of paper, separately torn into leaves like the reconstructed sheet above, and that the two unidentified leaves beginning "Calamus" no. 2 very likely came from the same sheet, although they were apparently not in any adjacent position—or at least from a similar sheet.

Three poems now remain. These are written on larger pieces of the white wove paper which represent a quarter of the original large sheet. The first is what seems to have been, rather curiously, the original no. 2 (folder 7) before the two smaller leaves of w2 paper were prefixed. This is the poem written, after cutting apart, on the back of the sheet which had originally contained the draft of the Brooklyn Waterworks editorial. The second is no. 12 "To a New Personal Admirer" (folder 14) on paper that cannot be connected with other pieces. Finally there is no. 18 (folder 20), written in much the same ink on the back of an early draft for "Enfans d'Adam" no. 1. This leaf fits sideways to "Enfans d'Adam" no. 9, the interesting "Once I Passed through a Populous City" poem, itself written on the back of a draft for sec. 23 of "Premonition," to make up a half-sheet (w3).

Of the remaining white wove paper in the Valentine manuscripts the leaves in "Premonition" do not join with each other or with other pieces, nor can the two leaves of "Enfans d'Adam" no. 8 (folder 4) be identified as originally adjacent to other leaves. Paste-on slip no. 8 of "So Long" seems to be the top of a w1(b) leaf, part of leaf 20 of the "Live-Oak" notebook, and it is written in the same ink as the leaves in folder 8. The white paper in "Poem of Joys" cannot be identified.

When on the slim evidence available we attempt to place in some approximate order the inscription of the various poems on this white wove paper, it seems clear on the evidence of the ink that the later additions on the blank notebook leaves (nos. 44, 38, and 39) coincide substantially with the inscription of the poems on w2 paper measuring $6\frac{1}{4}$ vertically, and therefore that the writing-out of roman-numbered poems I–XII preceded the copying of these other poems on w2 paper. It also seems clear on the evidence of the draft for "Enfans d'Adam" no. 1 on the verso of "Calamus" no. 18 (originally part of the same sheet as the leaf of "Enfans d'Adam" no. 9) that the w2 paper, on which the final form of "Enfans d'Adam" no. 1 was written, and doubtless the rest of the poems on leaves from the same sheet, preceded the inscription of "Calamus" no. 18 (and its identified conjugate, "Adam" no. 9) on the w3 or quarter-sheet paper as represented by these two poems.[9]

It is unfortunate that the only poem in "Calamus" that can be dated with any confidence—that original part of no. 2 written on quarter-sheets containing the draft editorial on the verso—cannot be linked with other paper. Although the poem begins rather abruptly on the first leaf of the large paper with what is now verse 11, the fact that this leaf was numbered 81 in pencil, almost certainly with an original intent to place the poem in the long numbered series, indicates that the prefixed leaves on w2 paper which now begin the final version were inscribed at a later date. Although the paper of these two prefixed leaves cannot be physically connected with any of the white leaves, the ink establishes that they were doubtless written-out at substantially the same time as the rest of the w2 paper. However, this fact has no bearing on the important relation between the drafting of that part of no. 2 on the large paper (for it seems definitely to be a first draft, heavily revised) in March or April of 1859 and the inscription of the fair copies of the roman-numbered poems in the notebook.

---

9 Yet if this is so, it is extremely odd that a paste-on revision is made to no. 18 in the light ink though the lines of the poem on the w3 paper are written in a darker brown-black ink.

Nevertheless, it seems plausible to conjecture that the twelve roman-numbered poems preceded this original part of no. 2. There is good evidence that the earliest symbol which Whitman adopted for 'manly love' was the live oak, its leaves and moss. This symbol is worked out in poems I and II and is given as the original title for the sequence. On the other hand, the original part of no. 2 is closely concerned with the calamus leaves as the symbol for male friendship. Slight as the inference may be, it seems reasonable to hold that Whitman did not have these two associations simultaneously in his mind; but that instead the live oak preceded the calamus and was later engulfed by it. If so, the pencil-numbered 81 poem would seem to have been written later than the live-oak series and—as attested by its added number—to have been planned for inclusion in the long series independent of any cluster. Subsequently, Whitman decided upon the calamus as his basic symbol, altered the heading "Live Oak with Moss" to read "Calamus-Leaves," and in the same ink wrote two 'heading' poems—no. 1 and the prefixed leaves to no. 2—which performed for the calamus what poems I and II had done for the live oak as an association.[10]

On the available evidence the dating of the various forms of the white wove paper presents real difficulty. We know that the five leaves of larger paper which comprised the original form of "Calamus" no. 2 must have been written after 16 March 1859, but how soon after is indeterminable. If the date of June, 1859, in the notebook containing the early draft of "Premonition" sec. 23 has any bearing on the verses, as seems probable, it would follow that the intermediate draft on the verso of "Enfans d'Adam" no. 9 would place the inscription of this no. 9 after late June, and with no. 9 we should, on the evidence of the paper, include "Calamus" no. 18.

10 The suggestion has been made above that at least in part the spurt of poetic energy that produced the large number of added poems for the earliest planned stage of the third edition was motivated by some specific emotional experience. That this perhaps occurred as early as 1856 or in the winter of early 1857 might be inferred from various of the pink-paper poems which celebrate this experience and were transferred in the 1860 edition to the full "Calamus" section. Moreover, it is significant that when the original set of pink-paper poems was expanded after the summer of 1857, the added poems on white wove paper group themselves almost exclusively in what became in the 1860 printed edition "Calamus" and its later derivative, "Enfans d'Adam." The date of the expansion, at least as concerns the fair copies made on white wove paper, is the crucial point, however, and this seems to have occurred as late as 1859. But we do not know how long Whitman worked over the drafts before making the final copies. If the "praised in the Capitol" poem is truly autobiographical—and the ocean bathing before dawn in February, 1856 makes this somewhat doubtful in all details if Professor Allen's conjectural identification is to be accepted—the experience was early and the literary fruits came later.

Since the verso of no. 18 contains a draft for "Enfans d'Adam" no. 1, part
of a whole sheet of w2 paper that can be reconstructed, the various poems
on this w2 paper ought to have been inscribed at some indeterminate
date before no. 18. From the draft of "Calamus" no. 11 on the verso of
leaf 15 of "Premonition" we know that the notebook roman-numbered
poems were inscribed as a unit before the insertion of leaf 15 in "Premonition." Unfortunately, no physical connection can be established between
leaf 15 and leaf 12 (containing the final form of sec. 23) in "Premonition."
It seems probable that these two leaves were added after leaves 13, 14, and
16; but whether together or separately is not known. It would seem to
be a reasonable inference, however, that the use of this white wove paper
did not extend over a period of many months, and certainly not years.
Attention has already been called to the fact that the white-paper additions in "Premonition" sift a calamus fragrance into this poem not found
in its earliest form. We may well believe, therefore, that the additions to
"Premonition" and the inscription of the white-paper poems later found
in "Calamus" and "Enfans d'Adam" were made at substantially the same
time. If this is so, the inscription of the fair copies of the roman-numbered
poems in the notebook was very likely made in the spring of 1859; but
since they are fair copies not much can be told about the actual date of
composition. The draft of no. III on the back of leaf 15 of "Premonition"
is very likely not the first composition. Hence it is as possible that the
actual writing-out of the notebook was later than the composition of the
first form of "Calamus" no. 2 as that no. 2 followed on the notebook.
The late spring to early summer of 1859 seems a plausible rough date for
both.

However, the fact that no. 2 was, some time after its composition, assigned a number in the long series, and also "Enfans d'Adam" no. 8, as no.
81 and no. 82 respectively, demonstrates that at least as late as April, 1859,
Whitman was still thinking in terms of a non-cluster arrangement. The
roman-numbered notebook, on the other hand, may seem to represent a
modification of his earliest plans and the insertion of one cluster somewhere in the long series, this cluster being confined to twelve poems.[12]
The question then arises whether before the whole batch of Valentine
manuscripts was turned over to Rome Brothers this plan was revised and
a larger cluster planned. The inscription of "Calamus" no. 1 and the significant prefixed new leaves to no. 2, together with the inscription of nos.

12 The fact that the remaining three leaves
in the notebook were originally left blank
helps to re-inforce this inference. Yet the
original plan may have been to withhold
the notebook poems altogether.

38, 39, and 44 on what had been the two blank leaves of the notebook, and the inscription of no. 4—to which we may add "Enfans d'Adam" no. 9 addressed in the manuscript to a man—seem to be coincidental with the alteration of the heading of notebook poem no. I from "Live Oak with Moss" to "Calamus-Leaves." This alteration is certainly significant, for without various of the additional poems "Calamus-Leaves" would have no point attached merely to poems I–XII. It would seem, then, that before sending his manuscripts to be set up in proof, Whitman had determined to expand his first idea for a cluster, had changed its basic symbolism, brought over no. 81 from the long series and revised it, and added to the sequence the poems mentioned above.[13] If this is so, there is every reason to suppose that no. 18 should also be added to this list. No. 12 is less certain, since it is the single titled poem on the white paper and seems, as a consequence, not to have been written with the sequence in mind. Whether the foliation, either original or revised, found on the leaves of some of these poems refers to a separate organization or to their inclusion in the expanded series cannot be determined.[14]

Of the remaining Valentine-Barrett poems found printed in "Calamus" in 1860, those on pink paper are all titled and numbered in the long series and thus cannot have been composed for the purposes of the cluster. Of the three poems on the backs of tax blanks, no. 27 (folder 27) is also titled and numbered in the long series and is therefore manifestly a revision of some earlier pink-paper poem. A second, no. 15 (folder 17), is not numbered but is entitled "Confession Drops." The title is rather against the theory that it was inscribed or revised for the purposes of the "Calamus" cluster. The third, no. 7 (folder 9), has neither title nor number: possibly it was revised for insertion in "Calamus" from some pink-paper poem, but evidence is lacking. No. 40 (folder 40) on ruled blue wove paper, without title or number, is equally ambiguous. We cannot know whether just before he gave the manuscripts to Rome Brothers Whitman abstracted these

---

13 It is somewhat odd that Whitman chose to substitute the heading "Calamus-Leaves" for "Live Oak with Moss" and therefore presumably to begin his cluster with the live oak poems I and II instead of with nos. 1 and 2 which seem designed to introduce the calamus theme, as they do in the 1860 edition. It may be that he was hurried and thought he could make all necessary rearrangements in proof.

14 "Calamus" no. 4 was foliated 3–6, revised to 1–4 (this last probably an independent unit-foliation not in any series). The two prefixed leaves to no. 2 were foliated 8–9 but have been altered in blue pencil to 2 and 1 respectively. No. 37 was numbered 9, altered in blue pencil to 3. No. 39 has what seems to be a blue-pencil numbering, somewhat like the start of a 4, but whether this is written over a pencil number cannot be seen. Rearrangement of some earlier plan is certainly indicated, but the details are obscure.

poems, including those on pink paper, from their series and arranged them under the "Calamus-Leaves" heading. My own feeling is that this was performed later, in proof, but the single evidence that can be offered is the inscription of white-paper no. 12 with a title which seems to dissociate it from the "Calamus" cluster though it was later printed as a part of the expanded grouping.

If we may take it as a general rule that poems printed in 1860 but not found in the Valentine collection or Rome printed list represent composition, or at least final inscription,[15] after the date when the manuscripts were turned over for setting up into proof, then it is possible that the nine poems in the 1860 printed "Calamus" section not preserved in manuscript are pieces composed or written-out in final form at a date subsequent to the release of the manuscripts and thus that they may be assigned to the second half of 1859 or to early 1860.[16]

Although it seems clear that before he sent off his manuscripts Whitman had designed a "Calamus" cluster of about twenty odd poems, no evidence exists to suggest that the 1860 groupings of "Chants Democratic" or "Messenger Leaves" had been evolved at this time.

The case is less certain for "Enfans d'Adam." What was no. 1 in this group in 1860 was demonstrably inscribed at the same time as the other poems on the reconstructed sheet of w2 paper, and is known in draft before the inscription of "Calamus" no. 18. It is, therefore, intimately associated in point of time with the expansion of the "Calamus" cluster; but its subject sets it off from "Calamus" and its heading "Leaves-Droppings" sounds rather as if it were intended as the head-title for a sequence.[17]

From two of Whitman's notes we know that at some indeterminate time after the writing of the twelve notebook poems he was meditating a balancing cluster on the subject of the love of women. The first was clearly written before the expansion of the original twelve "Live Oaks" poems into a modified "Calamus" sequence:

A string of Poems, (short etc.) embodying the amative love of woman—the same as *Live Oak Leaves* do the passion of friendship for man.[18]

15 It seems probable that some poems were in process of composition or revision when Whitman sent off his manuscripts: for example, verses which formed part of "Enfans d'Adam" no. 6, known only in print, are found on the back of pink-paper "Thought" in folder 46.

16 This may be true in general though not in particular application to any specific poem not found in the manuscripts.

17 This heading is in the text ink and therefore presumably written at the same time as the fair copy of the verses. It is not found in the draft. Below the heading is a pencilled arabic figure 1, but it is doubtful whether this is Whitman's.

18 Bucke, *Notes and Fragments*, p. 169; Camden ed., X, 18.

The second comes later, seemingly after the alteration of the sequence title:

Theory of a Cluster of Poems the same *to the passion of Woman-Love* as the *Calamus-Leaves* are to adhesiveness, manly love. Full of animal fire, tender, burning.—. . . . Adam, as a central figure and type.[19]

Unless we are to suppose that the new title "Calamus-Leaves" had been in Whitman's mind for some time before he altered the original manuscript title "Live Oak with Moss," it would seem possible that this note was written after the inscription of "Enfans d'Adam" no. 1, which seems to have been performed very close to the time that the title change was made.

Thus it may be an open question whether the composition of a poem about Adam and Eve led Whitman to the idea of an "Adam" cluster, or whether no. 1 was written after the concept of such a cluster had been formulated. At any rate, "Leaves-Droppings" may seem to be a rather neutral title for such a cluster. Thus whether this title was given to no. 1 in manuscript to introduce a woman-love grouping of poems or else some much more general section is doubtful,[20] and the case for the title to introduce the "Adam" cluster is not aided by the fact that only five of the fifteen poems in the 1860 "Enfans d'Adam" are preserved in the Valentine manuscripts, of which two are early pink-paper poems from the long series, and another, No. 9, celebrates manly love in the manuscript though the sex has been altered in the 1860 revised version. Of the remaining two, on white wove paper, no. 8 has been given a long-series number and thus was certainly not composed as an "Adam" poem, although it might have been brought over into such a sequence, as its companion, "Calamus" no. 2, was later revised for apparent insertion in that cluster. We are left, then, only with no. 1 which might have been composed for an "Adam" series. It would seem, therefore, that the cluster which was later to become "Enfans d'Adam" was perhaps forming in Whitman's mind at the time he sent off his manuscripts, but that it is unlikely the manuscripts reflect any real plan for such a cluster. If so, "Leaves-Droppings" may very well reflect only a general series which he had in mind, the details of which are lost.[21]

19 Bucke, p. 150; Camden ed., IX, 150.
20 It had, in fact, been used in the second edition as the title for a catch-all group.
21 It is somewhat tempting, on the basis of its title, to speculate that "Calamus" no. 15, on a tax blank, entitled "Confession Drops" in manuscript, may have been a poem planned for the "Leaves-Droppings" series. Almost any other poem, however, would have had to be removed from the long numbered-series on pink paper.

The Texts

[FOLDER 1]

[Leaf 1, blue tax blank (8½ × 4¾), many pinholes in center. Written in black ink. This is a revision of the early draft preserved in part at the top of leaf 2 (see Appendix I).]

Premonition.

Free, fresh, savage,

Fluent, luxuriant, self-content, fond | of persons and places,

Fond of fish-shape Paumanok where | I was born, fond of the sea, | large-begotten,

Boy of the Mannahatta, Boy of | the south savannas,

5 Full-breath'd on Cuban, Californian, | Arizonian air,

Resounding Niagara, resounding | Mississippi,

Rude in my home in Kanuck | woods,

A prairie-man, a mountain-man, | my drink water,

Stars, rain, snow, grass, wind, trees, my amaze, my love,

10 Aware of the buffalo, the peace-|herds, the bull strong-breasted | and hairy,

Aware of the mocking-bird of the | wilds at daybreak,

Solitary, singing in the west, I | strike up for a | new world.—

[Leaf numbered 2 in pencil written over 1; pink paper (4¾ × 5 1/16); originally a full leaf as shown by the pinholes near the top. The leaf is headed by four verses deleted by a vertical pen stroke (for the text, see Appendix I), these verses representing an earlier form of verses 4-12 on leaf 1. Wishing to revise his opening, Whitman wrote the final form on the tax-blank leaf 1 and cut off the top of the present leaf, destroying the first few verses and preserving only so much of the paper as was convenient. On the evidence, this half-leaf represents the remains of the original first leaf of the manuscript for this series. Verse 13, given below, follows on the deleted lines after a space and concludes the leaf.]

13 Victory, union, faith, democracy, | prudence, the soul, space, | time, the present and future | lands, yourself, the mysteries, kosmos, | invisible riches, and the modern reports.—

2 Fluent] an ink blot largely obscures the capital *F*, which seems to be mended from another letter, possibly a capital *T*.
9 Stars . . . love,] interlined in pencil.
10 herds] the *r* is written over an *a*, and the *ds* added at the same time.

12 for] interlined in the light ink above original *the songs of*, deleted in the same ink.
13 Victory,] the original reading 'Victory,' was excised and a caret placed after the deleted comma. Interlined is 'Vista,', which is thereupon deleted (save for the comma)

Proto-Leaf.

1. FREE, fresh, savage,
    Fluent, luxuriant, self-content, fond of persons and places,
    Fond of fish-shape Paumanok, where I was born,
    Fond of the sea—lusty-begotten and various,
    Boy of the Mannahatta, the city of ships, my city,
    Or raised inland, or of the south savannas,
    Or full-breath'd on Californian air, or Texan or Cuban air,
    Tallying, vocalizing all—resounding Niagara—resounding Missouri,
    Or rude in my home in Kanuck woods,
    Or wandering and hunting, my drink water, my diet meat,
    Or withdrawn to muse and meditate in some deep recess,
    Far from the clank of crowds, an interval passing, rapt and happy,
    Stars, vapor, snow, the hills, rocks, the Fifth Month flowers, my amaze,
      my love,
    Aware of the buffalo, the peace-herds, the bull, strong-breasted and
      hairy,
    Aware of the mocking-bird of the wilds at daybreak,
    Solitary, singing in the west, I strike up for a new world.

2. Victory, union, faith, identity, time, the Soul, yourself, the present
      and future lands, the indissoluble compacts, riches, mystery, eternal
      progress, the kosmos, and the modern reports.

---

and in the light ink 'Victory' is restored
on the line above. Two ink spots resembling a colon before 'Vista' have been deleted in the light ink.

13 time] the *m* is heavily mended.

[Leaf numbered 3; pink paper, numerous pinholes in the center. Written in blackish ink. Originally the lower part of the left margin had been folded over slightly and the first numbering, a '3,' written in pencil on the folded part as well as on the body of the leaf.]

14 This then is life,
   Here is what has risen on the | earth after so many throes | and
      convulsions.

16 How curious! How real!
   Under-foot, the divine soil—Over-|head the sun.

18 Take my Leaves America! Make | places everywhere for them, | for
      they are your offspring,
   O inland and seaboard perpetuate them!
   Waft them O winds! Buoy | them, liquid lakes!

15 Here] interlined with a caret above deleted 'This'.

17 soil] a deleted exclamation mark originally preceded the dash.

17 sun.] the upper stroke of an exclamation mark has been deleted to form a period.

18 Leaves] L mended from l when the ink was still wet.

18 Make . . . everywhere,] originally this ran, 'Yield | places to them, every-where,'. 'Yield' was deleted and 'Make' interlined, accompanied by the interlineation of 'for' above a caret placed after deleted 'to'. (A large ink blot obscures the certainty of this deletion, but a stroke may perhaps be seen.) There seems to have been an interval between the alteration of 'Yield' to 'Make' and the change of 'to' to 'for', since a pencilled 'for' also is interlined, now excised by a horizontal ink stroke. After this stroke appears the interlined 'everywhere for their roots,' above deleted 'them, every-where'. The words 'everywhere for' were written with the fine pen in black ink, and this same pen has drawn a curved line after 'for' leading down to a caret placed after original deleted 'to'. The words 'their roots' are placed over independently deleted 'every-where' and are in a large script and with a different pen, seemingly a later addition. Then 'their roots' was deleted with the light ink, and in the same ink 'them' was interlined above and the curving line mended to begin after it. The order seems to have been: 'everywhere for' interlined with fine pen, the 'for' being repeated and the space to the right chosen because of a large ink blot which had spread over the first interlined 'for'. Later, 'them' on the original line was deleted and 'their roots' added after interlined 'everywhere for'. Finally, 'their roots' was deleted and in the light ink 'them' added to achieve the final reading.

19 O inland . . . them!] the original lines read, 'O my native Earth and Sun | perpetuate them ! | Waft them. . . .' First 'Soil' was interlined above deleted 'Earth' and then the whole line crossed out, with the following line crowded in below, 'O native Sons and [ ] Daughters'. This in turn was deleted, in part so heavily that one word before 'Daughters' is obscure, though probably it is 'native'. The final version of the line is written with the fine pen and crowded in below the deleted part-line 'perpetuate them!'.

20 liquid lakes] interlined with the fine pen above deleted 'O waters'. The undeleted exclamation mark after 'waters' is retained in the transcript.

3. This then is life,
    Here is what has come to the surface after so many throes and con-
        vulsions.

4. How curious! How real!
    Underfoot the divine soil—Overhead the sun.

5. See, revolving,
    The globe—the ancestor-continents, away, grouped together,
    The present and future continents, north and south, with the isthmus
        between.

6. See, vast, trackless spaces,
    As in a dream, they change, they swiftly fill,
    Countless masses debouch upon them,
    They are now covered with the foremost people, arts, institutions
        known.

7. See projected, through time,
    For me, an audience interminable.

8. With firm and regular step they wend—they never stop,
    Successions of men, Americanos, a hundred millions,
    One generation playing its part and passing on,
    And another generation playing its part and passing on in its turn,
    With faces turned sideways or backward toward me to listen,
    With eyes retrospective toward me.

9. Americanos! Masters!
    Marches humanitarian! Foremost!
    Century marches! Libertad! Masses!
    For you a programme of chants.

10. Chants of the prairies,
    Chants of the long-running Mississippi,
    Chants of Ohio, Indiana, Illinois, Wisconsin, Iowa, and Minnesota,
    Inland chants—chants of Kanzas,
    Chants away down to Mexico, and up north to Oregon—Kanadian
        chants,
    Chants of teeming and turbulent cities—chants of mechanics,
    Yankee chants—Pennsylvanian chants—chants of Kentucky and Ten-
        nessee,
    Chants of dim-lit mines—chants of mountain-tops,

21 Surround them, east and west, | for they would surround you— |
    and north and south, for they | would you,
    And you precedents connect lovingly | with them, for they | con-
       nect lovingly with you.

[Leaf numbered 4, half of a blue tax form ($4\frac{1}{16} \times 4\frac{11}{16}$), the form seemingly having been cut down only to hold verses 23–25 since the pinholes are in the
center. These lines, written in black ink, revise lines deleted at the head of
leaf 5 (for the text, see Appendix I). The only revisions on leaf 4 are in the
light ink.]

23 I returned to old times,
    I sat, a child, a listener, | at the feet of the great masters,
    Now, if it be eligible, let | the great masters return | and listen to
       me.—

[Leaf numbered 5; pink paper, many pinholes. At the head is an early version
of verses 23–25 (see Appendix I), deleted by a vertical stroke. Verses 26–32 follow after a space.]

26 Antiques of men,
    Dead poets, philosophs and priests,
    Martyrs, artists, | inventors, language-shapers, | governments long
      since,
    Nations once powerful, now reduced, | withdrawn, or desolate,
30 I dare not proceed till I respect-|fully credit | what you have left,

22 they connect] originally 'they are to connect'. First 'are to' was deleted and 'would'
interlined; then 'would' in turn was
crossed out.

24 at the feet of] interlined in light ink with
a caret above deleted 'among'.

25 masters return] a caret pointing to interlined 'themselves' follows 'masters'. This
interlineation and the caret are deleted
in the light ink.

26 Antiques . . .] the original line was 'Ancestors of men,', which was deleted and above
it written 'Ancient of man,' the *t* of 'Ancient' and the *a* of 'man' being mended in
such a way as to suggest that the first form
was 'Ancients of men'. This was excised
in turn and above it written 'Antiques of
men,'. When this was deleted, there was
no more space above it, and therefore 'Ancestors of men' was interlined as a sub-

stitute below the original line. When this
was excised, the final reading 'Antiques
of men,' was written with the fine pen in
the only remaining space, in the right
half of the page.

27 poets,] interlined in the light ink above
a caret.

28 Martyrs . . . -shapers,] the line first read
'Captains, mothers, martyrs,'. The word
'artists,' looks as if it were added later
after 'shapers' in the line below had
been written in as a revision. 'Captains,
mothers' was later crossed out in the light
ink and the *m* of 'martyrs' mended in
this ink to a capital. Above deleted 'makers' is interlined 'shapers' in the light ink.

30 dare] this was also the deleted reading of
the original line. A now illegible word
(perhaps 'do') was interlined above the
original in pencil; over this pencil word

Chants of sailors—chants of the Eastern Sea and the Western Sea,
Chants of the Mannahatta, the place of my dearest love, the place sur-
 rounded by hurried and sparkling currents,
Health chants—joy chants—robust chants of young men,
Chants inclusive—wide reverberating chants,
Chants of the Many In One.

11. In the Year 80 of The States,
 My tongue, every atom of my blood, formed from this soil, this air,
 Born here of parents born here,
 From parents the same, and their parents' parents the same,
 I, now thirty-six years old, in perfect health, begin,
 Hoping to cease not till death.

12. Creeds and schools in abeyance,
 Retiring back a while, sufficed at what they are, but never forgotten,
 With accumulations, now coming forward in front,
 Arrived again, I harbor, for good or bad—I permit to speak,
 Nature, without check, with original energy.

13. Take my leaves, America!
 Make welcome for them everywhere, for they are your own offspring;
 Surround them, East and West! for they would surround you,
 And you precedents! connect lovingly with them, for they connect lov-
 ingly with you.

14. I conned old times,
 I sat studying at the feet of the great masters;
 Now, if eligible, O that the great masters might return and study me!

15. In the name of These States, shall I scorn the antique?
 Why These are the children of the antique, to justify it.

16. Dead poets, philosophs, priests,
 Martyrs, artists, inventors, governments long since,
 Language-shapers, on other shores,
 Nations once powerful, now reduced, withdrawn, or desolate,
 I dare not proceed till I respectfully credit what you have left, wafted
 hither,

---

was written in ink (above a caret) the substitute 'dare'.

30 credit] interlined with a medium fine pen
above deleted original 'turn my eyes upon'.

[[7]]

I own how admirable, | it is—I think none | can ever deserve more
    than | it deserves—I regard it | fixedly a long while,
Then I take my place for good | with | my own day here.

[Leaf numbered 6 written over original 5; pink paper, many pinholes. Written in brown-black ink. In verses 40–41 the ink is slightly lighter.]

33 Here lands female and male,
    Here the heirship and heiresship of the | world—Here the flame
        of materials,
    Here Spirituality, the translatress, | the openly-avowed, the | ever-
        tending, the finale of | visible forms,
    The satisfier—after due long-|waiting, now advancing,
37 Yes, here comes the mistress, the | Soul.

    The Soul!
39 Forever and forever—longer than | soil is brown and solid— |
    longer than water ebbs and | flows.—

    I will make the poems of materials, | for I think they are to be | the
        most spiritual poems,
41 And I will make the poems of | my body and of mortality, | for I
    think I shall then | supply myself with the poems | of my soul
    and of immortality.—

31 admirable] the original line read, 'admi-
rable, how in-|credible', the last two words
being deleted in the light ink. The comma
after 'admirable' seems to have been left
in by oversight.

32 with my own day here.] the first version
was, '. . . good, | on my own ground, with
| my own race,—to-day.—'. The phrase 'on
my own ground' was crossed out and 'in
my own days,' interlined above. This was
then excised, and immediately below
the original line 'on my own ground' was
repeated and then deleted. The word 'to-
day' and its preceding dash were deleted
and below them written in fine pen 'my
own day.—'. Below this revision appears
the pencil words 'and here—', with 'my
own day' being crossed out in pencil.
The comma after 'good' in the part line
above was crossed through in the light

ink, as was the pencilled 'and here—'.
Finally, the period and dash after revised
'day' were excised in the light ink and the
final word 'here.' appended. This conclusion of a sentence by a revision in light
ink after other stages of revision demonstrates that it was the ink used in the
final stage. The stage of the pencilled
word here is uncertain, but since it would
appear to be a note to the fine-pen revision 'my own day', it was probably not
the earliest here.

33 Here . . . male,] first version was, 'Here
are the lands that have ar-|rived,'. First,
'the' was crossed out; a single stroke de-
letes 'lands that have ar-|rived'. Above a
caret in medium fine pen is interlined
'proofs, and accumulations,', the 'and' of
this revision then being deleted. The fine
pen then deleted 'Here are proofs, accu-

I have perused it—I own it is admirable,
I think nothing can ever be greater—Nothing can ever deserve more
    than it deserves;
I regard it all intently a long while,
Then take my place for good with my own day and race here.

17. Here lands female and male,
    Here the heirship and heiress-ship of the world—Here the flame of
        materials,
    Here Spirituality, the translatress, the openly-avowed,
    The ever-tending, the finale of visible forms,
    The satisfier, after due long-waiting, now advancing,
    Yes, here comes the mistress, the Soul.

18. The SOUL!
    Forever and forever—Longer than soil is brown and solid—Longer
        than water ebbs and flows.

19. I will make the poems of materials, for I think they are to be the most
        spiritual poems,
    And I will make the poems of my body and of mortality,
    For I think I shall then supply myself with the poems of my Soul and
        of immortality.

---

mulations' and wrote above it, 'Here are the lands that [ ] arrived, female and male,'. There is some question whether 'female and male,' was written *seriatim* after 'arrived' or was an afterthought. This line was then revised, 'lands' being deleted and 'days' interlined above it. Then 'days' was excised and in the fine pen 'lands' was replaced below the same word in the revised line. The phrase 'that [ ] arrived,' was crossed out with a thick heavy line. The illegible word or words marked by brackets may possibly be 'have', although the first letter looks somewhat like an *I*. Finally, with the light ink 'are the' was deleted and the final form of the line achieved.

34 Here . . . materials,] the first version read, 'Here the last descendants of the | world,'. After 'Here' is placed a caret and then the interlineation 'are' in the medium fine pen, this 'are' then being deleted in favor of 'is', this last finally crossed out in pen-cil. 'last descendants' was crossed out, the two words at different times, and above a caret in the fine or medium fine pen is interlined 'heirship and heiressship', the *a* of 'and' being mended. The comma after 'world' is crossed through and '—Here the flame of materials,' added in the fine pen.

35 Here Spirituality] an original 'is' between these words is deleted first in pencil and then in ink.

36 The satisfier . . . advancing,] crowded in as an afterthought after 'forms,' is '—after due long-|waiting, now advancing,'. Then in the light ink over a caret is interlined just before it '¶ The satisfier'.

40 of materials,] the first version read, 'of forms,'. Between these two words the fine pen has interlined above a caret 'materials and', then crossed out the interlined 'and', and the 'forms' in the line below.

41 immortality.—] the period is mended, just possibly over a comma.

[Leaf numbered 7; pink paper (6⅝ × 5⅛). Written in blackish ink. As shown by only the one cluster of pinholes positioned in what would have been the center of a full leaf, a small portion of the bottom of leaf 7, with writing, has been cut off. This cut-off piece (containing verses 46–47) is now found glued to the foot of leaf 8, below the later deleted lines for "I am a child of Democracy," an intermediate version of verses 58–61.]

42 I will make a song for These | States that no one State | may under any circumstances | be subjected to another State,

And I will make a song that | there shall be faith and | comity by day and by night | between all The States, and | between any two of them,

And I will make a song of the | organic compacts of The | States— and a shrill song | of curses on him who would | dissever the union of The States,

45 And I will make a song for | the ears of the President, full | of weapons with menacing | points—and behind the weapons | countless dissatisfied faces.—

[Leaf numbered 8; blue wove paper (6¾ × 5⅛) torn into about three-quarters of a normal leaf. The leaf-number 8 is placed on the fragment of pink paper (containing verses 46–47) which had originally comprised the foot of leaf 7 and had been cut off and glued near the foot of blue-paper leaf 8. A cluster of pin-holes appears near the center, some of these tying the pink and blue paper together. On the blue paper in a light-brown ink, excised by a vertical stroke, is written an intermediate version of verses 58–61 found in revised form on leaf 12 (see Appendix I for these deleted verses). No alterations appear in the deleted lines. A still earlier version of verses 58–61 (see Appendix I) was written on a leaf the back of which was later utilized for "Enfans d'Adam" [no. 9], in folder 5. The undeleted verses 46–47 are given here from the pink paper.]

46 I will be the preparer of what is | to come,—I will take exception to nothing,

I will trail the whole geography | of the globe, and salute | court-eously every city large | and small.

42 may] originally 'shall'. This was deleted, a caret placed after it and 'is' interlined and then deleted. Another caret was placed before 'shall'; above this, 'may' was inter-lined and then deleted. Following inter-lined deleted 'is' is crowded in 'must', slanting to make use of the caret. This 'must' is first deleted in pencil and then

20. I will make a song for These States, that no one State may under any
circumstances be subjected to another State,
   And I will make a song that there shall be comity by day and by night
between all The States, and between any two of them,
   And I will make a song of the organic bargains of These States—And a
shrill song of curses on him who would dissever the Union;
   And I will make a song for the ears of the President, full of weapons
with menacing points,
   And behind the weapons countless dissatisfied faces.

21. I will acknowledge contemporary lands,
   I will trail the whole geography of the globe, and salute courteously
every city large and small;

---

in ink. Finally, just before original 'shall',
the word 'may' is returned, traced in ink
over pencil.

42 be] above a caret preceding 'be' is interlined a 'to', which has been deleted.

44 shrill] medium fine-pen interlineation in
black ink above deleted 'fierce'.

45 points] the *ts* heavily mended, perhaps
consequent upon the addition of the *s*.

45 countless] interlined in the light ink with
a caret above deleted 'the.'

45 faces.—] the first version read 'faces of
people.' In the light ink, 'of people' was
crossed out and the period and dash added
after 'faces'.

46 I will take . . . nothing,] with the spelling 'exciption' this was crowded in with
the fine pen as an afterthought follow-

ing 'come,—'. A single pen stroke crosses
out 'I will take exci' and also 'nothing' in
the part-line below, and 'I will take exception to nothing,' was restored by interlineation, in the light ink.

47 trail] interlined in the light ink above deleted 'sing'.

47 globe] originally 'earth', which was deleted and 'New World,' interlined; this
was deleted and below 'earth' was crowded
in 'globe'. A caret appears closeup beneath 'globe' but may be associated with
the earlier interlining of 'New World'.

47 small.] the punctuation is so close to the
bottom of the page that it is not quite
certain whether the mark is intended as
a period or a comma.

[Leaf numbered 9; a pink-paper half-leaf (4⅜ × 5) irregularly cut across at the foot. Two clusters of pinholes, one in the normal center for a full leaf and the other in the center of the half-leaf, indicate that before stabbing into the present series the leaf contained other writing below. This cut-off section from leaf 9 became leaf 17 (verses 98–99).]

48 And employments! I will make | a song that with you is | heroism
      upon land and | sea—And I will report all | heroism from an
      American | point of view.
   And sexual organs and acts! do | you concentrate in me—for | I
      am determined to tell | you with courageous clear | voice, to
      prove you illustrious.

[Leaves numbered 10 and 11; blue wove paper. Leaf 11 is torn into about three-quarters of a leaf, but leaf 12 (3⅜ × 5⅛) is only about one-third of normal size. However, central pinholes in each indicate that no writing has been lost, and that leaf 11 was torn to size to economize on paper. The verses are written in a light-brown ink.]

[leaf 10]

50 I will make the song of companionship,
   I will show what alone can compact | These States,
   I believe the main purport | of America is to found | a new ideal
      of manly | friendship, more ardent, | more general,
   I will therefore let appear these | burning fires | that were threat-
      ening to | consume me,
   I will lift what has too | long kept down those | smouldering fires
      —I will | now expose them and use them.

[leaf 11]

55 I will make the new evangel-|poem of lovers and comrades,
   (For who but I should understand | love, with all its sorrow | and
      joy?
   And who but I should be | the poet of comrades?)

48 And I will] A of 'And' triple underscored.
51 I . . . States,] the original line was, 'I will show love to compact | Democracy,'. The words 'love to' are deleted and above a caret is interlined 'what alone can', 'alone' being written currently after de-

leted 'only'. 'These States,' is interlined above excised 'Democracy,'.
52 America] interlined above deleted 'These States'.
52 ideal] interlined above deleted 'type'.
53 therefore] interlined.
53 these] the s written over an r, suggesting

And employments! I will put in my poems, that with you is heroism,
   upon land and sea—And I will report all heroism from an American point of view;
And sexual organs and acts! do you concentrate in me—For I am determined to tell you with courageous clear voice, to prove you
   illustrious.

22. I will sing the song of companionship,
   I will show what alone must compact These,
   I believe These are to found their own ideal of manly love, indicating
      it in me;
   I will therefore let flame from me the burning fires that were threaten-
      ing to consume me,
   I will lift what has too long kept down those smouldering fires,
   I will give them complete abandonment,
   I will write the evangel-poem of comrades and of love,
   (For who but I should understand love, with all its sorrow and joy?
   And who but I should be the poet of comrades?)

that the first intention was to write 'I will let appear therefore' but that Whitman stopped, interlined 'therefore' after 'will' and mended 'there' to 'these'.

53 fires] interlined above 'flames'; following this, original 'of adhesivesness' is deleted and 'were' is interlined above a caret after 'that'.

54 what] the *w* mended over some other letter, possibly an *h* or *th*.

54 fires] interlined over deleted 'flames'.

54 expose . . . use them.] the line originally ended with 'expose them,'. The comma was crossed out and 'and use them.' crowded in. The period after final 'them' may be mended from a comma.

[Leaf numbered 12; made up of two pasted-together sections of white wove paper, the lower section lapping over the foot of the upper. The upper section measures $2\frac{9}{16} \times 6\frac{3}{8}$ and contains verses 58–61. In the upper right corner of this piece is the pencil number '7', the hand uncertain. If the numbering is Whitman's, presumably it indicates the intention, subsequently altered, to place the piece before leaf 8, which contains deleted lines for which the present version substitutes. On the other hand, the figure might be the annotator's as an indication of the assumed position of the lines. No pinholes appear on this upper piece. The lower section, containing pinholes, measures $5\frac{1}{2} \times 6\frac{3}{8}$ and is numbered in pencil '12' in the lower left corner, thus proving that the numbering was made after the rearrangement, or at least the secting of the original leaf. The contours demonstrate that the upper piece was originally the foot of the whole leaf and that it has been torn off and pasted above the original head of the leaf in order to reverse the order of the two sections. Thus before the rearrangement, verses 62–68 preceded verses 58–61 as originally copied on the leaf. Both sections are written in a brown-black ink. On the verso appear deleted drafts for verses 69–73 later copied out fair on leaf 13. Since these deleted verses were written before the leaf was cut apart, it is clear that the inscription of leaf 13 preceded that of leaf 12.]

[*upper section*]

 I am all-credulous,
 I am the child of the commonalty,
60 I advance from the people en-masse in | their own spirit,
 Here is what sings unrestricted faith

[*lower section*]

62 Here myself I give,
 Here is my blood—Here are my pulses and | breaths,
 My inward joys are here, and my sorrows | are all here.

65 In what I compass here I | accept what others scorn,
 I make the dark poems of sin,
 I do not ignore what is called evil— | I commemorate it also,
 I am myself just as much evil | as good.—

[Leaf numbered 13; white wove paper ($7\frac{7}{8} \times 6\frac{5}{16}$); a few centered pinholes. Written in dark-brown ink. Verses 69–76 were subsequently cut up into different sections and much revised or excised in the 1860 edition, but they are transcribed here continuously as in the manuscript. For deleted drafts of these lines, see Appendix I.]

 I dart forth Religion,
70 I will yet utter the free canticles of it— | they shall rise and soar
  into the air,

23. I am the credulous man of qualities, ages, races,
    I advance from the people en-masse in their own spirit,
    Here is what sings unrestricted faith.

24. Omnes! Omnes!
    Let others ignore what they may,
    I make the poem of evil also—I commemorate that part also,
    I am myself just as much evil as good—And I say there is in fact no evil,
    Or if there is, I say it is just as important to you, to the earth, or to me,
        as anything else.

25. I too, following many, and followed by many, inaugurate a Religion—
    I too go to the wars,
    It may be I am destined to utter the loudest cries thereof, the con-
    queror's shouts,
    They may rise from me yet, and soar above every thing.

26. Each is not for its own sake,
    I say the whole earth, and all the stars in the sky, are for Religion's sake.

---

65 In what . . . scorn,] the original line read 'From what I compass here I reject | nothing,'. 'From' was deleted and 'In' interlined in pencil; also in pencil 'reject nothing' was deleted and 'accept all' was added. Then 'all' was deleted in pencil and above it was written in pencil 'what others scorn,'.

67 ignore] interlined in ink over excised 'condemn'.

69 I dart] originally 'I will dart', the 'will' being excised in pencil.

70 yet utter] 'utter' interlined in ink above deleted 'shout', the 'yet' being inserted before it in pencil. However, there may be some very slight doubt, in spite of its position, whether 'yet' belongs before 'utter' as interpreted here, or whether it is a substitute, below the line, for pencil-deleted 'will' in the verse above.

I see that none have ever yet been devout enough—none have ever
yet worship'd | half enough,

None have ever begun to think how divine | himself is, or how
sure the | future is.

I distinctly announce that the greatest part | of America, or of any
nation, must | be its Religion.—

Of all a man needs, I say he needs | nothing any more than he
needs Religion,

75 Always he needs Love—but he does not need | it any more than
he needs Religion—per-|haps not as much as he needs Re-
ligion,

Perhaps even the best of Love is that where | it is there is the prep-
aration and readiness | for Religion.—

[Leaves numbered 13 and 14. The section comprising verses 77–82 begins near
the foot of leaf 13 and carries over to leaf 14, which is the same white wove paper
($7\frac{15}{16} \times 6\frac{5}{16}$) with a few pinholes in its center. The verses on both leaves are
written in the same dark-brown ink. Verses 83–84, another section, conclude
leaf 14 written in the same ink.]

[*leaf 13 cont.*]

77 The unseen something in all life,

The prophetic spirit of materials shifting | and flickering around
me,

The wondrous interplay between the divinity | of the future and
the divinity of | the present,

---

71 been devout . . . ever yet] interlined in
pencil above a caret which has been inked
over a pencil caret.

71 worship'd] *d* is mended from *t*, and possibly the apostrophe added at the same
time.

72 himself] interlined in a lighter ink above
deleted 'a man'.

72 or] interlined in pencil above deleted 'nor'.

73 or of] 'of' interlined in a lighter ink.

74 all a man] originally 'all that a man', the
'that' being deleted in ink.

77 The] interlined above deleted 'This'.

77 life,] interlined in lighter ink above deleted 'things,'.

78 The] the *e* is written over original *is*.

27. I say no man has ever been half devout enough,
    None has ever adored or worship'd half enough,
    None has begun to think how divine he himself is,
        and how certain the future is.

28. I specifically announce that the real and permanent grandeur of These
        States must be their Religion,
    Otherwise there is no real and permanent grandeur.

29. What are you doing, young man?
    Are you so earnest—so given up to literature, science, art, amours?
    These ostensible realities, materials, points?
    Your ambition or business, whatever it may be?

30. It is well—Against such I say not a word—I am their poet also;
    But behold! such swiftly subside—burnt up for Religion's sake,
    For not all matter is fuel to heat, impalpable flame, the essential life of
        the earth,
    Any more than such are to Religion.

31. What do you seek, so pensive and silent?
    What do you need, comrade?
    Mon cher! do you think it is love?

32. Proceed, comrade,
    It is a painful thing to love a man or woman to excess—yet it satisfies
        —it is great,
    But there is something else very great—it makes the whole coincide,
    It, magnificent, beyond materials, with continuous hands, sweeps and
        provides for all.

33. O I see the following poems are indeed to drop in the earth the germs
        of a greater Religion.

34. My comrade!
    For you, to share with me, two greatnesses—And a third one, rising
        inclusive and more resplendent,
    The greatness of Love and Democracy—and the greatness of Religion.

35. Melange mine!
    Mysterious ocean where the streams empty,
    Prophetic spirit of materials shifting and flickering around me,
    Wondrous interplay between the seen and unseen,

[*leaf* 14]

80 This extasy touching and thrilling me,
    This contact daily and hourly that will | not release me.
    How effective at last it all has become upon | me!

83 Not he whom I love, kissing me so long | with his daily kiss, has
        winded and | twisted around me that which holds | me to him
        forever,
    Any more than I am become welded | to the heavens, to the spirit-
        ual | world, and to the identities of | the Gods, my unseen
        lovers, after what | they have done to me.—

[Leaf numbered 15; white wove paper ($6\frac{1}{2} \times 6\frac{1}{2}$). The lower part of the leaf
(containing verses 92–93) has been cut off and pasted above leaf 16, where it
substitutes for the removed top of that leaf. Verses 85–88 and 89–91 are written
in the same brown-black ink. These verses are written on the back of a deleted
draft for "Calamus" [no. 11], folder 13, which must have been earlier inscribed,
the draft continuing on the cut-off part of leaf 15 which now heads leaf 16. For
the text of these deleted lines see after "Calamus" [no. 11], folder 13.]

85 States!
    You do not need maternity only,
    You do not need to be born and | matured only,
    There is a subtler influence still | to go with your conformation.

    As I have walked my walk through the rows of the | orchard-trees,
        I have seen where the | she-bird faithfully sat on her | nest,
        hatching her brood,
90 I have seen the he-bird also—I heard him | where he sat by himself
        every day near at hand, | inflating his throat and joyfully |
        singing,
    And I have perceived that what he really sang | for must be some-
        thing beyond the | she-bird.—

82 How . . . me!] the line read originally,
'How   —how effective at last upon | me!'
The space seems to have been left for a
word to be inserted later; but subsequently Whitman deleted '—how' and its
preceding space in pencil. After 'last' was

Living beings, identities, now doubtless near us, in the air, that we
    know not of,
Extasy everywhere touching and thrilling me,
Contact daily and hourly that will not release me,
These selecting—These, in hints, demanded of me.

36. Not he, adhesive, kissing me so long with his daily kiss,
    Has winded and twisted around me that which holds me to him,
    Any more than I am held to the heavens, to the spiritual world,
    And to the identities of the Gods, my unknown lovers,
    After what they have done to me, suggesting such themes.

37. O such themes! Equalities!
    O amazement of things! O divine average!
    O warblings under the sun—ushered, as now, or at noon, or setting!
    O strain, musical, flowing through ages—now reaching hither,
    I take to your reckless and composite chords—I add to them, and cheer-
      fully pass them forward.

38. As I have walked in Alabama my morning walk,
    I have seen where the she-bird, the mocking-bird, sat on her nest in the
      briers, hatching her brood.

39. I have seen the he-bird also,
    I have paused to hear him, near at hand, inflating his throat, and joy-
      fully singing.

40. And while I paused, it came to me that what he really sang for was not
      there only,
    Nor for his mate nor himself only, nor all sent back by the echoes,
    But subtle, clandestine, away beyond,
    A charge transmitted, and gift occult, for those being born.

---

interlined in pencil above a caret the words 'they are', these being later deleted in ink and 'it all has become' interlined.

84 Any] The word was first 'And', but while still wet the 'd' was smudged out and the 'y' traced in.

84 spiritual] interlined above deleted 'unseen'.

84 unseen] interlined above a caret.

89 have walked] 'have' interlined above a caret.

89 my walk through] interlined above a caret.

89 have seen] interlined with a caret above deleted 'saw'.

89 she-bird] in 'bird' the letters *ird* are heavily mended above some slip.

90 have seen] interlined above deleted 'saw'.

90 by himself] interlined above a caret.

90 at hand] interlined above deleted 'by'. The text comma is drawn from that after 'by'.

91 have] interlined above a caret.

91 really] interlined above a caret.

[Leaf numbered 16; white wove paper. The pasted-on upper piece ($1\frac{1}{2} \times 6\frac{1}{4}$) was cut off from the foot of leaf 15 and attached to the lower piece ($4 \times 6\frac{1}{4}$) as a substitute for something removed from the head of the original leaf. All verses are written in the same brown-black ink used for leaf 15. Verses 92–93 are on the upper section; 94–97 on the lower.]

92 Democracy!
    For you a throat is now inflating itself | and joyfully singing.—

    Ma femme!
95 Our offspring shall be provided for,
    None could come to do what was | wanted till I have come,
    For you, and something beyond you, I will send | forth strong
        and haughty chants | different from those of all the rest | of
        the earth.—

[Leaf numbered 17; a half-leaf of pink paper ($4\frac{1}{4} \times 5\frac{1}{8}$) backed for strength by a glued-on piece of plain blue wove paper. A few pinholes at the top indicate this piece was once the lower portion of a full leaf, and the pattern of the tear demonstrates that originally it comprised the lower part of leaf 9 (verses 48–49). Written in blackish ink.]

    ¶ I will make the songs of passions, | to give them their way.—
    And your songs offenders, | for I scan you with kindred | eyes,
    and carry you with me the same as any;
99 And I will make the true | poem of riches, namely, to | earn for
    the body and the | mind what adheres and goes | forward, and
    is not dropt by | death,

[Leaf numbered 18; pink paper with many pinholes; written in blackish ink.]

100 And I will effuse egotism, and | show egotism underlying all— |
    and I will be the Bard of Per-|sonality,
    And I will show of male and | female that either is but | the equal
    of the other, |
    And I will show that there is no | imperfection in male or | fe-
    male, or in the earth, or | in the present, and can be | none
    in the future,
    And I will show that whatever | happens to anybody it may | be
    turned to beautiful results— | and that nothing can happen
    | more beautiful than death |

41. Democracy!
Near at hand to you a throat is now inflating itself and joyfully singing.

42. Ma femme!
For the brood beyond us and of us,
For those who belong here, and those to come,
I, exultant, to be ready for them, will now shake out carols stronger
and haughtier than have ever yet been heard upon the earth.

43. I will make the songs of passions, to give them their way,
And your songs, offenders—for I scan you with kindred eyes, and carry
you with me the same as any.

44. I will make the true poem of riches,
Namely, to earn for the body and the mind, what adheres, and goes
forward, and is not dropt by death.

45. I will effuse egotism, and show it underlying all—And I will be the
bard of Personality;
And I will show of male and female that either is but the equal of the
other,
And I will show that there is no imperfection in male or female, or in
the earth, or in the present—and can be none in the future,
And I will show that whatever happens to anybody, it may be turned to
beautiful results—And I will show that nothing can happen more
beautiful than death;

93 is] interlined above a caret.
93 and] a following 'is' is deleted.
93 singing.—] the period and possibly the dash were added later when the original concluding words were excised: 'for you and | and something beyond you.—' The final part-line is under the paste-over.
97 will] interlined above a caret.
97 forth strong] originally 'forth my strong', the 'my' being excised.
97 chants] interlined above deleted 'ballads.—' It would seem that the poem first ended here, and then was continued

using the pen that interlined 'chants', and thus probably at the same time as the alteration.
98 ¶] the paragraph mark is added in the light ink.
98 make the songs] 'songs' interlined in light ink over deleted 'poems'.
98 And your songs] *A* of 'And' triple underscored; 'songs' interlined in light ink above deleted 'poems'.
100 Bard] *B* written over *b*.
100 Personality] *P* written over *p*.

And I will thread a thread | through my poems that no | one thing in the universe is | inferior to another thing— | and that all the things of | the universe are perfect mira-|cles, each as profound as any;

[Leaf numbered 19; pink paper with many pinholes; written in blackish ink.]

105 And I will not make poems | with reference to parts, | but I will make Leaves, | poems, poemets, songs, says, | thoughts, with reference to | ensemble,

And I will not sing with refer-|ence to a day, but with | reference to all days,

And I will not make a poem, | nor the least part of a | poem, but has reference | to the soul,

Because, having looked at the | objects of the universe, I find | there is no one, nor any | particle of one, but has | reference to the soul.

Was somebody asking to see the soul?

110 See! Your own shape and counte-|nance, persons, substances, | beasts, the trees, the birds, | the running rivers, the rocks | and sands.—

[Leaf numbered 20; pink paper with many pinholes; written in blackish ink.]

111 All hold spiritual joys, and af-|terward loosen them.

How can that which is really you, die | and be buried?

Of that which is really you, and | of any part of you, | item for item, it will elude | the hands of the corpse-cleaners, | and pass to fitting spheres, | carrying what has accrued to | it from the moment of birth | to the moment of death.

Not the types set up by the | printer return their impression, | the meaning, the main concern, | any more than a man's sub-|stance and life, or a woman's | substance and life, return in | the body and the soul indif-|ferently before death and | after death.—

[Leaf numbered 21; pink paper with many pinholes; written in blackish ink.]

115 Behold! the body includes and is the | meaning, the main con-cern, | and includes and is the soul;

And I will thread a thread through my poems that no one thing in the universe is inferior to another thing,

And that all the things of the universe are perfect miracles, each as profound as any.

46. I will not make poems with reference to parts,

But I will make leaves, poems, poemets, songs, says, thoughts, with reference to ensemble;

And I will not sing with reference to a day, but with reference to all days,

And I will not make a poem, nor the least part of a poem, but has reference to the Soul,

Because, having looked at the objects of the universe, I find there is no one, nor any particle of one, but has reference to the Soul.

47. Was somebody asking to see the Soul?

See! your own shape and countenance—persons, substances, beasts, the trees, the running rivers, the rocks and sands.

48. All hold spiritual joys, and afterward loosen them,

How can the real body ever die, and be buried?

49. Of your real body, and any man's or woman's real body, item for item, it will elude the hands of the corpse-cleaners, and pass to fitting spheres, carrying what has accrued to it from the moment of birth to the moment of death.

50. Not the types set up by the printer return their impression, the meaning, the main concern, any more than a man's substance and life, or a woman's substance and life, return in the body and the Soul, indifferently before death and after death.

51. Behold! the body includes and is the meaning, the main concern—and includes and is the Soul;

---

104 profound] above is interlined 'incredible', which has been deleted; 'profound' itself seems to be written with a finer pen than the context and may represent an addition in a blank space left for later insertion of a word.

105 to ensemble,] originally this read 'to the ensemble, of the world,' these words being crossed out including an interlined 'universe' above 'world'.

108 at] interlined above deleted 'upon'.

110 substances,] interlined with a finer pen above deleted 'materials,'.

112 that which is really you,] interlined in light ink above deleted 'the real body ever'.

113 that which is really you, and of any part of you,] interlined in light ink above excised 'your real body and each | man's or woman's real body,'.

114 than a] the tail of the 'a' is mended over the start of some other letter.

115 and is] interlined with a finer pen above a caret.

115 and is] interlined with a finer pen above a caret.

Whoever you are! how superb and | how divine is your body, or | any part of it!

Whoever you are! to you endless | announcements!

Daughter of the lands, did you wait | for your poet?
Did you wait for one with a | flowing mouth and indicative | hand?

120 Toward the female of The States, and | toward the male of The States,

Toward the President, the Congress, | the diverse Governors, the | new Judiciary,

Live words—Words to the lands.—

[Leaves numbered 22–26; pink paper with many pinholes; written in blackish ink.]

[*leaf 22*]

O The Lands!

Interlinked lands! Land of the common | people! | Food-yielding lands!

125 Lands of coal and iron! Land of gold! Land | of cotton, sugar, rice!

Odorous and sunny land! Floridian, | Alabamian, Texan land! Cu-|banese land!

Land of the spinal | river, the Mississippi! | Land of the Alleghanies! Ohio's land!

Land of wheat, beef, pork! Land | of wool and hemp! Land | of the potato, the apple, | and the grape!

Land of the pastoral plains, the | grass-fields of the world! | Land of those sweet-aired | interminable plateaus! Land | there of the herd, the garden, | the healthy house of adobe! | Land there of rapt thought, | and of the realization of the stars! | Land of simple, untamed, holy lives!

[*leaf 23*]

130 Lands | where the north-west | Columbia winds, and where | the south-west Colorado winds!

116 Whoever] the 'W' was written heavily over some other letter, possibly a 'T' which was smudged out while wet. The

letters 'oe' are also traced over some letter or letters. Possibly the original word was 'The'; but in the light of verse 117

Whoever you are! how superb and how divine is your body, or any
part of it.

52. Whoever you are! to you endless announcements.

53. Daughter of the lands, did you wait for your poet?
Did you wait for one with a flowing mouth and indicative hand?

54. Toward the male of The States, and toward the female of The States,
Toward the President, the Congress, the diverse Governors, the new
Judiciary,
Live words—words to the lands.

55. O the lands!
Lands scorning invaders! Interlinked, food-yielding lands!
Land of coal and iron! Land of gold! Lands of cotton, sugar, rice!
Odorous and sunny land! Floridian land!
Land of the spinal river, the Mississippi! Land of the Alleghanies!
Ohio's land!
Land of wheat, beef, pork! Land of wool and hemp! Land of the
potato, the apple, and the grape!
Land of the pastoral plains, the grass-fields of the world! Land of those
sweet-aired interminable plateaus! Land there of the herd, the gar-
den, the healthy house of adobie! Land there of rapt thought, and
of the realization of the stars! Land of simple, holy, untamed lives!
Lands where the northwest Columbia winds, and where the southwest
Colorado winds!

---

below, Whitman may first have written
'Whosoever'.
117 Whoever] the 'oe' heavily mended over
some letter or letters smudged out while
wet.
119 indicative] above this is interlined and
deleted 'determined'.
122 Live words] originally 'Live and severe
words', the 'and severe' then being crossed
out.
122 Words] the 'W' has a triple stroke beneath it to enforce capitalization.
123 The] *T* written over *t*.
124 Land . . . people!] 'Land of the common'
interlined in light ink above, and 'people!' beneath, deleted 'Hilarious lands!'.
125 Lands] the *s* added in light ink.

125 coal and] interlined above a caret with
a finer pen.
126 Odorous] interlined in a finer pen with
a caret above deleted 'Perfumed'.
127 spinal] original 'Mississippi, the' deleted
before this.
127 Land of the Alleghanies! Ohio's land!]
crowded in in the light ink.
130 Lands where] originally 'Ohio's land! Ka-
nadian lands! | Lands where'. In the
light ink all but the last word was crossed
through, 'Lands' being interlined above
'Ohio's' and connected with 'where' in
the line below by a stroke.
130 winds!] this may have been added later
with a different pen.

Land of the Chesapeake! Land of | the Delaware!

Full-draped land, tied at the | breast with the belt stringing |
    the oval lakes!

Land of the future! Land of | the ceaseless right of rebellion!

Land of the Old Thirteen! And of | all since! And of all to come!

135 Land of many oceans! Land of sierras and peaks!

Land of of boatsmen and sailors! | Fishermen's land!

Inextricable lands! The clutched | together! The passionate |
    lovers!

The side by side! The elder and | younger brothers! The bony-|
    limbed!

[*leaf* 24]

The great women's land! The | feminine! The experienced | sis-
    ters, and the inexperienced | sisters!

140 Far-breathed land! Arctic-braced! | Mexican-breezed! The di-
    verse! The compact!

The Pennsylvanian! The | Tennesseean! The double | Carolin-
    ian!

All and each well-loved by me! | my intrepid nations! O I | can-
    not be discharged from you!

O death! O for all that, I am | yet of you, unseen, this | hour,
    with irrepressible love,

Walking New England, a friend, | a traveler,

145 Splashing my naked feet in the | edge of the summer ripples on
    | Paumanok's sands,

Crossing the prairies—dwelling | again in Chicago—dwelling |
    in many towns,

Observing shows, births, improvements, | structures, arts,

[*leaf* 25]

Listening to the orators and oratresses | in the public halls,

Of and through The States as during life— | each man and
    woman my | neighbor,

150 The Louisianian, the Georgian, as | near to me, and I as near |
    to him and her,

135-6 Land of many . . . Fishermen's land!]
the lines read originally, 'Lands of many
oceans! Land | of boatsmen and sailors!

| Fishermen's land!'. The *s* in 'Lands'
was crossed out and 'of sierras and
peaks!' interlined above a caret with a

Land of the Chesapeake! Land of the Delaware!
Land of Ontario, Erie, Huron, Michigan!
Land of the Old Thirteen! Massachusetts land! Land of Vermont and
    Connecticut!
Land of many oceans! Land of sierras and peaks!
Land of boatmen and sailors! Fishermen's land!
Inextricable lands! the clutched together! the passionate lovers!
The side by side! the elder and younger brothers! the bony-limbed!
The great women's land! the feminine! the experienced sisters and the
    inexperienced sisters!
Far breath'd land! Arctic braced! Mexican breezed! the diverse! the
    compact!
The Pennsylvanian! the Virginian! the double Carolinian!
O all and each well-loved by me! my intrepid nations! O I cannot be
    discharged from you!
O Death! O for all that, I am yet of you, unseen, this hour, with irre-
    pressible love,
Walking New England, a friend, a traveller,
Splashing my bare feet in the edge of the summer ripples, on Pau-
    manok's sands,
Crossing the prairies—dwelling again in Chicago—dwelling in many
    towns,
Observing shows, births, improvements, structures, arts,
Listening to the orators and the oratresses in public halls,
Of and through The States, as during life—each man and woman my
    neighbor,
The Louisianian, the Georgian, as near to me, and I as near to him
    and her,

finer pen. At the start of what had first been a continuing verse, 'Land of' was prefixed to make 'Land of of [*sic*] boatsmen . . .' begin a new verse. The *e* of 'boatsmen' appears to be mended, possibly from an *a*.

140 Far-breathed. . . .] this line was first written, 'Far-breathed land! The arctic, | The Pennsylvanian! . . .' The 'The' before 'arctic' was crossed through, the *a* of 'arctic' mended to a capital *A*, the final *c* mended, perhaps over a comma, and '-braced!' added. Then 'Mexican-breezed! The diverse! The compact!' was

squeezed in between the lines with a finer pen, 'Mexican-' beginning over deleted 'The' before 'Pennsylvanian' which had started a new line. Then 'The' was prefixed out to the margin so as to begin a new verse with 'The Pennsylvanian'.

143 this] just possibly *is* was mended over another letter, but the irregularity may be no more than an ink blot.

144 New England,] interlined in the light ink above deleted 'the Mannahatta,'.

149 Of and through] interlined with a finer pen above deleted 'In and of'.

The Kentuckian, Mississippian, Arkan-|sian,—the workwoman |
and workman of Iowa, | Illinois, Indiana, Michigan, | Wis-
consin, Minnesota, Kansas, | Nebraska, Utah, Dacotah, yet
with | me, and I yet with any of them,

Yet in Oregon,—yet | upon the plains west of the | spinal river—
yet in my | house of adobie,

Yet returning eastward,—yet in | Virginia,—yet in the Sea-Side
| State, or in Maryland,

Yet a northern child—Yet Kanadian, | cheerily braving the win-
ter—the snow | and ice welcome to me,

[*leaf* 26]

155 Yet the true son either of Maine, | or of the Granite State, or
of | Vermont, Massachusetts, Connect-|icut, or of the Nar-
raganset Bay | State, or of the Empire State,

Yet sailing forth to other shores, | to annex the same—Yet wel-|
coming every new mate,

Hereby applying these Leaves to the | new ones, from the hour
| they unite with the old ones,

Coming among the new ones | myself to be their companion— |
coming personally to you now,

Enjoining you to acts, characters, | spectacles with me.

160 With me, with firm holding, yet | haste, haste on!

For your life, adhere to me,

I only can unloose you and toughen you,

I may have to be persuaded many times | before I consent to
give myself to you,— | but what of that?

Must not Nature be persuaded many times?

[Leaf 27; a cut-down blue tax form ($4\frac{5}{8} \times 4\frac{1}{2}$) numbered 27 at the foot and
containing verses 168–171 written in black ink. To the upper edge is pasted
a small piece of pink paper ($3\frac{1}{8} \times 5\frac{1}{4}$) on which are written verses 165–167. This
pink slip, numbered in pencil $26\frac{1}{2}$ (see Introduction), is the cut-off top of leaf
30 (verses 182 ff.), written in black ink. Pinholes show that this made-up leaf
was pinned in the series after the two sections had been pasted together.]

165 No dainty dolce affetuoso I,

151 Arkansian] after this, 'Missourian' is
crossed through in the light ink.
151 workwoman and workman] 'workwoman'

is interlined in light ink above deleted
'workman'. Before 'and' is crossed-out
'of', which had first been smudged out

The Mississippian and Arkansian—the woman and man of Utah, Da-
kotah, Nebraska, yet with me—and I yet with any of them,

Yet upon the plains west of the spinal river—yet in my house of adobie,

Yet returning eastward—yet in the Sea-Side State, or in Maryland,

Yet a child of the North—yet Kanadian, cheerily braving the winter—
the snow and ice welcome to me,

Yet a true son either of Maine, or of the Granite State, or of the Nar-
ragansett Bay State, or of the Empire State,

Yet sailing to other shores to annex the same—yet welcoming every
new brother,

Hereby applying these leaves to the new ones, from the hour they unite
with the old ones,

Coming among the new ones myself, to be their companion—coming
personally to you now,

Enjoining you to acts, characters, spectacles, with me.

56. With me, with firm holding—yet haste, haste on.

57. For your life, adhere to me,

Of all the men of the earth, I only can unloose you and toughen you,

I may have to be persuaded many times before I consent to give myself
to you—but what of that?

Must not Nature be persuaded many times?

58. No dainty dolce affettuoso I;

---

when wet. 'workman' is interlined in light ink above deleted 'workwoman'.

151 Dacotah,] interlined in light ink above a caret.

152 Yet in Oregon. . . .] originally written 'Yet in California or in Oregon, | Yet upon the plains. . . .' with 'Yet upon the plains' beginning a new verse. First, '—yet in Arizonia' was interlined with a finer pen and brought down by a curving stroke to follow 'Oregon,'. Then in the light ink 'in California or' was deleted and also '—yet in Arizonia'. In this same ink '—yet' was added after 'Oregon,' and the 'Yet' before 'upon the plains' was crossed through to indicate that a new verse was not to be printed.

154 Yet a] 'a' interlined in light ink above deleted 'the'.

155 or of Vermont] 'or' mended over 'as'.

156 other] this was the original reading, which was deleted and in the light ink 'new' written above it. Apparently before the ink was dry, 'new' was smudged-out, and to confirm 'other' the word was under-dotted.

156 Yet welcoming] the Y is triple under-scored to emphasize capitalization.

156 mate,] interlined above deleted 'equal,'.

158 personally] interlined above deleted 'directly'.

160 on!] an original period was mended to an exclamation mark in the light ink.

161 life,] following this is interlined above a caret with a fine pen 'as I move,', deleted first in pencil and then in ink, possibly the light ink.

165 I,] at the end of this line was subsequently added 'now arrived' in the fine pen, deleted by heavy strokes.

I have arrived, bearded, sun-|burnt, gray, forbidding, to be wres-
tled | with as I pass for the solid prizes of the | universe,
For such I afford whoever can per-|severe to win them.—

On my way a moment I | pause,
Here for you! And here for | America!
170 Still the Present I raise | aloft—Still the Future | of These States
I harbinge | glad and sublime,
And for the Past I pronounce | what the air hold of | the red
aborigines.—

[Leaf numbered 28; pink paper with various pinholes; written in black ink. A
title *'Aborigines.'* has been deleted. The cutting of the leaf differs from that of
any of the packs used in "Premonition" and it is evident that verses 172–175
represent the later insertion of an independent poem (see Introduction).]

The red aborigines!
Leaving natural breaths, | sounds of rain and wind, | calls as
of birds and ani-|mals in the woods, syl-|labled to us for
names,
Okonee, Koosa, Ottawa, Monon-|gahela, Sauk, | Natchez, Chat-
tahoochee, | Walla-Walla, Kaqueta, Orinoko,
175 Wabash, Miami, | Saginaw, | Chippewa, Oshkosh, | Alabama,
Leaving such to The States, they | melt, they depart, | charging
the water and | the land with names.—

[Leaf numbered 29; blue tax form; pinholes. Verses 177–180 are written in
black ink. Verses 181–182 were added later in the light revising ink.]

Elements, breeds, turbulent, quick auda-|cious,
A world primal again—Vistas | of glory, incessant and branching,

166 I have arrived] this phrase was heavily
corrected. Originally the line began, 'I
have arrived,'. Above 'have arrived' was
written 'step into' ['into' is uncertain].
The 'into' (?) was heavily stroked
through and 'forth' added. The original
words and this interlineation were deleted, perhaps at the same time. Beneath
the original line was written 'have arrived,' and then 'arisen' was written over
'arrived'. These words were then excised.
Beneath them, 'arrived' was written be-

low 'have', and 'arisen' written over 'arrived'. A caret after original deleted 'arrived', accompanied by fine directing
lines, leads to the top of the leaf and the
words written there 'I have arrived'.
Either this 'arrived' is written over some
other word, or some word over it (very
likely 'arisen'). In the same pen the line
continues, '—I stop for a moment | ['I'
deleted] on my journey, I pause,'. Above
'for a moment' is interlined 'on my journey'. All this at the top is then crossed

Bearded, sunburnt, gray-necked, forbidding, I have arrived,
To be wrestled with as I pass, for the solid prizes of the universe,
For such I afford whoever can persevere to win them.

59. On my way a moment I pause,
Here for you! And here for America!
Still the Present I raise aloft—Still the Future of The States I harbinge,
glad and sublime,
And for the Past I pronounce what the air holds of the red aborigines.

60. The red aborigines!
Leaving natural breaths, sounds of rain and winds, calls as of birds and
animals in the woods, syllabled to us for names,
Okonee, Koosa, Ottawa, Monongahela, Sauk, Natchez, Chattahoochee,
Kaqueta, Oronoco.
Wabash, Miami, Saginaw, Chippewa, Oshkosh, Walla-Walla,
Leaving such to The States, they melt, they depart, charging the water
and the land with names.

61. O expanding and swift! O henceforth,
Elements, breeds, adjustments, turbulent, quick, and audacious,
A world primal again—Vistas of glory, incessant and branching,

---

out, and finally 'have arrived' is squeezed in just above the original reading.

166 bearded] this was originally preceded by 'gray,', which has been deleted in light ink.

166 gray,] interlined in the light ink above a caret.

166 as I pass] interlined in the light ink above a caret.

170 aloft] the *al* written over two letters not now legible.

170 These] the capital *T* mended over a lower-case *t*.

172 The red aborigines!] perhaps at the time the title was deleted, this verse was squeezed in above the original opening verse 'Leaving natural breaths, . .'.

174 Okonee] the *k* is mended over a *c*.

174 Koosa] a capital *C* was smudged out while still wet and the *K* written over it.

174 Sauk] this was originally followed by 'Walla-Walla,' which has been deleted.

174 Kaqueta] the line first began 'Anahua, Kaqueta,'. 'Anahua' was deleted and 'Paumanok,' interlined and then excised. 'Walla-Walla' was later added with the fine pen above a caret.

175 Wabash] interlined in the light ink above a caret.

175 Miami] after this originally followed 'Alleghany, Connecti-|cut,' which have been separately deleted, 'Connecticut' last in the light ink.

175 Saginaw] after this originally followed 'Adiron-|dack,', which was deleted and above it written 'Mannahatta,' also deleted. 'Chippewa' is interlined in the light ink above a caret.

175 Oshkosh,] after this originally followed 'Chip-|pewa,' which was deleted in the light ink.

176 depart,] originally following this was 'leaving', but this was deleted before the next line continued with 'charging'.

177 Elements . . . audacious,] interlined in the light ink above the deleted original verses: 'Ships, men, elements, breeds, | [*new verse*] Settlements, youthful, plentiful, | turbulent, quick and audacious,'.

178 of glory] a preceding short dash may be only a slip of the pen.

178 incessant and branching,] interlined above deleted 'without end,'.

A new race, dominating | previous ones, and grander | far,
180 New politics—New literatures | and religions—New inventions
| and arts.—

These! These, my voice an-|nouncing—I will sleep | no more
but arise,
You oceans that have been | calm within me! how | I feel you,
fathomless, | stirring, preparing unprecedented | waves and
storms.—

[Leaves numbered 30–32: pink paper; pinholes. Leaf 30 (5½ × 5¼) has had its
top cut off to form leaf 26½ (verses 165–167) pasted at the head of leaf 27. Pinholes appear in the original center of the full leaf, and again in the new center.
Leaf 31 has had its number mended from 30. Leaf 32 is about three-quarters of a
leaf (6⅞ × 5⅛), the lower part torn off. Just above the tear is a horizontal pencil
line drawn below verse 192. Beneath this, at the tear, appear the upper parts of
some letters. The first of these that can be at all deciphered may just possibly
have formed the word 'Manahatta'; after this there is a gap and then, clearly, the
interlined and deleted word 'at'. The torn-off part of the leaf is not present in
the Valentine-Barrett collection. The verses on these three leaves are written
in black ink.]

[*leaf* 30]

See! steamers steaming through my | poems!
See in my poems immigrants con-|tinually coming and landing,
185 See in arriere, the wigwam, | the trail, the hunter's hut, | the
flat-boat, the maize-leaf, the claim, the rude fence, | and the
backwoods village,
See, on the one side the Western sea, | and on the other side the
Eastern | sea, how they advance and retreat | upon my poems,
as upon their | own shores,
See, pastures and forests in my | poems—See, animals wild and
| tame—See, beyond the Kansas, | buffalo feeding on the |
short curly grass.—

179 dominating] 'all' was originally written
after this word to end the line, and then
deleted.
180 New literatures] *N* mended over *n*.
181 voice] the *voi* is written over other
letters.

183 See!] interlined above a caret before this
is pencilled 'For' preceded by a question
mark, the whole deleted in ink.
183 steamers] interlined above deleted 'steamships'.

A new race, dominating previous ones, and grander far,
New politics—New literatures and religions—New inventions and arts.

62. These! These, my voice announcing—I will sleep no more, but arise;
    You oceans that have been calm within me! how I feel you, fathomless,
      stirring, preparing unprecedented waves and storms.

63. See! steamers steaming through my poems!
    See, in my poems immigrants continually coming and landing;
    See, in arriere, the wigwam, the trail, the hunter's hut, the flat-boat, the
      maize-leaf, the claim, the rude fence, and the backwoods village;
    See, on the one side the Western Sea, and on the other side the Eastern
      Sea, how they advance and retreat upon my poems, as upon their
      own shores;
    See, pastures and forests in my poems—See, animals, wild and tame—
      See, beyond the Kanzas, countless herds of buffalo, feeding on short
      curly grass;

---

183 poems!] the exclamation mark is written after a crossed-out comma.

185 See in arriere . . . village,] the original version was: 'See in arriere, the wigwam, the | war-scalp, the stone hatchet, | the trail, the hunter's hut, | and the backwoods village,'('backwoods' with a deleted apostrophe between *d* and *s*). 'the war-scalp,' is crossed through in black ink and 'the stone hatchet' crossed through first in pencil and then in the light ink. Between the lines was crowded in 'the maize-patch, the flat-boat, the claim, the rude fence,'. 'patch' was deleted and 'leaf' interlined. (Perhaps at the time of this last revision, the line was continued with 'the flat-boat . . .' since this part of the line is in a finer pen than 'the maize-patch'.) 'the flat-boat' was deleted and the same words interlined with a fine pen above a caret and directing line before 'the maize-leaf'.

186 See, on the one side . . . shores,] the first version read, 'See, the Mississippi and the Missouri, | how they run down

through | my poems, southerly, central, | moistening all,'. All this after 'See,' was crossed through in black and the revised form crowded in as an interlineation. After 'one side' a comma has been deleted. The latter part of the interlined revision first read, 'Eastern | sea, how they rise and decline | upon my poems'. 'decline' was crossed out and 'sink' added after it with a different pen. Finally, in the light ink 'rise and sink' was deleted and 'advance and retreat' interlined.

187 poems—See] a comma after 'poems' was smudged out while still wet. The *S* of 'See' is triple underscored to emphasize capitalization.

187 tame—See,] a comma after 'tame' is crossed through. 'See, beyond . . . grass. —' is a later addition in a finer pen.

187 Kansas] the final *s* is mended over some other letter, probably an *n*. The first version began, 'Kansas, vast herds of buffalo'. 'vast' is very heavily crossed through; but 'herds of' was deleted more lightly and at a later time.

[*leaf* 31]

¶ See, in my poems, old and new cities, solid, | vast, inland, with
paved streets, with | iron and stone edifices, and | ceaseless
vehicles, and commerce;

See, the populace, millions upon | millions, handsome, tall, |
muscular, both sexes, clothed | in easy and dignified clothes,
| teaching, commanding, marrying, | generating, equally elect-
ing and | elective;

190 See, the many-cylinder'd steam | printing-press—See, the elec-
tric | telegraph—See, the strong and quick | locomotive as
it departs, panting, blowing the | steam-whistle

[*leaf* 32]

See, ploughmen ploughing | farms—See, miners digging | mines
—See, the numberless | factories,

See, mechanics busy at their | benches with tools—See | from
among them superior | judges, philosophs, Presidents, |
emerge, dressed in working-|dresses;

See, lounging through the shops | and fields of The States, | me,
well-beloved, close-held | by day and night,

Hear the jocund echo | of my songs there—Read the hints come
at last.—

[Leaf numbered 33; blue tax form; pinholes. Written in the light revising ink,
without alteration. One of the "Thought" poems (CD 11) was written on the
back of pink paper containing a deleted version of verses 200–203, folder 46
(for the text of these deleted verses, see Appendix I).]

195 O rendezvous at last! O | us two only!

O power, liberty, eternity at | last! O to be so blithe!

O to be relieved of distinctions! | To make as much of vices |
as of virtues! To level occupa-|tions and the sexes! To | bring
all to common ground!

188 See in my poems] The leaf originally began with the following verse: 'See [final
e mended over a smudged-out letter,
perhaps an *a*], by the sea-side bathing,
free | from costumes, the full-grown |
and chaste body of a man, | or the full-
grown and chaste | body of a woman,'.

These were first set off at the left by a
brace and a question mark. Then a
pencil line was drawn beneath them.
Lastly, in the light ink they were crossed
through with three vertical strokes and
a short line drawn below them. In the
next line, now become the first on the

See, in my poems, old and new cities, solid, vast, inland, with paved streets, with iron and stone edifices, and ceaseless vehicles, and commerce;

See the populace, millions upon millions, handsome, tall, muscular, both sexes, clothed in easy and dignified clothes—teaching, commanding, marrying, generating, equally electing and elective;

See, the many-cylinder'd steam printing-press—See, the electric telegraph—See, the strong and quick locomotive, as it departs, panting, blowing the steam-whistle;

See, ploughmen, ploughing farms—See, miners, digging mines—See, the numberless factories;

See, mechanics, busy at their benches, with tools—See from among them, superior judges, philosophs, Presidents, emerge, dressed in working dresses;

See, lounging through the shops and fields of The States, me, well-beloved, close-held by day and night,

Hear the loud echo of my songs there! Read the hints come at last.

64. O my comrade!

O you and me at last—and us two only;

O power, liberty, eternity at last!

O to be relieved of distinctions! to make as much of vices as virtues!

O to level occupations and the sexes! O to bring all to common ground! O adhesiveness!

---

leaf, the paragraph sign was prefixed, and 'in my poems' was interlined above a caret; and further on 'inland,' was similarly interlined.

189 See, the populace,] between this verse and the line above ending 'vehicles and commerce;' was originally written, 'See, the President, ashamed, scouted | at by the people [smudged-out comma] for his de-| relictions,'. This was braced at the left and in the left margin added the notation 'out' with a fine pen, a question mark above it. This notation was crossed out in pencil at the time the lines were pencil-deleted by two horizontal strokes joined by a vertical. Lastly, a long stroke was drawn through the lines in the light ink, though by error this stroke did not excise 'for his de-'.

190 departs, panting,] interlined with a caret in the light ink above deleted 'passes'.

191 ploughing] a following 'the' is deleted.

191 digging] interlined above deleted 'working', with 'the' beginning the next line

being crossed out.

191 numberless] interlined with a fine pen above deleted 'iron-'.

192 superior] interlined with a fine pen above deleted 'new'.

194 Hear the jocund . . .] the first version read: 'Hear the echos of my jocund | songs there—Read the | hints come at last.—' The *s* of 'echos' was crossed through, and 'jocund' interlined before 'echo', the phrase 'of my jocund songs' being deleted and 'of my voice' interlined above deleted 'songs'. Then 'voice' was deleted and 'call' added. Lastly, in the light ink 'call' was excised and 'songs' interlined above a caret and directing stroke. In 'Read' the *R* was given a triple underscoring. At the end of the verse, the *s* of 'hints' was crossed out, then the word 'hint' was interlined and in a different ink was added 'that has', these two words then being deleted and an *s* added to the interlined 'hint'.

O adhesiveness! O the pensive | aching to be together—you |
    know not why and I | know not why;

O a word to clear one's path | ahead endlessly!

200 O something extatic and unde-|monstrable! | O music wild!

O now I triumph—and you | shall also,

O hand in hand—O wholesome | pleasure—O one more desirer
    | and lover!

O to haste, firm-holding—to haste, | haste on with me.—

APPENDIX I

Earlier versions of lines for "Premonition" from the Valentine-Barrett papers.

[Top of leaf numbered '2' over original '1'. These lines represent the original pink-paper inscription of verses 4–12 (and doubtless of verses 1–3, now cut off). The lines are marked for deletion by a vertical pen stroke and the top of the leaf cut away, destroying the original opening. The revised verses appear on leaf 1, a blue tax form.]

<Boy of the> Mannahatta—boy of | the prairies, Boy of the
    southern savannahs

Looking north | toward Niagara— | and through Kanada, with
    equal love,

Resounding the Alleghanies, re-|sounding the Mississippi— | —
    natural, vocal, spontaneous,

4 I, singing in the West, strike | up for The States.

1 boy of the prairies] the *b* of 'boy' written over some pencilled capital letter which might be a *D*. The remains of some pencilled letters appear above the dash but have been largely cut off.

1 Boy . . . savannahs] crowded in to the right as an afterthought. The *f* of 'of' is written over a deleted comma after 'Mannahatta' in the line above. A question mark precedes 'Boy'.

2 Looking . . . love] the original line read, 'Looking friendlily southward,— | looking toward Niagara,'. Above the *L* of 'Looking' some illegible letter has been deleted. The word 'friendlily' was crossed out and

the phrase 'and longing' interlined, this being deleted in turn with a stroke from the fine pen, the stroke being continued in order to excise 'southward,'. After 'southward,' a caret points to the interlineation 'to live there and never depart—', which has been deleted. The word 'northward' was interlined below 'friendlily', only to be deleted in favor of 'north' placed after it. Before 'toward' the original 'looking' is crossed out. Following 'Niagara' the comma is deleted and a dash added with the fine pen. Crowded below this part-line 'toward Niagara—' was added 'and beyond through Kanada, with

O the pensive aching to be together—you know not why, and I know not why.

65. O a word to clear one's path ahead endlessly!
O something extatic and undemonstrable! O music wild!
O now I triumph—and you shall also;
O hand in hand—O wholesome pleasure—O one more desirer and lover,
O haste, firm holding—haste, haste on, with me.

---

love,' the word 'beyond' being deleted. The word 'equal' is interlined above a caret.

3 Alleghanies,] the original comma following this word was deleted and a dash substituted. When the dash was also crossed out, the original comma was mended as a substitute.

3 Mississippi—] an original comma has been excised and a dash made with the fine pen.

3 —natural] this word is an interlined addition to the original part-line which had begun with 'vocal'.

3 vocal,] the comma was excised in favor of a dash, this being deleted in turn and another comma squeezed in before the first. Pencil marks of deletion are present for the dash, and also a pencil dash interlined above it but deleted in ink.

[Top of leaf numbered 5. These lines are the original pink-paper inscription and were deleted by a vertical stroke when verses 23–25 were revised from them and copied on the tax-form leaf 4.]

I do not discredit old times,
I returned,—I | sat among the great masters, | and listened to them,
3 Now if it be eligible, let them | return and | listen to me.

1 I do . . . times] the line first read 'I remember ancient things,' the revisions being written with a medium fine pen above the deleted words but the original comma remaining. The first form of the revision was, 'I do not forget', 'forget' being interlined above deleted 'remember'. Then with a finer pen 'forget' was excised and 'discredit' written above it, followed by 'old times'.

2 I returned . . . masters,] originally, 'I have listened to the past,—I have | heard the great masters,'. Above deleted 'listened to' was interlined 'retraced' in pencil, and above deleted 'heard' pencilled 'studied'. The next step seems to have been the deletion of 'have retraced the past' and 'have' ending the line. 'returned to' was written in, the line then reading, 'I have returned to the great masters,'. Next the

interlined 'to' was crossed out and a comma placed after 'returned'; 'sat among' (the *a* of 'among' mended) was interlined above 'great masters' and to the right of the pencilled interlineation 'studied', now deleted in ink. Finally, 'and listened to them,' was crowded in below as a separate part-line. All revisions were made with the fine pen.

3 return and . . . me.] the word 'and' was added after 'return' perhaps during the original writing following the deletion of 'with the rest'. Above the line between 'listen' and 'to' is the pencilled word 'study', with a pencil line drawn through 'listen to'. An ink stroke has deleted 'study', which seems to have been an early note to establish a parallelism with the pencil 'study' above, and 'listen to' was underdotted in ink for retention.

[Folder 5. Deleted draft on white wove paper for verses 58–61; presumably "Enfans d'Adam" [no. 9] was written on the back of this leaf after the deletion. Also on this same side of the leaf is a pencil verse later in "Chanting the Square Deific" published in *When Lilacs Last in the Door-yard Bloom'd* in 1865–66 (see after "Enfans d'Adam" [no. 9]). The deleted verses are written in pencil and crossed out by a vertical pencil stroke.]

> I am the child of Democracy,
> I will advance from the | people en-masse, in their | own spirit,
> 3 I will chant a | strong and haughty chant, | for you, my mother.—

2 I] indented 'I' is crossed out and another substituted out to the margin in order to indicate that a new verse begins.
3 a] interlined above deleted 'your own'.
3 for you,] added above a caret.

3 mother.—] the period mended over a comma and the dash added; originally, after a space another verse began, 'I will make', and then stopped. 'will make' is crossed out, but 'I' left untouched.

[Leaf 8 of "Premonitions." A form of verses 58–61 intermediate between those found on the back of "Enfans d'Adam" [no. 9] in folder 5 (see above), and the finally revised version on the white wove paper of leaf 12. These lines are written in a light brown ink on blue wove paper and deleted by a vertical stroke. There are no alterations.]

> I am the child of Democracy,
> I advance from the people | en-masse, in their own | spirit,
> 3 I chant a strong and haughty | chant for you, my mother.

[Leaf 12 verso. Drafts for verses 69–73; written in brown-black ink on white wove paper and deleted by vertical pencil strokes. Leaf 12 (verses 58–68 on the recto) has been cut apart horizontally and the top and bottom transposed in order to reverse the sequence of its recto lines. Since the drafts on the verso were written before this transposition (and doubtless before the inscription of the recto verses themselves), the following transcripts rearrange the draft lines in their original order as inscribed.]

[*original upper but present lower piece; the first three lines through 'canticles' are pasted over by the overlap of the upper piece. Verses 1–4 above the horizontal line have been deleted by a vertical ink stroke and various pencil strokes.*]

> I distinctly acknowledge Religion,
> I intend that America shall have the greatest,
> I will in due time make my canticles | of it, fit for These States,
> 4 I understand perfectly well that | a man or nation is little or nothing without | Religion.—
>
> [*horizontal line*]

2 I intend . . . greatest,] an addition, crowded in between the original verses.

4 that] following 'that' at the end of the line is deleted 'for'.

4 little or] interlined above a caret.

[below the horizontal line. These verses are deleted by a vertical pencil stroke. In the left margin opposite the second verse is the note in the text ink, 'very crude'.]

1 I distinctly acknowledge Religion,
     I understand perfectly well that Religion is the | greatest part of a man or nation | —and that no man or nation | can possibly be great without | it,

[present upper section, original lower]

    I will duly place the canticles of it | here

2 perfectly] interlined above a caret.

2 greatest] interlined above deleted 'vital'.

2 of a man or] Whitman first wrote after 'man' the words 'on a' (the *a* doubtful and possibly an *o*), and then deleted them before continuing 'or nation'.

3 I will . . . here] this line is written below several trials. Whitman first began, 'and I w' before crossing out the words and beginning again with a new verse, 'I know my poems were nothing without | it,'. A new verse was then added, beginning, 'I am to make its canticles here—I | will make', at which point he broke off and wrote in the line below, 'will duly bring them to', the word 'bring' written after currently deleted 'bind'. This last line was then crossed out, and then all above it, including the verse 'I know my poems . . .', before inscribing the final form 'I will duly . . . of it here.'

[Folder 46, verso of leaf 1 of "Thought" (CD 11); pink paper. Undeleted drafts of verses 200–203 subsequently revised on tax-form leaf 33. The drafts are written in a dark brown ink. The second line appears in "Enfans d'Adam" no. 6 in the 1860 edition, a poem not found in the Valentine-Barrett manuscripts.]

    O something wild and extatic! | Something undemonstrable!
    O something unproved! Something | in a trance!
    O now I triumph—and you | shall also!
    O hand in hand! O wholesome | pleasure! O one more desirer | and lover!
5 O to haste, firm holding—To haste, | haste on with me.—

2 unproved] *r* mended over another letter, perhaps an *a*.

4 wholesome] interlined in the same ink above deleted 'burning'.

5 with me.—] in the lower right corner within a semi-circle is written in the same ink, 'end of Poem'.

⟦ 39 ⟧

APPENDIX II

Leather-bound holograph notebook in the Charles E. Feinberg Collection, reproduced by kind permission of Mr. Feinberg. On page 1 (page 2 blank) is a brief copied extract from the New York *Express* dated 21 October 1856. Pages 76–78 contain lists of names and book titles. On page 77 is the name of Bronson Alcott and the date 'Oct. 4, '56'; page 78 is headed 'Sept. 16th'. (For details see the Introduction.) After page 38 the notebook was reversed and the writing continued from the other end; however, for convenience the pages have been numbered consecutively here as if they were in seriatim order. Most of the notebook is given over to drafts of lines for "Premonition"; nevertheless, because of the general interest of the material, all writing except for the editorial and name and book lists has been transcribed here. It will be observed that some of the writing on the versos of leaves (even-numbered pages) was added later than that on the next rectos (odd-numbered pages), and hence that much continuous inscription must be traced from recto to recto.

[Page 3 (p. 4 blank). A section of the leaf has been cut out at the foot excising at least one, and probably two or more lines of text.]

Proem.—

Proem of all

These are the candid | open-shown thoughts | of me, and of all | my body & soul

Lo the round globe, tumbling

Lo, friendly persons advancing, | tall, muscular, friendly with | sufficient hands and feet,

5   Lo—great women upon the world | and Lo | how they precede the beard-faced masters | upon the world.

---

3 Lo the round] above this is the deleted trial 'Lo, the one free amplitude'. In this, 'one' has been independently crossed out. 'free' was deleted and 'open' interlined. Immediately under the latter half of the line was added 'over and over', undeleted. It is difficult to know whether this was part of the trial or whether it was intended

as an interlined addition after 'globe,' in verse 3.

4 muscular, friendly] 'friendly' interlined above a caret.

5 great . . . world.] before 'great' is deleted 'the'; the original 'the' before 'beard-faced' appears to have been deleted at the same time. After 'women' original 'of | the New

World' has been crossed out. Above 'of' was interlined 'of the world', this 'of' then being deleted and 'upon' substituted. The 'and' after 'world' was interlined in the next line above the dash after original 'New World'. 'how they precede the' is an interlineation. Before the final 'the world.' the word 'upon' was interlined above deleted 'of'.

[Page 5 (p. 6 blank). The upper third of the leaf has been cut off. Except for the trial 'Lo', the verse has been deleted by a vertical stroke.]

Lo

1 Shall speak in the Presidents | Message from the porch | of the Federal Capitol, and in | the Governors' Messages | from the State Capitols, | and in the rulings of | the Judges of the | Supreme Court.

1 speak] *eak* written over other letters. 'Federal' interlined above a caret. In 'Messages' the *M* is mended from *m*. In 'Judges' the *d* appears to have been written currently over an *s*, as if Whitman had had *Justices* first in mind.

[Page 7 (p. 8 blank). The upper two-thirds of the leaf has been cut off.]

Commencement of Discourse | "Spiritualism"

1 Life is very great but there | is something greater than life, absorbing life, namely Death.— | When as we use in the midst | of affairs going to dinner &c, we | receive the news of the sudden | Death of—

1 there] apparently mended from original 'the'. In the next line 'is' is written currently after the start of another word with some deleted letter. After 'Death of—' is the circled word 'over'; but the cutting of the leaf has destroyed the continuation on the verso.

[Page 9 (p. 10 blank). All the writing down to the horizontal line after the second start following verse 4 is deleted by a vertical stroke.]

[*begin deleted verses*]

Proem

Preface of Endless Announcements |
Toward the perfect woman | of America
Toward the perfect man | of America,

4 Toward the President | of These States, and | the members of |
the Congress of These | States

Proem

Preface of Endless | Announcements

[*end deleted verses*]

[*horizontal line*]

After all is said, it | remains to be said, This | too is great in its
reference | to death

1 Preface of] interlined above a caret.   4 the Congress] 'the' is a later addition.
2 America] before this is currently deleted
'Thes'.

[Page 11 (p. 12 blank).]

Poem of Remorse

I now look back to the | times when I thought | others—slaves—
the ignorant | —so much inferior to my self
To have so much less right | than myself

[Page 13. All the writing is deleted by a vertical stroke.]

O you round Earth, | I

[*horizontal line*]

Savage and strong,
Free, luxuriant, im   , | I from Mannahatta, | speak up for The
States.

[*horizontal line*]

O my body, that gives | me identity!
5 O my organs all and every one. O that | which makes manhood!
O

[*horizontal line*]

A   Savage and strong
Primal
9   Free, luxuriant, | im   I, | from Mannahatta | speak up for
you and | for The States.—

5 all and every one] interlined first as 'all   7 strong] interlined above deleted 'luxuri-
and each,'. Then 'each' was deleted and   ant'.
'every one' written below the line and   9 Free] before this is currently deleted 'Am',
brought up by a guiding stroke.   itself written over some other letter or
7 A] this appears to be written in a different   letters.
ink. It probably represents an undeleted   9 luxuriant,] after this is what seems to be a
trial start.   deleted caret which might have indicated

the intention to bring down 'Savage and strong' from verse 7 to this place.

9 I, . . . States.—] these lines originally read, 'I come, [come *currently deleted*] | stand in the midst | of The States.' In this, 'The' is mended from 'the'. Also, interlined above 'stand' is the deleted 'an Amer'. When the major deletion was made, 'stand' was inadvertently not lined through. Immediately above it was interlined 'from Mannahatta', and presumably at this time a comma was added after 'I' in the line above. 'speak . . . States.—' is an addition; in this, 'The' was originally 'These' but the last two letters have been deleted.

[Page 14.]

(Simply

Endless Announcements

3 nothing more

3 nothing more] this is circled. Below it, and within the circle is drawn a fist pointing to the words.

[Page 15.]

[*begin deleted verses*]

Words of America

Free and severe words, | the master's words,

[*end deletion with a horizontal line*]

3 The mother's, father's, | husband's wife's, | son's, daughter's words,

[*horizontal line*]

[drawn fist] *The Proem must | have throughout | a strong saturation | of America, The | West, the Geography, | the representative | American man.*

[Page 16.]

All that you do | dissipates away

2 But all that you | do to your body, | mind, morals, last | in this sphere and | in other spheres

1 do] above this is interlined 'g' and then to the right, 'gain' left undeleted.

2 mind] currently mended over 'mora'.

[Page 17. After verse 3 a rectangle has been cut out from the leaf excising perhaps two verses separated from the rest by horizontal lines.]

Shall grow in the manly | muscle of men and | in the greatness of | perfect women

[*horizontal line*]

I do not say that life | is not beautiful,

But I say that whatever | it is, it all tends to | the beauty of death.

[excised part of leaf, and horizontal line]

4 To you, endless announcements | whoever you are, I | kiss you with lips of | personal love,

4 To you, . . . announcements] an addition. 'endless' is written after currently deleted 'endless'.

4 whoever] originally the verse began here with 'You whoever'. First 'To' was added before 'You' and then both words independently deleted, probably at different times.

4 personal] interlined following the earlier deleted interlineation 'real'.

[Page 18. All this page is deleted by a vertical stroke. A large asterisk appears in the left margin slightly above the verse 'Free, savage' etc. The cut-out portion excising verses on the recto of the leaf affects various lines. The preliminary '(last verse' is a later notation.]

Premonition.

(last verse

To you, endless announcements

Whoever you are, For your sake, these.

Free, fresh and savage;

5 Fluent, luxuriant, | self-compos

[excised portion of leaf]

I was < born fond > | of the sea-beach,
In Mannahatta's streets walking | I make poems | for The States.
In Mannahatta's streets walking | I make poems for The States

2 To you] in the left margin ıs an added question mark. In the line below is a deleted false start with a marginal question mark preceding, 'To America'.

3 Whoever you are,] crowded in as an addition in the left margin. The verse originally began 'For. . . .'

4 fresh and] interlined above a caret. After 'savage;' is deleted 'strong,'.

5 Fluent] interlined above deleted 'Cheerful'. Deleted original 'fluent' comes after 'luxuriant' and beginning the next line.

5 -compos] below this is the interlineation 'perso' to some deletion in the top excised line.

7 In Mannahatta's. . . .] the verse originally read, 'In Mannahatta I walking | and sound thence | the strong poems | of The States.' 'In' was deleted and 'In the streets of' interlined, the 'the' then being crossed out. When 'streets' was interlined above deleted 'I' before 'walking', the earlier interlineation was not excised. The apostrophe and s were added to 'Mannahatta'. When 'and sound thence the strong' was deleted, 'I sound' was interlined and then deleted in favor of 'I make'. Before 'The States' the word 'for' was interlined above deleted 'of'. The repetition of the line was to write out fair the almost illegibly worked-over verse.

[Page 19 (p. 20 blank). The upper two-thirds of the leaf is cut off. Before the first verse is an excised large asterisk. A fist in the left margin before the third verse points up and to the left. A horizontal line shows just below the cut-off. All the writing on this page is deleted with a vertical stroke.]

Free, savage, strong,

Cheerful, luxuriant, fluent, | self-composed, fond of | friends, fond of women and children

Fond of fish-shaped | Paumanok, where I | was born—fond of | the sea-beach,

4 From Mannahatta I send | the poems of The States.

2 composed] interlined above deleted 'sufficient'.
2 fond of friends . . . children] an addition.

Before 'friends' is a deleted 'my'.
3 Paumanok] ending the line above is currently deleted 'Paumanok'.

[Page 21 (p. 22 blank). All the writing is deleted by a vertical stroke.]

O intertwined lands!

O lands of the future! | copious land | Washington's land

3 O the lands! | copiously embracing, the interhanded, many-armed, the | knit together, the | passionate lovers, the | fused and clasped, | the | old and young brothers, | the side by side, the | experienced sisters | and the inexperienced | sisters, the equal ones, | the womb-offspring, the | well-|beloved of ages! ages! ages! | —the inextricable, | the river-tied and the | mountain-tied

1 intertwined] 'twined' written over 'locked'.
2 copious . . . Washington's land] these two phrases are additions. The first two verses on this leaf appear to be additions, and the leaf first to have started with the single word 'This', deleted. Below this was written, 'Ahold of hands,' and then after a space 'These interhanded', with 'The interhanded States' in the next line, all deleted. 'copious land' and 'Washington's land' were written one above the other to the right in the space below 'Ahold of hands,'.
3 the lands!] 'the' interlined above deleted 'my'.
3 copiously embracing, the] an addition interlined above a caret. Originally a new

verse had begun with 'The interhanded,', the 'The' being deleted in favor of 'O' and then that rejected.
3 many-armed] interlined above a caret.
3 and clasped,] interlined above the first part of deleted 'ones the equal | womb-offspring,'.
3 side by side,] interlined above deleted 'equal'. Before 'side' is deleted interlined 'world'.
3 well-|beloved] originally, 'well-attached, the', with deletion creating the text reading.
3 ages! ages!] the second and third 'ages!' interlined above the first two words of deleted 'and of | ages,—'.

[Page 23. The beginning of the first verse is excised by a cut-off at the top of the leaf. All the writing is deleted by a vertical stroke.]

breezed, the Ar< > | braced, the sea-bosomed, | the Mississippi-drained, | the fresh-breezed, the | ample-land, the wonderful, | the welcome, the inseparable | brothers!

O dear lands! O death! | O I will not | be | be discharged severed
from you by death

O I cannot be severed! I | visit you | yet with irrepressible love.

O I come | silently and invisibly

5 Again the

2 be | be discharged severed] the first 'be'
was inadvertently left undeleted after the
current excision of preceding 'desert you
by death'. 'discharged' is interlined above
deleted 'divested'; below the line is the
undeleted alternate 'severed'.

3 cannot be severed!] interlined above deleted 'do not care!'

3 I visit you yet] originally, 'I | will yet visit
you with'. First 'will' was deleted and
'shall' crowded in below and to the right
of 'I'. Then 'shall' was deleted, and also
'yet' after 'will'. Finally, 'yet' was interlined without a caret before 'with'.

4 I come] after 'I' appears currently deleted
'will visi' before 'come' was written.

[Page 24. The excision affecting the text at the head of page 23 was made to
delete a verse heading page 24 above a horizontal line. All the writing on the
page is deleted by a vertical stroke. The verses are continued on page 26.]

This then is life,

Here is what has come upon | the earth, out of | so many throes |
and convulsions.—

How curious! How real!

Underfoot the divine soil— | Overhead, the sun.—

5 Nourish my poems, Earth, and give | them roots, | for they are
your | offspring,

Bedew them, you | spring and summer dews—shelter

2 Here . . . out of] interlined above original
'This then is the earth | and what has ar-
rived | after', in which 'This' and 'the
earth' were inadvertently left undeleted.
In the interlineation, 'Here' is crowded in
above currently deleted 'This', 'been' was currently
deleted before 'come', and the trial 'arrived' was placed above 'come upon' but
deleted.

5 Nourish . . . roots,] 'Earth,' is an interlineation without a caret, consequent upon
the deletion of 'you earth,' after 'roots,'.
Above this verse is the deleted start, 'Af-
ford foothold to my poems, | you'.

6 them, . . . dews—] original 'dews,' was deleted after 'them,' and 'dews—' interlined
above a caret after 'summer—'.

[Page 25. Heading this leaf and separated by a horizontal line from the verses
below, are five lines headed 'Philip Holmes' with jotted directions for reaching
'Scroon lake' in the Adirondacks. These lines may follow on those from page
23.]

I will visit the Texan | in

[*short horizontal line*]

The jaunt over the | prairies as welcome as | ever
3 Shine upon them, sun, for | they

1 jaunt] before this is currently deleted 'wal', doubtless beginning 'walk'. Below this verse is the deleted verse, 'The long voyage | up the | Mississip'. In this 'long sail' was interlined above deleted 'banks' and then 'sail' deleted in favor of 'voyage'. After 'banks' the first version read, 'of the | Missouri', which was deleted, and at some time a superfluous 'the' added after deleted 'the'. 'up the | Mississip' was added after deleted 'Missouri'. The word was broken off after starting the first stroke of the second *p*.

2 Shine. . . .] this verse is a later addition.

[Page 26. A vertical stroke deletes all the text, which continues that on page 24.]

them, winter snows, for | they would make you

Favor them, all you | laws of materials, and | of vulgar and rejected | things, for they would | make you illustrious
You mothers

4 You young women, for | they would announce you | forever as capable | and eminent as | young men

1 would] before this is currently deleted 'are'.
2 Favor] above is interlined deleted 'Help'. Before 'all' is currently deleted 'to yo'.
2 and of vulgar] between 'and' and 'vulgar' is deleted original | 'all ponderable things | all'. The 'of' before 'vulgar' is interlined above deleted 'all'.

4 announce . . . forever] before 'announce' is currently deleted 'p'. 'would' is interlined above a caret. 'forever' is interlined above a caret after deleted original 'as just'.
4 young men] before this is deleted 'the'.

[Page 27. All writing is deleted by a vertical stroke.]

The man or woman of Texas, the Lousiain [*sic*] | the Floridian the Georgian, | the Carolinian, the Mississippian | the Arkansian, the Californian | as much my friend as ever, and I his friend | or her friend as much as ever, |
Oregon as much mine as | ever,
You Mannahatta | close | as ever! O close! close to me!
The man of Ohio and woman of Ohio real | to me, as ever
5 The Kentuckian for me and I for him as much as ever
Wisconsin, Iowa, | Michigan, Illinois, | Indiana, Missouri, | Kansas, Nebraska, Utah, | Minnesota! for me and I | for them the same as | ever!

1 man or woman of] interlined above a caret.
1 the Floridian. . . .] 'the' before each such name in this verse is either added in the left margin or interlined.
1 or her friend] interlined above a caret.

3 You] interlined above a caret. After 'Man-
nahatta' is deleted ' ! Mannahatta! | Man-
nahatta! still'.

3 to me] interlined after 'close!'.

4 The man . . . real] 'O' was currently deleted before 'The'. 'man of' is interlined,
as is 'and woman of Ohio'; The original
'Ohio' was altered by deletion of the last
two letters from 'Ohioan'.

5 The Kentuckian. . . .] the whole verse is

an addition. Before 'for me' is currently
deleted 'my'.

6 Utah, Minnesota!] the first was crowded in
as an addition, and the second interlined
above a caret.

6 and I . . . ever!] before 'and I' is deleted
'as ever', with interlined 'much as' also
deleted. After 'for them' is deleted 'as
much,' and its substitute 'the same' interlined and deleted. Final 'the same' is written below the line.

[Page 28. A vertical stroke deletes the writing.]

You old man and old woman, | for they would show that | you are
no less | admirable than any

2 You sexual organs, and | acts, for they are determined to tell | you
with glad | courageous loud | voice, to make | you illustrious.

1 would show] interlined above separately
deleted 'know see'.

1 admirable] an original comma after this
is deleted.

2 are determined to tell] interlined above
deleted 'behold'.

[Page 29 (p. 30 blank). All but the last verse is deleted by a vertical stroke.
The verses are intended to come after those on page 27.]

The Tennessee-man and | the Tennessee-woman | —no less to
me than ever
Pennsylvania, New Jersey, | Delaware, Maryland, | Virginia, yet
travelled | by me,
Maine, New-Hampshire, | Vermont, Massachusetts, | Connecti-
cut, Rhode Island, | New York, yet dwelt | in by me,

[end deleted verses]

4 Ontario, Erie, Huron, | Michigan, Superior, | yet sailed upon | by
me.

1 no less . . . ever] 'no less to me' is interlined above deleted original 'the same as
ever'. The words 'to me' had been added
after original 'as ever'; these are deleted,
and 'than ever' interlined.

3 Maine] before this is currently deleted
'The'.

4 Ontario. . . .] above this is the deleted
false start, 'Huron, Erie Mic'.

[Page 31 (p. 32 blank). The upper third of the leaf has been cut away above a
horizontal line. A vertical stroke deletes the verses.]

To you endless im
2 To you, these, to | report nature, man, | politics,   from | an
American | point of view.

2 man] an addition. A space is left after 'politics'; the 'from' is an addition made at the same
time as 'man'.

[Page 33. The central third of the leaf has been cut away. All the writing is deleted by a vertical stroke.]

These are the words of the | master
These

[*excised part of leaf*]
[*horizontal line*]

As long as the earth | is brown and | solid

[*horizontal line*]

Free, savage, strong,

5 Cheerful, luxuriant, fluent, self-sufficient | slender fond | of
Paumanok where I was born, | fond of the sea-beach
From Manhattan I | send the poems of The States.

5 fond of Paumanok] originally a new verse began after 'self-sufficient', with 'Out from the sea-beach, from'. First 'Out from' was deleted and 'Fond of' interlined, but inadvertently never deleted. Then 'the sea-beach, from' was crossed through and 'fond' written above the 'from', this being accompanied by the addition of 'of' before 'Paumanok'. The word 'slender' was added immediately below the 'from' of 'Out from' and thus starting above and slightly to the left of 'Paumanok'. Since there is no caret, its intended place is uncertain, and it may have been intended to precede 'Paumanok'.

5 fond of the sea-beach] an addition.
6 Manhattan] deleted 'Island' follows this.

[Page 34. The excised part of the leaf has destroyed some text below the last transcribed line.]

These shall live,
Shall grow in
Shall walk in the streets | Mannahatta,

4 Shall climb the Alleghanies | and

1 live] above this is written the later alternative 'abide'.

[Page 35 (p. 36 blank).]
[*begin deleted verses*]

Listen to me,
Out from Paumanok, where | I was born, I

[*end deletion above horizontal line*]

All is in yourself,

4 Things, thoughts, the stately | shows of the world, | the suns and
moons, | the landscape, summer | and winter, | poems, endearments,
All

[*horizontal line, verses below deleted*]

Free, Savage, and strong, | coarse, luxuriant, | fluent, self-sufficient,

7 Out from Manhattan Island | I send the poems | of The States.

2 born, I] above 'I' is the alternative 'and'; and after 'I' is deleted 'recite'.

4 Things . . .] above this is deleted the false start, 'The' followed by deleted 'All things, all thoughts,'. After 'winter,' is deleted 'the'.

6 coarse] before 'luxuriant' a new verse originally began with 'Primal,'. After this is interlined 'arrogant', deleted, followed by the addition 'coarse'. After 'luxuriant,'

original 'coarse, and' are independently crossed out; and in the line below, 'fluent' is written above deleted 'combative'.

7 Out from]. The verse originally began with two trials, 'A' followed by 'O' before 'From Manhattan' was written. 'Out from' is interlined, the 'from' following deleted 'of'.

7 send] interlined above deleted 'make'.

[Page 37 (p. 38 blank). A large asterisk is placed in the margin to the left of verse 7 'How curious!'. All the writing is deleted by a vertical stroke.]

Filled fill'd with such

Overhead, the splendid sun!

Under-foot, the

O divine soil,

5 Under-foot, O divine soil!

Overhead, O

How curious!—How real,

Underfoot, the divine soil!

Overhead, the sun!

10 Me,

1 Filled] an apostrophe appears above the *e*. 'such' interlined above deleted 'wonders'.

2 the splendid] 'the' is interlined above deleted 'how' and an original 'the' after

'splendid' is deleted.

3 the] written after deleted 'how'.

10 Me,] above this are two deleted lines, 'How curious | How curious I myself!'

[Page 39. Beginning here, Whitman reversed the notebook and wrote forward from the other end.]

I understand you, you | bards of other lands

2 I bear you in mind, you | ancestors of men.—

1 other] after this is deleted 'ages, and'.

2 bear . . . mind,] interlined above deleted 'understand you,'.

[Page 40.]

Lo! ships sailing!

Lo, intersecting | streets in cities, full | of living people, coming | and going!

Lo, iron and steam, | so grand, so welcome!
Lo,

[*horizontal line*]

5 How curious is the brown | real earth!
How curious, how | spiritual is the water

[*horizontal line*]

Politics

On the one side pledged to – – –.
On the other side to | – – – –
— On the one side – – –

10 On

1 ships] before this is deleted 'the'.
2 intersecting] interlined above deleted 'interminable', before which is independently deleted 'the the'.

3 iron] before this is deleted 'where'.
4 Lo,] after this is deleted 'th'.
5 real] the first letter is doubtful; before, is deleted 'wo'.

[Page 42 (p. 41 blank).] A large asterisk appears in the left margin opposite the horizontal line drawn above verse 5. Verses 1–4 are deleted by a vertical stroke.]

[*begin deletion*]

Forever and
Thy soul!
Forever and forever, longer | than ground is brown and solid,!
     longer | than water ebbs and | flows
They duly give place, in their order of millions of years.—but |
     you O my soul shall never | give place!

[*asterisk and horizontal line ending deleted matter*]

5 Life—how curious, how real
Space, and time how filled with such | wonders!
To walk, to breathe, how delicious
The day! the | animals,! identity,! | eyesight,!
Underfoot, the divine | soil,
10 Overhead, the sun.

1 Forever and] an addition.
2 Thy soul!] written above deleted 'To co< >'
3 longer . . . brown] interlined above deleted 'as long | as the'. 'ground' is written over some illegible word.
3 longer than water] the *er* of 'longer' is added, and a preceding 'as' to original

'long' is deleted. 'than' is written after currently deleted 'as'.
4 duly . . . years.—] 'duly' is interlined above deleted 'shall', before which is currently deleted 'gi'. 'in their order . . . years.—' is interlined above a caret. 'their order of' is interlined above deleted 'a few'.
6 and time] interlined above a caret. Before

'wonders' is deleted 'easy'.
8 day] before this is deleted 'dayly'. Before 'animals' is deleted 'these | curious, di-

vine,'. 'the' is interlined above separately deleted 'these'; and 'divine' is independently deleted.

[Page 43. The upper third of the leaf has been cut off, destroying some text, as a result of an excision of lines on page 44. The writing is deleted by a vertical stroke.]

| deserves more than | you, and never can deserve
I do not fail to | salute you with my hand and neck, you | poets of all ages | and lands,
3 I do not forget | any one of you, you fallen | nations,—to bless you —nor any | one of you, | ancestors of men

1 deserves] interlined above deleted 'to receive' and following deleted interlined 'shall' and 'ought to'. The final 'deserve' is an addition.
2 fail] interlined above deleted 'forget'.
2 with . . . neck] interlined without a caret.

3 any one of] interlined without a caret. At the end of the preceding line, following 'forget' is deleted 'to bless'.
3 to bless you—] interlined without a caret.
3 ancestors] before this, at the end of the preceding line, is deleted 'you'.

[Page 44. A horizontal line appears below the cut-off upper third of the leaf.]

How real is the ground! | Come let us set | our feet upon the | ground;
How perfect and beautiful | are the animals!
3 How much room, and | splendor! How inevitable! | How spacious!

1 set] before this is deleted *p*.
3 How much] above this is the false start, 'How vas'.

3 spacious] before this is deleted 'vast and'.

[Page 45. The upper two-thirds of the leaf has been cut off as a consequence of the excision of lines on p. 46. The writing is deleted by a vertical stroke.]

ancestors of men
Nor you | old poets
3 I do not forget to salute | you, young poets, | of all ages and | lands,

1 ancestors] before this is deleted 'my'; following, is a deleted comma; the *e* in 'men' is mended from an *a*.
2 you] interlined above deleted 'you, you'

followed by independently deleted 'the'.
3 you poets] 'you' interlined above deleted 'you old'. 'ages' is interlined above deleted 'times'.

[Page 46, the upper two-thirds cut off.]

1 Do you not know <that> | your soul has brothers | and sisters, just as | much as your body | has?

1 your soul] 'your' interlined above deleted 'the'. Later, the 'your' before 'body' is in- terlined, but the original 'the' is not de- leted.

[Page 47.]

This then is life, and | this the earth.—

How curious! How real.

Underfoot, the divine soil,— | overhead, the sun

Surround my poems, you | east and west, for | they are for you
5 And you north and | south, for they are | for you,
Imbue them, nights, for | they are of you, and | for you,
And you, days, for they | are for you.—
Lo

1 then] a following comma is crossed through. The period after 'earth' is mended from a comma.
3 overhead] a capital *O* was deleted and miniscule *o* interlined in order to change the start of a new verse.
4 Surround] a question mark is interlined above this. The next word 'my' is inter- lined above deleted 'these'.

[Page 48].

Great ideas dominate | over all—

[*short horizontal line*]

What has Shakespeare | done to England?

[*short horizontal line*]

Not – – not – – | are of any account | compared to the | few men of great | ideas

[*short horizontal line*]

Even One great idea vitalizes | a nation

[*short horizontal line*]

5 —Man of great ideas

4 Even] interlined without a caret.
5 Man] the reading is uncertain, possibly it is 'Men'.

[Page 50 (p. 49 blank)]

Personality!
Your Personality! you | whoever you are?
O you coward that | dare not | be audacious!
O you liar that | assume to | be modest and | deferential

5 O you slave

O you tongueless, eyeless, earless,

O you   that | will not receive me | for your own sake

1 Personality!] above this is the false start 'Your' deleted.
2 whoever] before this is deleted 'and'.
3 dare not] after this is currently deleted 'claim'. After 'audacious' is deleted 'for |

your own sake'. The exclamation after 'audacious' comes from the undeleted mark after 'sake'.
4 assume] before this is deleted 'falsely'.
6 tongueless,] interlined above a caret.

[Page 52.]

Personality!

You! whoever you are! | without one single | exception, in any | part of and of These | States!

3 I   you with | free and severe | hand—I know well, | whoever you are, you are my equal, | and the President's | equal,— and that there | is no one on this | globe any | greater than you — | and that there is | no existence in all | the universes any more | immortal than you,

3 you with] before this is 'seize' with a question mark over it, the word deleted. After 'with' is deleted s and some incomplete following letter probably an h.
3 severe] after this is deleted 'your'.
3 whoever you are,] interlined without a caret.

3 globe] after this is a deleted word, probably 'and'. After 'any' is deleted 'better'. Preceding 'greater' is deleted 'gr'.
3 immortal than you,] 'you' is mended from 'your', possibly from 'yours'.

[Page 54 (p. 53 blank).]

In Poem

The earth, model of poems | none need | discard what I | find in the theory | of the great, diversified round | earth, so beautiful, so rude.

The body of a man, that | is my model—I do | not reject what I | find in my body—I | am not ashamed—Why | should I be ashamed?

3 The body of a woman, | that is my perfect | model—I believe | in all the body of | the woman—I believe | the perfect woman | shall even precede | the man

1 model . . . need] interlined above 'that is my | model—I do not'. A question mark appears before 'none', but it is uncertain whether the mark refers to the interlined 'none need' or to the 'I do not' below.

1 diversified] interlined without a caret.
1 so beautiful, so rude.] an addition. Deleted 'and' appears after 'beautiful'.
2 man,] a deleted dash comes after this. Before 'is' is currently deleted 'I'.

[Page 56 (p. 55 blank).]

Poem of Maternity

O my dear child! My | Darling
(Now I am maternal | a child bearer— | I have from | my womb
  borne | a child, and | observe it

3 The life that is, not | underlaid by great | ideas is – –

2 have] before this is deleted 'bea'.   3 The life] above is the false start, 'For great ideas!'

[Page 58 (p. 57 blank). The upper two-thirds of the leaf has been cut off.]

For friendship!

[*line of dashes*]

2 For immortality!

[*line of dashes*]

[Page 59. The lower two-thirds of the leaf is cut off.]

Dwelling nigh the Ohioan | and Kentuckian, a | friendly neighbor,
2 Sauntering the streets of | Boston, Portland, | (long list of cities

1 nigh the] interlined above deleted 'neighbor to the'.   2 Sauntering] follows after the deleted false start *W* (for proposed 'Walking'?).

[Page 60. The writing is deleted by a vertical stroke. A large asterisk is placed in the left margin against the first line.]

National hymns,
The freeman's and freewoman's | songs,
3 The master's words, arrogant, | fluent, severe.—

3 arrogant, fluent,] interlined above deleted 'strong, | lawless,'.

[Page 62 (p. 61 blank). The lower two-thirds of the leaf cut off below a horizontal stroke.]

? For your own sake
To stand fast by me!
3 To stand unshaken, | tenacious,

3 unshaken,] after this is deleted 'and'; after 'tenacious' deleted '—to'. Below is a deleted verse, after a space, 'To believe in me—no | matter'.

[Page 64 (p. 63 blank). Below the center, a small section of the leaf has been cut away.]

The observer stand | *clear day* on the northeast | height of Washington Park, | some clear day in the year | 1900, (the year of These | States.) will look on

[*space, and excised part of leaf*]

[*horizontal line*]

Have you any doubt of mortality?
I say there can be no more | doubt of immortality than | there is of mortality.

[Pag 66 (p. 65 blank).]

> Primer of Words | and |
> Thoughts ⎫ (none of
> Ideas   ⎬   these
> Principles ⎭ suit

[Page 68 (p. 67 blank). A small excision in the leaf appears in the middle, cutting away no more than one line of isolated writing.]

American songs,
—in which prose, | (to be spoken—with a | low, or other musical | accompaniment.) is interlineated

[Page 73 (pp. 69–72, 74 blank).]

I had rather have the | good will of the butchers and | boatman of Manhattan Island | than all the nominations | of the government—literate | elegant persons

2 nominations] below this are the alternatives 'approbation' and 'rewards'. 'literate' is mended from 'literary'. Below the last line is the deleted word 'Jake'.

[Page 75. At the head of the page is the name 'Sam Matthews' circled.]

Walt Whitman stands to-day | in the midst of the American people, | a promise, a preface, an | overture a
Will he fulfil the half-distinct | half-indistinct promise?— | Many do not understand him, | but there are others, a few who | do understand him. Will | he justify the great prophecy | of Emerson? or will he | too, like thousands of others, | flaunt out one [*interlined above deleted* the] bright | announcement, the result of | gathered powers, only to sink | back exhausted—or to | give himself up to the seductions | of

[Pages 76–78: lists of books and of names.]

[FOLDER 2. Single piece of white wove paper (6¼ × 4); a few pinholes in the center. Written in the light ink, without alterations. 1860, p. 287; Camden, I, 110. For an earlier version on the verso of "Calamus" [no. 18] in folder 20, see below.]

Leaves-Droppings.

1

In the garden, the world, I Adam, | again wander,
Curious, here behold my resur-|rection after ages of | slumber,
The revolving cycles in their | wide sweeps having again | brought
    me—I return | the same,
All beautiful to me—all | wondrous—I am myself | most won-
    drous,
5 I exist—I peer and penetrate | still,
Content with the present, | content with the past,
By my side Eve following, | and I following her just | the same.—

[Earlier version of "Enfans d'Adam" [no. 1] above from folder 20. "Calamus" [no. 18] was written on the back of this leaf, presumably after the verses were copied out in ink. These verses are written in pencil and were not marked for deletion. White wove paper.]

In the garden, the world, I, Adam, | again wander,
Curious, here behold my resurrection | after ages of slumber,
The revolving cycles in their wide | sweep, have again brought |
    me—I return | the same,
All is beautiful to me—all is | wondrous—I am myself | most
wondrous,
5 I exist, I peer and | penetrate still, |
Content with the present, content with the | past,
By my side Eve, following, | and I following her in turn | just |
    the same.

1 the garden] 'the' interlined above deleted 'a'.
1 the world,] interlined between 'garden,' and 'I' but without a caret to make placement specific.
1 I, Adam] originally 'I, a new Adam', the words 'a new' being deleted.
2 my] written over some other letters, but appears to be merely a clarifying of an original 'my'.
2 slumber,] before this Whitman began 'dea' [*query* death] and then deleted it before continuing.
3 revolving cycles] interlined above these words is deleted 'mighty'.
3 wide] interlined above deleted 'mighty'.

Enfans d'Adam.

1.

To the garden, the world, anew ascending,
Potent mates, daughters, sons, preluding,
The love, the life of their bodies, meaning and being,
Curious, here behold my resurrection, after slumber,
The revolving cycles, in their wide sweep, having brought me again,
Amorous, mature—all beautiful to me—all wondrous,
My limbs, and the quivering fire that ever plays through them, for
    reasons, most wondrous;
Existing, I peer and penetrate still,
Content with the present—content with the past,
By my side, or back of me, Eve following,
Or in front, and I following her just the same.

---

3 return the same] the original read, 'have returned, for | awhile,'. 'for awhile' seems to be independently deleted. Above excised 'have returned' is interlined 'return'.

4 All is. . . .] the remainder of the poem except for one addition to be noted, appears to be written with a different pencil from that used up to this verse, a pencil which looks like that used for the interlineation 'return' in line 4.

5 I exist . . . penetrate still,] Above the first line of this verse is the false start 'The', and, below this, other false starts 'All is' and, below, 'I have con', all crossed through. The verse beginning 'I exist' starts after deleted 'All is', and 'penetrate' thus comes after deleted 'con'. A comma after 'penetrate' has been excised and 'still,' added with a different pencil. The following reconstruction is hypothetical, but seems warranted by an interpretation of the different pencils used and the position of the material. Below deleted 'I have con' is the false start 'The' crossed out, the word written with a different pencil. On the same line, beginning below and slightly to the left of 'con' is the verse 'By my side Eve, following, | and I following her in turn | just | the same.' Above 'side' is deleted 'following'; after

'Eve,' originally appeared '—and', then deleted. Before 'and I' beginning the line originally is 'I', deleted apparently before continuing. 'in turn' is interlined above deleted 'wherso', which was originally continued in the next line as 'ever she goes,', the last two words being crossed through but 'ever' left undeleted by a slip. It is faintly possible that 'just the same,' is an addition, made as a consequence of the revision of the verse. The odd position of this verse makes it possible to guess that it represents a note made at the time of the false starts when Whitman could have given over the poem temporarily. The deleted 'following' interlined above 'side' appears to be in the same pencil as that which wrote the verse above, 'I exist . . . penetrate.' Below this supposed note, in a light pencil at the very foot of the leaf is written 'Content with the present, content with the | past,'. After 'past' a squiggle deleted some mark, which may only have been a slip of the pencil. This verse is brought up above 'By my side Eve. . . .' by a guide line. The pencil is the same as that which added 'still' after 'penetrate', and thus may represent the final act of revision in this version.

[FOLDER 3. Three leaves of pink paper written in blackish ink; pinholes in the center. The poem number 85 is written above deleted 84. 1860, pp. 309–10; Camden, I, 132.]

[*leaf 1*]

85

You and I.

We two—What the earth is, | we are;
We lovers—how long we were fooled!
Now delicious, trans-|muted, swiftly we escape, | as nature escapes,
We are nature—Long have we been absent, but now we return,
5 We become plants, weeds, foliage, | roots, bark,
We are bedded in the ground | —we are rocks,
We are oaks—we grow in | the openings, side by side,
We browse—we are two among | the wild herds, spontaneous | as any,
We are two fishes, swimming | in the sea together,
10 We are what the locust-blossoms | are—we drop scent around the | lanes, mornings and evenings,

[*leaf 2*]

We are also the coarse smut | of beasts, vegetables, | minerals,
We are what the flowing wet | of the Tennessee is—We | are two peaks of the Blue | Mountains, rising up in | Virginia,
We are two predatory hawks— | we soar above, and look | down,
We are two resplendent suns— | we it is that balance | ourselves, orbic and stellar— | We are as two comets,
15 We prowl, fanged and four-footed | in the woods—we spring | on prey,
We are two clouds, forenoons and | afternoons, driving overhead,

[*leaf 3*]

We are seas mingling—we | are two of those cheerful | waves, rolling on and on | over each other, and | interwetting each other,
We are what the atmosphere | is, transparent, receptive, | pervious, impervious,
We are snow, rain, cold, darkness, | —We are each product and | influence of the globe,

7.

You and I—what the earth is, we are,
We two—how long we were fooled!
Now delicious, transmuted, swiftly we escape, as Nature escapes,
We are Nature—long have we been absent, but now we return,
We become plants, leaves, foliage, roots, bark,
We are bedded in the ground—we are rocks,
We are oaks—we grow in the openings side by side,
We browse—we are two among the wild herds, spontaneous as any,
We are two fishes swimming in the sea together,
We are what the locust blossoms are—we drop scent around the lanes,
    mornings and evenings,
We are also the coarse smut of beasts, vegetables, minerals,
We are what the flowing wet of the Tennessee is—we are two peaks of
    the Blue Mountains, rising up in Virginia,
We are two predatory hawks—we soar above and look down,
We are two resplendent suns—we it is who balance ourselves orbic
    and stellar—we are as two comets;
We prowl fanged and four-footed in the woods—we spring on prey;
We are two clouds, forenoons and afternoons, driving overhead,
We are seas mingling—we are two of those cheerful waves, rolling over
    each other, and interwetting each other,
We are what the atmosphere is, transparent, receptive, pervious, im-
    pervious,
We are snow, rain, cold, darkness—we are each product and influence
    of the globe,

---

1 We] originally 'Us', with 'We' traced over it in the light ink and also interlined.

3 delicious, transmuted] between these two words appears deleted 'escaped,' part of the original writing.

3 escape,] interlined above deleted 'go forth'.

3 escapes,] originally 'goes,' the comma being deleted in pencil and 'forth,' added in pencil. Then 'goes forth,' was crossed through and 'escapes,' interlined in ink.

4 We are nature . . . return,] this entire verse was crowded in as an addition; the 'we' of 'we have been' is interlined above a caret.

6 ground] Whitman began to write some word and got as far as 'ear' [earth?], but before the *r* was fully formed he crossed out the letters and went on to 'ground'.

8 spontaneous] interlined in pencil above deleted 'natural'.

10 drop] interlined in pencil above a caret and deleted 'toss'.

11 beasts] interlined in pencil above deleted 'animals'. The comma is retained from the original after 'animals'.

20 We have circled and | circled till we have | arrived home again—
     we two | have,
   We have voided all | but freedom, and | all but our own joy.—

20 We have circled . . . home again—] this
first read, 'We have passed on, and | then
turned back, and | become these—'. From
'passed' to 'these' the words are deleted
in pencil. Above deleted 'passed on, and'
is interlined in pencil 'circled and'. Above
deleted 'then turned back, and' is interlined in pencil 'circled till we have'. The
dash after pencil-deleted 'become these'
was excised in ink and a pencil caret
placed beneath it, above which was inter-

lined in pencil, 'returned again—'. Then
'returned' was deleted with a fine pen,
and 'arrived home' interlined above it in
ink, the pencilled 'again—' then being
traced over in ink.
21 voided all] interlined in pencil above deleted 'rejected every thing'.
21 and all] 'all' interlined in pencil above a
caret after deleted 'every|thing'.
21 joy.—] the dash is a fine line, perhaps
added later.

[FOLDER 4. One and one-half leaves of white wove paper (7⅜ × 6¼ and 4⅜ ×
6¼) written in blackish ink. At top left appears the pencilled poem number 82.
The upper margin of the first leaf is irregularly torn, removing the tops of the
letters of 'upon me' in the first line. The half leaf has been scissored off irregularly at the foot. The first leaf has pinholes at left center and along the left
margin; the half-leaf holes in its center and left margin. Wet ink from the half-
leaf has offset on the verso of the first leaf. 1860, pp. 310–11; Camden, I, 133–34.]

[*leaf 1*]

      82

   Now the hour has come upon me,
   Give me fierce pleasures only! Give | me life coarse and rank!
   Give me the weedy luxuriance! Give | me the drench of my
     passions!
   This day I consort with nature's | darlings—this night too,
5 I bear a part in the midnight | orgies of young men,
   I dance with the dancers and | drink with the drinkers,
   I take for my love some prosti-|tute—I pick out some low | person
     for my dearest friend,
   He shall be lawless, rude, illiterate—he | shall be one who has
     done wicked deeds,

[*leaf 2*]

   I will play a part no longer,
10 Why should I exile myself from | my companions?

   O you shunned men and women, I do | not shun you,
   I come forthwith in your midst—| I will be your poet,
   I will be more to you than to | any of the rest.—

We have circled and circled till we have arrived home again—we two
  have,
We have voided all but freedom, and all but our own joy.

8.

NATIVE moments! when you come upon me—Ah you are here now!
Give me now libidinous joys only!
Give me the drench of my passions! Give me life coarse and rank!
To-day, I go consort with nature's darlings—to-night too,
I am for those who believe in loose delights—I share the midnight
  orgies of young men,
I dance with the dancers, and drink with the drinkers,
The echoes ring with our indecent calls,
I take for my love some prostitute—I pick out some low person for my
  dearest friend,
He shall be lawless, rude, illiterate—he shall be one condemned by
  others for deeds done;
I will play a part no longer—Why should I exile myself from my com-
  panions?
O you shunned persons! I at least do not shun you,
I come forthwith in your midst—I will be your poet,
I will be more to you than to any of the rest.

1 Now] in the fine pen 'O' was prefixed as
a revision and then deleted, probably at
a time later than the addition of 82 above.
1 come upon me,] originally the verse con-
tinued after these words with, | '—I dilate,
an animal, sensuous, | divine,'. 'sensuous'
is very heavily crossed out, earlier than
the rest. Above this extra line is crowded
in, 'An uncontrolable aversion toward
what respectable | life arises | in me'. This
addition was intended to precede '—I di-
late. . . .' Above 'what' is interlined 'all
that is', which is then deleted. 'arises' is
crossed out and 'fills' interlined (the *f*

is uncertain, but is more like an *f* than a
t). Then the whole interlineation and addition was crossed through with one stroke
of the pen.
2 pleasures] the original 'pleasures' deleted
and 'joys' interlined, this being deleted
in turn and 'pleasures' written above it.
4 night too,] originally there came next the
verse 'I am for those who believe in loose
| delights,' which has been deleted.
12 come] the original 'come' was excised and
'go' interlined in light ink; this was then
crossed out and 'come' underdotted to
confirm.

[FOLDER 5. One leaf of white wove paper ($7\frac{1}{8} \times 6\frac{3}{16}$); a few central pinholes. 1860, p. 311; Camden, I, 134. On the verso appear deleted draft verses for "Premonition" verses 58–61 (see "Premonition" Appendix I for the text). A line later to be used in "Chanting the Square Deific" sec. 3 also appears on the verso (for the text, see below).]

Once I passed through a populous | celebrated city, imprinting on
    my brain for future use, its shows, | with its shows, architec-
    ture, customs and | traditions
But now | of all | that city I remember | only the man | who | wan-
    dered with me, there, for | love of me,
Day by day, and night by night, we were together,

4 All else has long been forgotten | by me—I remember, I say, only
    | one rude and ignorant man who, when I | departed, long and
    long held me by the | hand, with silent lip, sad | and trem-
    ulous.—

1 Once I . . . traditions] the original verse read, 'Once I ['pass'd' *crossed out*] passed through a | great city full of shows, | wealth, architecture and | traditions'. Above deleted 'passed through' was interlined 'remained awhile'. 'great' was deleted, and 'populous' interlined above, this then being excised and 'celebrated' written beneath 'great'. 'full of' was deleted, and 'studying its' interlined, this being crossed out and below the line written 'to study its'. The above revisions were performed in ink. The remaining revision of the verse is found in pencil. The interlined 'remained awhile' was deleted and 'passed through a populous' added above it. 'to study' was seemingly crossed out by a long pencil line beginning underneath 'celebrated' (it is uncertain whether this word was supposed to be excised by the line) and curving under the line of words to end by running through 'to study'. Beginning after 'city' was interlined 'imprinting on my brain for ['the' *crossed out*] future | use,'. 'wealth' was excised, and above it interlined 'its shows', 'its' probably later. Ahead of deleted 'wealth' was written in 'with' and then partly above the line, 'all', this latter being then crossed out. Most likely the preceding original ink 'its shows,'

was left undeleted by an oversight. Above 'architecture' was interlined 'noticing', this then being deleted. A comma was added after 'architecture' and then 'customs' interlined above a caret.

2 But now of all that city . . . love of me,] the first version began, 'But now, I remember all that | [*two illegible mended and then crossed-out letters, perhaps* 'po'.] ['city,' *crossed out*] city has—now I | remember nothing', at which point it appears that Whitman stopped and crossed through all he had written of the verse save the first word 'But'. Separate ink-strokes indicate that as he had been writing the original version, 'I remember' had been currently deleted. He then may have interlined 'now' after 'But' and continued with the verse 'of all | that city I remember | nothing except that there | I wandered day by day, with | one who loved me,'. First 'that there' was crossed through and 'how' interlined, this later being deleted and 'one' added after it. In the next line, 'I wandered' was deleted and 'who' interlined. The words 'with | one who loved me' were deleted and above 'loved me' interlined 'wandered with me, for | love of me,'. The above revisions were made in ink; those described next, in

9.

ONCE I passed through a populous city, imprinting my brain, for
    future use, with its shows, architecture, customs, and traditions;
Yet now, of all that city, I remember only a woman I casually met
    there, who detained me for love of me,
Day by day and night by night we were together,—All else has long
    been forgotten by me,
I remember I say only that woman who passionately clung to me,
Again we wander—we love—we separate again,
Again she holds me by the hand—I must not go!
I see her close beside me, with silent lips, sad and tremulous.

---

pencil. 'nothing except' was deleted and 'only the ['a *crossed out*] man' was interlined. 'one' was crossed through and 'day by day' also, 'there' being interlined above this last but then deleted (though the deleting stroke is rather high). Between 'me, for' was interlined 'there,' above a caret and apparently over an erasure.

3 Day by day . . . together] this verse was crowded in in pencil. Originally the insertion began 'We wa', but this was deleted immediately before beginning again with 'Day by day. . . .'

4 I remember] a preceding 'But' is deleted. After 'remember' the original 'well' is deleted and 'only' interlined. Before this, in pencil above a caret, was added 'I say,' and a pencil comma was placed after 'remember'.

4 one rude and ignorant] interlined in ink above deleted 'that youth'.

4 long and long] interlined in pencil above a caret; an original 'long' after 'held me' was deleted in pencil.

4 sad] interlined in pencil above deleted 'pale'.

[Verso of leaf. Below the "Premonition" draft appears the following undeleted verse in pencil at the foot of the leaf, but reversed so that it once headed the leaf. It is a natural inference that the verse was inscribed before the "Premonition" lines. A long parenthesis appears before, and another after, the verse. This is a draft for the seventh line of sec. 3 of "Chanting the Square Deific," first printed in 1865 in *When Lilacs Last in the Door-yard Bloom'd*.]

1 Though it was thought I was | baffled and destroyed—but | that
    will never be.

1 Though] above are two false starts, each deleted. The first reads 'Standing'; the
second, beneath it, 'Even con'.
1 will] interlined above deleted 'shall'.

[FOLDER 6. One leaf of pink paper with only a single set of pinholes in the center. Written in blackish ink. At top left is the poem number '80—' in ink above deleted ink '79—'. Above the title is a question mark in pencil between parentheses. 1860, p. 312; Camden, I, 135.]

80—

Hindustan, from the Western | Sea.—

I, a child, over waves, toward | the house of maternity, the | land
    of migrations, look | afar,
Look off the shores of my Western | Sea, | having arrived curiously
    where | I am—the | circle is almost circled,
For coming westward from Paradise, | from the Himmalehs, from
    | the vales of Kashmere, | from the north,
From the god Brahm, the sage Menu and the hero | Rama—
5 From the south from flowery | peninsulas, and the spice islands,
I face home again, joyous, after | long travel, growth, and sleep.—

2 Western] the capital is mended over a minuscule and triple underscored.

2 Sea, having arrived . . . am—the'] the original version read, | 'Sea, as toward the mother of me, | [*new verse*] Mother of Languages—Mother | at distant removes of | These States.—' Beginning with 'as toward' and ending with 'States', all is crossed through in light ink. In a space first left between stanzas, 'having arrived . . . am—the' is crowded in in the light ink. A guide line curves downward to connect 'Sea' with 'having'.

2 circle] the original line began as a new verse, 'The circle. . . .'; but then 'The' was deleted in the light ink.

3 For coming] interlined with a caret in the light ink above deleted 'I came'

3 Kashmere] originally the word began with a capital *C*, but while it was still wet the letter was smudged out and capital *K* mended over it.

4 From] this was originally 'from' and continued the verse after 'north'. The *f* was crossed through in the light ink and capital *F* interlined, before which was placed a paragraph sign to indicate a new verse.

4 god Brahm, the] interlined with the fine pen.

4 Rama—] a comma after this word and before the dash is partly smudged out, probably as an act of deletion.

5 From the south] originally the phrase started 'from' and continued the verse above. First 'Also' was interlined before it with the fine pen. Then this was deleted and 'From the south' interlined in the light ink above a caret, with a paragraph sign placed before it.

5 from flowery] originally 'from the flowery', the 'the' being crossed through in the light ink.

[FOLDER 7. Eight leaves of assorted paper. The first leaf is a quarter sheet of white wove paper (6¼ × 3¹⁵⁄₁₆), pinholes at top and in center, written in a rather light-brown ink without alterations. These verses seem to represent a fair copy. 1860, pp. 341–42; Camden, I, 137 and (for another version) III, 137.]

[*leaf* 1]

Long I was held by the life | that exhibits itself,
By what is done in the | houses or streets, or in | company,

⟦ 66 ⟧

13324

10.

INQUIRING, tireless, seeking that yet unfound,
I, a child, very old, over waves, toward the house of maternity, the land
  of migrations, look afar,
Look off the shores of my Western Sea—having arrived at last where
  I am—the circle almost circled;
For coming westward from Hindustan, from the vales of Kashmere,
From Asia—from the north—from the God, the sage, and the hero,
From the south—from the flowery peninsulas, and the spice islands,
Now I face the old home again—looking over to it, joyous, as after
  long travel, growth, and sleep;
But where is what I started for, so long ago?
And why is it yet unfound?

Calamus.

1.

IN paths untrodden,
In the growth by margins of pond-waters,
Escaped from the life that exhibits itself,
From all the standards hitherto published—from the pleasures, profits,
  conformities,
Which too long I was offering to feed to my Soul;
Clear to me now, standards not yet published—clear to me that my
  Soul,
That the Soul of the man I speak for, feeds, rejoices only in comrades;
Here, by myself, away from the clank of the world,
Tallying and talked to here by tongues aromatic,
No longer abashed—for in this secluded spot I can respond as I would
  not dare elsewhere,

The usual adjustments and | pleasures—the things which | all con-
form to and which | the writers celebrate;
But now I know a life | which does not exhibit | itself, yet contains
all the | rest,
5 And now, escaping, I celebrate | that concealed but substantial |
life,
I celebrate the need of the love | of comrades.—

[FOLDER 7, *continued.* Seven assorted leaves of white wove paper. Of the
eight in the folder the second and third (the first and second of this poem) are a
conjugate folded half-sheet of the same size and paper as leaf 1 and are written
in the same ink as the first leaf. The pinholes in the three leaves also match.
At the top right corner of leaf 2, probably in Whitman's hand, appears a '1'
written in blue pencil over a lead pencil '7.' On the third leaf appears in blue
pencil '2' written over a pencil figure '8'. Below the last line on leaf 3 (verse
10) Whitman wrote '×More'. Leaves 4–8 are larger pieces of the same wove
paper ($7\frac{7}{8} \times 6\frac{3}{16}$) written in a darker ink. These leaves contain pinholes dif-
fering from those in leaves 1–3. Whitman's own poem numbering '81' is found
in pencil in the top left corner of leaf 4 above verse 11. This number, and
the change in paper at leaf 4, appears to indicate that the first ten verses were
attached to the poem as an afterthought. 1860, pp. 342–44; Camden, I, 138–39.
On the versos of leaves 4–6 appears the pencil draft of an editorial or prose article
entitled *Important Questions in Brooklyn.*—, beginning "The most prominent
public question in Brooklyn, just now, (coincident with the April charter"
(see Introduction).]

[*leaf 2*]

Was it I who walked the | earth disclaiming all except | what I
had in myself?
Was it I boasting how complete | I was in myself?
O little I counted the comrade | indispensable to me!
O how my soul—How the | soul of man feeds, re-|joices in its
lovers, its | dear friends!
5 And now I care not to | walk the earth unless | a lover, a dear
friend, | walk by my side.

[*leaf 3*]

Scented herbage of my breast
Leaves here I write, to be | perused best afterwards,
Tomb-leaves, breast-leaves, | growing up above me, above | death,
Perennial leaves—tall leaves— | O the winter shall not | freeze
you, delicate leaves!

5 care] *c* written over *w*.

Strong upon me the life that does not exhibit itself, yet contains all the
    rest,
Resolved to sing no songs to-day but those of manly attachment,
Projecting them along that substantial life,
Bequeathing, hence, types of athletic love,
Afternoon, this delicious Ninth Month, in my forty-first year,
I proceed, for all who are, or have been, young men,
To tell the secret of my nights and days,
To celebrate the need of comrades.

2.

SCENTED herbage of my breast,
Leaves from you I yield, I write, to be perused best afterwards,
Tomb-leaves, body-leaves, growing up above me, above death,
Perennial roots, tall leaves—O the winter shall not freeze you, delicate
    leaves,

10 Every year shall you bloom | again—Out of your roots, | where
you retired, you shall | emerge again

[*leaf* 4]

8₁

I do not know whether | many, passing by, will discover you, | or
inhale your | faint odor—but I believe a | few will

O slender leaves! O blossoms of my blood! I permit you to tell, in
your | own way, of the heart that is | under you, where your
roots | are!

O aching and throbbing! O these hungering | desires!

Surely one day they will be | pacified—all will be accomplished

15 O I know not what you mean—you | are not happiness—you are
often too | bitter!

[*leaf* 5]

Yet you are beautiful to me, | you faint-tinged roots! you | make
me think of death,

Death is beautiful from you— | —what is so beautiful | as death
and love?

I think it is not for life | I am chanting here my chant of | lovers—
I think it must | be for death,

For how calm, how solemn it | grows, to ascend to the | atmos-
phere of lovers,

11 I do not know] a second 'not' (presumably a slip of the pen) has been deleted in pencil after the first. Above this verse appear two false starts. Whitman first wrote 'The flowers' and crossed it out in the same ink. Below, and indented, he began '—you shall not fail to | appear, for your own sake,' this being crossed through, just possibly in a different ink.

11 many, passing by, will discover] before 'many' was first written 'you' (*or* 'your'), deleted before 'many' was written. 'passing by,' is interlined. 'discover' is interlined with a caret above deleted 'perceive'.

11 or inhale] before this the original read, 'where you are,' which has been deleted, perhaps in a different ink.

12 O slender leaves! . . . to tell] the original read, 'Breast-blossoms! O tell,'. Before 'tell' and after deleted 'O' was interlined above a caret 'O little blossoms leaves! I per-
mit you to', this apparently as a substitute or alternate. 'to such' was interlined above 'I permit', but deleted. 'little blossoms' was crossed through and 'slender' interlined. 'Breast-' was deleted, 'O' prefixed to it, and a caret placed before 'O', a guide line bringing down before 'O blossoms' the revised interlined 'O slender leaves!'. Underneath 'blossoms' was written 'of my breast,' and later an exclamation mark was added. Then 'breast' was excised and 'blood' in light ink crowded in above it, a long guide line being drawn intended to bring these words up after 'blossoms'.

12 of the heart] 'of' is later interlined above a caret.

12 where] interlined above deleted 'that'. The *h* of 'where' is mended over some other letter.

13 O aching] between the two words was interlined 'this' above a caret, later deleted.

Every year shall you bloom again—Out from where you retired, you
    shall emerge again;

O I do not know whether many, passing by, will discover you, or inhale
    your faint odor—but I believe a few will;

O slender leaves! O blossoms of my blood! I permit you to tell, in your
    own way, of the heart that is under you,

O burning and throbbing—surely all will one day be accomplished;

O I do not know what you mean, there underneath yourselves—you
    are not happiness,

You are often more bitter than I can bear—you burn and sting me,

Yet you are very beautiful to me, you faint-tinged roots—you make me
    think of Death,

Death is beautiful from you—(what indeed is beautiful, except Death
    and Love?)

O I think it is not for life I am chanting here my chant of lovers—I
    think it must be for Death,

For how calm, how solemn it grows, to ascend to the atmosphere of
    lovers,

---

13 these] interlined above a caret.

14 they] interlined above deleted 'we all'.

14 pacified] *c* mended over *s*.

15 often too bitter!] originally, 'often bitter,
bitter bitter as gall to me,'. The first two
words 'bitter' are crossed through in ink,
the second apparently at a later time.
Then after 'often' is added 'very' in pencil,
which is then deleted in pencil and 'too'
interlined. An exclamation mark is added
in pencil after the remaining 'bitter', and
'as gall to me,' crossed out.

16 Yet you are beautiful to me,] at the top
of the leaf the first verse began, 'Surely
one day I will find the dear | friend, the
lover, who will' | . 'will' is deleted and
'am to' interlined. At this point Whitman
seemingly began again, although not out
to the margin as for a new verse, with
'You are no'. A curving guide line joins
'Surely' to 'You' as if to read 'Surely you'.
But all this material, except 'You are no',
was crossed out, and Whitman wrote,
one above the other, the false starts
'Many' and 'Much', but deleted them before achieving (once more not out to the
margin), 'O you are beautiful to me,', the
e of 'me' being mended over some other
letter. 'yet' is interlined in ink above a
caret after 'are' but deleted in pencil. 'Yet'
is then interlined above a caret in pencil
after deleted 'O'.

16 -tinged roots] interlined with a caret over
deleted 'blossoms'.

17 from you—] interlined in lighter ink above
deleted 'also'.

18 is not] written currently after deleted 'no'.

18 I am chanting here my] the original read,
'life | I chant this chant of' | . 'chant this'
is excised and 'proceed to chant my' interlined, with 'now' interlined with a
caret before 'proceed'. Above 'my' is interlined in pencil 'here'. 'proceed to chant
my' is crossed through in pencil and in
ink, leaving 'I now' and the pencil-interlined 'here' unexcised through error. Then
'I am chanting here my' is interlined in
a light ink.

19 how calm] *h* mended over *n*. 'calm' is written currently after deleted 'soothing'. After 'calm,' is interlined above a caret,
'how solemn'.

[*leaf* 6]

20 Death or life, I am then indifferent | —my soul declines to |
    prefer,

I am not sure but the high | soul of lovers welcomes | Death most,

Indeed Death! I think | these leaves mean you;

Grow up, taller, sweet leaves that I may see! Grow | up out of my
    breast!

Spring from the heart | that is there,

25 Do not any longer hide | yourselves, you timid leaves,

[*leaf* 7]

Do not remain down there, so | ashamed, blossoms of my breast!

Come I am determined to unbare | my breast—I have stifled | and
    choked too long

I will escape from | the costume, the play which | was proposed to
    me

I will sound myself and love—I | will utter the | cry of friends—I
    will | raise new reverberations through The States

30 I will | give an example to lovers till they take | shape, and will in
    The States,

20 then] interlined above a caret with a finer pen.

20 prefer,] after this was added in pencil, 'one to the other,' which was then deleted in ink.

21 Death most] 'most' written after currently deleted 'with'.

22 Indeed Death! I think] originally, 'Death! Death! why I think'. In pencil above a caret placed at the start of the verse was interlined 'you'; a pencil 'O' was written over this; and finally, over this, 'Indeed' in ink above a caret. The second 'Death' was crossed out in pencil, and also the following 'why'. Before this deleted 'Death' was placed a caret, and 'you' was interlined in pencil, this being deleted also in pencil.

22 you;] the original punctuation was a comma, and the verse continued in the line below, 'growing as growing'. These words were crossed through in ink (the second 'growing' independently), and the comma after 'you' altered to a dash, which was then deleted and the semi-colon added.

23 Grow up . . . see!] the first part of this verse read initially, 'Grow up, little leaves,'.

'little' was deleted. The comma after 'leaves' was made into a caret (the exclamation mark being added) and 'that I may see' interlined. The vertical stroke of an exclamation mark, without the dot, appears after 'see'. Later, in a lighter ink, 'taller, sweet' was interlined above a caret.

24 Spring] after this is deleted 'up'.

24 heart] apparently as part of the original composition, Whitman wrote 'fiery' and then crossed it through, interlining 'heart' before proceeding.

25 Do not any longer hide] Whitman began, 'Do not be af' [*query* 'afraid'?] and then crossed out 'be af' before continuing, 'altogether hide'. First 'any further' was added above a caret (smudged) after deleted 'altogether'; then 'further' was deleted and 'longer' interlined.

27 stifled and choked too long] Whitman first wrote, 'stifled | ['too l' *deleted*] too long'. Between 'l' and 'too' is a caret pointing to the interlineation 'my heart and choked', 'my heart' then being deleted. Possibly 'and choked' was added only after the deletion of 'my heart'.

28 I will escape] Whitman began to write, 'I will' ['un' (?) *deleted*] ['arm myself' *de-*

Death or life I am then indifferent—my Soul declines to prefer,

I am not sure but the high Soul of lovers welcomes death most;

Indeed, O Death, I think now these leaves mean precisely the same as
you mean;

Grow up taller, sweet leaves, that I may see! Grow up out of my breast!

Spring away from the concealed heart there!

Do not fold yourselves so in your pink-tinged roots, timid leaves!

Do not remain down there so ashamed, herbage of my breast!

Come, I am determined to unbare this broad breast of mine—I have
long enough stifled and choked;

Emblematic and capricious blades, I leave you—now you serve me not,

Away! I will say what I have to say, by itself,

I will escape from the sham that was proposed to me,

I will sound myself and comrades only—I will never again utter a call,
only their call,

I will raise, with it, immortal reverberations through The States,

I will give an example to lovers, to take permanent shape and will
through The States;

---

leted] before continuing with 'escape'.

28 costume, the] originally, 'mask, and'. 'the'
is interlined in ink above deleted 'and';
and 'costume,' in pencil above deleted
'mask,'. To the left of the lines beginning
originally 'the mask' and 'is prepared' is
a large pencil question mark in a circle,
deleted in pencil.

28 was] interlined in lighter ink above deleted 'is'.

28 proposed to me] between the end of this
verse and the start of the next was crowded
in, 'It is ['played' *deleted*] acted on all
sides around me, but I swear I | cannot
| do it,'. All except 'do it,' (this last by
oversight presumably) was crossed through
first in pencil and then in ink.

29 sound myself and love—] originally, 'I
will enact life only—'. Under 'life only'
is the pencilled 'myself' crossed out in
ink. Above deleted 'only' is a caret and
the interlineation in a different ink 'and
myself,'. This was deleted as was 'enact
life', in the light ink, and under the
original line written 'sound myself and
love—'. The purpose is uncertain of a
capital 'I' in the lighter ink below the
line after 'only'.

29 utter] written currently after deleted 'invoke'. Opposite the lines beginning originally 'will invoke' and 'cry of love' is an
undeleted pencil question mark in a circle.

29 friends] interlined in a lighter ink above
deleted 'love'.

29 raise new] interlined above a caret after
deleted 'raise the'.

29 through The States] interlined above the
latter part of 'reverberations'. Whitman
began to mend 'The' to 'These' but
stopped with the *s* partly formed.

30 I will give an example to lovers] the first
version read, 'I will press the keys of | new
music—through | me shall lovers'. In pen-
cil 'strike' is written above deleted 'press'
and then in ink Whitman deleted 'strike
the keys of new music'. 'through | me'
was deleted; 'by' was added after deleted
'through'; and 'my example' was interlined above 'me'. The 'my' was then
crossed out and 'give an' interlined, with
'to' added after 'example'. By inadvertence, the 'by' ending the line above was
not deleted.

30 till they . . . States,] after 'lovers' appears
a caret and the interlineation 'till they'.
Before 'shape' the original had 'definite,'
which was deleted in pencil and 'free' interlined, this then being deleted. After
'shape' appeared originally, 'and wishes'.
These words were deleted in ink. Later
'in The States,' was interlined in a lighter
ink, and then preceded by 'and will' in
pencil.

Through me shall the words be said to make death | exhilarating.

[*leaf* 8]

    Give me | your tone therefore O Death and | manly Love that I
        may accord | with it!

    Give me yourselves—for I see | that you belong to me now above
        all, | and have folded | yourselves here above all—you | Love
        and Death have,

    Nor will I henceforth allow | you to balk me with life, | ostensible
        life,

35 For these leaves, these blossoms out of my breast | flash upon me
        | that you yourselves | and not they are the life,

    That you lie enfolded within | all ostensible life.—

31 Through me . . . exhilarating,] this verse was crowded in at the bottom of the leaf as an addition. The first form read 'shall something come to make'. Above deleted 'something' was written in pencil 'the words', and above 'come' in pencil 'be sung', the 'sung' then being deleted and 'said' added in pencil.

31 Give me . . . it!] the verse originally began, 'Unclose, natural leaves!', which was deleted. The 'Unclose' had originally been written over 'A' smudged out. In 'me' after 'Give' the *m* is written over two other letters. Before 'tone' originally appeared 'free', which was deleted in ink; and after 'tone', 'therefore' was interlined above a caret. Instead of 'O Death and manly love' the first version read, 'O love and | death!'. In a different ink the miniscule initial letters of 'love' and 'death' were mended to capitals, and 'manly' was prefixed to 'Death', the upper part of the original exclamation mark after 'Death' being crossed through and the dot extended to a comma. In pencil, 'Death' was then interlined above 'Love' and 'Love' above 'Death'.

[*Cont. on page 75*]

[FOLDER 8. Four leaves of white wove paper (6¼ × 4), the same as leaves 1–3 in folder 7, and inscribed in the same light-brown ink. Pinholes at top left and in left-center margin. The leaves are numbered in pencil from 1 to 4 over erased 3–6, but in whose hand is uncertain. 1860, pp. 347–48; Camden, I, 142–44.]

[*leaf* 1]

    These I, singing in spring, collect | for lovers,

    (For who but I should understand | love, with all its sorrow | and
        joy?

    And who but I should be the | poet of comrades?)

    Collecting, I traverse the garden, | —but soon I pass the gates,

3 comrades?] the question mark added after a period or comma had been smudged out.

Through me shall the words be said to make death exhilarating,
Give me your tone therefore, O Death, that I may accord with it,
Give me yourself—for I see that you belong to me now above all, and
    are folded together above all—you Love and Death are,
Nor will I allow you to balk me any more with what I was calling life,
For now it is conveyed to me that you are the purports essential,
That you hide in these shifting forms of life, for reasons—and that they
    are mainly for you,
That you, beyond them, come forth, to remain, the real reality,
That behind the mask of materials you patiently wait, no matter how
    long,
That you will one day, perhaps, take control of all,
That you will perhaps dissipate this entire show of appearance,
That may be you are what it is all for—but it does not last so very long,
But you will last very long.

[*Cont. from page 74*]
32 belong] written currently after deleted 'are'. 'to me now above all' was interlined above deleted 'here,'.
33 yourselves] written currently after deleted 'yourself'.
33 you Love and Death] the 'you' is an addition during the course of writing, made after commas following 'here' and 'all' had been crossed through and the dash added. Originally, a new verse began 'And the', at which point Whitman seems to have stopped, made the revision in the line above, deleted 'And the', and continued with 'Love and Death'.
34 henceforth] interlined in pencil above deleted 'any longer'.
34 ostensible life,] Whitman first began to continue the line after 'life,' with '—for', but stopped and deleted the continuation in order to begin with a new verse, as shown in line 35. At some later time he

interlined in ink 'the padding of life,' but deleted this in pencil.
35 out of my breast] interlined later above a caret with a guide line.
35 flash upon] the original reading was, | 'suddenly indicate to'. 'indicate to' was crossed through and 'flash upon' interlined. Then in the next line the original 'the thought' before 'that' was deleted. Apparently at a later time 'suddenly' was excised.
35 and not they] interlined in pencil above a caret.
36 That you lie] interlined in pencil above a caret after 'life,'. Apparently at a later time the dash after 'life' was interlined in ink and followed by a paragraph sign before 'That' to indicate the start of a new verse.
36 within] originally 'there in'. 'there' was deleted and 'with' interlined and brought down to connect with 'in'.

4.

THESE I, singing in spring, collect for lovers,
(For who but I should understand lovers, and all their sorrow and joy?
And who but I should be the poet of comrades?)
Collecting, I traverse the garden, the world—but soon I pass the gates,

5 Along the pond-side, wading | in a little, fearing not the | wet,

Along the post and rail fences, | where the old stones, | thrown there, picked from the | fields, have accumulated,

Wild-flowers and vines and weeds | come up through the stones | and partly cover them—Be-|yond these I pass,

Far, far in the forest before | I think where I go,

[*leaf 2*]

Solitary, smelling the earthy | smell, stopping now and | then in the silence,

10 Alone I thought—yet soon | a silent troop gathers | around me,

Some walk by my side, and | some behind, and some | embrace my arms or | neck

They, the spirits of dear friends, | lovers, comrades dead or | alive,
—Thicker they come, | and I in the middle,

Collecting, dispensing, singing in | spring, there I wander with | them

Plucking something for tokens | —something for these till I | hit upon a name,

15 Tossing toward whoever is near | me,

[*leaf 3*]

Here! lilac with a branch of pine,

Here, out of my pocket, some | moss which I pulled off | a live-oak in Florida | as it hung trailing down,

Here, some pinks and laurel-|leaves, and a handful of | sage,

And here what I drew from | the water where I waded | in the pond-side,

20 (O there I saw him that tenderly | loves me, and never separates | from me

Therefore this shall be the | special token of comrades— | this calamus-root shall,

Interchange it, youths, with each | other—Let none render it back,)

And twigs of maple, and a | bunch of wild orange, and | chesnut,

[*leaf 4*]

And stems of currants, and | plum-blows, and the ar-|omatic cedar,

25 These I, singing, compassed round | by a thick cloud of spirits,

Wandering, point to or touch | as I pass, or throw them | loosely from me,

Now along the pond-side—now wading in a little, fearing not the wet,
Now by the post-and-rail fences, where the old stones thrown there,
    picked from the fields, have accumulated,
Wild-flowers and vines and weeds come up through the stones, and
    partly cover them—Beyond these I pass,
Far, far in the forest, before I think where I get,
Solitary, smelling the earthy smell, stopping now and then in the
    silence,
Alone I had thought—yet soon a silent troop gathers around me,
Some walk by my side, and some behind, and some embrace my arms
    or neck,
They, the spirits of friends, dead or alive—thicker they come, a great
    crowd, and I in the middle,
Collecting, dispensing, singing in spring, there I wander with them,
Plucking something for tokens—something for these, till I hit upon a
    name—tossing toward whoever is near me,
Here! lilac, with a branch of pine,
Here, out of my pocket, some moss which I pulled off a live-oak in
    Florida, as it hung trailing down,
Here, some pinks and laurel leaves, and a handful of sage,
And here what I now draw from the water, wading in the pond-side,
(O here I last saw him that tenderly loves me—and returns again, never
    to separate from me,
And this, O this shall henceforth be the token of comrades—this cala-
    mus-root shall,
Interchange it, youths, with each other! Let none render it back!)
And twigs of maple, and a bunch of wild orange, and chestnut,
And stems of currants, and plum-blows, and the aromatic cedar;
These I, compassed around by a thick cloud of spirits,
Wandering, point to, or touch as I pass, or throw them loosely from
    me,

11 my arms] *m* of 'my' written over some   14 these] *se* over some smudged-out letter(s).
smudged letter.

Indicating to each one what | he shall have—giving some-|thing to each,

But that I drew from the | pond-side, that I reserve,

I will give of it but | only to those comrades who love | as I my-self am capable | of loving.—

29 comrades] interlined above a caret.

[FOLDER 9. Two leaves, both blue tax forms, a few central pinholes and a few at the head. Written in a medium-brown ink. 1860, pp. 352–53; Camden, I, 145–46.]

[*leaf* 1]

Of the doubts, the uncertainties | after all,

That may-be reliance and hope | are but speculations after all,

That may-be identity beyond | the grave is a beautiful | fable only,

May-be all the things I | perceive—the animals, | men, hills, shin-ing and | flowing waters—the skies | of day and night—colors, | densities, forms—May-be these | are, (as doubtless they are,) only ap-|pearances,

5 (How often they dart something out of | themselves to confound me and | mock me!

How often I think neither I nor | any man knows aught of them!)

May-be they only seem to me what | they are, (as doubtless they only | seem,) from my present point | of view—And might prove, | (as of course they would,) naught | of what they ap-pear, or naught | any-how, from entirely changed | points of view:

[*leaf* 2]

To me all these, and the | like of these, are curiously | answered by my lovers, my dear | friends,

When he whom I love travels | with me, or sits a long while | holding me by the hand,

10 When the subtle air, the impalpable, | the sense that words and reason | hold not, surround us and | pervade us,

Then I know and am silent— | I require nothing further,

I cannot answer the terrible | questions of appearances, | and of identity beyond the | grave,

But I walk or sit indif-|ferent—I am satisfied— | My comrade has made | me so.—

Indicating to each one what he shall have—giving something to each,
But what I drew from the water by the pond-side, that I reserve,
I will give of it—but only to them that love, as I myself am capable
    of loving.

7.

OF the terrible question of appearances,
Of the doubts, the uncertainties after all,
That may-be reliance and hope are but speculations after all,
That may-be identity beyond the grave is a beautiful fable only,
May-be the things I perceive—the animals, plants, men, hills, shining
    and flowing waters,
The skies of day and night—colors, densities, forms—May-be these
    are, (as doubtless they are,) only apparitions, and the real some-
    thing has yet to be known,
(How often they dart out of themselves, as if to confound me and
    mock me!
How often I think neither I know, nor any man knows, aught of
    them;)
May-be they only seem to me what they are, (as doubtless they indeed
    but seem,) as from my present point of view—And might prove,
    (as of course they would,) naught of what they appear, or naught
    any how, from entirely changed points of view;
To me, these, and the like of these, are curiously answered by my
    lovers, my dear friends;
When he whom I love travels with me, or sits a long while holding
    me by the hand,
When the subtle air, the impalpable, the sense that words and reason
    hold not, surround us and pervade us,
Then I am charged with untold and untellable wisdom—I am silent—
    I require nothing further,
I cannot answer the question of appearances, or that of identity beyond
    the grave,
But I walk or sit indifferent—I am satisfied,
He ahold of my hand has completely satisfied me.

---

4 May-be these] *M* is triple underscored.
7 view:] an original comma has been
smudged out and then a colon added
in a dark ink.
8 To me. . . .] opposite this line in the left

margin is a question mark in blue pencil
followed by a parenthesis.
12 I] heavily mended.
13 comrade] the tail of the *e* is mended over
a currently smudged-out *s*.

[FOLDER 10. Three pieces of white wove paper, the first two $5\frac{3}{4} \times 3\frac{5}{8}$, the third a small piece $2\frac{1}{2} \times 3\frac{11}{16}$; sets of pinholes at top center. Written in black ink. Whitman's pencil figure 7 appears in the lower left corner of the first leaf. The second leaf he numbered 8, and the third $8\frac{1}{2}$. The roman 'V' heading the poem is drawn ornamentally; a wavy line appears at the conclusion. 1860, pp. 354–55; Camden, III, 298–99. The poem was rejected in 1867.]

[*leaf* 1]

V.

Long I thought that knowledge | alone would suffice me—O | if I could but obtain | knowledge!

Then the Land of the Prairies engrossed me—the south savannas engrossed me— | For them I would live—I | would be their orator;

Then I met the examples of old | and new heroes—I heard | of warriors, sailors, | and all dauntless persons— | And it seemed to me I too | had it in me to be as | dauntless as any, and would | be so;

And then to finish all, it | came to me to strike up the | songs of the New World—And | then I believed my life must | be spent in singing;

5 But now take notice, Land of | the prairies, Land of the south | savannas, Ohio's land,

[*leaf* 2]

Take notice, you Kanuck woods | —and you, Lake Huron—and | all that with you roll toward | Niagara—and you Niagara | also,

And you, Californian mountains— | that you all find some one else | that he be your singer of songs,

For I can be your singer of songs | no longer— | I have ceased to enjoy them.

I have found him who loves me, | as I him, in perfect love,

10 With the rest I dispense—I sever | from all that I thought would | suffice me, for it does not—it | is now empty and tasteless | to me,

I heed knowledge, and the grandeur | of The States, and the examples | of heroes, no more,

[[80]]

8.

LONG I thought that knowledge alone would suffice me—O if I could
  but obtain knowledge!
Then my lands engrossed me—Lands of the prairies, Ohio's land,
  the southern savannas, engrossed me—For them I would live—
  I would be their orator;
Then I met the examples of old and new heroes—I heard of warriors,
  sailors, and all dauntless persons—And it seemed to me that I too
  had it in me to be as dauntless as any—and would be so;
And then, to enclose all, it came to me to strike up the songs of the
  New World—And then I believed my life must be spent in singing;
But now take notice, land of the prairies, land of the south savannas,
  Ohio's land,
Take notice, you Kanuck woods—and you Lake Huron—and all that
  with you roll toward Niagara—and you Niagara also,
And you, Californian mountains—That you each and all find some-
  body else to be your singer of songs,
For I can be your singer of songs no longer—One who loves me is
  jealous of me, and withdraws me from all but love,
With the rest I dispense—I sever from what I thought would suffice
  me, for it does not—it is now empty and tasteless to me,
I heed knowledge, and the grandeur of The States, and the example
  of heroes, no more,

---

2 Then . . . savannas engrossed me—] the
line first read simply, 'Then my lands engrossed me—'. In pencil 'the Land of the
Prairies' was interlined above deleted 'my
lands'. Beginning over the end of the
original 'engrossed', in pencil was inter-
lined '—the south | savannas engrossed
| me—'.

3 heard of] first written, 'heard the | ex-

amples of', with 'the examples' deleted
in the same ink. 'of' is written over an
illegible smudge.

5 land,] the comma is uncertain, but is
more like a comma than a period.

6 Lake] original *l* mended to capital *L*.

8 longer—I have ceased] originally, 'longer
—I have passed ahead— | I have ceased',
the deletion being made in pencil.

[*leaf 3*]

> I am indifferent to my own | songs—I am to go with | him I love, and he is to | go with me,
>
> It is to be enough for each | of us that we are together— | We never separate again.—

[FOLDER 11. Two leaves of white wove paper; pinholes at the top of both leaves, and one set in the center of the upper section of the second leaf. The writing is in black ink. The first leaf measures $3\frac{3}{4} \times 3\frac{5}{8}$. The second is composed of two sections pasted together at the back with a strip of pink paper. The upper section measures $5\frac{11}{16} \times 3\frac{5}{8}$, and the lower $2 \times 3\frac{5}{8}$. In pencil, erased, in the right-hand portion of the text of verse 2 in the first leaf is '(finished, in | the other city)' in Whitman's hand. In part owing to the position, and in part to the difficulty of knowing whether the text was written over these words, or these words added, one may only speculate whether the application is to this poem, or else was a note added after the inscription of no. VII (folder 12), which originally headed the full leaf from which the first piece of this present poem has been cut off. The poem number 'VIII' is drawn ornamentally above deleted ornamental 'IX.'. Whitman numbered the leaves in the lower left corner in pencil, the first as 11, the initial digit written over some other, doubtfully a 7; the second leaf is numbered 12, the first digit over an erased number, doubtfully an 8. A short wavy line ends the poem. Beneath this, and mostly cut off, is the top of an ornamental roman 'IX'. A short piece of white thread adheres to a hole at the top of the first leaf. 1860, pp. 355–56; Camden, III, 299. The poem was rejected in 1867.]

[*leaf 1*]

VIII.

> Hours continuing long, sore | and heavy-hearted,
>
> Hours of the dusk, when I | withdraw to a lonesome and | unfrequented spot, seating | myself, leaning my face | in my hands,
>
> Hours sleepless, deep in the night, | when I go forth, speeding | swiftly the country roads, or | through the city streets, or | pacing miles and miles, stifling | plaintive cries,

[*leaf 2, upper section*]

> Hours discouraged, distracted, | —For he, the one I cannot | content myself without — | soon I saw him content | himself without me,
>
> 5 Hours when I am forgotten — | (O weeks and months are | passing, but I believe I am | never to forget!)
>
> Sullen and suffering hours — | (I am ashamed—but it is | useless —I am what I am;) |

I am indifferent to my own songs—I will go with him I love,
It is to be enough for us that we are together—We never separate
again.

9.

HOURS continuing long, sore and heavy-hearted,
Hours of the dusk, when I withdraw to a lonesome and unfrequented
spot, seating myself, leaning my face in my hands;
Hours sleepless, deep in the night, when I go forth, speeding swiftly
the country roads, or through the city streets, or pacing miles and
miles, stifling plaintive cries;
Hours discouraged, distracted—for the one I cannot content myself
without, soon I saw him content himself without me;
Hours when I am forgotten, (O weeks and months are passing, but I
believe I am never to forget!)
Sullen and suffering hours! (I am ashamed—but it is useless—I am
what I am;)

---

2 dusk] *k* heavily mended, with just a bare
possibility that it is over a *t*.
2 seating] *ing* written over *ed* smudged out
while still wet.

4 him content] *c* mended over another letter, perhaps the start of *w*.
5 forgotten] *en* heavily mended over some
letters.

Hours of torment—I | wonder if other men ever | have the like, out of the | like feelings?

Is there even one other like | me—distracted—his friend, | his lover, lost to him?

Is he too as I am now? Does | he still rise in the morning, | dejected, thinking who is lost to him?

10 And at night, awaking, think who is | lost?

[lower paste-on section]

Does he too harbor his friendship si-|lent and endless? Harbor his anguish | and passion?

Does some stray reminder, or the | casual mention of a name, bring | the fit back upon him, taciturn | and deprest?

Does he see himself reflected in me? | In these hours does he see the | face of his hours reflected?

8 me] written over a smudge, probably rep-   9 lost to him?] written over a smudged era-
resenting an erasure.   sure.

[FOLDER 12. Two pieces of white wove paper. The first measures $3\frac{1}{4} \times 3\frac{1}{2}$; the second, a paste-together, the upper section $5\frac{3}{4} \times 3\frac{5}{8}$, and the lower $2\frac{1}{16} \times 3\frac{5}{8}$. Pinholes appear at the top of both leaves and a few in the center of the upper part of the second. Written in black ink. In the lower left corner Whitman numbered the leaves in pencil. The first is $9\frac{1}{2}$ to the right of a pencil-deleted two-digit number, the first digit of which is 1 and the second perhaps 4. The second leaf is numbered 10, the 0 being drawn over what looks like a 1. The poem number is drawn ornamentally and a wavy line appears at the conclusion. A short piece of white thread adheres to a hole at the top of the first leaf. 1860, pp. 356–57; Camden, I, 147–48.]

[leaf 1]

VII.

You bards of ages hence! when | you refer to me, mind not | so much my poems,

Nor speak of me that I pro-|phesied of The States and led | them the way of their glories,

But come, I will inform you | who I was underneath that | impassive exterior—I will | tell you what to say of me,

[leaf 2, upper section]

Publish my name and hang up | my picture as that of the | tenderest lover,

1 hence!] the exclamation mark added after a deleted comma.

Hours of my torment—I wonder if other men ever have the like, out
    of the like feelings?
Is there even one other like me—distracted—his friend, his lover, lost
    to him?
Is he too as I am now? Does he still rise in the morning, dejected,
    thinking who is lost to him? and at night, awaking, think who is lost?
Does he too harbor his friendship silent and endless? harbor his anguish
    and passion?
Does some stray reminder, or the casual mention of a name, bring the
    fit back upon him, taciturn and deprest?
Does he see himself reflected in me? In these hours, does he see the face
    of his hours reflected?

10.

You bards of ages hence! when you refer to me, mind not so much my
    poems,
Nor speak of me that I prophesied of The States, and led them the way
    of their glories;
But come, I will take you down underneath this impassive exterior—I
    will tell you what to say of me:
Publish my name and hang up my picture as that of the tenderest lover,

5 The friend, the lover's portrait, of | whom his friend, his lover, | was fondest,

Who was not proud of his songs, | but of the measureless ocean | of love within him—and | freely poured it forth,

Who often walked lonesome walks | thinking of his dearest friends, | his lovers,

Who pensive, away from one he | loved, often lay sleepless and | dissatisfied at night,

Who, dreading lest the one he loved | might after all be indifferent | to him, felt the sick feeling— | O sick! sick!

10 Whose happiest days were those, far | away through fields, in woods, on hills, he | and another, wandering hand in | hand, they twain, apart from | other men.

[*lower paste-on section*]

Who ever, as he sauntered the | streets, curved with his arm | the manly shoulder of his | friend—while the curving | arm of his friend rested | upon him also.

8 and] *a* heavily mended over another letter.
10 through fields,] interlined above a caret; after 'woods' an original 'or' is then deleted.

[FOLDER 13. Two leaves of white wove paper of the same cutting, $5\frac{7}{8} \times 3\frac{11}{16}$ each. The second leaf has had pasted over its lower part a piece of white paper, measuring $3\frac{1}{8}$ vertically, which contains revised lines. Pinholes appear at the top of the leaves and a few in the center. Whitman's leaf numbers, in pencil at lower left, are 4 and 5. The poem number is drawn ornamentally. A fragment of an earlier version of this poem is preserved on the verso of "Premonitions" leaves 15–16 in folder 1. The text is given below, at the end of the poem. 1860, pp. 357–58; Camden, I, 148–49.]

[*leaf* 1]

III

When I heard at the close of | the day how I had been | praised in the Capitol, still | it was not a happy night | for me that followed;

Nor when I caroused— | —Nor when my favorite plans were accom-|plished—was I really happy,

But that day I rose | at dawn from the bed of | perfect health, electric, in-|haling sweet breath,

When I saw the full moon | in the west grow pale and | disappear in the morning light,

The friend, the lover's portrait, of whom his friend, his lover, was
  fondest,
Who was not proud of his songs, but of the measureless ocean of love
  within him—and freely poured it forth,
Who often walked lonesome walks, thinking of his dear friends, his
  lovers,
Who pensive, away from one he loved, often lay sleepless and dissatisfied
  at night,
Who knew too well the sick, sick dread lest the one he loved might
  secretly be indifferent to him,
Whose happiest days were far away, through fields, in woods, on hills,
  he and another, wandering hand in hand, they twain, apart from
  other men,
Who oft as he sauntered the streets, curved with his arm the shoulder
  of his friend—while the arm of his friend rested upon him also.

11.

WHEN I heard at the close of the day how my name had been received
  with plaudits in the capitol, still it was not a happy night for me
  that followed;
And else, when I caroused, or when my plans were accomplished, still
  I was not happy;
But the day when I rose at dawn from the bed of perfect health, refreshed, singing, inhaling the ripe breath of autumn,
When I saw the full moon in the west grow pale and disappear in
  the morning light,

---

1 followed] *ed* mended over *d*.
2 Nor when I caroused . . . happy,] 'Nor' is
  interlined in pencil at the beginning of
  the verse above deleted 'And else,'. The
  line first ended 'caroused—Or'. The 'Or'
  was deleted in pencil and another dash
  placed above the original. At the start of
  the next line, before 'when' was interlined in pencil above a caret, '—Nor'.
  Further on, 'favorite' was interlined in
  pencil above a caret. The *s* of 'plans' is
  smudged as if for excision, but this ap-

pears to be accidental. 'was I really
  happy,' was interlined in pencil above
  deleted 'it was well enough—'. The origi-
  nal continuation, | 'Still I was not happy;'
  is deleted in pencil.
3 that] deleted in ink and 'the' interlined.
  On either side was then written in pencil
  'the' and 'that', the 'the' then being deleted in pencil.
3 day I rose] originally 'day when I rose', the
  'when' being deleted in pencil, with a
  pencil-interlined 'when' also deleted.

5 When I wandered alone over the | beach, and undressing, bathed, | laughing with the waters, and | saw the sun rise,

[*leaf 2*]

And when I thought how | my friend, my lover, was | coming, then O I was happy;

Each breath tasted | sweeter—and all that day my | food nourished me more—And | the beautiful day passed well,

And the next came with equal | joy—And with the next, at | evening, came my friend,

[*paste-over revision*]

And that night, while all | was still, I heard the | waters roll slowly continually | up the shores

10 I heard the hissing rustle of | the liquid and sands, as directed | to me, whispering, to congratulate | me,—For the friend I love lay | sleeping by my side,

In the stillness his face was in-|clined towards me, while the | moon's clear beams shone,

And his arm lay lightly over my | breast—And that night I was happy.

6 O] interlined in pencil above a caret.
7 Each] originally 'O then each'. The 'O' was deleted in pencil and the *t* of 'then' made into a capital; then the word was deleted in pencil and *e* of 'each' mended to capital *E*.

8 with the next,] the comma is smudged out, probably by accident in the process of erasing some illegible word in the line below, over which now appears 'friend'.
10 liquid] the *i* is inserted after *u*.

[*earlier version on the original second leaf beneath the paste-over; no alterations*]

And that night O you happy | waters, I heard you beating | the shores—But my heart | beat happier than you— for | he I love is returned and | sleeping by my side,

And that night in the stillness | his face was inclined toward | me while the moon's clear | beams shone,

And his arm lay lightly over my | breast—And that night I | was happy.

When I wandered alone over the beach, and, undressing, bathed,
    laughing with the cool waters, and saw the sun rise,
And when I thought how my dear friend, my lover, was on his way
    coming, O then I was happy;
O then each breath tasted sweeter—and all that day my food nour-
    ished me more—And the beautiful day passed well,
And the next came with equal joy—And with the next, at evening,
    came my friend;
And that night, while all was still, I heard the waters roll slowly con-
    tinually up the shores,
I heard the hissing rustle of the liquid and sands, as directed to me,
    whispering, to congratulate me,
For the one I love most lay sleeping by me under the same cover in
    the cool night,
In the stillness, in the autumn moonbeams, his face was inclined to-
    ward me,
And his arm lay lightly around my breast—And that night I was happy.

[Verso of leaves 15–16 of "Premonition," folder 1. Written in black ink on
white wove paper and deleted with a vertical pencil stroke.]

V.

When I heard at the close of | the day how I had been | praised
    in the Capitol, still | it was not a happy night | for me that
    followed,
And else, when I caroused—Or | when my plans were accom-
    plished— | it was well enough—Still I | was not happy;
But that day when I rose at dawn | from the bed of perfect health,
    electric, inhaling sweet breath,
When I saw the full moon in the | west grow pale and disappear
    [*end of verso leaf* 15] | [*begin verso leaf* 16] in the morning
    light,
5 When I wandered alone over the | beach, and undressing, bathed,
    laughing | with the waters, and saw the | sun rise, [*the remain-
    ing is cut off*]

1 night] interlined above deleted 'day'.
2 caroused] a following comma has been
smudged out while still wet.
3 that day] interlined with a fine pen above
'that day', previously excised.

3 health,] the comma is partly smudged; it
is not clear whether this was intended
for a deletion, but the appearance suggests that the comma was first wiped for
excision and then mended.

FOLDER 14. Two pieces of white wove paper 5 × 4½ and 7$\frac{15}{16}$ × 6¼; pinholes in the center and left margin. Written in a dark ink. 1860, pp. 358–59; Camden, I, 149.

[*leaf* 1]

To a new personal | admirer.

Be careful—I am | perhaps | different from what you | suppose;
Do you suppose you will | find in me your ideal?

[*leaf* 2]

Do you suppose you can easily | be my lover, and I yours?
Do you suppose I am trusty | and faithful?
5 Do you trust this pliant and | and tolerant manner of mine?
Do you suppose yourself advancing | on real ground toward a real
    heroic person?
Have you no thought, O | dreamer, that it is all | maya, illusion?
O let some wise serpent hiss | in your ears how many | have trusted
    the same as you,
How many have fondly supposed what you | do now—only to be
    disappointed.—

1 Be . . . perhaps] 'careful—' was interlined above deleted 'cautious'. Whitman first wrote, 'I am not | this' and then deleted 'this' before continuing 'that probably', whereupon he seems to have stopped, deleted 'that probably' and interlined 'perhaps' before continuing 'very | different'. 'very' is later deleted.

2 your ideal?] the question mark is an addition, since the verse originally continued, | 'of ['w' *crossed out*] manliness and | of love, and of continual | trust'. All this continuation except the 'of' [*inadvertently?*] before 'love' was crossed through. Beginning a new verse before this 'of', Whitman started 'Do' (o mended [*Cont. on page 91*]

[FOLDER 15. One leaf of pink paper written in dark ink. Two sets of pinholes at the top, and one in the center. The poem number 52 is mended in ink from 51. 1860, pp. 359–60; Camden, I, 149–50.]

52—

Buds.

Earth's and Mine, offered fresh to you, | after natural ways, folded,
  | silent,

1 Earth's and Mine,] originally 'Mine' began the verse (the retention of its capital is accidental), and after it was interlined above a caret 'from the earth,', which was deleted and 'Earth's and' with a caret placed before and above 'Mine'.

12.

ARE you the new person drawn toward me, and asking something significant from me?

To begin with, take warning—I am probably far different from what you suppose;

Do you suppose you will find in me your ideal?

Do you think it so easy to have me become your lover?

Do you think the friendship of me would be unalloyed satisfaction?

Do you suppose I am trusty and faithful?

Do you see no further than this façade—this smooth and tolerant manner of me?

Do you suppose yourself advancing on real ground toward a real heroic man?

Have you no thought, O dreamer, that it may be all maya, illusion? O the next step may precipitate you!

O let some past deceived one hiss in your ears, how many have prest on the same as you are pressing now,

How many have fondly supposed what you are supposing now—only to be disappointed.

[*Cont. from page 90*]

over *ou*) and then continued after deleted 'trust' with 'suppose I can | be trusted'. Above deleted 'love' and thus following 'Do' is deleted 'you anticipate'. All is then excised with a single vertical pen stroke.

5 pliant] interlined above deleted 'easy'.

5 and tolerant] interlined above a caret after deleted | 'pliant'. The 'and' ending the line above after deleted 'easy' was inadvertently not excised.

6 yourself advancing] interlined above deleted 'you are not'.

6 on real] 'on' written currently after deleted 'in'.

6 toward . . . person?] the first version was simply 'on real ground?' | . The question mark was deleted and above a caret was

interlined 'toward a real | man?', the 'man?' being placed on the same line as 'ground'. 'man' was then crossed out and between it and 'toward a real' was crowded in 'heroic person?'.

7 Have . . . thought] this verse originally started 'Do you', but Whitman stopped, deleted it, and started the present verse on the line below. 'thought' was written currently after deleted 'idea,'.

8 trusted the same as you,] the original version was 'supposed' [*immediately crossed out and followed by*] 'thought the same,'. This was deleted and 'trusted too the same as you' interlined, 'too' then being deleted.

9 fondly] interlined above a caret.

13.

CALAMUS taste,

(For I must change the strain—these are not to be pensive leaves, but leaves of joy,)

Roots and leaves unlike any but themselves,

Thoughts, says, poems, poemets, | put before you and within | you, to be unfolded by | you on the old terms;

If you bring the warmth of the | sun to them they will | open and bring form, color, | perfume, to you,

If you become the aliment and | the wet, they will become | flowers, fruits, tall branches | and trees,

5 They are comprised in you | just as much as in | themselves, perhaps more than in themselves,

They are not comprised in one season | or succession, but in many successions,

They have come slowly up out of the | earth and me, and are to come slowly | up out of you.—

3 and bring] *b* mended over *f*.
5 just as] 'just' is interlined above a caret;
the *a* of 'as' is mended over some other letter, perhaps the start of *i*.

[FOLDER 16. One leaf of white wove paper $5\frac{3}{4} \times 3\frac{9}{16}$; pinholes at top and center. Written in black ink. Whitman (presumably) has numbered the leaf as 1 at the bottom left. The left margin of the leaf looks as though it had been torn from a made-up notebook: paste, and possibly some lavender paper, adhere to the recto left margin. The original title was *'Live Oak, with Moss.'*, above which has been written *'Calamus-Leaves.'* in light ink. 1860, p. 360; Camden, I, 150.]

Calamus-Leaves.

I.

Not the heat flames up and con-|sumes,

Not the sea-waves hurry in and | out,

Not the air, delicious and dry, the | air of the ripe summer, bears | lightly along white down-balls | of myriads of seeds, wafted, | sailing gracefully, to drop | where they may,

Not these—O none of these, more | than the flames of me, con-|suming, burning for his love | whom I love—O none, more | than I, hurrying in and out;

5 Does the tide hurry, seeking some-|thing, and never give up?— O | I, the same, to seek my life-long | lover;

5 some-] the hyphen has been mended in blue pencil.
5 to] *t* mended over a smudged-out letter.

Scents brought to men and women from the wild woods, and from the
   pond-side,
Breast-sorrel and pinks of love—fingers that wind around tighter than
   vines,
Gushes from the throats of birds, hid in the foliage of trees, as the sun
   is risen,
Breezes of land and love—Breezes set from living shores out to you on
   the living sea—to you, O sailors!
Frost-mellowed berries, and Third Month twigs, offered fresh to young
   persons wandering out in the fields when the winter breaks up,
Love-buds, put before you and within you, whoever you are,
Buds to be unfolded on the old terms,
If you bring the warmth of the sun to them, they will open, and bring
   form, color, perfume, to you,
If you become the aliment and the wet, they will become flowers, fruits,
   tall branches and trees,
They are comprised in you just as much as in themselves—perhaps
   more than in themselves,
They are not comprised in one season or succession, but many suc-
   cessions,
They have come slowly up out of the earth and me, and are to come
   slowly up out of you.

14.

Not heat flames up and consumes,
Not sea-waves hurry in and out,
Not the air, delicious and dry, the air of the ripe summer, bears lightly
   along white down-balls of myriads of seeds, wafted, sailing grace-
   fully, to drop where they may,
Not these—O none of these, more than the flames of me, consuming,
   burning for his love whom I love!
O none, more than I, hurrying in and out;
Does the tide hurry, seeking something, and never give up? O I the
   same;

O nor down-balls, nor perfumes, nor | the high rain-emitting clouds, | are borne through the open air, | more than my copious soul is | borne through the open air, wafted | in all directions, for friendship, for | love.—

[FOLDER 17. One blue tax form, pinholes at top and center; written in light ink. 1860, p. 361; Camden, I, 151.]

Confession Drops.

Trickle, slow drops,
Candid, from me falling—drip, | bleeding drops,
From wounds made to free | you whence you were | prisoned,
From my face—from my fore-|head and lips,
5 From my breast—From within, | where I was concealed— | press forth, red drops,
Stain every page—stain every | song I sing, every word I | say, bloody drops,
Let them know your scarlet | heat—let them glisten,
Saturate them with yourself, | all ashamed and wet,
Glow upon all I have written or | shall write, bleeding drops,
10 Let it all be seen in your light, | blushing drops.—

[FOLDER 18. Two leaves of pink paper; cluster of pinholes in the center and a set in the left margin. Written in black ink, including the poem number. In pencil at the top of the second leaf is written '43', followed by a figure 1 in parentheses; then in blue pencil this 1 has been made into '½'. The title was originally 'Leaflet.', the last three letters being deleted and a new period added. 1860, pp. 361–62; Camden, III, 300. The poem was rejected in 1867.]

[*leaf* 1]

43—

Leaf.

May-Be one will read this | who recollects some | wrong-doing of my life,
Or may-be a stranger will read | this who has secretly | loved me,

O nor down-balls, nor perfumes, nor the high rain-emitting clouds, are
    borne through the open air,
Any more than my Soul is borne through the open air,
Wafted in all directions, O love, for friendship, for you.

15.

O DROPS of me! trickle, slow drops,
Candid, from me falling—drip, bleeding drops,
From wounds made to free you whence you were prisoned,
From my face—from my forehead and lips,
From my breast—from within where I was concealed—Press forth, red
    drops—confession drops,
Stain every page—stain every song I sing, every word I say, bloody
    drops,
Let them know your scarlet heat—let them glisten,
Saturate them with yourself, all ashamed and wet,
Glow upon all I have written or shall write, bleeding drops,
Let it all be seen in your light, blushing drops.

16.

1. WHO is now reading this?

2. May-be one is now reading this who knows some wrong-doing of my
    past life,
    Or may-be a stranger is reading this who has secretly loved me,

---

1 who recollects . . . life,] the original version read, 'May-Be one will read this | who is knowing to some | folly of my past life, | —or knowing to some | defection, or deed of the | night,'. 'is knowing to' was deleted and 'remembers' interlined, this in turn being deleted and "recollects' added over a caret. 'wrong-doing' was interlined over deleted 'folly'; and 'past' deleted. 'recollects' was interlined above deleted 'knowing to', and subsequently the preceding 'or', and then the interlined 'recollects' and 'some defection, or' was deleted. This last revision must have taken place at a point later than the revision substituting 'a stranger' in the verse below, since this latter displaces upward an early addition after 'night,' reading 'or unsupplied defect,' which is crossed out with the same pen stroke that excised 'night'. Above the last letter of 'defection' appears deleted 'as'. Since in the same line two pen strokes were used, one to excise 'defection, as' and the other 'deed of the', it is possible that the excision of 'defection, as' was the earlier.

2 a stranger] in pencil 'some stranger' was interlined with a caret above deleted 'one'. Then 'some' was deleted in ink and 'a' placed above it, 'stranger' being traced over in ink.

Or may-be one | who meets all my grand | assumptions and ego-tisms with | derision,—Or may-be one who is puzzled | at me.—

As if I were not puzzled at | myself! Or As if I never | deride my-self! | —(O conscience-struck!—O self-convicted!)

5 Or as if I do not secretly | love strangers—O tenderly, a long time, and | never exhibit it!

[*leaf 2*]

Or as if interior in me | were not the stuff of | wrong-doing (fol-lies, defections, | deeds of the night)

Or as if it | could cease transpiring | from me until it must cease!

3 one who meets . . . egotisms] the original version was, 'one will read | this who looks back | and remembers me'. 'will read this' is deleted (including some illegible letter or mark above 'this'), and above deleted 'looks back' (possibly there was a dash af-ter 'back') is interlined 'meets all my grand', while in the next line 'assumptions and egotisms' is interlined above deleted 'and remembers me'.

3 —Or may-be one who] interlined in pen-cil above a caret after deleted 'and'.

3 me.—] an original comma is crossed out, and the period and dash added.

4 As] above and to the left is placed a para-graph mark, probably to indicate a space and the start of another stanza.

4 Or As . . . deride] 'Or' is interlined above a caret, and by inadvertence the capital-ization of the *A* of 'As' was not reduced.

[*Cont. on page* 97]

[FOLDER 19. Two leaves of pink paper; cluster of pinholes in the center. Written in black ink. The poem number 79 is written in this ink over some other number: although the 7 is somewhat smudged, no digit seems to be ap-parent under it, but the 9 is written over an 8. The original title was '*Leaf.*' This has been deleted and '*Poemet.*' placed after it in the light ink. 1860, pp. 362–63; Camden, II, 225–26.]

[*leaf* 1]

79—

Poemet.

Of him I love day and | night, I dreamed I heard | he was dead,

And I dreamed I went where | they had buried the man | I love but he was not | in that place,

And I dreamed I wandered | searching | among burial places, to find him,

And I found that every place | was a burial place,

5 The houses full of life were | equally full of death, | —(this house is now,)

Or may-be one who meets all my grand assumptions and egotisms with
    derision,
Or may-be one who is puzzled at me.

3. As if I were not puzzled at myself!
    Or as if I never deride myself! (O conscience-struck! O self-convicted!)
    Or as if I do not secretly love strangers! (O tenderly, a long time, and
        never avow it;)
    Or as if I did not see, perfectly well, interior in myself, the stuff of
        wrong-doing,
    Or as if it could cease transpiring from me until it must cease.

[*Cont. from page 96*]
'never' is interlined in pencil traced over in ink above pencil-deleted 'do not'. Before 'deride' and originally starting the line the word 'sometimes' has been crossed through in pencil and in ink.

4 (O conscience- . . . -convicted!)] this is crowded in between the end of the original verse above 'deride myself!' and the next verse, in the center. 'conscience-struck!' was interlined with a caret above deleted original 'bitterly'. The *ed* of '-convicted' is altered over 'ion', and the word 'with' before 'self-' has been deleted.

5 strangers] interlined in pencil above and to the left of deleted 'people'. This revision by its position seems to have been made later than the ink interlining above a caret and guide lines of '—O tenderly,'.

6 wrong-doing] interlined above a caret, originally as 'wrong-doings,'. In pencil a *g* has been written over *gs*, and the comma deleted. The parentheses before 'follies' and after 'night' are in pencil, an original exclamation mark after 'night' being deleted in pencil.

6 defections,] an original following 'and' has been deleted.

7 if it] originally, 'if from me it', the 'from me' being crossed out.

7 transpiring] interlined with a caret above deleted 'going forth'.

17.

OF him I love day and night, I dreamed I heard he was dead,
And I dreamed I went where they had buried him I love—but he was
    not in that place,
And I dreamed I wandered, searching among burial-places, to find
    him,
And I found that every place was a burial-place,
The houses full of life were equally full of death, (This house is now,)
The streets, the shipping, the places of amusement, the Chicago, Bos-
    ton, Philadelphia, the Mannahatta, were as full of the dead as of the
    living,
And fuller, O vastly fuller, of the dead than of the living;

1 Of him I love] 'him' interlined in the light ink above deleted 'a man'; a final *d* is crossed off 'love' in black ink.

2 love] a final *d* and comma excised in pencil.

3 wandered searching] between these two words originally appeared 'to find | the man I love,' all except the comma crossed through in the light ink.

3 to find him,] interlined in the light ink above a caret.

5 —(this house is now,)] crowded in between the lines in the light ink.

The streets, the shipping, the | places of amusement, the Chicago, | the Mannahatta, were | as full of the dead | as of the living, and fuller | of the dead than of the | living.—

[*leaf 2*]

And what I dreamed I will | henceforth tell to every | person and age,

And I stand henceforth bound to | what I dreamed;

And now I am willing to | disregard burial places, | and dispense with them,

10 And if the memorials of the | dead were put up indif-|ferently everywhere, even in | the room where I eat | or sleep, I should be | satisfied,

And if the corpse of any one | I love, or if my own corpse, | be duly rendered to powder | and poured into the sea, | or distrib-uted to the winds, | I shall be satisfied.—

6 places] interlined in dark ink above de-leted 'houses'.
6 the Chicago] 'the' interlined in the light ink above a caret.
6 were as full] originally, 'were as | just as full', 'as just' being crossed through in dark ink before continuing.
6 living.—] an original semi-colon has been deleted and the period and dash added in black ink.

[FOLDER 20. One leaf of white wove paper consisting of a large piece ($7\frac{3}{8}$ × $6\frac{5}{16}$), with a small piece ($3\frac{1}{4}$ × $3\frac{15}{16}$) pasted on at top left, the area of paste-over being $1\frac{1}{4}$. To the right of the paste-on, the large piece has been trimmed off by $\frac{7}{16}$, destroying some of the unrevised text. (What can be read is detailed in the notes.) Clearly, the upper part of the large piece has been cut off, and revised opening lines written on the attached small piece. The large piece is written in a dark-brown ink, the small in a lighter-brown ink. A torn-off fragment in the right margin of the main leaf has been repaired by gluing on a strip of white backing paper. 1860, p. 363; Camden, I, 151–52. On the verso of the large piece is written in pencil the opening lines of "Enfans d'Adam" (no. 1), for which see under folder 2.]

[*top section, paste-on*]

City of my walks and joys!

City—whom that I have lived | and sung there will one day | make you illustrious!

Not the infinite pageants of | you—Not your shifting | tableaux, your spectacles, | repay me

—And what I dreamed I will henceforth tell to every person and
    age,
And I stand henceforth bound to what I dreamed;
And now I am willing to disregard burial-places, and dispense with
    them,
And if the memorials of the dead were put up indifferently every-
    where, even in the room where I eat or sleep, I should be satisfied,
And if the corpse of any one I love, or if my own corpse, be duly ren-
    dered to powder, and poured in the sea, I shall be satisfied,
Or if it be distributed to the winds, I shall be satisfied.

18.

City of my walks and joys!
City whom that I have lived and sung there will one day make you
    illustrious,
Not the pageants of you—not your shifting tableaux, your spectacles,
    repay me,

Not the interminable rows of | your houses—nor the | ships at the wharves,

5 Nor to

[*start of original large piece below paste-on*]

converse with | learned persons, or bear | my share in the soiree, or | feast, or in politics, |

But as I pass, the frequent and swift flash | of eyes offering me | love—offering me | the response and equal of | my own,

These repay me—Lovers, continual Lovers | only repay me.—

4 nor] *r* mended over *t*.
5 Nor] *r* mended over *t*. 'Nor to' on the small piece leads down above a caret on the large piece to continue with 'converse'. The original version had been 'I converse with educated and | fashionable persons,'. Above deleted 'educated' was interlined 'eminent', in turn excised. A pencil guide line brings down half-erased 'learned' in pencil. The same pen stroke that crossed through 'educated', continued with 'and' and, in the next line, 'fashionable'. 'learned' is interlined above a caret. Above this point where the two pieces join, the excised text is fragmentary. In the original large-sized hand there is the following: 'Manhattan—little you $_\wedge$ < > | Not ['your' *interlined above* deleted 'these'] crowded rows of houses | attract me | Not to'. The last two words break off the sense, and seem to represent a false start on the verse that began 'I converse', revised to 'Nor converse'. 'repay' is placed under deleted 'attract'. In these lines under the paste-over there is a great deal of revision. Under the line 'Manhattan— . . . ' is crowded in 'You [ ] City, what do [*Cont. on page 101*]

[FOLDER 21. Two pieces of white wove paper ($6\frac{7}{8}$ × $3\frac{11}{16}$); several sets of pin-holes in the center and at the top. Written in black ink. Whitman numbered the leaves in pencil at the lower left corner 2 and 3. The poem number is ornamentally drawn. 1860, pp. 364–65; Camden, I, 152–53. In the Berg Collection at the New York Public Library is another holograph of these verses without substantive change. Bucke (p. 51) prints exactly the same text for the first leaf only, perhaps from what is now the Berg MS.]

II

[*leaf 1*]

I saw in Louisiana a | live-oak growing,

All alone stood it, and the | moss hung down from the | branches,

Without any companion it grew | there, glistening out | joyous leaves of dark green,

And its look, rude, unbending, | lusty, made me think of | myself;

5 But I wondered how it could | utter joyous leaves, standing | alone there without its friend, | its lover—For I knew I could | not;

3 out] originally 'with' followed to end the line, but this was deleted in pencil.

Not the interminable rows of your houses—nor the ships at the
wharves,

Nor the processions in the streets, nor the bright windows, with goods
in them,

Nor to converse with learned persons, or bear my share in the soiree
or feast;

Not those—but, as I pass, O Manhattan! your frequent and swift flash
of eyes offering me love,

Offering me the response of my own—these repay me,

Lovers, continual lovers, only repay me.

[Cont. from page 100]

y<o >' |, all except the 'you' crossed
through. Above this, 'little you' in the
line following 'Manhattan—' is deleted.
Between the deleted 'what do yo' and
the line containing 'crowded rows of
houses' has been added, the first word beginning immediately below 'do': 'you re-
pay me for | daily walks'. After 'for' is
deleted 'my' and after 'walks' is 'joys'
above deleted 'silen'. The whole has been
crossed through. Below the 'Not' which
begins 'Not your crowded rows' and
against the left margin is the single word
'Not' with some illegible deletion above it.
Below this are the words 'Not to', already
commented on as a false start. To the
right of 'Not to' is crowded in considerable material in pencil, 'the bright win-
dows or the goods in them, or the | pro-
cessions in the streets'. The 'or' after 'windows' is interlined above deleted 'and'.
The phrase 'in them, or the' may be a
later pencil addition.

5 in politics] a preceding 'even' has been
heavily crossed out.

6 frequent and] interlined above a caret.

6 offering] Whitman first wrote 'speaking'
and then seemingly continued with the
alternate 'offering'. Apparently 'offering'
was first deleted, since 'speaking' is also
crossed through, and interlined is 'offering' over the original.

6 me love] the original read, | 'delicious
love'. 'delicious' was deleted in pencil and
another word started with two letters,
which may be 'ro' [query robust] before being heavily excised and above a caret, in
pencil, added 'athletic'; probably later
there was also pencil-interlined after this,
'fresh as nature's air and | herbage—'.
'athletic' is heavily excised, and the following phrase more lightly, both in pencil.

6 response and] interlined in pencil above a
caret, the second s is mended, perhaps
from a d. In this line before 'the equal'
the original had read | 'full repo', deleted
before continuing.

7 continual] interlined above a caret, apparently in mid-thought when in the next
line before 'only', the letters 'contin' are
broken off and crossed through.

20.

I saw in Louisiana a live-oak growing,

All alone stood it, and the moss hung down from the branches,

Without any companion it grew there, uttering joyous leaves of dark
green,

And its look, rude, unbending, lusty, made me think of myself,

But I wondered how it could utter joyous leaves, standing alone there,
without its friend, its lover near—for I knew I could not,

And I broke off a twig with a certain number of leaves upon it, and
twined around it a little moss,

And I plucked a twig with | a certain number of leaves | upon it, and twined around | it a little moss, and brought | it away— And I have placed | it in sight in my room,

[*leaf 2*]

It is not needed to remind | me as of my friends, (for I | believe lately I think of little | else than of them,)

Yet it remains to me a | curious token—it makes | me think of manly love,

For all that, and though the | live oak glistens there in Louis-|iana, solitary in a wide | flat space, uttering joyous | leaves all its life, without | a friend, a lover, near—I | know very well I could | not.

7 lately] interlined above a caret in the same ink.

8 —it makes me think of manly love,] the first version read, '—I write | these pieces, and name | them after it;'. This has been deleted and 'it makes | me . . . love,' interlined in the light ink.

9 live oak] interlined with a caret in a light ink above deleted 'tree'.

[FOLDER 22. Two leaves of pink paper; a cluster of pinholes in the center, and a few in the left margin. The poem number is in a darker ink. 1860, pp. 365–66; Camden, II, 228–29.]

[*leaf 1*]

34—

As of Eternity.

That music always around me, | unceasing, unbeginning—yet | long untaught I did not | hear,

Now the underlying chorus I hear, | and am elated,

A tenor, strong, ascending with | power and health, with glad | notes of day break, I hear,

A soprano, at intervals, sailing | buoyantly over the tops of im-|mense | waves,

5 A transparent bass, shuddering | lusciously through the uni-|verse,

The triumphant tutti—the fu-|nereal wailings, with sweet | flutes and violins—all | these I fill myself with;

[*leaf 2*]

I hear not the volumes of | sound merely—I am moved | by the exquisite meanings,

And brought it away—and I have placed it in sight in my room,
It is not needed to remind me as of my own dear friends,
(For I believe lately I think of little else than of them,)
Yet it remains to me a curious token—it makes me think of manly
love;
For all that, and though the live-oak glistens there in Louisiana, soli-
tary, in a wide flat space,
Uttering joyous leaves all its life, without a friend, a lover, near,
I know very well I could not.

21.

MUSIC always round me, unceasing, unbeginning—yet long untaught I
did not hear,
But now the chorus I hear, and am elated,
A tenor, strong, ascending, with power and health, with glad notes
of day-break I hear,
A soprano, at intervals, sailing buoyantly over the tops of immense
waves,
A transparent base, shuddering lusciously under and through the
universe,
The triumphant tutti—the funeral wailings, with sweet flutes and
violins—All these I fill myself with;
I hear not the volumes of sound merely—I am moved by the exquisite
meanings,

---

1 unbeginning] a comma before the dash
has been crossed out.

4 soprano] final o mended over a smudged
out letter with a tail like an e or a.

4 buoyantly] u mended currently over o.

4 the tops of] interlined in the same ink
above a caret.

5 bass] final s mended in pencil over original e.

6 tutti—] a comma before the dash has
been crossed out.

⟦ 103 ⟧

I listen to the different voices, | winding in and out, striving, |
contending with fiery vehe-|mence to excel each other | in
emotion,
I do not think the performers | know themselves—But now | I
think I begin to know | them.—

[FOLDER 23. Two leaves of pink paper; cluster of pinholes in the center.
Written in black ink. The poem number 95 is written above deleted '94—',
both inks apparently different from that of the verses. 1860, pp. 366–67; Camden, I, 153.]

[*leaf* 1]

95

To A Stranger.—

Passing Stranger, you do not know | how longingly I look | upon
you,
You must be he I was seeking, | or she I was seeking,
I have somewhere surely lived | a life of joy with you,
All is recalled as we flit | by each other, fluid, | affectionate, chaste,
| matured,
5 You grew up with me, were | a boy with me, or a | girl with me,
I ate with you, and slept | with you—Your body has | become not
yours only, | nor my body mine only,

[*leaf* 2]

You give me the pleasure | of your eyes, face, | flesh, as we pass
—You | take of my beard, breast, | hands, in return,
I am not to speak to you— | I am to think of you | when I sit alone,
or | wake at night alone,
I am to wait—I do not | doubt I am to meet | you again,
10 I am to see to it that | I do not lose you.—

1 Passing] interlined in the light ink above
a caret; probably the capital of 'Stranger'
was not reduced through inadvertence.
4 affectionate] deleted 'refreshed,' begins the
line before this.

7 pass—] a smudged-out comma appears before the dash.
8 sit] interlined in a very black ink above
deleted 'walk'.

I listen to the different voices winding in and out, striving, contending
   with fiery vehemence to excel each other in emotion,
I do not think the performers know themselves—But now I think
   I begin to know them.

22.

PASSING stranger! you do not know how longingly I look upon you,
You must be he I was seeking, or she I was seeking, (It comes to me,
   as of a dream,)
I have somewhere surely lived a life of joy with you,
All is recalled as we flit by each other, fluid, affectionate, chaste, ma-
   tured,
You grew up with me, were a boy with me, or girl with me,
I ate with you, and slept with you—your body has become not yours
   only, nor left my body mine only,
You give me the pleasure of your eyes, face, flesh, as we pass—you
   take of my beard, breast, hands, in return,
I am not to speak to you—I am to think of you when I sit alone, or
   wake at night alone,
I am to wait—I do not doubt I am to meet you again,
I am to see to it that I do not lose you.

[FOLDER 24. One leaf of white wove paper (5⅛ × 3¾); pinholes at top and in center. Black ink. The poem number ornamentally drawn. Whitman's leaf number 6 appears in pencil in lower left corner. 1860, p. 367; Camden, I, 154.]

IV.

This moment as I sit alone, | yearning and pensive, it | seems to me there are other | men, in other lands, yearning | and pensive.

It seems to me I can look | over and behold them, in | Germany, France, Spain—Or | far away in China, India, or | Russia— talking other dialects,

And it seems to me if I | could know those men | I should love them as I | love men in my own lands,

It seems to me they are as | wise, beautiful, benevolent, | as any in my own lands;

5 O I think we should be | brethren—I think I should | be happy with them.

2 It] Whitman began the line with 'I', and then mended it to a *t,* prefixing capital *I.*

2 India,] interlined in pencil above a caret. After the following 'or' the word 'in' (ending the original line) was deleted in pencil consequentially.

2 dialects,] comma only a faint scratch.

3 men] originally 'men better', the latter word being deleted in pencil. A pencil comma was then placed after 'men' but deleted.

5 think . . . think] interlined in pencil respectively over 'know . . . . know'.

[FOLDER 25. One leaf of pink paper; cluster of pinholes in the center. Written in dark ink. The poem number was originally 53, the 4 being mended over the 3. 1860, p. 368; Camden, I, 155.]

54—

Prairie-Grass.

I demand the spiritual | that corresponds with it— | I demand the blades to rise, | of words, acts, beings,

Those of the open atmosphere, | coarse, sunlit, fresh, nu-|tritious,

Those that go their own gait, erect, stepping | with freedom and command, | leading, not following,

Those with a never-quelled | audacity—Those with | sweet and lusty flesh, | clear of taint, choice | and chary of love-power,

5 Those that look carelessly in | the faces of Presidents and | Governors, as to say, Who | are you?

Those of earth-born passion, | simple, never constrained, never | obedient—Those of inland America.—

23.

THIS moment as I sit alone, yearning and thoughtful, it seems to me
   there are other men in other lands, yearning and thoughtful;
It seems to me I can look over and behold them, in Germany, Italy,
   France, Spain—Or far, far away, in China, or in Russia or India—
   talking other dialects;
And it seems to me if I could know those men better, I should become
   attached to them, as I do to men in my own lands,
It seems to me they are as wise, beautiful, benevolent, as any in my
   own lands;
O I know we should be brethren and lovers,
I know I should be happy with them.

25.

THE prairie-grass dividing—its own odor breathing,
I demand of it the spiritual corresponding,
Demand the most copious and close companionship of men,
Demand the blades to rise of words, acts, beings,
Those of the open atmosphere, coarse, sunlit, fresh, nutritious,
Those that go their own gait, erect, stepping with freedom and com-
   mand—leading, not following,
Those with a never-quell'd audacity—those with sweet and lusty
   flesh, clear of taint, choice and chary of its love-power,
Those that look carelessly in the faces of Presidents and Governors,
   as to say, *Who are you?*
Those of earth-born passion, simple, never constrained, never obedient,
Those of inland America.

---

1 I demand] the verse originally began 'Now
I demand'. 'Now' was deleted and 'Always'
interlined in a darker ink, it also then
being deleted.
3 go their own gait,] interlined in a darker

ink with a caret over deleted 'stand'.
Originally, the interlineation continued
after 'gait' with '—those'. This is crossed
through in pencil, and a comma in pencil
placed after 'gait'.

[FOLDER 26. One leaf of pink paper; various pinholes in the center. Written in dark ink. The poem number 84 has been mended over 83, both in ink. 1860, p. 369; Camden, I, 156.]

84—

Razzia.

Up and down the roads | going—North and South | excursions making,
Power enjoying—elbow stretch-|ing—fingers clutching,
Armed and fearless—eating, | drinking, sleeping, loving,
No law less than myself | owning—Sailing, soldiering, | thieving, threatening,
5 Misers, menials, priests, alarming— | Air breathing, water drink-ing, | on the turf or the sea-beach | dancing,
With birds singing—with fishes | swimming—with trees | branch-ing and leaving,
Cities wrenching, ease scorning, | statutes mocking, feebleness | chasing,
Fulfilling my foray.—

6 with trees] Whitman began with a capital *W* but crossed it out before continuing 'with'.

[FOLDER 27. One blue tax form; pinholes in center and at top. Written in dark-brown ink. 1860, pp. 369–70; Camden, II, 230.]

44—

Leaf.

O dying! Always dying!
O the burials of me, past and present!
O me, while I stride ahead, ma-|terial, visible, imperious | as ever!
O me, what I was for | years, now dead, (I | lament not—I am | content,)
5 O to disengage myself | from those corpses of me | which I turn and | look at, where I cast | them!
To pass on, (O living! | Always living!) and leave | the corpses be-hind!

26.

WE two boys together clinging,
One the other never leaving,
Up and down the roads going—North and South excursions making,
Power enjoying—elbows stretching—fingers clutching,
Armed and fearless—eating, drinking, sleeping, loving,
No law less than ourselves owning—sailing, soldiering, thieving,
     threatening,
Misers, menials, priests alarming—air breathing, water drinking, on
     the turf or the sea-beach dancing,
With birds singing—With fishes swimming—With trees branching
     and leafing,
Cities wrenching, ease scorning, statutes mocking, feebleness chasing,
Fulfilling our foray.

27.

O LOVE!
O dying—always dying!
O the burials of me, past and present!
O me, while I stride ahead, material, visible, imperious as ever!
O me, what I was for years, now dead, (I lament not—I am content;)
O to disengage myself from those corpses of me, which I turn and
     look at, where I cast them!
To pass on, (O living! always living!) and leave the corpses behind!

---

2 burials] original preceding 'ceaseless' is deleted.

2 past and present!] the verse originally ended 'burials of me!' Between the added comma and the original exclamation was inserted a caret and above this interlined 'past, present and | future', the 'and' perhaps being a later addition. A stroke of the pen deleted this (except for 'and') and passed through the original exclamation mark. Then above was interlined 'past and present!'.

3 while] interlined with a caret above deleted 'as'.

3 stride ahead,] after 'stride' was originally written 'on!', which has been deleted with a heavy pen and then later with the fine pen used for the subsequent revisions. 'ahead, yet' seems to have been first inter-

lined above deleted 'on' and then 'yet' deleted in pencil and interlined once more in pencil, above a caret placed before 'stride'. This was then traced over in ink and deleted in ink.

3 ever] interlined above deleted 'before'.

5 myself] originally this ended the line with an exclamation mark, and the next line began 'O those corpses'. With the fine pen the exclamation and 'O' have been deleted, and 'from' interlined above a caret.

6 To pass on,] originally 'O to pass'. The 'O' has been deleted and the *t* of 'to' mended to a capital first in pencil and then in ink. 'on,' is interlined above a caret.

6 leave the] the line originally began 'them', which was currently deleted after an attempt at mending to 'the'.

[FOLDER 28. One leaf of pink paper, a few pinholes in the center. Written in dark ink. The second digit of the poem number 71 is written over a zero and is not quite certain. Above and to the right of the title appears what seems to be an alternate title 'Leaflet', which has been deleted. 1860, p. 371; Camden, I, 156.]

71—

Leaf.—

A promise to Indiana, | Nebraska, Kansas, Iowa, | Minnesota, and
    others:
Sojourning east awhile longer, | soon I travel toward | you, to re-
    main westward,
For I know well that I | belong westward, and am | to be inland,
4 For These States tend inland | and cheerfully concentrate | west-
    ward—and I will | also.—

4 These] capital *T* mended over miniscule *t*.   4 inland] a following comma has been smudged out while still wet.

[FOLDER 29. One leaf of pink paper, some pinholes in center. The poem number 69 has the 9 written over an 8. The title was originally 'Leaflet.—' but the *let* has been crossed out. The upper part of the leaf contains a heavily revised draft deleted by a vertical pen stroke running between horizontal strokes placed above and below. The revised verses follow after the bottom stroke. 1860, p. 372; Camden, I, 14.]

69—

Leaf.—

What place is besieged, and has | tried in vain to raise the | seige?
A commander, brave, swift, immortal, | I send to that place—and
    | with him horse and foot,
3 And parks of artillery, the deadliest | that ever fired gun.—

1 seige] the *ei* may be mended, or perhaps only written with an over-full pen.

[*draft version at head of leaf*]

What place is besieged | and cannot raise the seige?
A commander brave, swift, immortal, I | send to that place, | and
    with him horse and foot,
3 And parks of artillery, the | deadliest that ever | fired gun.—

30.

A PROMISE and gift to California,
Also to the great Pastoral Plains, and for Oregon:
Sojourning east a while longer, soon I travel to you, to remain, to teach robust American love;
For I know very well that I and robust love belong among you, inland, and along the Western Sea,
For These States tend inland, and toward the Western Sea—and I will also.

31.

1. WHAT ship, puzzled at sea, cons for the true reckoning?
   Or, coming in, to avoid the bars, and follow the channel, a perfect pilot needs?
   Here, sailor! Here, ship! take aboard the most perfect pilot,
   Whom, in a little boat, putting off, and rowing, I, hailing you, offer.

2. What place is besieged, and vainly tries to raise the siege?
   Lo! I send to that place a commander, swift, brave, immortal,
   And with him horse and foot—and parks of artillery,
   And artillerymen, the deadliest that ever fired gun.

---

1 What place . . . seige?] originally, 'What place is beleaguered | and needs defence?'. In pencil, 'besieged' is interlined above deleted 'beleaguered', and in the next line, 'raise the seige?' above deleted 'defence?'. Then in dark ink 'needs' is deleted and 'seeks' interlined. Finally, the ink 'seeks' and the following pencil 'to' are crossed through by a single stroke, and 'cannot' interlined in dark ink.

2 A commander . . . foot,'] originally, 'A commander I send to | that place, bringing horse | and foot with him,'. The comma after 'place' is mended and may not be original. In ink above a caret after 'commander' is interlined 'immortal,', and above that, 'brave, swift,'. This revision must have been made after the rejection to be noted in the line below, or else the words were written above both lines as alternates. 'send' is deleted and 'offer' interlined; and then 'offer' and the follow-

ing original 'to' are excised in pencil. In the next line of the verse, 'send to' is interlined in pencil before 'that'. Above a caret after 'place,' is interlined in ink 'immortal', and above that 'the brave, swift'. The 'the' is independently crossed through in ink, and subsequently the rest of this interlineation. Above deleted 'bringing' is interlined 'carrying', deleted. 'horse' is crossed out, and in the next line 'and foot with him'. Above this last is interlined 'and with him horse and foot,'.

3 deadliest . . . gun—] originally, | 'fiercest and most | effective that' . . . . 'fiercest and' is crossed through in pencil; then in ink it is deleted and also 'most effective'. Above a caret placed before 'that' is interlined 'deadliest'. 'ever' was first written 'every' but the y smudged out while wet. A little squiggle, to indicate the end, starts after the final dash.

[FOLDER 30 + 37. One small piece of white wove paper (5¾ × 3⅝); pinholes at top and one set in the center. Written in a medium-brown ink. The two poems are separated by a short wavy line. No revisions are present in the first poem. (1) 1860, p. 377; Camden, I, 156. (2) 1860, p. 375; Camden, I, 160.]

Here the frailest leaves of me, and | yet the strongest-lasting,—the | last to be fully understood,

Here I shade down and hide | my thoughts—I do not | expose them,

3 And yet they expose me more | than all my other poems.

~~~~~~~~~~~~~~~~

[*below*]

Primeval my love for the | woman I love!

O bride! O wife! more re-|sistless, more enduring than | I can tell, the thought of | you,

3 Then, separate as disembodied, | ethereal, a further-born | real-ity, my consolation, | I ascend to the regions | of your love, O man, | O friend.

3 a] interlined in the same ink above deleted 'the'.

[FOLDER 31. One small piece of white wove paper (5¾ × 3 9/16), on the left edge what appear to be remains of glue and small pieces of paper to which it has been attached at some time. Pinholes are in the center and at upper left. Writ-ten in black ink. Whitman originally numbered the leaf as 9 in the upper right corner, but wrote 3 over it in blue pencil. 1860, p. 375; Camden, I, 157–58.]

A leaf for hand-in-hand!

You processions in the streets!

You friendly boatmen and | workmen! You roughs!

You natural persons, old | and young!

5 I wish to encourage you, | till I see it | common for you | to walk hand-in-hand.

5 common] interlined in pencil in the third line of the verse above excised 'uncom-mon', with a preceding 'not' ending the line above also deleted in pencil.

5 hand-in-hand.] the period is almost a comma, and may originally have been one.

44.

HERE my last words, and the most baffling,
Here the frailest leaves of me, and yet my strongest-lasting,
Here I shade down and hide my thoughts—I do not expose them,
And yet they expose me more than all my other poems.

38.

PRIMEVAL my love for the woman I love,
O bride! O wife! more resistless, more enduring than I can tell, the
  thought of you!
Then separate, as disembodied, the purest born,
The ethereal, the last athletic reality, my consolation,
I ascend—I float in the regions of your love, O man,
O sharer of my roving life.

37.

A LEAF for hand in hand!
You natural persons old and young! You on the Eastern Sea, and you
  on the Western!
You on the Mississippi, and on all the branches and bayous of the
  Mississippi!
You friendly boatmen and mechanics! You roughs!
You twain! And all processions moving along the streets!
I wish to infuse myself among you till I see it common for you to walk
  hand in hand.

[FOLDER 32. One small piece of white wove paper ($5\frac{11}{16} \times 3\frac{5}{8}$), the remains of glue and adhering paper on the verso at the left margin. Pinholes appear across the top, with one set in the upper center. Written in black ink. The poem number is ornamentally drawn. In the lower left corner Whitman numbered the leaf 15 in pencil. 1860, p. 374; Camden, I, 158.]

XI.

Earth! Though | you look so impassive, | ample and spheric there | —I now suspect that | is not all,

I now suspect there is | something terrible in you, | ready to break forth,

For an athlete loves me, | —and I him—But toward | him there is something | fierce and terrible in me,

4 I dare not tell it in words— | not even in these songs.

1 Earth!] after this originally appeared 'My likeness!', which has been deleted (except for the exclamation) in a light ink. The *n* of 'likeness' is heavily mended over some smudged-out letter.

1 there] a semi-colon following has been smudged out while wet. There is a strong possibility that 'there' was added later, since its ink seems to be lighter and the pen finer.

3 For] *o* mended over *a*.

4 dare] *d* mended over the start of another letter, which may be a *c* (*query*, was 'can' about to be written?).

[FOLDER 33. One small piece of white wove paper ($3\frac{11}{16} \times 3\frac{5}{8}$), pinholes at the top and a few in the center. Written in black ink. The poem number is ornamentally drawn and has been partly cut off at the top. Whitman numbered the leaf in the lower left corner 13 with pencil, the 3 just possibly being written over another pencil digit. 1860, p. 373; Camden, I, 158.]

IX.

I dreamed in a dream of a | city where all the men | were like brothers,

O I saw them tenderly love | each other—I often saw | them, in numbers, walking | hand in hand;

I dreamed that was the city | of robust friends—Nothing | was greater there than | manly love—it | led the rest,

It was seen every hour in the | actions of the men of that city, | and in all their looks and | words.—

3 than manly] between these two words originally appeared, 'the | quality of', then deleted in pencil.

36.

EARTH! my likeness!
Though you look so impassive, ample and spheric there,
I now suspect that is not all;
I now suspect there is something fierce in you, eligible to burst forth;
For an athlete is enamoured of me—and I of him,
But toward him there is something fierce and terrible in me, eligible
  to burst forth,
I dare not tell it in words—not even in these songs.

34.

I DREAMED in a dream, I saw a city invincible to the attacks of the whole
  of the rest of the earth,
I dreamed that was the new City of Friends,
Nothing was greater there than the quality of robust love—it led the
  rest,
It was seen every hour in the actions of the men of that city,
And in all their looks and words.

[FOLDER 34. One leaf of white wove paper ($5\frac{1}{2} \times 3\frac{5}{8}$) made up from two smaller pieces pasted together, the upper measuring $3\frac{5}{16} \times 3\frac{9}{16}$ and the lower $2\frac{5}{8} \times 3\frac{5}{8}$. Pinholes appear along the top of the upper section and one set at the foot. One set at the top of the lower section goes through the paste-over and thus represents a pinning of the made-up leaf at its center. Both sections are written in black ink; but the lower is darker and written with a thicker pen. The poem number is ornamentally drawn. A short straight line appears below the final verse. Whitman numbered the leaf 9 in pencil in the lower left corner. The alterations in the lower section, and the lack of revision in the upper, lead to the view that the upper represents a fair-copy revised opening. 1860, pp. 372–73; Camden, I, 159.]

VI.

[upper section]

What think you I have | taken my pen to record?

Not the battle-ship, perfect-|model'd, majestic, that I saw | to day arrive in the offing, | under full sail,

Nor the splendors of the past | day—nor the splendors of | the night that envelopes me— | Nor the glory and growth of | the great city spread around | me,

[paste-on lower piece]

But the two men I saw | to-day on the pier, parting | the parting of dear friends.

5 The one to remain hung on | the other's neck and passionately | kissed him—while the one | to depart tightly prest the | one to remain in his arms.

[FOLDER 35. One small piece of white wove paper ($3\frac{11}{16} \times 6\frac{3}{4}$), pinholes at top and one set in the center. Written in light-brown ink. At the upper right is a short vertical stroke in blue pencil with a slightly curving horizontal stroke beginning at its foot and going right, rather like a 4 with a light or erased down stroke, but the purport is not clear. To the right is a circled figure 1 in light pencil, which is very likely the annotator's. Inverted in the lower right corner and partly cut off is the blind impression of a papermaker's lozenge die. At the bottom is 'MASS' and in the middle appears < > 'S. LEE'. Some word or words at the top are so flattened out as not to be read with certainty. Possibly this is the die of Platner and Smith, of Lee, Mass. 1860, pp. 375–76; Camden, I, 160.]

Sometimes, with one I love | I fill myself with rage | for fear I effuse unreturned | love;

1 love;] after an original comma has been added a semicolon in the same ink.

32.

WHAT think you I take my pen in hand to record?
The battle-ship, perfect-model'd, majestic, that I saw pass the offing
  to-day under full sail?
The splendors of the past day? Or the splendor of the night that en-
  velops me?
Or the vaunted glory and growth of the great city spread around me?
  —No;
But I record of two simple men I saw to-day, on the pier, in the midst
  of the crowd, parting the parting of dear friends,
The one to remain hung on the other's neck, and passionately kissed
  him,
While the one to depart, tightly prest the one to remain in his arms.

---

4 two men] originally, 'two young men', the deletion being made in the same ink.
5 to remain] interlined in the same ink above deleted 'who remained'.

5 to depart] interlined in the same ink above deleted 'who departed'.
5 to remain] interlined in the same ink above deleted 'who remained'.

39.

SOMETIMES with one I love, I fill myself with rage, for fear I effuse
  unreturned love;

But now I think there | is no unreturned love, | —the pay is certain, | one way or another,

3 Doubtless I could not | have perceived the universe | or written one of my | songs, if I had not | freely given myself to | comrades, to love.—

[FOLDER 36. One small piece of white wove paper (5¾ × 3⅝), thinned in the left margin as if once pasted and torn away. Pinholes appear across the top, with one set in the center. Written in black ink. The poem number is drawn ornamentally. Whitman numbered the leaf 16 in pencil in the lower left corner after it had been detached from whatever it was pasted to. 1860, p. 377; Camden, I, 160.]

XII

To the young man, many | things to absorb, to engraft, | to develop, I teach, that | he be my eleve,

2 But if through him speed | not the blood of | friendship, hot | and red—If he be not | silently selected by lovers, | and do not silently select | lovers—of what use were | it for him to seek to | become eleve of mine?

[FOLDER 38. One leaf of pink paper, a few pinholes in the center. Written in black ink. The original poem number 101 was crossed out, but before the deletion the final digit had been altered to a zero and then back to '1'. Later, to the right and with a different pen, was written '?100'. In the title the word 'One', traced first in pencil and then in ink, is interlined above 'Those' deleted first in pencil and then in ink. 1860, p. 376; Camden, I, 161.]

?100

To One Who Will Understand.

Among the men and women | of all times, I perceive that you pick me | out by secret and divine | signs,

You acknowledge none else—not | parent, wife, husband, friend, | any nearer or dearer to you than I am.—

Some are baffled—But you are not baffled—you | know me.—

O my lover and equal! I | meant that you should | discover me so by my faint | indirections,

5 And I, when I meet you, mean | to discover you by the | same in you.—

But now I think there is no unreturned love—the pay is certain, one
way or another,
Doubtless I could not have perceived the universe, or written one of
my poems, if I had not freely given myself to comrades, to love.

42.

To the young man, many things to absorb, to engraft, to develop,
I teach, to help him become élève of mine,
But if blood like mine circle not in his veins,
If he be not silently selected by lovers, and do not silently select lovers,
Of what use is it that he seek to become élève of mine?

1 develop] an original final *e* is crossed out
in pencil.
2 speed] interlined in pencil above deleted
'rolls'.
2 blood] 'red' originally appeared before
this but is crossed through in the same
ink.

2 friendship] before this, and beginning the
line, was originally 'divine', then deleted
in pencil.
2 mine?] just possibly the question mark has
been inserted or mended, although it is
in the same ink.

41.

1. AMONG the men and women, the multitude, I perceive one picking
me out by secret and divine signs,
Acknowledging none else—not parent, wife, husband, brother, child,
any nearer than I am;
Some are baffled—But that one is not—that one knows me.

2. Lover and perfect equal!
I meant that you should discover me so, by my faint indirections,
And I, when I meet you, mean to discover you by the like in you.

1 I perceive that] interlined above a caret,
and probably in a different pen.
1 signs,] after this was added and then deleted in pencil, '—You know me—you
draw close'.
2 nearer or dearer to you] first 'dearer to
you' was interlined in pencil above a caret
and deleted 'nigher'. Later, with the fine
pen, 'nearer or' was prefixed and the pencil interlineation, and its caret, traced
over in ink.
3 Some are . . . me.—] This verse was
crowded in, written with the fine pen, between the stanzas.

4 O my lover] originally, 'O young man! O
woman! O | my lover. . . .' All of the line
except for the first 'O' was crossed
through and a guide line brings down the
'O' to precede 'my lover'.
4 so] interlined above a caret.
5 And] the *A* is written over an original 'I',
smudged out while still wet.
5 I meet you] this was the original reading,
deleted to admit interlined 'we meet,',
which was deleted and the original words
restored below the line.

[FOLDER 39. One small piece of white wove paper (5¾ × 3¾), pinholes across the top and several in the upper center. Written in black ink. The poem number is ornamentally drawn. Whitman numbered the leaf 14 in the lower left corner. 1860, p. 377; Camden, I, 161.]

X

O you whom I often and silently come | where you are, that | I
    may be with you,
As I walk by your side, or | sit near, or remain in | the same room
    with you,
3 Little you know the subtle | electric fire that for | your sake is
    playing | within me.—

1 often and] interlined above a caret.
1 you are] before 'you' is the pronoun 'I', immediately crossed out before proceeding with 'you'.

[FOLDER 40. One leaf of ruled light-blue wove paper (6¾ × 3¹³⁄₁₆), two sets of pinholes in the center. Written in pencil. 1860, p. 376; Camden, I, 161.]

That shadow, my likeness, | that goes to and fro | seeking a liveli-
    hood, | chattering, chaffering,
How often I find | myself standing and looking | at it where it flits!
How often I question | whether that is really | me!
4 But in these, and among | my lovers, and among | my songs, O I
    never | question whether that | is really me!

2 find] Whitman first wrote 'stand' and then crossed it out before proceeding with 'find'.

43.

O YOU whom I often and silently come where you are, that I may be
with you,
As I walk by your side, or sit near, or remain in the same room with
you,
Little you know the subtle electric fire that for your sake is playing
within me.

40.

THAT shadow, my likeness, that goes to and fro, seeking a livelihood,
chattering, chaffering,
How often I find myself standing and looking at it where it flits,
How often I question and doubt whether that is really me;
But in these, and among my lovers, and carolling my songs,
O I never doubt whether that is really me.

[FOLDER 41. One leaf of pink paper consisting of two pasted-together sections, the whole measuring 7⅜ × 5⅛. Since the bottom section measures (from the verso side) 3⅞ vertically, and the top 4 9/16, it is clear that these two pieces without paste-over would make up a typical leaf of pink paper. Moreover, there is every evidence that the foot of the lower section once fitted the bottom of the upper piece, and thus that the two once formed a whole leaf which has been cut apart. What seems to have happened is this. Whitman wrote the poem originally on one side of a full leaf of this pink paper, but at the latest stage of revision, as indicated by the light ink of the upper section, he wanted to expand the beginning. Instead of retranscribing the whole poem, with these additions, he cut the leaf apart. On the verso of the original upper section he wrote in the light ink the new beginning, having turned the piece end-to-end. The beginning, therefore, is on the verso of the original top section, turned end-for-end. Below this verso section he then pasted the original ending of the poem from its recto lower section. No number or title appear above the revised opening, but they are not deleted at the head of the original start. There is only one set of pinholes toward the head of the original upper section. Whitman numbered the original start of the poem in ink as '101—', and at some time altered the final digit to '2'; later, he deleted the number and added in a fine pen '?101'. In the transcription given here the poem number and title come from the original opening but the verses below from the revised lines, the rejected verses being provided at the close. 1860, p. 378; Camden, I, 162.]

?101

To one a century hence, | or any number of cen-|turies hence —

[*rewritten lines, light ink, upper section*]

Throwing far, throwing over the head | of death, I, full of affection,

Full of life, compact, visible, | thirty-eight years old the | eighty-first year of The States,

To one a century hence, or any number | of centuries hence,

To you, yet unborn, these, | seeking you.—

[*lower section*]

5 When you read these, I that was | visible am become invisible,

Now it is you, compact, full | of life, realizing my poems, | seeking me;

If I were with you, I should | expect love and understanding | from you,

Be it as if I were with you—Be | not too certain but I am | with you.—

45.

1. FULL of life, sweet-blooded, compact, visible,
   I, forty years old the Eighty-third Year of The States,
   To one a century hence, or any number of centuries hence,
   To you, yet unborn, these, seeking you.

2. When you read these, I, that was visible, am become invisible;
   Now it is you, compact, visible, realizing my poems, seeking me,
   Fancying how happy you were, if I could be with you, and become your
       lover;
   Be it as if I were with you. Be not too certain but I am now with you.

---

1 head] what may be an original final *s* has been erased.

2 -eight] actually, spelled 'eght'. The final *t* is mended, while still wet, over one or more other letters, one of which is a *t*.

2 eighty-] *t* mended over original *y*.

3 centuries hence,] originally the line continued 'these,', but then this was deleted, probably immediately.

[*original opening, now on verso*]

   I, full of life, compact, visible, | thirty-eight years old the | eighty-
       first year of The | States,
   To you, yet unborn, these, seeking you.——

[FOLDER 42. Sixteen leaves of pink paper, numbered by Whitman in pencil in lower left corner 1–9 9½ 10–15. Leaf 9½ is of the same cutting as the rest of the paper. Written in blackish ink. Clusters of pinholes in center, and several sets at top. The poem number 90 is written above deleted '89—'. 1860, pp. 159–66; Camden, I, 206–12.]

[*leaf 1*]

90—

Feuillage

America always! Always me | joined! Always our own | feuillage!

Always Florida's green peninsula! | Always the priceless delta of Louisiana! Always the | cotton-fields of Alabama and | Texas!

Always California's golden | hills and hollows—and the | silver mountains of New | Mexico! Always soft-breathed Cuba!

Always the vast slope drained | by the Southern Sea—insep-|erable with the slopes drained | by the Eastern and Western | Seas,

[*leaf 2*]

5 The area the Eightieth year of | These States, the three millions | of square miles,

The eighteen thousand miles of | sea-coast and bay-coast | on the main—The twenty-six thousand miles | of river passage,

The seven millions of distinct | families, and the same | number of dwellings—Always | these and more, branching forth into | numberless branches,

Always the range and diversity | of America—the roominess and | space, previously unknown among | nations

Always the prairies, pastures, forests, vast | cities, travelers, Kanada the snows, | the great lakes, and the sea-beach,

[*leaf 3*]

10 Always The West, with strong native | persons, the increasing density, | friendly, threatening, ironical, | scorning invaders,

All sights, South, North, East— | All deeds, promiscuously done | at all times—All characters, | movements, attitudes—a few | noticed, myriads unnoticed,

1 feuillage] the *i* is inserted by mending.
2 peninsula] an original final *s* has been smudged out while still wet and the tail of the *a* mended over it.

3 golden hills] Whitman first wrote 'golden valleys—' and began the next line with a dash before stopping, deleting 'valleys—' and continuing the next line with 'hills' written over the dash.

Chants Democratic.

4.

AMERICA always!

Always me joined with you, whoever you are!

Always our own feuillage!

Always Florida's green peninsula! Always the priceless delta of Louisiana! Always the cotton-fields of Alabama and Texas!

Always California's golden hills and hollows—and the silver mountains of New Mexico! Always soft-breath'd Cuba!

Always the vast slope drained by the Southern Sea—inseparable with the slopes drained by the Eastern and Western Seas,

The area the Eighty-third year of These States—the three and a half millions of square miles,

The eighteen thousand miles of sea-coast and bay-coast on the main— the thirty thousand miles of river navigation,

The seven millions of distinct families, and the same number of dwellings—Always these and more, branching forth into numberless branches;

Always the free range and diversity! Always the continent of Democracy!

Always the prairies, pastures, forests, vast cities, travellers, Kanada, the snows;

Always these compact lands—lands tied at the hips with the belt stringing the huge oval lakes;

Always the West, with strong native persons—the increasing density there—the habitans, friendly, threatening, ironical, scorning invaders;

All sights, South, North, East—all deeds, promiscuously done at all times,

---

3 Always soft-breathed Cuba!] a later insertion in a blacker ink.

5 States,] a dash following the comma has been deleted and the comma strengthened.

5 square miles,] the next verse was originally, 'The Thirty-Two Supreme States, each | with its cluster of counties,'; in this verse 'Supreme' is interlined above a caret. The whole verse has been deleted.

6 twenty-] t written over some other letter.

7 seven] interlined above deleted 'five'.

7 forth] interlined above a caret.

7 numberless] interlined above a caret.

8 the range] originally 'the welcome range,'

but a single slanting stroke is drawn through the lc of 'welcome' to delete the word.

9 Always the prairies . . . sea-beach,] this verse is crowded in at the bottom of the page, and since the ink looks blacker and the pen thicker than the main text, it is just barely possible that the verse represents a later addition.

10 the increasing density,] originally 'many millions,'. In ink 'the increasing' is interlined above deleted 'many'; then, later, in pencil, 'millions' is deleted and 'density,' interlined.

In Mannahatta's streets I walking, | on these things feeding,

On interior rivers by night, | by the glare of pine knots, | steamboats wooding up,

Sunlight by day on the valley | of the Susquehannah, and on | the valleys of the | Potomac and Rappahannock, | and the valleys of the Roanoke | and of the Delaware,

[*leaf* 4]

15 In their northerly wilds, beasts of | prey haunting the Adiron-| dacks, the hills—or lapping | the Saginaw waters to drink,

In a lonesome inlet, the | sheldrake, lost from the | flock, sitting on the water, | rocking silently,

In farmers' barns, oxen in the | stable, their harvest labor | done, they resting standing— | they are too tired;

Afar on the Arctic ice the | she-walrus lying drowsily | while her cubs play around,

The hawk sailing where men | have not yet sailed, the | farthest polar sea, open, | ripply, crystalline, beyond the | floes;

20 White drift spooning ahead where the | ship in the tempest dashes;

[*leaf* 5]

On solid land what is done | in cities during the sound of bells | all striking midnight | together,

In primitive woods the sounds there also | sounding—the howl of the | wolf, the scream of the | panther, and the hoarse | bellow of the elk,

In winter, beneath the hard | blue ice of Moosehead | lake—in summer, visible | through the clear waters, | the great trout swimming,

In lower latitudes, in warmer air, | in the Carolinas, the large | black buzzard floating slowly, | high beyond the tree-tops.— | Below, the red-cedar, festooned | with green-gray tylandria— the | pines and cypress growing out of | the white sand that spreads far | and flat,

14 valleys of the Potomac] originally, 'valley of the Roanoke'|. Apparently 'Roanoke' was crossed out and the *s* added to 'valley' before beginning the next line with 'Potomac'.

15 northerly] interlined above a caret.

15 waters] an original following comma has been deleted, probably in consequence of continuing with (or adding) 'to drink,'.

18 Arctic ice] an interlineation above a caret, 'in the cold daylight,' has been crossed through.

All characters, movements, growths—a few noticed, myriads unnoticed,

Through Mannahatta's streets I walking, these things gathering;

On interior rivers, by night, in the glare of pine knots, steamboats wooding up;

Sunlight by day on the valley of the Susquehanna, and on the valleys of the Potomac and Rappahannock, and the valleys of the Roanoke and Delaware;

In their northerly wilds beasts of prey haunting the Adirondacks, the hills—or lapping the Saginaw waters to drink;

In a lonesome inlet, a sheldrake, lost from the flock, sitting on the water, rocking silently;

In farmers' barns, oxen in the stable, their harvest labor done—they rest standing—they are too tired;

Afar on arctic ice, the she-walrus lying drowsily, while her cubs play around;

The hawk sailing where men have not yet sailed—the farthest polar sea, ripply, crystalline, open, beyond the floes;

White drift spooning ahead, where the ship in the tempest dashes;

On solid land, what is done in cities, as the bells all strike midnight together;

In primitive woods, the sounds there also sounding—the howl of the wolf, the scream of the panther, and the hoarse bellow of the elk;

In winter beneath the hard blue ice of Moosehead Lake—in summer visible through the clear waters, the great trout swimming;

In lower latitudes, in warmer air, in the Carolinas, the large black buzzard floating slowly high beyond the tree-tops,

Below, the red cedar, festooned with tylandria—the pines and cypresses, growing out of the white sand that spreads far and flat;

---

19 farthest] interlined above deleted 'northernmost'.

21 during the sound of bells] the line first read | 'when in cities the bells'|. After 'the' was first placed a caret and above this 'sound of'. Then 'during the' was interlined above a caret after 'cities', the original 'the' crossed out, and 'sound of' traced over. At some indeterminate time 'when' was deleted by a heavy stroke.

21 all striking midnight] the line first read | 'at noon strike twelve'|. 'all' was inter-

lined above a caret, and *ing* mended over final *e* of 'strike'. 'midnight' is written over deleted 'twelve'. 'at noon' is crossed through with the same heavy stroke that excised 'when' in the line above and which differs from the other deleting strokes in these two lines.

22 woods the] interlined with a caret (the two words seemingly at different times) above deleted 'their'.

22 there] interlined above a caret.

[*leaf* 6]

25 Rude boats descending the Big | Pedee—climbing plants, | parasites | with colored flowers and | berries, enveloping huge trees —the waving drapery | on the live-oak, | trailing long and low, noise-|lessly waved by the wind,

The camp of Georgia wagoners | after dark—the supper-fires, | and the cooking and eating | by whites and negroes— | Thirty or forty great wagons— | the mules, cattle, horses feeding | from troughs—The shadows, | gleams, | up under the leaves of the | old sycamore trees—also | the flames and the black smoke of the pitch-|pine fires, curling and rising;

[*leaf* 7]

Southern fishermen fishing—the | sounds and inlets of the | North Carolina coast—the | shad-fishery and the herring-|fishery— the large sweep-|seines—the windlasses on | the shore, worked by horses— | the cleaning, curing, and | packing-houses;

Deep in the forest in the piney | woods, turpentine and tar | dropping from the incisions | in the trees—There is the | turpentine distillery—there | are the negroes at work, in | good health—the ground | in all directions is covered | with pine straw;

In Tennessee and Kentucky, slaves busy in the | coalings, at the forge, by | the furnace-blaze, or at the | corn-shucking,

[*leaf* 8]

30 In Virginia, the planter's son | returning after a long absence, | joyfully welcomed and kissed | by the aged mulatto nurse;

On rivers, boatmen safely moored | at night-fall in their boats, | under high river-banks— | Some dance to the sound | of the banjo and fiddle, | and the singing of the | chorus—some sit on the | gunwales, smoking and talking;

Late in the afternoon the | mocking-bird, the American | mimic, singing in the Great | Dismal Swamp—There are | the greenish waters, the | resinous odor, the plenteous | moss, the cypress tree, and | the juniper tree;

25 plants,] after this originally appeared 'en-vel-|oping huge trees,' which has been deleted.

25 enveloping huge trees—] interlined with a caret before the original dash after 'berries'.

Rude boats descending the big Pedee—climbing plants, parasites, with colored flowers and berries, enveloping huge trees,

The waving drapery on the live oak, trailing long and low, noiselessly waved by the wind;

The camp of Georgia wagoners, just after dark—the supper-fires, and the cooking and eating by whites and negroes,

Thirty or forty great wagons—the mules, cattle, horses, feeding from troughs,

The shadows, gleams, up under the leaves of the old sycamore-trees— the flames—also the black smoke from the pitch-pine, curling and rising;

Southern fishermen fishing—the sounds and inlets of North Carolina's coast—the shad-fishery and the herring-fishery—the large sweep-seines—the windlasses on shore worked by horses—the clearing, curing, and packing houses;

Deep in the forest, in the piney woods, turpentine and tar dropping from the incisions in the trees—There is the turpentine distillery,

There are the negroes at work, in good health—the ground in all directions is covered with pine straw;

In Tennessee and Kentucky, slaves busy in the coalings, at the forge, by the furnace-blaze, or at the corn-shucking;

In Virginia, the planter's son returning after a long absence, joyfully welcomed and kissed by the aged mulatto nurse;

On rivers, boatmen safely moored at night-fall, in their boats, under the shelter of high banks,

Some of the younger men dance to the sound of the banjo or fiddle— others sit on the gunwale, smoking and talking;

Late in the afternoon, the mocking-bird, the American mimic, singing in the Great Dismal Swamp—there are the greenish waters, the resinous odor, the plenteous moss, the cypress tree, and the juniper tree;

---

25 drapery] after this was written, and then deleted 'of moss'.

26 negroes] *e* mended over an *s*.

26 gleams,] after this originally followed 'flicker, and the glare'|, then deleted.

26 old] an inadvertent repetition 'of the' beginning the line has been deleted.

26 flames and the] interlined above a caret.

29 and Kentucky,] interlined above a caret.

31 night-fall,] a hyphen has been added to 'night', and 'fall' interlined above a caret.

32 mimic] first minim of the second *m* mended over some letter like an *s*.

[*leaf* 9]

> Northward, young men of | Mannahatta—the target | company,
> from an excursion | returning home at evening, | the musket-
> muzzles each | bearing a bunch of | flowers, presented by
> women;

> Children tired at play— | —Or on his father's lap A young | boy
> fallen asleep—how | his lips move! how he | smiles in his sleep!

35 The scout riding on horseback | over the plains west of | the Mis-
> sissippi—he ascends | a knoll, and sweeps his | eye around;

> In the crowd of Oregonese, | one old hunter leaning on | his rifle
> and standing taller | than any of the rest;

[*leaf* 10 (9½)]

> The Texas cotton-field and | the negro-cabins—drivers | driving
> mules or oxen before | rude carts—cotton-bales | piled on rude
> wharves,

> A slave approaching sulkily— | he wears an iron necklace | and
> prong—he has raw | sores on his shoulders,

> The runaway, steering his course | by the north star—the | pack of
> negro-dogs chained | in couples pursuing;

40 The American soul with equal | hemispheres—one Love, | one
> Dilation or | Pride;

> In arriere, the peace-talk with the | Cherokees, the aborigines—
> the | calumet, the pipe of friendship, | arbitration, and en-
> dorsement—the | sachem blowing the smoke first toward the
> | sun, and then toward the earth,

[*leaf* 11 (10)]

> The drama of the scalp-dance | enacted with painted faces | and
> guttural exclamations— | the setting out of the war-|party—
> the long and stealthy | march—the swinging hatchets—the
> surprise and | slaughter of enemies;

> All the acts, growths, scenes, ways, | persons, reminiscences, of
> These | States—any thing, small or large;

33 Mannahatta] a preceding 'the' ending the line above has been deleted, as well as a comma following 'Mannahatta'.

33 each] interlined above deleted 'every'. Following at the start of the next line, 'one'

has been crossed through at the same time.

34 play— | —Or on . . . lap'] originally 'play —on the | playground—'. This has been deleted and after its last dash (not de-

Northward, young men of Mannahatta—the target company from an excursion returning home at evening—the musket-muzzles all bear bunches of flowers presented by women;

Children at play—or on his father's lap a young boy fallen asleep, (how his lips move! how he smiles in his sleep!)

The scout riding on horseback over the plains west of the Mississippi— he ascends a knoll and sweeps his eye around;

California life—the miner, bearded, dressed in his rude costume—the stanch California friendship—the sweet air—the graves one, in passing, meets, solitary, just aside the horse-path;

Down in Texas, the cotton-field, the negro-cabins—drivers driving mules or oxen before rude carts—cotton-bales piled on banks and wharves;

Encircling all, vast-darting, up and wide, the American Soul, with equal hemispheres—one Love, one Dilation or Pride;

In arriere, the peace-talk with the Iroquois, the aborigines—the calumet, the pipe of good-will arbitration, and indorsement,

The sachem blowing the smoke first toward the sun and then toward the earth,

The drama of the scalp-dance enacted with painted faces and guttural exclamations,

The setting out of the war-party—the long and stealthy march,

The single file—the swinging hatchets—the surprise and slaughter of enemies;

All the acts, scenes, ways, persons, attitudes of These States—reminiscences, all institutions,

All These States, compact—Every square mile of These States, without excepting a particle—you also—me also,

---

leted) above a caret was first written '—Or a yo', at which point Whitman deleted 'a yo' [*query*, 'young'?] before proceeding with the interlineation 'on his father's lap'. The following capital 'A' was not reduced through oversight.

34 move!] the exclamation point has been added after a dash was deleted.

37 The Texas. . . .] the numbering as 9½ of this leaf is odd, the more especially since its last verse is written progressively smaller to crowd it in on this leaf, as if Whitman were working from copy and could not extend the limits of his numbering. On the other hand, if this page is an addition, which the numbering might suggest, and which might be indicated by a presumed close connection between the end of leaf 9 and the beginning of leaf 10, which the first lines of leaf 9½ seem to break off, then it must be considered that there is no sign of any difference in pen or ink, and the leaf of paper itself, is cut precisely like the rest of the batch for this whole poem, and obviously belongs with it. Possibly Whitman merely numbered two successive leaves as 9, by a slip, and then repaired the anomaly by adding the ½ to the second leaf-number.

40 Dilation] written immediately after deleted 'Dlation'. The following 'or' has a mended *o* but probably only a touching up of an original *o*.

42 —the swinging hatchets—] interlined above a caret placed below the original dash after 'march'.

Me pleased, rambling in lanes and | country fields—Me observing | the spiral flight of two little | yellow butterflies, shuffling between | each other, ascending high in | the air,

45 The darting swallow, the destroyer | of insects, the fall traveler | southward, but returning northward | early in the spring,

[*leaf* 12 (11)]

The country-boy at the close | of the day driving the herd | of cows, and shouting to | them as they stop to | browse by the roadside;

The city-wharf—the departing | ship, and the sailors | heaving at the capstan,

In the low dance-cellar at | night the bloat-faced | prostitutes drinking at the | bar with the men,

In the circus, the rider | riding his daring feats on | a swift true-footed horse;

50 The setting summer sun shining | in my open window, showing | me flies balancing athwart | the centre of the room, up | and down, casting swift shadows in | specks on the opposite wall where the | glare is;

[leaf 13 (12)]

The athletic American matron | speaking in public to thou-|sands of listeners;

Males, females, immigrants, com-|binations, the large diversity | of The States, and the money-|makers,

Factories, machinery, the mechanical | forces, the windlass, lever, | pulley—all certainties,

The certainty of space, increase, | freedom, futurity, individualism,

55 In space, the sporades, the scattered | islands, the stars—On the | firm earth, the lands, my lands!

Southward there I, screaming, with | wings slow flapping, with | the myriads of gulls wintering | along the coast of Florida— | Or in Louisiana, with | pelicans breeding,

[*leaf* 14 (13)]

Otherways there, atwixt the banks | of the Arkansaw, the Rio | Grande, the Nueces, the | Brazos, the Tombigbee, | the Red River, the | Saskatchawan, or the Osage, | I with the spring waters | running;

Me pleased, rambling in lanes and country fields, Paumanok's fields,

Me, observing the spiral flight of two little yellow butterflies, shuffling between each other, ascending high in the air;

The darting swallow, the destroyer of insects—the fall traveller southward, but returning northward early in the spring;

The country boy at the close of the day, driving the herd of cows, and shouting to them as they loiter to browse by the road-side;

The city wharf—Boston, Philadelphia, Baltimore, Charleston, New Orleans, San Francisco,

The departing ships, when the sailors heave at the capstan;

Evening—me in my room—the setting sun,

The setting summer sun shining in my open window, showing me flies, suspended, balancing in the air in the centre of the room, darting athwart, up and down, casting swift shadows in specks on the opposite wall, where the shine is;

The athletic American matron speaking in public to crowds of listeners;

Males, females, immigrants, combinations—the copiousness—the individuality and sovereignty of The States, each for itself—the money-makers;

Factories, machinery, the mechanical forces—the windlass, lever, pulley—All certainties,

The certainty of space, increase, freedom, futurity,

In space, the sporades, the scattered islands, the stars—on the firm earth, the lands, my lands,

O lands! all so dear to me—what you are, (whatever it is,) I become a part of that, whatever it is,

Southward there, I screaming, with wings slow flapping, with the myriads of gulls wintering along the coasts of Florida—or in Louisiana, with pelicans breeding,

Otherways, there, atwixt the banks of the Arkansaw, the Rio Grande, the Nueces, the Brazos, the Tombigbee, the Red River, the Saskatchawan, or the Osage, I with the spring waters laughing and skipping and running;

45 northward] the last few letters are mended in order to insert the *r*.

49 rider] interlined in pencil above deleted 'circus-boy'.

50 flies] a preceding 'the' has been deleted.

50 casting] *c* written over the start of some other letter, perhaps *s*.

52 The] *T* mended from *t*.

56 myriads] *a* written over original *d* before the *ds* added.

⟦ 133 ⟧

Northward, on the sands, on | some shallow bay of | Paumanok, I, with parties | of snowy herons, wading in the | wet to seek worms and | aquatic plants,

Retreating, triumphantly twittering, | the king-bird, from piercing | the crow with its bill | for amusement—and I | triumphantly twittering,

[leaf 15 (14)]

60 The migrating flock of wild-|geese alighting in autumn | to refresh themselves—the | body of the flock feed— | the sentinels outside move | around with erect heads | watching, and are from time | to time relieved by new sentinels— | and I feeding and taking | turns with the rest;

In Kanadian forests, the moose, | large as an ox, cornered by | hunters, rising desperately on | his hind-feet, and plunging | with his fore-feet, the | hoofs as sharp as knives— | And I plunging at the | hunters, cornered and desperate;

[*leaf* 16 (15)]

In the Mannahatta, streets, piers, | shipping, store-houses, and | the countless workmen | working in the shops—and | I of the Mannahatta, and | no less in myself than | the whole of the Manna-|hatta in itself;

Nativities, climates, the grass of | the great Pastoral Plains,

Cities, labors, death, animals, | products, good and evil— | These me,

These affording in all their particulars | endless feuillage to me | and to America, how can | I do less than pass them | to afford the like to you?

65 How can I but offer you divine leaves, | that you also be eligible as I am?

How can I but invite you for yourself | to collect bouquets of the incomparable | feuillage of These States?

---

57 Otherways there,] interlined with a caret above deleted 'Downward'.
57 waters] while still wet three letters after *wa* were smudged out and *ter* written over them, *s* then being added. The general impression is that of a slip in the spelling being mended.

Northward, on the sands, on some shallow bay of Paumanok, I, with parties of snowy herons wading in the wet to seek worms and aquatic plants;

Retreating, triumphantly twittering, the king-bird, from piercing the crow with its bill, for amusement—And I triumphantly twittering;

The migrating flock of wild geese alighting in autumn to refresh themselves—the body of the flock feed—the sentinels outside move around with erect heads watching, and are from time to time relieved by other sentinels—And I feeding and taking turns with the rest;

In Kanadian forests, the moose, large as an ox, cornered by hunters, rising desperately on his hind-feet, and plunging with his fore-feet, the hoofs as sharp as knives—And I, plunging at the hunters, cornered and desperate;

In the Mannahatta, streets, piers, shipping, storehouses, and the countless workmen working in the shops,

And I too of the Mannahatta, singing thereof—and no less in myself than the whole of the Mannahatta in itself,

Singing the song of These, my ever united lands—my body no more inevitably united, part to part, and made one identity, any more than my lands are inevitably united, and made ONE IDENTITY,

Nativities, climates, the grass of the great Pastoral Plains,

Cities, labors, death, animals, products, good and evil—these me,

These affording, in all their particulars, endless feuillage to me and to America, how can I do less than pass the clew of the union of them, to afford the like to you?

Whoever you are! how can I but offer you divine leaves, that you also be eligible as I am?

How can I but, as here, chanting, invite you for yourself to collect bouquets of the incomparable feuillage of These States?

---

58 some] written immediately after the deletion of original 'the'.
58 wading] interlined above a caret.
59 with] a vertical stroke, evidently the start of some letter, has been deleted before continuing with 'with'.

60 turns] *s* written over smudged-out *w*.
61 And] *A* written over *d*.
62 no less] this was written after deletion of the false start 'I'.
65 leaves] *l* mended over *L*.

⟦ 135 ⟧

[FOLDER 43. Six leaves of pink paper; clusters of pinholes in the center. Written in blackish ink, the section numbered in pencil. Whitman has numbered the leaves in pencil in the right top corner 1–6. The original title was 'Poemet.—'. This was deleted and in the light revising ink 'Evolutions.—' written above it. The poem number is written in a darker ink than the text, 1860, pp. 174–76; Camden, I, 292–94.]

[*leaf 1*]   41—

Evolutions.——

With antecedents—With my | fathers and mothers—with | the
    accumulations of | past cycles,
With all which, had it not | been, I would not now | be here as
    I am,
With Egypt, India, Phenicia, | Greece, | and Rome,
With the Celt, the Scandina-|vian, the Alb, and the | Saxon,
5 With antique maratime | ventures—With laws, | artisanship,
    wars, and | journeys,
With the poet, the skald, the saga, | the myth, and the oracle,

[*leaf 2*]
With the sale of slaves— | with enthusiasts—with | the trouba-
    dour, the | crusader, and the | monk,
With those old continents | whence we have come | to this new
    continent,
With the fading kingdoms | and kings over there— | with the
    fading religions | and priests,
10 With the small shores | we look back to, from | our own large and
    present | shores,
With countless thousands | of years drawing themselves | onward,
    and arrived at | these years, and making | this year,

[*leaf 3*]
With this year sending itself | ahead countless | years to come.—

2

O but it is not the years— | It is I,
I touch all laws and tally | all antecedents,
15 I am the skald, the oracle, | the monk, and the knight— | I easily
    include them, | and far more,
I stand amid time beginningless | and endless—I stand | between
    evil and good,

7.

1. WITH antecedents,
   With my fathers and mothers, and the accumulations of past ages,
   With all which, had it not been, I would not now be here, as I am,
   With Egypt, India, Phenicia, Greece, and Rome,
   With the Celt, the Scandinavian, the Alb, and the Saxon,
   With antique maritime ventures—with laws, artisanship, wars, and
      journeys,
   With the poet, the skald, the saga, the myth, and the oracle,
   With the sale of slaves—with enthusiasts—with the troubadour, the
      crusader, and the monk,
   With those old continents whence we have come to this new continent,
   With the fading kingdoms and kings over there,
   With the fading religions and priests,
   With the small shores we look back to, from our own large and pres-
      ent shores,
   With countless years drawing themselves onward, and arrived at these
      years,
   You and Me arrived—America arrived, and making this year,
   This year! sending itself ahead countless years to come.

2. O but it is not the years—it is I—it is You,
   We touch all laws, and tally all antecedents,
   We are the skald, the oracle, the monk, and the knight—we easily in-
      clude them, and more,
   We stand amid time, beginningless and endless—we stand amid evil
      and good,

---

2 as I am,] beneath this verse and the beginning of the next was crowded in later
in a fine pen 'With what the Eastern
Hemisphere has pass'd down to me,'. The
E of 'Eastern' was written over a *W* before
the rest of the word was written. This
interlineation was then in part revised.
'what' was deleted and 'all' written above
it in pencil. In ink, 'down' was deleted
and 'over' interlined above a caret, but
this has been crossed through in pencil.
Finally, the whole interlineation was taken
out with a line drawn in the light ink.

3 Greece] before this was first written, |
'China, Persia,' which was deleted in the
light ink.

8 those] mended with the fine pen from
original 'the'.

10 our own] interlined in the light ink above
deleted 'these'.

11 this year,] interlined above deleted 'these
years,'.

12 this year,] interlined with the fine pen
above a caret and deleted 'that'.

12 ahead countless] 'ahead' interlined in the
same ink above deleted 'onward'. In the
light ink, 'countless' interlined above deleted 'thousands of'.

15 them] *th* written over another letter, perhaps an *m*.

16 endless—] a comma after this word and
before the dash was smudged out while
wet.

16 evil] the tail of the *l* is mended over the
start of an *s*.

All swings around me—there | is as much darkness as | light,
The very sun swings itself and | its system of planets around
    me— | Its sun and system the same,

[*leaf* 4]

I have the idea of all and | am all, and believe in | all,

20 I believe materialism is | true, and spiritualism | is true—I reject
    no | part,
    (Have I forgotten any part? | Come to me whoever and | whatever,
    till I give you | recognition,)
I respect Assyria, China, | Teutonia | and the Hebrews,
I recognize each theory, | myth, god, and demigod,
I see that the old accounts, | bibles, | genealogies, are true, | with-
    out exception,

[*leaf* 5]

25 I promulge that all past | days were what they | should have been
    — | And that to-day is what | it should be—And | that
    America is,
And that they could no-how | have been better than they | were—
    And that to-day | could no-how be better | than it is.

3

I am he who means the past,
And I am he who means the | present time—Always | the present
    time, in | myself or yourself,
I know the past was great, | and the future will be | great—And
    I know both | conjoint in the present | time, in myself or |
    yourself,

[*leaf* 6]

30 And that there is no untruth | in time, and no imper-|fection in
    time, past, | present, or future,
And that time, materials, | spirits, go with me— | And that com-
    pleteness | goes with me,

18 Its] *I* mended over *i.*
18 same,] a dash after 'same' was deleted
when the comma was added. Beginning
a new line, Whitman wrote 'I have' and
then deleted the words in favor of starting a new verse on the next leaf with the
same opening.

19 am all, and believe in] 'am' was interlined above deleted 'believe in' and 'believe in' interlined farther on with a caret
and guide line above deleted 'am'.
22 China] interlined without a comma in the
light ink above deleted 'Syria,'. At the
start of the next line, a stroke of the

All swings around us—there is as much darkness as light,
The very sun swings itself and its system of planets around us,
Its sun, and its again, all swing around us.

3. As for me,
   I have the idea of all, and am all, and believe in all;
   I believe materialism is true, and spiritualism is true—I reject no part.

4. Have I forgotten any part?
   Come to me, whoever and whatever, till I give you recognition.

5. I respect Assyria, China, Teutonia, and the Hebrews,
   I adopt each theory, myth, god, and demi-god,
   I see that the old accounts, bibles, genealogies, are true, without ex-
      ception,
   I assert that all past days were what they should have been,
   And that they could no-how have been better than they were,
   And that to-day is what it should be—and that America is,
   And that to-day and America could no-how be better than they are.

6. In the name of These States, and in your and my name, the Past,
   And in the name of These States, and in your and my name, the Pres-
      ent time.

7. I know that the past was great, and the future will be great,
   And I know that both curiously conjoint in the present time,
   (For the sake of him I typify—for the common average man's sake—
      your sake, if you are he;)

---

pen in this light ink has crossed through 'Hindostan', originally written before 'Teutonia'.

24 accounts,] interlined with the fine pen above deleted 'histories,'. Beginning the next line, the original 'lives, legends,' has been deleted before 'bibles' with a pen stroke in the light ink.

26 have been] interlined with a caret above deleted 'be'.

27 I am he . . . past,] crowded in, written in the light ink in the stanza space. A paragraph sign precedes the verse.

28 And] interlined, with a preceding paragraph sign, above a caret and in the light ink.

And that where I am | and the present day is, | there is the centre
    of | all days, all races,
And there is the meaning of all that has ever | come of races and
    days, | or that ever will come.

33 there is the meaning] interlined in the text ink above a caret. Deleted 'central' appears before 'meaning'.

[FOLDER 44. Six leaves of pink paper; a cluster of pinholes in the center and in left margin. Written in a blackish ink. In the upper right corner Whitman numbered the leaves in pencil 1–6. The first leaf consists of two pasted-together pieces, the upper measuring 3¾ vertically, and the lower 6⅞, the whole totaling 10 1/16 when pasted together. Since the upper section is written in the light revising ink, including the title, it seems clear that the opening lines have been expanded from those cut off from the original leaf, or lower section, and that the first three verses are a revision. Owing to the length of the made-up leaf (a normal leaf of pink paper measures about 8⅜ vertically), the foot has been severely worn and the early letters of the opening words have been lost. 1860, pp. 176–79; Camden, II, 278–80.]

[*leaf 1, upper section*]

A Sunset Carol.

Splendor of falling day floating and | filling me,
How prophetic—hour resuming the | past,
Inflating my throat—you, Earth | and Life! till the last ray |
    gleams, I sing.—

[*pasted-on lower section*]
    Open mouth of my soul, | uttering gladness!
5 Eyes of my soul, seeing per-|fection!
Natural life of me, faithfully | praising things,
Corroborating forever the triumph | of things.

Illustrious every one!
Illustrious what we name | space, the sphere of | unnumbered
    spirits
10 Illustrious the mystery of motion | in all beings, even the | tiniest
    insect
    <   >strious the attribute of speech— | < s>enses—the
    body,

And that where I am, or you are, this present day, there is the centre
    of all days, all races,
And there is the meaning, to us, of all that has ever come of races and
    days, or ever will come.

8.

1. SPLENDOR of falling day, floating and filling me,
    Hour prophetic—hour resuming the past,
    Inflating my throat—you, divine average!
    You, Earth and Life, till the last ray gleams, I sing.

2. Open mouth of my Soul, uttering gladness,
    Eyes of my Soul, seeing perfection,
    Natural life of me, faithfully praising things,
    Corroborating forever the triumph of things.

3. Illustrious every one!
    Illustrious what we name space—sphere of unnumbered spirits,
    Illustrious the mystery of motion, in all beings, even the tiniest insect,
    Illustrious the attribute of speech—the senses—the body,

---

5 Eyes] originally this word had concluded the previous line after 'gladness!', but it was there crossed out in light ink and put in the left margin of the continuing line below in order to form the start of a new verse.

[leaf 2]

Illustrious the yet shining light! | Illustrious the soft reflection | of the moon in the eastern sky

Illustrious world | whatever I see or hear | or touch

Good in all!

15 In the satisfaction and aplomb | of animals,
In the annual return of the | seasons,
In the hilarity of youth,
In the strength and flush | of manhood,
In the grandeur and exqui-|siteness of old age,
20 In the superb vistas of | death.—

Wonderful to be here!
The heart to jet the all-alike | and innocent blood,
To breathe the air, how de-|licious!

[leaf 3]

To speak! To walk! To | seize something by the | hand!
25 To be conscious of my | body, so perfect, so | large!
To be this incredible God | I am!
To move among these other | Gods—these men and | women!

Wonderful how I celebrate | you and myself!
How my thoughts play | subtly at the spectacles | around!
30 How clouds pass silently overhead!
How the earth darts on and | on! And how the sun, | moon, stars, dart on and on!

[leaf 4]

How the water sports and | sings! (Surely it is alive!)
How the trees stand out | there with strong trunks— | with branches and leaves!
(Surely there is something more | in each of the trees— | some living soul!)

35 O amazement of things! Even | the least particle!
O spirituality of things!

12 yet shining] interlined in light ink above deleted 'shining'.   12 the moon . . . sky] interlined in the light ink above deleted 'moons at night!'

Illustrious the passing light! Illustrious the pale reflection on the moon
    in the western sky!
Illustrious whatever I see, or hear, or touch, to the last.

4. Good in all,
    In the satisfaction and aplomb of animals,
    In the annual return of the seasons,
    In the hilarity of youth,
    In the strength and flush of manhood,
    In the grandeur and exquisiteness of old age,
    In the superb vistas of Death.

5. Wonderful to depart!
    Wonderful to be here!
    The heart, to jet the all-alike and innocent blood,
    To breathe the air, how delicious!
    To speak! to walk! to seize something by the hand!
    To prepare for sleep, for bed—to look on my rose-colored flesh,
    To be conscious of my body, so amorous, so large,
    To be this incredible God I am,
    To have gone forth among other Gods—those men and women I love.

6. Wonderful how I celebrate you and myself!
    How my thoughts play subtly at the spectacles around!
    How the clouds pass silently overhead!
    How the earth darts on and on! and how the sun, moon, stars, dart
      on and on!
    How the water sports and sings! (Surely it is alive!)
    How the trees rise and stand up—with strong trunks—with branches
      and leaves!
    (Surely there is something more in each of the trees—some living
      Soul.)

7. O amazement of things! even the least particle!
    O spirituality of things!

---

13 Illustrious world . . . touch] the stanza
originally ended with the line 'Illustrious
the soul!'. At first 'the soul!' was deleted
and 'the whole' interlined, then the line
continued, all in the light ink, 'world |
whatever . . . hear | or touch'. Then 'the
whole' was crossed through. There is a
strong possibility that 'the whole' is in a
slightly different ink from the rest of the
addition, and may precede it in point of
time. This is somewhat buttressed by
an ambiguous vertical stroke following
'whole', which may represent an exclamation point.
26 God] G is triple underscored.
27 Gods] a currently deleted comma follows.

O strain musical, flowing | through ages and continents | —now reaching me and | America!

I take your strong chords— | I intersperse them, and | cheerfully pass them | forward.—

I too carol the sun, ushered, or at | noon, or, as now, setting,

[*leaf* 5]

40 I too throb to the brain | and beauty of the earth, | and of all the growths | of the earth,

I too have felt the resistless | call of myself.—

As I sailed down the | Mississippi,

As I wandered over the | prairies,

As I have lived—As I | have looked through | my windows, my eyes,

45 As I went forth in the | morning—as I beheld | the light breaking in | the east,

As I bathed on the beach | on the Eastern Sea, and | again on the beach on | the Western Sea,

[*leaf* 6]

As I roamed the streets of | inland Chicago—Whatever | streets I have roamed,

Wherever I have been, I have | been charged with a | charge of contentment | and triumph.—

I sing the endless finales | of things,

50 I say Nature continues—Glory | continues.—

I praise with electric voice,

For I do not see one im-|perfection in the universe,

And I do not see one law | at last lamentable in | the universe.—

O setting sun!

55 I warble under you, if none else does, | unmitigated adoration.—

37 America!] an original comma after the word has been crossed through and the exclamation added in the same ink.   39 I too carol . . . setting,] crowded in at the bottom of the leaf in the light ink as an addition.

O strain musical, flowing through ages and continents—now reaching me and America!
I take your strong chords—I intersperse them, and cheerfully pass them
forward.

8. I too carol the sun, ushered, or at noon, or setting,
I too throb to the brain and beauty of the earth, and of all the growths
of the earth,
I too have felt the resistless call of myself.

9. As I sailed down the Mississippi,
As I wandered over the prairies,
As I have lived—As I have looked through my windows, my eyes,
As I went forth in the morning—As I beheld the light breaking in the
east,
As I bathed on the beach of the Eastern Sea, and again on the beach
on the Western Sea,
As I roamed the streets of inland Chicago—whatever streets I have
roamed,
Wherever I have been, I have charged myself with contentment and
triumph.

10. I sing the Equalities,
I sing the endless finales of things,
I say Nature continues—Glory continues,
I praise with electric voice,
For I do not see one imperfection in the universe,
And I do not see one cause or result lamentable at last in the universe.

11. O setting sun! O when the time comes,
I still warble under you, if none else does, unmitigated adoration!

---

44 —As] *A* is triple underscored.
44 through] apparently written immediately
after deleted 'forth'.
44 windows,] the comma is added in pencil.
46 Eastern Sea] the capitals are triple underscored.

47 Whatever] *W* mended from *w* and triple
underscored.
54-55 O setting . . . adoration.—] added in
the light ink.

[FOLDER 45. Two leaves of pink paper. The first is a normal leaf measuring 8⅜ × 5¹⁄₁₆. The second is composed of two pasted-together pieces, the upper measuring 2¼ vertically, and the lower 7¼; together, the measurement is 8⅝. The single verse (5) in the upper section is written in the light revising ink, whereas the rest are in a very dark ink; hence Whitman seems to have cut off the original verse from the top of the leaf and revised it by means of the paste-on upper section. On the verso of this added upper section are three deleted draft verses for "So Long" (see Appendix to that poem). A cluster of pinholes appears in the center of the two leaves. Within a half circle in the top right corner of the first leaf Whitman wrote in black ink with a fine pen '2ᵈ | piece | in Book'. 1860, pp. 179–80; Camden, II, 275–76.]

[leaf 1]

Thought.

Of these years I sing—how | they pass through convulsed | pains,
    as through parturitions;

How America illustrates birth, | gigantic youth, the promise, | the
    sure fulfilment, despite | of people,—illustrates evil as well as
    good,

How many hold despairingly | yet to the models departed, | castes,
    myths, authorities, | the laws, and to infidelity,

How few see the arrived models, | The States—or see | freedom,
    or spirituality,— | or hold any faith in the | results, (But I see
    that | the results are glorious | and inevitable—and that | they
    again but lead to | other results,)

[leaf 2, upper section]

5 How the great cities appear— | How the people, the democ-|racies,
    coarse, wilful, as | I love them

[leaf 2, lower section]

How the divine whirl, the | contest, the wrestle of evil with good,
    the sounding and | resounding, keep on and | on,

How society waits unformed, | and is between things ended | and
    things begun,

How America is the continent | of glories and of the triumph |
    of freedom, and of the Democracies, | and of the fruits of
    society, and of all | that is begun,

---

2 illustrates evil as well as good,] added in the light ink. The *e* in 'illustrates' is mended over some letter, perhaps an *s*. 'as well' is interlined above a caret.

9.

A THOUGHT of what I am here for,

Of these years I sing—how they pass through convulsed pains, as through parturitions;

How America illustrates birth, gigantic youth, the promise, the sure fulfilment, despite of people—Illustrates evil as well as good;

Of how many hold despairingly yet to the models departed, caste, myths, obedience, compulsion, and to infidelity;

How few see the arrived models, the Athletes, The States—or see freedom or spirituality—or hold any faith in results,

(But I see the Athletes—and I see the results glorious and inevitable— and they again leading to other results;)

How the great cities appear—How the Democratic masses, turbulent, wilful, as I love them,

How the whirl, the contest, the wrestle of evil with good, the sounding and resounding, keep on and on·

How society waits unformed, and is between things ended and things begun;

How America is the continent of glories, and of the triumph of freedom, and of the Democracies, and of the fruits of society, and of all that is begun;

---

3 hold] a preceding 'are' has been deleted before continuing with 'hold'.

3 models departed,] before 'models' an original 'old' has been deleted in the light ink. 'departed,' is interlined above a caret in the light ink.

4 arrived models,] originally 'coming | athletes,'. First, 'coming' was deleted in pencil and 'arrived' interlined in pencil. Later, 'athletes,' was deleted in the light ink and 'arrived' traced over in this ink, 'models,' then being added.

6 whirl,] a following caret has been smudged out while wet.

6 the wrestle of evil with good,] interlined above a caret in the light ink.

7 waits] 'is' was deleted before continuing with 'waits'.

8 glories, and of the] interlined in very black ink above deleted 'the completion and'.

8 the Democracies,] interlined in the light ink above deleted 'transitions,'. 'Democracies' is written over some erased word, probably in pencil, of which only the final *y* can be seen, though it may have begun with a *d*. Probably it was 'democracy'.

8 the fruits of] interlined in black ink above a caret.

And, how America is complete in itself—And how | triumphs and
 glories are complete in themselves, | to lead onward, |
10 And how these of mine and of | America will in their | turn be
 convulsed, and serve | other parturitions and transitions,
And how now or at any time | each serves the exquisite | transition
 of death.—

9 America is . . .—And how] interlined above a caret in black ink.

9 triumphs and glories] interlined above a caret in black ink at the start of the line. At the end of the previous line after 'all' the same words, in the original writing, have been crossed through and 'parturitions' interlined above them in pencil, this in turn being deleted in pencil.

9 to lead onward,] the original version was, | 'but do not end in themselves,'. First, 'but' was deleted and above a caret 'yet' was interlined in pencil. Then this interlined 'yet' and 'not end in themselves' was crossed through with a pencil stroke and 'to lead onward,' interlined in pencil.

In the black ink Whitman later crossed through 'do' which had not been caught by the deleting pencil stroke, traced over in ink the interlineation of the word 'to' and the *l* of 'lead', but no more except for touching up in ink the comma after 'onward'.

10 in their] original 'yet' before 'in' has been deleted in pencil and 'their' appended to the line.

10 and serve] first, original 'and' of 'and serve' was deleted and above a caret was interlined in pencil 'as we are, to'. Then this was deleted in the black ink and 'and' restored, the caret being touched up.

[FOLDER 46. Two leaves of pink paper. The first is composed of two pasted-together pieces, the upper measuring 3⅜ vertically, the lower 7⅛, and the whole 9½. The much crumpled upper section contains the first two verses and title written in the light revising ink, and thus it represents a revision of what was probably the title and one verse cut away from the original leaf. The other verses are written in a dark ink. This paste-on upper section fits by its cutting beneath the piece used as a paste-on revision in folder 45. On its verso are five undeleted draft verses for "Premonition" (see Appendix I to that poem). 1860, pp. 182–83; Camden, II, 276–77.]

[*leaf* 1] [*upper section*]

Thought.

Of closing up my songs by these | shores,
Of California—Of Oregon, and | I journeying thither to live |
 and sing there,

[*lower section*]
Of the Western Sea—Of the | spread inland between | it and the
 spinal | river,
Of the American pastoral | area, athletic and feminine,
5 Of all sloping down | south-westerly from the | flowing Missouri,
 the | fresh free-giver, the |mother,

And how The States are complete in themselves—And how all triumphs and glories are complete in themselves, to lead onward,

And how these of mine, and of The States, will in their turn be convulsed, and serve other parturitions and transitions,

And how all people, sights, combinations, the Democratic masses too, serve—and how every fact serves,

And how now, or at any time, each serves the exquisite transition of Death.

11.

THE thought of fruitage,

Of Death, (the life greater)—of seeds dropping into the ground—of birth,

Of the steady concentration of America, inland, upward, to impregnable and swarming places,

Of what Indiana, Kentucky, Ohio and the rest, are to be,

Of what a few years will show there in Missouri, Kansas, Iowa, Wisconsin, Minnesota and the rest,

Of what the feuillage of America is the preparation for—and of what all the sights, North, South, East and West, are;

Of the temporary use of materials for identity's sake,

Of departing—of the growth of a mightier race than any yet,

Of myself, soon, perhaps, closing up my songs by these shores,

Of California—of Oregon—and of me journeying hence to live and sing there;

Of the Western Sea—of the spread inland between it and the spinal river,

Of the great pastoral area, athletic and feminine,

Of all sloping down there where the fresh free-giver, the mother, the Mississippi flows—and Westward still;

1 shores] the lower part of *h* and then all of *ores* has been traced over in an almost blue-black ink, apparently only to make legible a blot.

3 it] interlined in the fine pen with a caret over deleted 'that'.

5 sloping] a preceding 'flowing' has been crossed out before writing 'sloping'.

⟦ 149 ⟧

Of future men and women | there—Of happiness in | those high plateaus, ranging | three thousand miles, warm | and cold,

Of cities yet unsurveyed and un-|suspected, (As I am also, and | as it must be,)

[leaf 2]

Of the new and good names— | Of strong developements— | Of the inalienable home-|steads,

Of a free original life there— | Of simple diet and clean | and sweet blood,

10 Of litheness, majestic faces, | clear eyes, and perfect | physique there,

Of immense spiritual results, future years, | inland, spread there each side of | the Anahuacs,

Of these Leaves established there, and | well understood there.—

Of the native scorn of grossness | and gain there, (O it lurks | in me night and day—What | is gain, after all, to savage-|ness and freedom?)

---

8 Of the new. . . .] heading the leaf and above this verse, but deleted in the light ink is the verse, 'Of me in those cities wel-comed, well-beloved, many years | hence,'.

9 diet] an original comma following this has been deleted in the same ink.

9 clean] the final letter is mended and [*Cont. on page 151*]

[FOLDER 47. One large pasted-together piece of ruled white laid paper writ-ten across in a dark-brown ink. The upper piece measures $7\frac{1}{8} \times 6\frac{3}{16}$; the lower, $4\frac{5}{16} \times 6\frac{3}{8}$. The continuity of prose writing on the versos of both pieces, in combination with the matching of cut letters at the verso foot of the large piece and the top of the small, shows that the smaller piece is the cut right-hand half of the original lower portion of the large piece. One pinhole appears in the center. The title was originally, as here, 'To a Historian'; but later, in a darker ink, 'a' was deleted and s added to 'Historian', the underlining being extended to take in the addition. Finally, this s was deleted and 'a' restored by interlining. The remaining piece of the full sheet of paper is found in folder 68. 1860, p. 181; Camden, I, 4.]

[upper section]

To a Historian.

All you have said, | I find good.

After carefully perused it, I proceed to | make use thereof,

You have celebrated the life that has ex-|hibited itself,

Of future men and women there—of happiness in those high plateaus,
  ranging three thousand miles, warm and cold,
Of cities yet unsurveyed and unsuspected, (as I am also, and as it
  must be,)
Of the new and good names—of the strong developments—of the in-
  alienable homesteads,
Of a free original life there—of simple diet, and clean and sweet blood,
Of litheness, majestic faces, clear eyes, and perfect physique there,
Of immense spiritual results, future years, inland, spread there each
  side of the Anahuacs,
Of these Leaves well-understood there, (being made for that area,)
Of the native scorn of grossness and gain there,
(O it lurks in me night and day—What is gain, after all, to savage-
  ness and freedom?)

[Cont. from page 150]
blotted so heavily in the same ink as to
defy positive identification. The word just
possibly might have been 'clearer', and
the intention to mend or to delete *er*.
11 results] interlined in black ink above deleted 'things'. The comma is taken from
that after 'things'.
12 established] before this is a deletion crossing out two or three letters, very likely
'be'.

13 Of the native . . . freedom?)] this verse
was originally written between the verse
beginning 'Of litheness' (verse 10) and
that beginning 'Of immense' (verse 11). In
the black ink a large parenthesis is drawn
about the whole verse in the left margin,
and below an asterisk is written 'down'.
Then in the same ink and fine pen, a
short line is drawn at the very foot of
the page followed by an asterisk, and
beneath the line is written 'take in'.

10.

HISTORIAN! you who celebrate bygones!
You have explored the outward, the surface of the races—the life that
  has exhibited itself,

---

1 All you have said,] above this is the deleted initial start, 'Having read your pro-
ductions'. After 'said,' is deleted 'and will
always say'.
1 good,] interlined in a light ink above deleted 'indispensable enough,'.

2 After] interlined in pencil above deleted
'Having'. In the same line the failure to
alter 'perused' consequentially to 'perus-
ing' was a slip.
3 celebrated the life . . . itself,] interlined in
the same ink above deleted 'treated man as
the creature | of politics,'.

You have **explored** the outward surface | and lineaments of the races,

5 You have **told** of man as he | has been—and the world as it | has been,

You have treated man as the creatures of politics | and rulers and priests

Now advancing, and first saluting you and all your entourage with | love,)

I, an American, painting the spirit of the traits of | my own age —(the future shall | behold them in me, so turbulent, so | contradictory,—me the most loving and haughty | democrat,)

I paint man as he is in the | influences of nature, in himself,— and of all nature

[lower piece pasted on]

10 I do not tell facts—those half-truths,

I do not tell any thing that requires | further proof than he or she | who will hear me will furnish by silently meditating alone,

I press the pulse of the life that seldom or never exhibits itself, | but generally seeks concealment,

I illuminate feelings, faults, | hopes, desires—I have come at last —I am not ashamed | nor afraid,

I sketch the ideal | man, the American of the future,

15 I project that which shall | make the history of a race | yet to be.—

4 explored] after this an original 'all' is deleted in pencil.

4 and lineaments] interlined in pencil above a caret.

5 told] after this the original 'the world' has been heavily crossed through.

5 it has] *as* heavily mended over one or two letters, as though 'he' had been changed to 'his' and then to 'has'.

6 treated man . . . priests] interlined in the same ink above deleted original 'celebrated the life that has | exhibited itself,'. Inadvertently, in the original line 'has' was not crossed through.

7 Now] originally 'Now I', the 'I' being deleted.

7 and first] the 'and' is interlined above a caret. An original parenthesis before 'first'

has been crossed out, but inadvertently the closing parenthesis after 'love' in verse 8 was not also deleted. The whole latter part of the verse from 'first' on to 'love,)' is almost certainly a later addition, since it seems to be written with a different pen and ink, and the second line to be crowded in.

8 an American,] interlined above a caret and deleted 'will' in the same ink, a comma being also placed after preceding 'I'. After 'American' appears a heavily deleted short word which may have been 'sing' or 'say', more likely the latter.

8 painting] *ing* added in pencil. After this 'in' is added above a caret, but then deleted.

8 the traits of] 'the' is interlined above and

You have treated man as the creature of politics, aggregates, rulers,
and priests;
But now I also, arriving, contribute something:
I, an habitué of the Alleghanies, treat man as he is in the influences
of Nature, in himself, in his own inalienable rights,
Advancing, to give the spirit and the traits of new Democratic ages,
myself, personally,
(Let the future behold them all in me—Me, so puzzling and contradic-
tory—Me, a Manhattanese, the most loving and arrogant of men;)
I do not tell the usual facts, proved by records and documents,
What I tell, (talking to every born American,) requires no further proof
than he or she who will hear me, will furnish, by silently meditating
alone;
I press the pulse of the life that has hitherto seldom exhibited itself,
but has generally sought concealment, (the great pride of man, in
himself,)
I illuminate feelings, faults, yearnings, hopes—I have come at last, no
more ashamed nor afraid;
Chanter of Personality, outlining a history yet to be,
I project the ideal man, the American of the future.

---

to the left of deleted 'life'; 'traits' is interlined above and to the right. A preceding
hyphen (showing the original intention
was to revise to 'life-traits') has been deleted along with 'life'. The 'of' is added
on the line after deleted 'in'.
8 them] interlined in the same ink above
deleted 'it'.
8 so] interlined before the start of 'turbulent' without a caret.
8 contradictory] second *c* mended over a *t*.
8 —me the most] interlined in the same ink
with a caret above deleted 'so'.
9 paint] interlined above deleted 'will treat'.
9 —and of all nature] an addition crowded
in at the end of the line.
10 I do not tell facts—those] originally, 'I
will not tell facts—no half-truths,'. First
the 'not' was crossed out and 'no' interlined with a caret after 'tell'. Then this
interlineation was deleted, 'will' excised,
and 'do not' interlined above deleted 'no'.
'those' is inter-
lined above deleted 'no'.
11 do] interlined above deleted 'will'.
11 further] before this was original 'any',
deleted.

11 than] *n* mended over *t*.
11 will hear me . . . alone,'] interlined in
the same ink above delated 'hears me
furnishes', the final *es* of 'furnishes' having previously been crossed through. In
the interlineation, 'by' is written above a
caret.
12 I press . . . concealment,] this verse was
crowded in as an addition.
13 illuminate] a preceding original 'will' has
been deleted.
13 feelings] before he wrote this Whitman
started 'fe', crossed it out, wrote 'un', and
then finally 'feelings,'.
13 —I have come at last—] interlined in the
same ink above a caret placed after the
original dash following 'desires'.
14 sketch] before writing this, Whitman wrote
'will paint the'; the last two words were
crossed out before he continued with
'sketch', then the preceding 'will' deleted
at a later time.
15 project] a preceding 'will' has been deleted.
15 that] *a* mended over *e*.

⟦ 153 ⟧

[FOLDER 48. Five leaves of pink paper, cluster of pinholes in the center. Written in black ink. In the upper right corner is the partly erased pencil note in Whitman's hand, 'Needs to be | re-written | or excluded'. In the lower left corner the leaves are numbered in pencil 1–5. The 8 of the poem number 68 is written over a 7. 1860, pp. 183–85; Camden, II, 157–59.]

[*leaf* 1]

68—

Orators.

To one of these—Also to a | lecturer, lecturess, or-|atress, or
   myself,
Vocalism, breath, measure, | concentration, determination, | and
   the divine power | to use words.—

Are you eligible?
Are you full-lunged and | limber-lip'd from long | trial? from
   vigorous | practice? from physique?

5 Do you understand that all | depends on physique?
Do you move in these broad States | as broad as they?—
Remembering inland America? the high | plateaus, stretching far?
Remembering Kanada—Remembering what | edges the vast
   round edge | of the Mexican Sea?

[*leaf* 2]

Come duly to the divine | power to use words?

10 For only at last after many | years—after chastity, friendship, |
   procreation, prudence and | nakedness,
After treading ground, and | breasting river and lake,
After an athletic throat— | after absorbing eras, races, | tempera-
   ments—after | knowledge, freedom, | crimes,

3 eligible?] the question mark added after the next word 'yourself?' was deleted.
7 inland America? . . . far?] interlined in the light ink above deleted 'the Eastern Ocean and | the Western Ocean—' which has been crossed through in pencil.
8 Remembering Kanada] a new verse was begun by prefixing *Remem* in the light ink to original | *ber*; the *Remem-* ending the line above having been crossed through

in pencil as part of the major deletion described above.
11 ground] a preceding 'the' has been deleted in the same ink.
11 river] a preceding 'the' has been deleted in the same ink.
12 absorbing] interlined above deleted 'observing'.
12 freedom,] after this an 'and' concluding the line has been deleted in the same ink.

[Prose text in folder 47 consisting of the left-hand section on the back of "To a Cantatrice" (folder 68), and the right-hand section from the lower paste-on of "To a Historian".]

Georgia, no Roman Catholic could be | elected or appointed to any high office of | the state—and I believe this exclusion is | still the case in New Hampshire. | [new paragraph] In Deleware all office holders were required | to profess their belief in the Trinity—in | South Carolina they were required to believe | in a future state of rewards and punishments | —in Pennsylvania they were required to acknowledge | the inspiration of the old and new testaments. | In Connecticut the law as that debtors unable | to pay, could be sold by the creditor into temporary | slavery to get the demand.—Something of the same | sort prevailed in many states, with respect | to debts incurred for passage at sea.— | [one-line space and new paragraph] In 1782 the officers of the army, because they could | not get their pay, proposed to Washington that they | would make him king.—

12.

1. To oratists—to male or female,
    Vocalism, breath, measure, concentration, determination, and the divine power to use words.

2. Are you eligible?
    Are you full-lung'd and limber-lipp'd from long trial? from vigorous practice? from physique?
    Do you move in these broad lands as broad as they?
    Remembering inland America, the high plateaus, stretching long?
    Remembering Kanada—Remembering what edges the vast round edge of the Mexican Sea?
    Come duly to the divine power to use words?

3. For only at last, after many years—after chastity, friendship, procreation, prudence, and nakedness,
    After treading ground and breasting river and lake,
    After a loosened throat—after absorbing eras, temperaments, races—after knowledge, freedom, crimes,

After complete faith—after | clarifyings, elevations, and | removing obstructions,

After these, and more, it is | just possible there comes | to a man, a woman | the divine power to use words.—

[*leaf* 3]

15 Then toward that man or | that woman swiftly | hasten all—None refuse, | all attend,

Armies, ships, antiquities, the | dead, libraries, paintings, | machines, cities, hate, | despair, amity, pain, | theft, murder, aspiration, | form in close ranks,

They debouch as they are | wanted, to march obedi-|ently through the mouth | of that man or that | woman.—

[leaf 4]

O Now I see arise orators | fit for America,

And I see it is as slow to | become an orator as | to become a man,

20 And I see that all power | is folded in a great | vocalism.—

[*leaf* 5]

Of a great vocalism, when | you hear it, the merciless | light shall pour, and the | storm rage around,

Every flash shall be a revela-|tion, an insult—Now | you are struck, exposed,

Is it you then—such a booby, | fanatic, fop? Is it | yours—such a needlessly | ennuyeed life?

No respect for you—No | politeness, forbearance, | soft hands,

25 The glaring flame turned on | depths, on heights, on suns, | on stars,

On the interior and exterior of man or woman | —on the laws of nature—on passive materials,

On what you called death, and what to you | therefore was death.—

[After verse 17 ending 'that woman.—' the remaining part of leaf 3, and the upper part of leaf 4 before the start of verse 18, is occupied by a series of deleted verses. The horizontal lines drawn across the page inclose different deletions made independently.]

[*Cont. on page 158*]

After complete faith—after clarifyings, elevations, and removing obstructions,

After these, and more, it is just possible there comes to a man, a woman, the divine power to use words.

4. Then toward that man or that woman swiftly hasten all—None refuse, all attend,

Armies, ships, antiquities, the dead, libraries, paintings, machines, cities, hate, despair, amity, pain, theft, murder, aspiration, form in close ranks,

They debouch as they are wanted to march obediently through the mouth of that man, or that woman.

5. O now I see arise orators fit for inland America,

And I see it is as slow to become an orator as to become a man,

And I see that power is folded in a great vocalism.

6. Of a great vocalism, when you hear it, the merciless light shall pour, and the storm rage around,

Every flash shall be a revelation, an insult,

The glaring flame turned on depths, on heights, on suns, on stars,

On the interior and exterior of man or woman,

On the laws of Nature—on passive materials,

On what you called death—and what to you therefore was death,

As far as there can be death.

---

13 complete] interlined above a caret and deleted 'ceaseless' first in pencil and then traced over, with a fresh caret, in the light ink.

14 divine] interlined in the light ink above a caret.

15 all—] before the dash an original comma has been smudged out while still wet.

17 march] *c* mended over *t* smudged out while still wet.

18 O] interlined above a caret in a different

pen. The capital *N* of 'Now' was inadvertently not reduced.

23 —such] interlined above a caret, the original comma after 'then' being crossed out.

23 —such a] interlined above deleted 'that'. A comma following 'yours' has been crossed out.

24 soft hands,] in the light ink the original verse below this has been deleted, 'Your wants, callosities, | obesities, blue-balls, exposed,'.

[*Cont. from page 156*]

O action and [*a false start, deleted separately*]

O joy! To feel the solid and | turbulent masses of The | States un-
der your control,

[line]

Invisible within, memory, | passions, judgment, | all busy, [*end
leaf* 3]

[*begin leaf* 4] [line]

Visible without, every muscle, | every nerve excited—Not | a limb,
not a feature | but speaks,

[line]

Knowing in yourself | You are moulding | The States—the Many
In | One—people, lands, | proud, friendly, equal, sensual,
spiritual.

[line]

[*Cont. on page 159*]

[FOLDER 49. Three leaves of pink paper, measuring $8\frac{3}{8} \times 5$, except for the
first leaf, which is $7\frac{5}{8}$. The portion of a horizontal line that can be seen at the
head of the first leaf, and the fact that the poem's title (underlined) is written
in the light revising ink, suggest that the original title and very likely the poem
number has been cut off. In Whitman's list, this appears as '38. Walt Whitman's Laws'. A cluster of pinholes appears in the center, and a few holes are
in the left margin. The verses are written in a dark ink. In the lower left
corner Whitman numbered the leaves 1–3. 1860, pp. 185–86; Camden, II,
160–61.]

[*leaf* 1]

American Laws.

For Creations,

For strong artists and oratists—For fresh | broods of teachers and
perfect | literats for America,

For diverse savans, and for the | coming musicians:

There shall be no subject | but it shall be treated | with reference
to the | ensemble of the world and the compact truth of the
world— | And no coward or copyist | shall be allowed,

5 There shall be no subject | too pronounced—All | works shall il-
lustrate | the divine law of indi-|rections;

[Cont. from page 158]

NOTE: As shown by the different deleting pen strokes, these rejected lines were excised in two parts at different times. First, a horizontal line was drawn on leaf 3 above verse 3 ('Invisible within' . . .; and a line at the head of verse 4 and at its foot. Then verses 3–4 were crossed out with slanting vertical strokes. At a later time, verse 2 was deleted, the strokes descending into the already deleted verse 3 at the foot of leaf 3. Since the next pen strokes to be described were made seemingly with a finer pen, the final deletion on leaf 4 of verse 5 may have been made at a different time, but whether earlier or later is impossible to judge although the odds are the deletion was the final one. At any rate, a horizontal line was drawn beneath verse 5, and two vertical pen strokes, extending up to the top of the leaf and thus passing through the already deleted verse 4 heading the leaf, were drawn. The only alterations appear in verse 5. This originally began, 'Knowing in yourself, Orator! | Oratress!'. The last two words have been deleted, and also the comma after 'yourself'. Further on, 'moulding' was written with a finer pen above deleted 'addressing'. The capitals in 'Many In One' were triple underscored. Before 'people' originally appeared 'races,' deleted.

13.

1. LAWS for Creations,
   For strong artists and leaders—for fresh broods of teachers, and perfect
       literats for America,
   For diverse savans, and coming musicians.

2. There shall be no subject but it shall be treated with reference to
       the ensemble of the world, and the compact truth of the world—
   And no coward or copyist shall be allowed;
   There shall be no subject too pronounced—All works shall illustrate
       the divine law of indirections;

2 and oratists—] interlined with a finer pen above a caret placed before the original dash following 'artists'.

4 and the compact truth of the world—] interlined with a finer pen above a caret and guide line placed before the original dash after 'world'. Between 'and the' appear perhaps two deleted letters, the first of which is probably a *t*.

There they stand—I see them | already, each poised in | its place,

[*leaf 2*]

Statements, models, censures, |poems, dictionaries, biog-|raphies, essays, theories— | How complete! How rel-|ative and inter-fused! No | one supersedes another;
They do not seem to me | like the old specimens,
They seem like Nature at | last, (America has given | birth to them, and I | have also,)
10 They seem to me at last as | perfect as the animals, | and as the rocks and weeds, | —fit to range beside them,
They seem to me fit to move along the sky | with floating clouds— | to rustle in the trees with rustling leaves— | — to stretch with stretched and level | waters, where ships silently | sail in the distance.—

[*leaf 3*]

What do you suppose Creation is?
What do you suppose will | satisfy the soul except | to walk free | and own no superior?
What do you suppose I have | intimated to you in a | hundred ways, but that | man or woman is as | good as God?
15 And that there is no God | any more divine than | Yourself?
And that that is what the | oldest and newest myths finally | mean?
And that you or any one | must approach Creations | through such laws?

7 essays,] in the finer pen above a caret af-ter this is interlined 'orations,', then de-leted.

10 —fit to range beside them,] originally crowded in with the finer pen as '—fit to [*Cont. on page 161*]

[FOLDER 50. Two conjugate leaves of white wove paper (6¼ × 4) in a fold; pinholes in the left margin and upper left corner. Written in a light-brown ink. At upper right Whitman numbered the leaves 1–2 in pencil. These verses doubtless represent a fair copy. 1860, pp. 186–87; Camden, I, 15.]

[*leaf 1*]

To Poets to Come.

Not to-day is to justify me,
But you, a new brood, native, | athletic, continental, you | must justify me.—

There they stand—I see them already, each poised and in its place,

Statements, models, censuses, poems, dictionaries, biographies, essays, theories—How complete! How relative and interfused! No one supersedes another;

They do not seem to me like the old specimens,

They seem to me like Nature at last, (America has given birth to them, and I have also;)

They seem to me at last as perfect as the animals, and as the rocks and weeds—fitted to them,

Fitted to the sky, to float with floating clouds—to rustle among the trees with rustling leaves,

To stretch with stretched and level waters, where ships silently sail in the distance.

3. What do you suppose Creation is?

What do you suppose will satisfy the Soul, except to walk free and own no superior?

What do you suppose I have intimated to you in a hundred ways, but that man or woman is as good as God?

And that there is no God any more divine than Yourself?

And that that is what the oldest and newest myths finally mean?

And that you or any one must approach Creations through such laws?

[*Cont. from page 160*]
stand up with them,'; then 'range beside' was interlined in pencil above deleted 'stand up with'.

11 fit to move along] interlined with the finer pen above a caret and deleted 'like'.

11 to rustle in the] interlined with the finer pen above a caret placed before 'trees'. In the line above the final word 'like' is deleted.

11 —to stretch with] interlined with the finer pen at the start of the line above deleted 'like'.

11 where] interlined with the finer pen above deleted 'with'.

11 sail] originally 'sailing', the *ing* being crossed out.

11 distance.—] the lower part of a semi-colon has been smudged out while wet to form

the period.

12 What] a paragraph sign in pencil is placed before this.

13 except to walk free.] originally, 'but | to stand up haughtily'. 'but' and 'stand up' are deleted and 'except' and 'walk' interlined respectively with the finer pen. Later, 'free,' was interlined in the light ink above deleted 'haughtily'.

14 suppose] interlined with the finer pen above deleted 'think'.

14 as God] originally 'as any God', the 'any' being deleted first in pencil and then in the light ink.

15 Yourself] in the light ink *y* is mended to *Y* and triple underscored.

16 and newest] interlined with a caret in the finer pen.

14.

1. POETS to come!

Not to-day is to justify me, and Democracy, and what we are for,

But you, a new brood, native, athletic, continental, greater than before known,

You must justify me.

Indeed if it were not for you | what would I be?
What is the little I have | done, except to arouse | you?

5 I depend on being realized by | you where the Mississippi | flows,
    and thence to Oregon | and California inclusive,
I expect that the Texan and | the Arizonian, ages hence, | will
    understand me,
I expect that the future | Ohioan and Missourian | will understand
    me and love | me,

[*leaf 2*]

I expect that Kanadians, | a hundred, and perhaps | many hundred
    years from | now, in the splendor of | the snow and woods, or |
    on the icy lakes, will take | me with them and permanently |
    enjoy themselves with me.—

Of to-day I know I am mo-|mentary, untouched—I am | the man
    of the future,
10 I have but written one or two | indicative words for the future,
I have but advanced a moment, | only to wheel and hurry | back
    in the darkness.
I am a man who, sauntering | along, without stopping, turns | a
    casual look upon you, and | then averts his face,
Leaving it to you to prove and | define it,
Expecting the main things from | you.—

8 me.—] the period was placed over a comma smudged out while still wet.

[FOLDER 51. Two leaves of pink paper; a cluster of pinholes in the center.
Written in a dark ink. 1860, pp. 189–90; Camden, II, 262–63.]

[*leaf 1*]

    48

Mediums.—

They shall arise in The States,
They shall report nature, | laws, physiology, and | happiness,
They shall illustrate America | and the kosmos,

1 They shall arise. . . .] after this opening
verse, the poem originally continued:
‘They shall be complete women | and
men, their pose | brawny and supple,

their | drink water, their blood | clean
and clear,
They shall test all things by | the body
and the soul’.

2. Indeed, if it were not for you, what would I be?
What is the little I have done, except to arouse you?

3. I depend on being realized, long hence, where the broad fat prairies
spread, and thence to Oregon and California inclusive,
I expect that the Texan and the Arizonian, ages hence, will understand me,
I expect that the future Carolinian and Georgian will understand me
and love me,
I expect that Kanadians, a hundred, and perhaps many hundred years
from now, in winter, in the splendor of the snow and woods, or on
the icy lakes, will take me with them, and permanently enjoy themselves with me.

4. Of to-day I know I am momentary, untouched—I am the bard of the
future,
I but write one or two indicative words for the future,
I but advance a moment, only to wheel and hurry back in the darkness.

5. I am a man who, sauntering along, without fully stopping, turns a
casual look upon you, and then averts his face,
Leaving it to you to prove and define it,
Expecting the main things from you.

16.

THEY shall arise in the States—mediums shall,
They shall report Nature, laws, physiology, and happiness,
They shall illustrate Democracy and the kosmos,

The last verse is crossed through in the same ink. A left marginal brace was drawn about the first verse, and in the left margin written 'tr | (or | out) | down | *', the 'or out', within a parenthesis, being deleted. In the light ink appears crowded in above the opening line of the above verse and the initial verse of the poem, 'They shall report Nature, laws, physiology,' which is crossed through in the light ink. This appears over a caret placed after individually deleted 'They shall' of the braced verse, and therefore represents the intended revised start of the verse, together with its continuation (inadvertently not deleted) in the next line 'and happiness'. The next step seems to have been to delete the remainder, 'be complete women

| and men,' and, perhaps inadvertently, 'their pose' | . Above 'be complete' was started in the light ink 'illustrate Amer', which was then deleted and below the line written as the start of a new verse 'They shall illustrate America and the kosmos,'. Finally, the whole revised lines below the initial verse and extending through 'clean and clear,' were deleted by two slanting vertical strokes in the light ink, these strokes extending down into the earlier deleted verse beginning 'They shall test. . . .' Some of this material was then transferred below, see note. It is extremely puzzling, however, that with the original pen and ink the poem continued, 'They shall report nature . . .' with the same wording found in the revising ink above.

They shall be alimentive, | amative, perceptive,

5 They shall be complete women and men—their pose | brawny and supple, their drink water, their blood | clean and clear,

They shall enjoy materialism | and the sight of products— | they shall enjoy the beef, | lumber, bread-stuffs of Chicago, the | great city,

[*leaf 2*]

They shall train themselves | to go in public, to become | oratists, (orators and oratresses,)

Strong and sweet shall their | tongues be—poems and | materials of poems shall | come from their lives— | they shall be makers | and finders,

Of them, and of their works, | shall emerge divine con-|veyers, to convey gospels,

10 Characters, events, retrospections, | shall be conveyed in gos-|pels —Trees, animals, | waters, shall be conveyed,

Death, the future, the in-|visible faith, shall all | be conveyed.—

5 They shall be complete . . . clean and clear,] crowded in later in the light ink, introduced in the left margin by an asterisk and guide lines in the original ink, presumably placed there at the time the notation of transfer and the asterisk was placed beside the braced lines above.
7 oratists,] interlined with a fine pen above a caret. The parenthesis before 'orators' and after 'oratresses,' seems to have been added at a later time, since the first is definitely smaller and cramped by reason of the interlined 'oratists,'.
9 gospels] the final *s* is written over a smudge, which might represent a rubbed out wet letter.

[FOLDER 52. Two leaves of pink paper; a cluster of pinholes in the center. Written in dark ink. The poem number 51, in ink, has been altered from 50. 1860, pp. 190–91; Camden, I, 11.]

[*leaf 1*]

51—

Wander-Teachers.—

Now we start hence, I with | the rest, on our journeys | through The States,

We willing learners from all | teachers of all, | and lovers of | all.—

I have watched the seasons | dispensing themselves and | passing on—and I have | said, Why should not a | man or woman do as | much as the seasons, and | effuse as much?

They shall be alimentive, amative, perceptive,

They shall be complete women and men—their pose brawny and supple, their drink water, their blood clean and clear,

They shall enjoy materialism and the sight of products—they shall enjoy the sight of the beef, lumber, bread-stuffs, of Chicago, the great city,

They shall train themselves to go in public to become oratists, (orators and oratresses,)

Strong and sweet shall their tongues be—poems and materials of poems shall come from their lives—they shall be makers and finders,

Of them, and of their works, shall emerge divine conveyers, to convey gospels,

Characters, events, retrospections, shall be conveyed in gospels—Trees, animals, waters, shall be conveyed,

Death, the future, the invisible faith, shall all be conveyed.

17.

1. Now we start hence, I with the rest, on our journeys through The States,
We willing learners of all, teachers of all, and lovers of all.

2. I have watched the seasons dispensing themselves, and passing on,
And I have said, Why should not a man or woman do as much as the seasons, and effuse as much?

---

1 Now] interlined with a fine pen above deleted 'Soon'.

1 journeys] just possibly the *s* has been added in the same ink.

2 teachers] a preceding 'and' beginning the line has been deleted with the fine pen.

Inadvertently a comma was not thereupon placed after 'all' ending the line above.

2 and] interlined with the fine pen above 'already' in the deleted original 'as | we are already'.

We dwell awhile in every city and town,

5 We pass through Kanada, the north-|east, the vast valley of the | Mississippi, and the Southern | States,

[*leaf 2*]

We confer on equal terms with | each of The States,

We make trial of ourselves, | and invite men and women | to hear

We say to ourselves, Remember, | fear not, be candid, promulge the body and the | soul,

Promulge real things,— | never forget the equality | of human-kind, and never | forget immortality,

10 Dwell awhile and pass on—Be | copious, temperate, chaste, mag-netic— | And what you effuse | may then return as the | seasons return, and may | be as much as the | seasons.—

8 say] a comma following this has been crossed through in the same ink.

9 Promulge] this was originally written, with the rest of the verse, as a continuing line of the verse above. In the light ink *p* has been mended to *P* and a paragraph sign placed before it.

9 things,—] the dash was added in the light ink.

10 temperate, chaste,] interlined with a caret in the fine pen above deleted 'lawless,'.

[FOLDER 53. One leaf of pink paper; a few pinholes in the center. Written in dark ink, but beginning with verse 7 a different pen and a slightly lighter ink is used. The poem number 74 is mended in ink from 73. 1860, p. 191; Camden, I, 12.]

74—

Leaf.

Me imperturbe!

Me standing at ease in Nature,

Master of all, or mistress of | all—aplomb in the midst of | irra-tional things,

Imbued as they—passive, receptive, | silent as they,

5 Finding my occupation, poverty, | notoriety, less important | than I thought;

Me private or public or menial | or solitary—all those sub-|ordinate,

Me toward the Mexican Sea, or in | the Mannahatta, or the Ten-|nessee, or far north, or inland, | a man of the prairies, | a man of the woods, or of any farm-life of | These States, or of the coast, | or of the lakes, or of Kanada,

3. We dwell a while in every city and town,
    We pass through Kanada, the north-east, the vast valley of the Mississippi, and the Southern States,
    We confer on equal terms with each of The States,
    We make trial of ourselves, and invite men and women to hear,
    We say to ourselves, Remember, fear not, be candid, promulge the body and the Soul,
    Promulge real things—Never forget the equality of humankind, and never forget immortality;
    Dwell a while, and pass on—Be copious, temperate, chaste, magnetic,
    And what you effuse may then return as the seasons return,
    And may be just as much as the seasons.

18.

ME imperturbe,
Me standing at ease in Nature,
Master of all, or mistress of all—aplomb in the midst of irrational things,
Imbued as they—passive, receptive, silent as they,
Finding my occupation, poverty, notoriety, foibles, crimes, less important than I thought;
Me private, or public, or menial, or solitary—all these subordinate,
    (I am eternally equal with the best—I am not subordinate;)
Me toward the Mexican Sea, or in the Mannahatta, or the Tennessee, or far north, or inland,
A river-man, or a man of the woods, or of any farm-life of These States, or of the coast, or the lakes, or Kanada,

---

3 in the midst of] interlined with a different pen and ink above deleted 'and quiet | amidst'.

7 a man of the prairies,] a preceding 'or' has been deleted.
7 a man of the woods,] interlined in a blacker ink above a caret.

Me wherever my life is to be lived, O | it is self-balanced for con-
tingencies,

It confronts night, storms, hunger, | ridicule, accidents, rebuffs, as
| the trees and animals do.—

9 accidents] following this is deleted 'ob-   9 and] interlined above deleted 'or'.
stacles,'.

[FOLDER 54. One leaf of pink paper; a few pinholes in the center. Written in
a dark ink. The poem number 76 is mended in a blacker ink over 75. Above
and to the right of the title Whitman wrote in pencil 'Leaflet' but deleted this
with a fine pen. 1860, p. 192; Camden, II, 162.]

76—

Leaf.—

I was looking a long while | for the History of the | past for my-
self, and | now I have found it,

It is no more in those paged fables in the libraries, | (them I
neither accept nor reject,)

It is no more in the | legends than in all |else,

It is in the present—It is | this Earth to-day, and | this America,
and | the old world also,

5 It is the life of one man or one woman to-day,

It is in all politics, languages, social customs, literatures | and arts,

It is the broad show of ar-|tificial things, ships, | machinery, mod-
ern im-|provements, and the inter-|changes of nations.—

[FOLDER 55. Two leaves of pink paper; a cluster of pin-holes in the center.
Written in black ink. The poem number 55 has been mended from 54. The
original title was 'Leaf.—'. This was deleted and above it written 'Songs—
always wanted.'; then in a different ink 'Mouth-' was prefixed, a period placed
after 'Songs', and '—always wanted.' deleted. 1860, pp. 192–93; Camden, I,
13–14.]

[*leaf* 1]

55—

Mouth-Songs.

Those of mechanics— | each one singing his own, as it should be,
| blithe and strong,

The carpenter singing his, as | he measures his plank | or beam,

1 Those] interlined in the light ink above   songs—Those | mouth-songs', the first line
a caret at the end of original 'American   deleted in the light ink, the second,

Me, wherever my life is to be lived, O to be self-balanced for con-
tingencies!

O to confront night, storms, hunger, ridicule, accidents, rebuffs, as
the trees and animals do.

19.

I WAS looking a long while for the history of the past for myself, and
for these Chants—and now I have found it,

It is not in those paged fables in the libraries, (them I neither accept
nor reject,)

It is no more in the legends than in all else,

It is in the present—it is this earth to-day,

It is in Democracy—in this America—the old world also,

It is the life of one man or one woman to-day, the average man of to-
day;

It is languages, social customs, literatures, arts,

It is the broad show of artificial things, ships, machinery, politics,
creeds, modern improvements, and the interchanges of nations,

All for the average man of to-day.

1 History] interlined in blacker ink above
deleted 'poem'.

2 It is no more in those paged . . . reject,)]
added later, crowded in in blacker ink.

3 legends] ending the line above, a preceding original 'rythmic' has been deleted in
darker ink.

3 than] after this original 'it is' has been
deleted.

4 the old world also,] interlined with a finer
pen and possibly a slightly lighter ink
above deleted 'all | languages and inven-
tions,'.

5 It is the life . . . to-day,] interlined probably with the pen and ink as in the line
immediately above. Originally this addition had 'in' after 'is', which has been

deleted; the 'one' before 'man' is interlined above a caret; after 'man' Whitman
began 'an' but crossed it out and finished
'or one woman'. It is probable that 'to-
day,' was added later, since its ink seems
to differ.

6 It is in all politics . . . arts,] this verse
was added in pencil at the foot of the leaf
and brought up to its present position by
guide lines. Before 'politics' an original
'the' has been deleted in a black ink.
'languages, social customs.' is added over
a caret with guide lines. The *s* in 'languages' is clearly an addition. Before 'and
arts,' is a false start, the letter *s* deleted in
pencil (*query, intent to write* science ?).

20.

1. AMERICAN mouth-songs!

Those of mechanics—each one singing his, as it should be, blithe and
strong,

The carpenter singing his, as he measures his plank or beam,

earlier, in text ink. In this original deleted version, the *ose* of 'Those' was
mended from 'The'.

1 mechanics—] a comma before the dash
has been crossed out.

1 singing his own,] interlined above a caret.

The mason singing his, as | he makes ready for work, | or leaves off work,

The boatman singing what belongs to him in his | boat—The deck-hand | singing on the steamboat | deck,

5 The shoemaker singing as he sits on | his bench—The hatter | singing as he stands,

[*leaf 2*]

The delicious singing of the | mother or of the young | wife at work, or of the girl sewing or washing—each | singing what belongs to | her, and to none else,

The day what belongs to the | day—At night the party | of young fellows, | robust, friendly, clean-blooded, | singing with melodious | voices, melodious thoughts.—

Come! some of you! | still be flooding The | States with hundreds | and thousands of mouth-songs, fit for The | States only.—

4 boatman] the second *a* mended over *e*.
4 what belongs to him] interlined above a caret.
4 The] *T* mended from *t*.
5 as he sits] interlined above a caret.
5 The] *T* mended over *t*.

6 or of the girl . . . washing—] interlined above a caret with guide line placed before the original dash after 'work,'. Just possibly the comma after 'work' was added at this time.

[*Cont. on page 171*]

[FOLDER 56. Three blue tax forms; cluster of pinholes in the center, a few at the top. Written in a rather black ink. 1860, pp. 231–32; Camden, II, 160.]

[*leaf* 1]

42—

Confession and Warning.—

I go no farther till I | confess myself in the | open air, in the hearing | of this time and future | times,
Also till I make a leaf of | fair warning.—

I am he who has been sly, | thievish, mean, a prevar-|icater, greedy,
And I am he who remains so | yet.—

5 What foul thought but I think it?
What in darkness in bed at | night, alone or with a | companion, but that too | is mine?

2 a] interlined above deleted 'my'.

The mason singing his, as he makes ready for work, or leaves off work,

The boatman singing what belongs to him in his boat—the deck-hand
singing on the steamboat deck,

The shoemaker singing as he sits on his bench—the hatter singing
as he stands,

The wood-cutter's song—the ploughboy's, on his way in the morning,
or at the noon intermission, or at sundown;

The delicious singing of the mother—or of the young wife at work—
or of the girl sewing or washing—Each singing what belongs to her,
and to none else,

The day what belongs to the day—At night, the party of young fellows,
robust, friendly, clean-blooded, singing with melodious voices,
melodious thoughts.

2. Come! some of you! still be flooding The States with hundreds and
thousands of mouth-songs, fit for The States only.

[*Cont. from page 170*]

7 robust] at the end of the preceding line is
the deleted slip of the pen 'rop'.

8 Come! . . . you!] the exclamation marks
are mended over original commas.

8 you! still] two verses have been joined
here by deleting after 'you!' the original
'write true | American [A *mended over* a]

mouth-songs,' and before 'still' the start
of a new verse, 'And come!'. A guide line
brings the two parts together.

8 hundreds and] Whitman first started 'hun-
dreds of' | and then deleted 'of' before
continuing with 'and'.

8 of mouth-songs,] interlined above a caret.

13.

1. O BITTER sprig! Confession sprig!
In the bouquet I give you place also—I bind you in,
Proceeding no further till, humbled publicly,
I give fair warning, once for all.

2. I own that I have been sly, thievish, mean, a prevaricator, greedy,
derelict,
And I own that I remain so yet.

3. What foul thought but I think it—or have in me the stuff out of
which it is thought?
What in darkness in bed at night, alone or with a companion?

You prostitutes flaunting over the |trottoirs, or obscene in your rooms?

Who am I that I should call you | more obscene than myself?

[*leaf* 2]

You felons on trial in courts,

10 You convicts in prison-cells—You | sentenced assassins, chained | and handcuffed with iron,

Who am I, that | I am not on trial or in | prison?

Me, ruthless and devilish as | any, that my wrists are | not chained with iron, | or my ankles with iron?

O I acknowledge! I expose!

Beneath this impassive face | the hot fires of hell | continually burn—within me | the lurid smutch and the smoke;

15 Not a crime can be named | but I have it in me | waiting to break forth,

Lusts and wickedness are ac-|ceptable to me,

I walk with delinquents | with passionate love,

[*leaf* 3]

And I say I am of them— | I belong to them myself,

And henceforth I will not | deny them—For how | can I deny myself?

20 —This leaf I specially sign with | my name, to signify to | any one concerned;

Let no man complain but | I have given him his | fair warning,

Let no woman complain but | I have given her hers.

[FOLDER 57. Three leaves of pink paper; a cluster of pinholes in the center and in left upper margin. Leaves 2 and 3 measure $8\frac{5}{16}$ vertically, but leaf 1 $7\frac{7}{8}$. This first leaf is composed of two pasted-together pieces, the upper measuring $1\frac{7}{16}$ and containing on its recto the title 'Night on the Prairies.' written in the light revising ink. On the verso, in the dark ink of the rest of the poem, appears '73—*Leaf.*— | Night on the prairies,'. This poem number 73 is mended from 72. What has happened presents no difficulties. 'Night on the prairies' was originally the first verse of the poem. Whitman excised this verse when he made it into the title simply by cutting off the top of the leaf and reversing it, writing the new title on the verso of the small piece. In the lower left corner the leaves are numbered in pencil 1–3 placed after deleted 16–18. 1860, p. 234; Camden, II, 231–32.]

4. You felons on trials in courts,
    You convicts in prison cells—you sentenced assassins, chained and
        handcuffed with iron,
    Who am I, that I am not on trial, or in prison?
    Me, ruthless and devilish as any, that my wrists are not chained with
        iron, or my ankles with iron?

5. You prostitutes flaunting over the trottoirs, or obscene in your rooms,
    Who am I, that I should call you more obscene than myself?

6. O culpable! O traitor!
    O I acknowledge—I exposé!
    (O admirers! praise not me! compliment not me! you make me wince,
    I see what you do not—I know what you do not;)
    Inside these breast-bones I lie smutch'd and choked,
    Beneath this face that appears so impassive, hell's tides continually
        run,
    Lusts and wickedness are acceptable to me,
    I walk with delinquents with passionate love,
    I feel I am of them—I belong to those convicts and prostitutes myself,
    And henceforth I will not deny them—for how can I deny myself?

---

9 courts,] the comma inserted after an original dash crossed out and smudged while wet.
11 Who am I,] originally there followed 'O brothers,', which has been deleted.
13 O I acknowledge! I expose!] interlined, preceded by a paragraph sign, and in a different ink, above deleted 'O I know— I am ['fully' *independently deleted*] aware | I deny' (*but possibly* say). The whole of this deleted matter is also clearly an addition, the original verse having begun 'Beneath this. . . .'
14 'within me . . . smoke;] crowded in as a later addition.
15 forth,] the original reading was 'forth,' which was deleted in favor of interlined

'out,', in turn deleted to restore 'forth,' written with a fine pen.
16 me] before this is deleted 'be'.
17 delinquents] *q* is heavily mended; possibly there had been a misspelling, or a letter formed too like a *q*.
20 —This leaf I specially sign] the original beginning of the verse read, '—Having read it over, this leaf | I particularly sign'. The first line is crossed out and '—This leaf' prefixed above a caret to the second line. 'specially' is interlined above deleted 'particularly'.
20 any one] interlined with a caret in the fine pen above deleted 'all'.
21 man] interlined above deleted 'woman', apparently before completing the rest of the verse.

[*leaf* 1]

Night on the Prairies.

I walk by myself—I stand and look | at the stars, which I | think
   now I never realized | before.—
Now I absorb immortality and | peace,
I admire death, and test | propositions.—
How plenteous! How | spiritual! How resumé!
5 The same old man and soul— | The same old aspirations, | and
   the same content. —
I was thinking the day most | splendid, till I saw what | the not-
   day exhibited,

[*leaf* 2]

I was thinking this globe | enough for me till there | descended to
   me myriads | of other globes;
Now, while the great thoughts | of space and eternity | are upon
   me, I will | measure myself by them,
And now while there is upon | me the thought of the | lives of
   other globes | arrived as far along | as those of the earth, | or
   waiting to arrive, or | passed on farther than | those of the
   earth, I no | more ignore them, than I | ignore my own life,
   or the | lives on the earth arrived | as far as mine, or waiting
   | to arrive there.—

[*leaf* 3]

10 O I see now that life | cannot exhibit all to | me—as the day can-
   not,
O I see now that I | wait for what will | be exhibited by death.

[FOLDER 58. Two leaves of pink paper; a cluster of pinholes in the center.
Written in blackish ink. The poem number 72 has been altered from 71. No
alterations appear in these verses. 1860, p. 235; Camden, II, 21.]

[*leaf* 1]

   72—

Leaf.—

Sea-water, and all breathing | it, and all living below | it,
Forests at the bottom of the | sea—the branches and | leaves, the
   sea-lettuce, | the vast lichens, the | strange flowers and seeds, |
   the thick tangle, the | openings, and the pink turf,

15.

1. NIGHT on the Prairies;
    I walk by myself—I stand and look at the stars, which I think now I
      never realized before.

2. Now I absorb immortality and peace,
    I admire death and test propositions.

3. How plenteous! How spiritual! How resumé!
    The same Old Man and Soul—the same old aspirations, and the same
      content.

4. I was thinking the day most splendid, till I saw what the not-day ex-
      hibited,
    I was thinking this globe enough, till there tumbled upon me myriads
      of other globes.

5. Now while the great thoughts of space and eternity fill me, I will meas-
      ure myself by them,
    And now, touched with the lives of other globes, arrived as far along
      as those of the earth,
    Or waiting to arrive, or passed on farther than those of the earth,
    I henceforth no more ignore them than I ignore my own life,
    Or the lives on the earth arrived as far as mine, or waiting to arrive.

6. O how plainly I see now that life cannot exhibit all to me—as the day
      cannot,
    O I see that I am to wait for what will be exhibited by death.

---

1 walk] interlined in black ink above deleted 'stand'.
1 —I stand] interlined in black ink above
a caret.
1 now] interlined in black ink above a caret.
2 immortality] interlined in the regular ink
above deleted 'spirituality'.
4 plenteous] originally 'still and plenteous',

the first two words being deleted in the
same ink.
4 How resumé!] just possibly some change
in pen is exhibited here and these words,
in slightly smaller letters, written in later; but the case is doubtful and they
may well be original.
10 me—] before the dash a comma has been
smudged out while still wet.

16.

SEA-WATER, and all living below it,
Forests at the bottom of the sea—the branches and leaves,
Sea-lettuce, vast lichens, strange flowers and seeds—the thick tangle,
  the openings, and the pink turf,

Different colors, pale gray and | green, purple, white | and gold—
the play of | light through the water,

Dumb swimmers there among | the rocks, coral, gluten, grass, |
rushes—and the | aliment of the swimmers,

[*leaf 2*]

5 Vast sluggish existences | grazing there, suspended | or slowly crawl-
ing close | to the bottom,

The sperm whale at the | surface blowing air | and water, or dis-
porting | with his flukes,

The leaden-eyed shark, | the walrus, the turtle, | the hairy sea-
leopard, | and the sting-ray;

Passions there—wars, pursuits, | tribes—sight in those ocean
depths—breathing | that thick-breathing air, as so many do,

The change thence to the sight here, | and to the subtle air
breathed | by beings like us who walk | this sphere,

10 The change onward from ours to that | of beings who walk other
spheres.

[FOLDER 59. Two leaves of pink paper; a cluster of pinholes in the center.
Written in blackish ink. The poem number 78 is altered from 77. 1860, p. 236;
Camden, II, 34.]

[*leaf 1*]

78—   *Leaf.—*

I sit and look out upon all | the sorrows of my race, | and upon
all oppression | and shame,

I hear secret convulsive sobs | from young men and women at |
anguish with themselves | for their late behaviour,

I see the mother misused by | her children, dying, neg-|lected, hun-
gered, desperate,

I see the wife misused by her | husband—I see the | treacherous
seducer of the | young woman,

5 I mark the stabs of jealousy | and unrequited love,

I see the workings of battle, | pestilence, tyranny—I | see martyrs
and prisoners,

[*leaf 2*]

I observe a famine at sea— | I observe the sailors | casting lots who
shall be | killed to preserve the lives | of the rest,

Different colors, pale gray and green, purple, white, and gold—the play
    of light through the water,
Dumb swimmers there among the rocks—coral, gluten, grass, rushes—
    and the aliment of the swimmers,
Sluggish existences grazing there, suspended, or slowly crawling close
    to the bottom,
The sperm-whale at the surface, blowing air and spray, or disporting
    with his flukes,
The leaden-eyed shark, the walrus, the turtle, the hairy sea-leopard,
    and the sting-ray;
Passions there—wars, pursuits, tribes—sight in those ocean-depths—
    breathing that thick-breathing air, as so many do,
The change thence to the sight here, and to the subtle air breathed
    by beings like us, who walk this sphere;
The change onward from ours to that of beings who walk other spheres.

17.

I SIT and look out upon all the sorrows of the world, and upon all op-
    pression and shame,
I hear secret convulsive sobs from young men, at anguish with them-
    selves, remorseful after deeds done;
I see, in low life, the mother misused by her children, dying, neglected,
    gaunt, desperate,
I see the wife misused by her husband—I see the treacherous seducer
    of the young woman,
I mark the ranklings of jealousy and unrequited love, attempted to be
    hid—I see these sights on the earth,
I see the workings of battle, pestilence, tyranny—I see martyrs and
    prisoners,
I observe a famine at sea—I observe the sailors casting lots who shall
    be killed, to preserve the lives of the rest,

---

2 and women] interlined in pencil above a caret.
2 for] interlined with a fine pen above deleted 'and'.

2 late] interlined with a fine pen above a caret.
5 mark] interlined with a fine pen above deleted 'know'.

I behold the slights and degra-|dations cast by arrogant | persons
　upon laborers, | the poor, and upon negros, | and the like;
All these—All the meanness | and agony of the world, | I sit, look
　out upon, see, | hear, and am silent.—

9 meanness] interlined in pencil above de-   9 agony] interlined in pencil above deleted
leted 'horrors'.   'agonies'.

[FOLDER 60. Four leaves of pink paper; a cluster of pinholes in the center,
and one set in the left margin and at the head. Written in a dark ink. The upper part of the second leaf has been cut off and a paste-on, measuring $2\frac{3}{4}$ vertically, attached to the foot. The recto lines on this attached piece are written
in the light revising ink. On the verso appear deleted lines (given in the notes
to verse 4) which, on the evidence of the contours of the paper and matching
cut-off letters, originally appeared on the recto before this piece was cut from
the top and attached to the foot of the leaf. Whitman numbered the leaves
(after the making-up of leaf 2) in the lower left corner as 35–38. In the title
the *T* of 'The' has been mended from a miniscule. 1860, pp. 237–38; Camden,
II, 257–58.]

[*leaf* 1]

　　　35—

As of The Truth.—

O me, man of slack faith | so long! | Standing aloof! | Denying
　portions so long!
Me with mole's eyes, not | yet risen to buoyancy | and vision—not
　yet free,
Me, just aware to-day | of compact all-|diffused Truth.—

[*leaf* 2, *upper section*]

Discovering to-day there is | no lie, or form of lie, | and can be
　none, but | grows just as inevitably | upon itself, as the truth
　| does upon itself, or as | any law of the | earth, or any natural |
　production of the earth.

5 (This is a curious saying, | and may not be realized | immediately
　—But it must | be realized.

1 O me, man . . .] this was originally the   on unseen branches!'. These first two
third verse, the first being 'O my reached   verses were encircled by an ink line and
hands!' and the second, 'O fruit for my   in the left margin written 'tr | down',
hungry | soul! O hanging everywhere | but without indication of planned posi-

I observe the slights and degradations cast by arrogant persons upon
   laborers, the poor, and upon negroes, and the like;
All these—All the meanness and agony without end, I sitting, look
   out upon,
See, hear, and am silent.

18.

1. O ME, man of slack faith so long!
Standing aloof—denying portions so long;
Me with mole's eyes, unrisen to buoyancy and vision—unfree,
Only aware to-day of compact, all-diffused truth,
Discovering to-day there is no lie, or form of lie, and can be none, but
   grows just as inevitably upon itself as the truth does upon itself,
Or as any law of the earth, or any natural production of the earth does.

2. (This is curious, and may not be realized immediately—But it must
   be realized;

---

tion. Then they were deleted by three diagonal strokes, all this being done in a dark ink, possibly the original although it may be slightly blacker.

1 Standing aloof!] originally 'Man of | standing aloof so long—'. In the original ink 'of' was crossed out and the dash excised in favor of the added exclamation mark. Then 'so long' was crossed through in the light ink. Finally, 'Man' was deleted in pencil and the miniscule *s* of 'standing' altered in pencil to a capital. The original addition of an exclamation after 'long' was not excised and so was probably intended eventually to refer back to 'aloof'.

1 long!] the exclamation was added after the deletion of a comma.

3 to-day] originally 'this day', the 'to-' being added over deleted 'this' and brought down to connect with 'day'.

3 compact] originally 'the compact', the first word being deleted in the original ink.

3 Truth.—] interlined above deleted 'light.—', probably in the same ink. The miniscule *t* has been altered to *T*.

4 Discovering to-day] interlined in the light ink above deleted 'Because I discover'. Be-

fore this originally appeared the following two verses, which are found on the verso of the paste-over, crossed out in light ink. The final line is reconstructed from the cut-through letters of the two sections. First verse, 'I thought ['the' *deleted*] Truth [T *mended from* t] sublime— | But how far more sub-|lime it is than I thought!' Second verse, 'Now it is proved to me by | itself, and it is proved | to me by lies,'.

4 grows] originally 'is'. This was deleted and 'stands' written above a caret in the same ink. Then this was deleted in turn and 'grows' added in black ink.

4 inevitably] *y* written in the light ink over original *e*.

4 upon] interlined in the same ink above deleted 'after'.

4 law] before this appears a false start consisting of 'la' written over one of two other letters and then deleted.

5 realized.] a parenthesis closing this word has been deleted in the light ink consequent upon the addition of the the next verse written in light ink on the paste-on.

[*lower section*]

I feel in myself that I represent | falsehoods equally with the | rest
—and that the universe | does.)

[*leaf 3*]

Where has failed a perfect | return indifferent of lies or the truth?

Is it upon the ground, or | in water or fire, or in | the spirit of
man, or | in the meat and blood?

Meditating among liars, and | retreating sternly into | myself, I
see that there | are really no liars or | lies, after all,

10 And that nothing fails its | perfect return—and | that what are
called | lies are perfect returns,

And that each thing exactly | represents itself and what | has pre-
ceded it,

[*leaf 4*]

And that the truth includes | all, and is compact, | just as much as
space | is compact,

And that there is no flaw | or vacuum in the amount | of the truth,
—but that all is | truth, without exception,

And henceforth I will go | celebrate anything I | see or am, and
sing and | laugh, and deny nothing.—

[FOLDER 61. One leaf of pink paper ($9 \times 5\frac{1}{16}$) composed of three pasted-together sections measuring vertically, in order from the top, $2\frac{1}{2}$, then $3\frac{1}{4}$, and finally $4\frac{15}{16}$. The cutting of the edges indicates that no part of these three sections was originally attached to another, at least without a lost interval. A cluster of pinholes toward the foot of the lowest section shows that it was originally the top of a full leaf and has had its lower third or more cut away. No pinholes occur in the upper section, and only one set toward the top of the middle section. The title and the first verse contained on the upper piece are written in the light revising ink, and at a later time than the inscription of Whitman's list on the evidence that in the list the poem is given as 'A Handful of Air' numbered 33. The ink of the middle and lower sections appears to be of the same dark variety. 1860, p. 238; Camden, II, 31.]

As of Origins.

[*upper piece*]

Forms, qualities, lives, humanity, lan-|guage, thoughts,

[*second piece*]

The ones known and the ones | unknown—the ones on the | stars,

I feel in myself that I represent falsehoods equally with the rest,
And that the universe does.)

3. Where has failed a perfect return, indifferent of lies or the truth?
   Is it upon the ground, or in water or fire? or in the spirit of man? or
      in the meat and blood?

4. Meditating among liars, and retreating sternly into myself, I see that
      there are really no liars or lies after all,
   And that nothing fails its perfect return—And that what are called lies
      are perfect returns,
   And that each thing exactly represents itself, and what has preceded it,
   And that the truth includes all, and is compact, just as much as space
      is compact,
   And that there is no flaw or vacuum in the amount of the truth—but
      that all is truth without exception,
   And henceforth I will go celebrate anything I see or am,
   And sing and laugh, and deny nothing.

---

7 indifferent of lies or the truth?] interlined in the light ink above a caret placed between 'return' and its deleted original question mark.

10 And] interlined in black ink above deleted 'But'.

13 vacuum] interlined in the light ink above deleted 'speck'.

13 —but that all . . . exception,] added in the light ink.

14 go celebrate] the first version was 'go | look jubilant at all | things, and sing and | laugh, and deny nothing.' First, 'jubilant' seems to have been deleted and then 'trust' written over deleted 'look', and 'in whatever' over deleted 'at all', with the succeeding 'things' beginning the next line consequentially deleted. Then 'I see,' was interlined above a caret after deleted 'things,', the 'see,' later being deleted and with a different pen above another caret interlined 'hear or see,'. Finally, all of the verse after 'go' was crossed through in the light ink and the revised ending written in below, 'celebrate' being connected with 'go' by a guide line. Before 'anything' was written 'all' but this deleted immediately before 'anything' was written.

19.

FORMS, qualities, lives, humanity, language, thoughts,
The ones known, and the ones unknown—the ones on the stars,

The stars themselves, some formed, | others unformed,
Wonders as of those countries— | the soil, trees, liquids, | inhabi-
    tants, whatever they | may be,

[*third piece*]

5 Splendid suns—the moons and | rings—the countless com-|bina-
    tions and effects,
Such-like, or as good as such-like, | stand provided for I say in a |
    handful of air which I extend | my arm and half-enclose | with
    my hand—That | contains them all—in that the germs of all
    lie waiting;
This is the eternal theory | as of origins.—

[FOLDER 62. Two leaves of pink paper. Cluster of pinholes in the center, and
a set in left margin. Written in a blackish ink. 1860, p. 240; Camden, II,
158–59.]

[*leaf* 1]

       47—

Voices.

Now I make a Leaf | of voices—for I have found | there is nothing
    mightier | than they are,
And I discover that not a | word spoken but is | beautiful, | in its
    place.—
O what is it in me that | makes me tremble so | at voices?
Surely whoever speaks to me | in the right voice, him | or her I
    shall follow, | as the waters follow the | moon, silently, with |
    fluid steps, any where | around the globe.—

[*leaf* 2]

5 Now I believe that all | waits for the right voices;
Where is the perfect and | practised organ? Where | is the devel-
    oped soul?
I see now every word ut-|tered thence has deeper, | sweeter, new
    sounds— | further meanings, im-|possible on less terms,
I see brains and lips closed— | I see tympans of tem-|ples unstruck,
    until | that comes which has | the quality to strike and | to un-
    close,
Until that comes with the | quality slumbering forever | ready in
    all words.—

The stars themselves, some shaped, others unshaped,
Wonders as of those countries—the soil, trees, cities, inhabitants, what-
ever they may be,
Splendid suns, the moons and rings, the countless combinations and
effects,
Such-like, and as good as such-like, visible here or anywhere, stand
provided for in a handful of space, which I extend my arm and half
enclose with my hand,
That contains the start of each and all—the virtue, the germs of all;
That is the theory as of origins.

---

6 I say] interlined in the original ink above a caret.
6 of air] interlined above a caret with a finer pen and blacker ink.
6 hand—] a comma before the dash has been smudged out while still wet. Above 'hand' written and then deleted in the black ink appears '—That contains'.
6 —in that . . . waiting;] interlined in the black ink above a caret.

21.

1. Now I make a leaf of Voices—for I have found nothing mightier than
they are,
And I have found that no word spoken, but is beautiful, in its place.

2. O what is it in me that makes me tremble so at voices?

3. Surely, whoever speaks to me in the right voice, him or her I shall
follow, as the waters follow the moon, silently, with fluid steps,
any where around the globe.

4. Now I believe that all waits for the right voices;
Where is the practised and perfect organ? Where is the developed
Soul?
For I see every word uttered thence has deeper, sweeter, new sounds,
impossible on less terms.

5. I see brains and lips closed—I see tympans and temples unstruck,
Until that comes which has the quality to strike and to unclose,
Until that comes which has the quality to bring forth what lies slum-
bering, forever ready, in all words.

---

1 make] a preceding 'will' deleted in the same ink.
1 have found] interlined in a blacker ink above deleted 'discover'.
1 mightier] interlined in the light ink above the first word of deleted 'more | beau-tiful'.
2 beautiful, in] originally 'also beautiful, and | in', both 'also' and 'and' being de-leted in the light ink.
7 every] interlined in the blacker ink above deleted 'any'.
7 sounds—] a comma before the dash has been partly smudged out while wet.

[FOLDER 63. One leaf of pink paper; a few pinholes in the center. The first verse seems to be written in a different ink and pen from the rest, although the only real difference may lie in the use of a finer pen for the remainder. The poem number 70 is written above and to the right of deleted '69'. 1860, p. 241; Camden, II, 166–67.]

70—

Leaf.—

What am I after all but a | child, pleased with the | sound of my own name? | repeating it over and over,

I cannot tell why it affects | me so much, when I | hear it from women's | voices, or men's voices, or from my own voice,

I stand apart to hear—It | never tires me.—

To you, Your name also.

5 Did you think there was nothing | but two or three pronuncia-tions | in the sound of your own name?

1 pleased with] 'pleased' is interlined in a slightly blacker ink above deleted 'ever attracted'. Later, 'with' was interlined in pencil above deleted 'by'. This 'with' has been traced over the same word written first more faintly in pencil.

1 name? repeating . . . over,] first an origi-nal question mark after 'name' was deleted and the continuation crowded in below the line, 'and repeating it myself,', the last word then being deleted and 'over and over,' interlined above it. Then the 'and' before 'repeating' was deleted in pencil, a question mark placed after 'name', and what seems to be an elon-gated comma after the final 'over'.

2 I cannot tell why . . .] above this verse appear two deleted verses, the first read-ing 'How I return to it!—How | impas-sive—How curious to me!'. This verse was later revised in the darker ink by pre-fixing 'it is' above a caret before 'to me!' and after 'to me!' adding 'It is not a dead word—'. The second verse reads, 'It is living—It looks me in | the face,

[*Cont. on page 185*]

[FOLDER 64. Two leaves of pink paper; a cluster of pinholes in the center. Written in a blackish ink. The poem number 96 is mended from 95. 1860, p. 398; Camden, II, 230–31.]

[*leaf* 1]

96—

To One Shortly To Die.

From all the rest I single | out you, having a message | for you:

You are to die—Let | others tell you what they | please, I cannot prevaricate,

I am exact and merciless, | but I love you—there | is no escape for you.

22.

1. WHAT am I, after all, but a child, pleased with the sound of my own
   name? repeating it over and over,
   I cannot tell why it affects me so much, when I hear it from women's
   voices, and from men's voices, or from my own voice,
   I stand apart to hear—it never tires me.

2. To you, your name also,
   Did you think there was nothing but two or three pronunciations in
   the sound of your name?

[Cont. on page 184]
as with eyes,'. These two verses have seemingly been crossed out at different times, the strokes through the first being heavy, with a thick pen; but those through the second lighter with a finer pen. If, as seems possible, the deleted strokes through the second verse are in the same ink as the original, perhaps it was the first to be rejected.

2 it affects] 'affects' was interlined in the darker ink above deleted 'pleases'. Later, the preceding 'it' was struck through in pencil and 'my name' interlined, this being in turn deleted and 'it' placed before in pencil.

2 or men's] the 'or' is interlined above deleted 'and from' in the darker ink.

2 or from my own voice,] added above a caret and guide line, presumably at the same time 'or' was substituted for 'and from'.

4 To you, Your name also.] the verse originally read, 'Do you want an inkling how much | there is in sound? I give you | the sound of your own name,'. This was crossed through in the blacker ink and above the first part of the deletion was written 'Your own name also, to you;'. Finally, 'to you' (but not the semi-colon) was crossed through and above a caret was prefixed to the verse 'To you,'; the failure to reduce the capitalization of 'Your' was an oversight. What looks like a faint comma after 'also' seems to have been mended to a period.

To One Shortly To Die.

1. FROM all the rest I single out you, having a message for you:
   You are to die—Let others tell you what they please, I cannot prevari-
   cate,
   I am exact and merciless, but I love you—There is no escape for you.

---

1 you:] a comma before the colon has been smudged out while wet.

2 to die] preceding 'shortly' has been deleted.

2 please,] originally 'will', then 'choose,' interlined above deleted 'will' and a caret; finally 'choose' crossed out in pencil and 'please' added. The undeleted comma after 'choose' is presumably intended to apply to 'please'.

3 exact] interlined above deleted 'melancholy'.

3 merciless,] interlined with a finer pen above deleted 'stern'.

3 you—] some mark of punctuation before the dash has been partly smudged out.

Softly I lay my right hand | upon you—you just feel it,

5 I do not argue—I bend my | head close, and half-envelope | it,

I sit quietly by—I remain faithful,

I am more than nurse, more than | parent or neighbor,

[*leaf 2*]

I absolve you from all except | yourself, spiritual, bodily— | that
is eternal,

(The corpse you will leave will | be but excrementitious.)

10 The sun bursts through in unlooked-|for directions!

Strong thoughts fill you, and con-|fidence—you smile,

You forget you are sick, as I | forget you are sick,

You do not see the medicines— | you do not mind the weeping |
friends—I am with you,

I exclude others from you— | there is nothing to be com-|mis-
serated,

15 I do not commisserate you—I | congratulate you.—

[**FOLDER** 65. One leaf of pink paper, a few pinholes in the center. Written
in a medium dark ink. The poem number 99 is altered from 98. On the verso
appear a number of deleted verses, given below. 1860, p. 399; Camden, II,
34–35.]

99—

To Rich Givers.—

What you give me I | cheerfully accept,

A little sustenance, a hut | and garden, a little | money—these as
I ren-|dezvous with my poems,

A traveler's lodging and | breakfast as I journey | through The
States—Why | need I be ashamed to | own such gifts? Why to
| advertise for them?

For I myself am not one | who will bestow nothing | upon man and
woman,

5 For I know that what I | bestow upon any man | or woman is
no less | than the entrance to all the | gifts of the universe.—

3 —Why] *w* is triple underscored.   light ink.
3 Why to advertise for them?] added in the   5 all] interlined in pencil above a caret.

2. Softly I lay my right hand upon you—you just feel it,
   I do not argue—I bend my head close, and half-envelop it,
   I sit quietly by—I remain faithful,
   I am more than nurse, more than parent or neighbor,
   I absolve you from all except yourself, spiritual, bodily—that is eternal,
   (The corpse you will leave will be but excrementitious.)

3. The sun bursts through in unlooked-for directions!
   Strong thoughts fill you, and confidence—you smile!
   You forget you are sick, as I forget you are sick,
   You do not see the medicines—you do not mind the weeping friends
       —I am with you,
   I exclude others from you—there is nothing to be commiserated,
   I do not commiserate—I congratulate you.

To Rich Givers.

WHAT you give me, I cheerfully accept,
A little sustenance, a hut and garden, a little money—these as I ren-
    dezvous with my poems,
A traveller's lodging and breakfast as I journey through The States—
    Why should I be ashamed to own such gifts? Why to advertise for
    them?
For I myself am not one who bestows nothing upon man and woman,
For I know that what I bestow upon any man or woman is no less than
    the entrance to all the gifts of the universe.

[In folder 65, on verso of leaf. Verses written in black ink and deleted with a
single slanting stroke in a somewhat lighter ink and with a finer pen. These
verses have some small relation to a single verse in "To an Exclusive" (Camden,
III, 267), which was never printed; but the resemblance is slight.]

Therefore I put upon record that | I am well aware what | floats
suspended in you, you future, | as qualities float suspended in
the | air,

1 Therefore I . . .] two false starts were made and deleted: the first, 'Therefore I', and below it 'This'; then to the right the verse was begun.

1 well aware] interlined above 'not un-aware'.
1 suspended] interlined above a caret.
1 suspended] interlined above a caret.

[*Cont. on page 189*]

[FOLDER 66. One blue tax form without pinholes. Written with a fine pen in black ink. The title is added in the light revising ink below the original title, which has been cut off leaving only traces of a few descenders, two of which may just possibly represent some poem number. 1860, p. 400; Camden, II, 165.]

To a Pupil.

Is reform needed? Is it through | you?
The greater the reform needed, | the greater the Personality |
    you need to accomplish | it.—

You! do you not think it | would serve to have eyes, | blood, com-
    plexion, clean | and sweet?
Do you not think it would | serve to have such a | body and soul
    that | when you enter the | crowd, an atmosphere | of desire
    and command | shall accompany you, and | every one be im-
    pressed | by your Personality?

5 O the Magnet over and over!
  Go! give up all else, and commence | to-day to inure yourself to
    pluck reality, | self-esteem, definiteness, elevatedness,
  Rest not till you rivet and publish yourself | of your own Per-
    sonality.—

5 O the Magnet . . .] this final stanza was probably an addition, as shown by its being crowded in and by the heavy corrections in comparison to the lack of revision in what is presumably the fair copy of the lines above. The start of this stanza was originally, 'Freedom over and over!'. 'Freedom' was deleted and 'The Magnet' interlined, then 'The' deleted and 'O the' interlined above a caret. After 'over!' appears deleted original 'Yourself over and over!'.

6 Go! The verse originally started, 'This day go!'. Above deleted 'This day' was then interlined 'O to-day'. When this was deleted, 'go' was capitalized by mending.

6 to-day to] interlined above a caret placed after deleted 'and'.

6 definiteness,] a following 'and' has been crossed through.

[Cont. from page 187]

And therefore I charge the young | men, should I myself | not extract the thousand | poems, (as I now intend) that they nudge | others to extract them and | embody them,

And therefore I commit this, | as a charge to you, you | future, intertwined with | the large, compact, | idiomatic volume,

4 And therefore I infuse it in the | air, indestructible addressing you you future—for | fear I myself may not make | the divine volume.—

2 should I myself] Whitman first began to write, 'should I no more | be', but then stopped, deleted 'no more be' and interlined 'myself' above the first two words before continuing 'not extract'.

2 (as I now intend)] interlined above a caret.

3 to you] y mended over some other letter, just possibly an s.

4 And] to the left of this and slightly above the line is deleted 'Side', apparently a false start.

4 therefore] interlined above a caret.

4 addressing you you future—] interlined with a caret over deleted 'as'.

4 myself] interlined above a caret.

To a Pupil.

1. Is reform needed? Is it through you?
  The greater the reform needed, the greater the PERSONALITY you need to accomplish it.

2. You! do you not see how it would serve to have eyes, blood, complexion, clean and sweet?
  Do you not see how it would serve to have such a body and Soul, that when you enter the crowd, an atmosphere of desire and command enters with you, and every one is impressed with your personality?

3. O the magnet! the flesh over and over!
  Go, mon cher! if need be, give up all else, and commence to-day to inure yourself to pluck, reality, self-esteem, definiteness, elevatedness,
  Rest not, till you rivet and publish yourself of your own personality.

[FOLDER 67. Two leaves of pink paper; a cluster of pinholes in the center and a few sets in the left margin. Written in a dark ink. In the upper right corner, in blue pencil, is Whitman's notation '1858', deleted in blue pencil. 1860, pp. 400–401; Camden, II, 39.]

[*leaf* 1]

40—

A Past Presidentiad, and | one to come also.

Why reclining, interrogating? | Why myself and all drowzing?
What deepening twilight! Scum | floating atop of the waters!
Who are they as bats and | night-dogs askant in the | Capitol?
What a filthy Presidentiad! O | South, your torrid suns! O | North,
    your arctic freezings!
5 Are those really Congressmen? | Are those the great | Judges? Is
    that the Presi-|dent?

[*leaf* 2]

Then I will sleep awhile | yet—for I see that | These States sleep,
    for | reasons;
With gathering murk—with | muttering thunder and | lambent
    shoots, we all | duly awake.—
South North, East West, | inland and seaboard, we | will surely
    awake.—

[FOLDER 68. One small piece of ruled white laid paper ($3\frac{9}{16} \times 6\frac{3}{8}$); a few pinholes in the center. Written in a dark-brown ink across the rules. The title '*To a Cantatrice.*—' is found below two deleted titles. Immediately above it is '*To an architect.*', and above that, '*To an artist.*'. Perhaps as a suggestion for a later title, in the upper left corner in the light revising ink Whitman sketched in '*Lectures*' (or perhaps '*Lecturer*'); this is preceded by an illegible short word or two, and above this was placed '*To*'. But the whole notation was smudged out while the ink was still wet. This piece of paper fits into the missing half of the leaf in folder 47 containing "To a Historian." The pencil prose lines on its verso are transcribed in the reconstruction given in folder 47. 1860, p. 401; Camden, I, 11–12.]

To a Cantatrice.—

Here take this gift,
I was reserving it waiting for some hero or general,—

To The States,

To Identify the 16th, 17th, or 18th Presidentiad.

WHY reclining, interrogating? Why myself and all drowsing?

What deepening twilight! Scum floating atop of the waters!

Who are they, as bats and night-dogs, askant in the Capitol?

What a filthy Presidentiad! (O south, your torrid suns! O north, your arctic freezings!)

Are those really Congressmen? Are those the great Judges? Is that the President?

Then I will sleep a while yet—for I see that These States sleep, for reasons;

(With gathering murk—with muttering thunder and lambent shoots, we all duly awake,

South, north, east, west, inland and seaboard, we will surely awake.)

---

4 torrid] interlined with a fine pen above 'fiery'.

4 arctic] interlined with a fine pen above 'icy'. The *z* in 'freezings' has been mended, probably from an *s*.

5 President] *P* has been enlarged by mending, but was always a capital.

7 all] the original 'all' was deleted in pencil and 'will' interlined in pencil above a caret; this then was deleted and 'all' pencilled below the original.

7 duly] with the fine pen 'South and North' was interlined above a caret preceding 'duly' but then deleted in pencil.

8 South North, East West, . . .] this verse was added in pencil. Pencilled 'and' placed between 'South' and 'North' and also between 'East' and 'West' have been crossed out in black ink. After 'East' a pencil comma has been deleted in pencil, no doubt currently.

8 inland] a preceding false start, with a capital 'I' has been deleted in pencil before the writing of 'inland'.

8 will] the original 'will' was crossed out and 'all' interlined in pencil; then this was deleted and 'will' returned below the line.

To a Cantatrice.

HERE, take this gift!

I was reserving it for some hero, orator, or general,

---

1 gift,] Whitman proceeded, 'more precious than' before halting and deleting the words.

2 was reserving] interlined in pencil above deleted 'reserved'.

2 waiting] interlined above a caret.

2 general,—] the dash was added in pencil.

One who should serve the good old | cause, the freedom of my
    race, | the cause of my soul, the cause *en-avant*,
But I see that it belongs to you| just as much as to any of them.—

[FOLDER numbered 69, 70, 72. One leaf of pink paper ($9\frac{1}{16} \times 5\frac{1}{8}$) composed
of two pasted-together pieces, the top measuring $3\frac{1}{2}$ vertically and the bottom
8 inches. Although some $2\frac{3}{8}$ inches of the lower section is covered by the paste-
over, no writing appears underneath. The top of the upper piece is considerably
rumpled and has been pressed out flat. The section numbers 1 and 2 were
added in the light revising ink, the '2' after the pieces had been pasted together.
The first section is written with a slightly finer pen than the other, but both
are in the dark ink. 1860, p. 403 (printed in reverse order); Camden, I, 15,
and III, 300 (verses 3–6 rejected in 1871).]

[*upper section*]

To You.

1

If you, passing, meet me, | and desire to speak | to me, why should
    you not speak | to me?
And why should I not | speak to you?—

[*lower section*]

2

Come, let us twain walk | aside awhile from the rest;
Now we are together pri-|vately, do you discard | ceremony,
5 Vouchsafe to me what has yet | been vouchsafed to none,
Tell me the whole story— | Tell me what you would | not tell
    your brother, | wife, husband, or | physician.—

1 passing,] interlined with a finer pen above
deleted 'should'.
1 should you] interlined above a caret.
6 what you would . . .] this last part of the
verse is a later addition. The original read,
'Tell me more than you | would the phy-
sician.—'. Starting with 'more', the verse
is deleted and the addition linked to
'me' by a guide line. In the addition before 'wife' is the slip 'wh' deleted.

[FOLDER numbered 69, 70, 72. Second part. Five leaves of pink paper of the
same cutting, pasted together in the left margin by a strip of linen tape at front
and back, each pink leaf being mounted on a white paper stub. The tape at the
back shows signs that it has been torn away from other leaves since paper
adheres to its back and it is also torn irregularly. A cluster of pinholes in the
centers. Written in blackish ink. The poem number 57 was altered from 56.
Whitman numbered the leaves in pencil 1–5 in the lower left corner. 1860, pp.
404–5; Camden, II, 256–57.]

One who should serve the good old cause, the progress and freedom
    of the race, the cause of my Soul;
But I see that what I was reserving belongs to you just as much as to
    any.

3 One who should serve] originally this verse only continued the one above, and was written | 'who should strike for'. First 'who should' was deleted and the *e* of 'strike' mended to *ing*. A deleted 'of' is found above and to the right of 'for'. Then 'striking for' was crossed through and 'who should serve' interlined. Finally, in pencil, 'One' was prefixed to start a new verse.

3 cause,] after this an original 'for' has been deleted.
3 the cause of my soul] interlined with a caret above deleted 'and'.
4 just as much as to any] Whitman first began the line 'just as much' but then stopped and deleted the words before continuing 'before any'. Later, 'before' is deleted and 'just as much as to' interlined above a caret in pencil.

To You.

LET us twain walk aside from the rest;
Now we are together privately, do you discard ceremony,
Come! vouchsafe to me what has yet been vouchsafed to none—Tell
    me the whole story,
Tell me what you would not tell your brother, wife, husband, or
    physician.

To You.

STRANGER! if you, passing, meet me, and desire to speak to me, why
    should you not speak to me?
And why should I not speak to you?

Mannahatta.

I was asking for something | specific and perfect for | my city—and
  behold! | here is the aboriginal | name!

Now I see what there is | in a name, a word, | liquid, sane, unruly,
  | musical, self-sufficient,

I see that the word of my | city is that word up there,

Because I see that word | nested | in nests of water-bays, | superb,
  with tall and | wonderful spires,

[*leaf* 2]

5 Rich, hemmed thick all | around with sailships | and steamships
    —an | island sixteen miles | long, solid-founded,

Numberless crowded streets, | —high growths of iron, | slender,
  strong, light, | splendidly uprising | toward clear skies,

Tides swift and ample, | well-loved by me toward | sun-down,

The flowing sea-currents, | the little islands, the | larger adjoining
  islands, | the heights, the villas,

The countless masts, the | white shore-steamers, | the lighters, the
  ferry-|boats, the black sea-|steamers, well-model'd,

[*leaf* 3]

10 The down-town streets, | the jobbers' houses of | business,—the
    houses of | business of the ship-|merchants, money-brokers, |
    factors,

Immigrants arriving, fifteen | or twenty thousand in | a week,

The carts hauling goods— | the manly race of | drivers of horses
    —The | river streets—the brown-|faced sailors;

The summer air, the bright | sun shining, and the | sailing clouds
  aloft,

The winter snows, the | sleigh-bells, the broken ice | in the river,
  passing slowly | up or down with the | flood-tide or ebb-tide,

[*leaf* 4]

15 The mechanics of the city, | the masters, well-formed, | beautiful-
    faced, looking | you straight in the eyes,

Trottoirs thronged— | vehicles—Broadway— | the women, the
  | shops, the shows,

The parades, processions, bugles | playing, flags flying, | drums
  beating,

Mannahatta.

I WAS asking for something specific and perfect for my city, and behold!
    here is the aboriginal name!
Now I see what there is in a name, a word, liquid, sane, unruly, mu-
    sical, self-sufficient,
I see that the word of my city, is that word up there,
Because I see that word nested in nests of water-bays, superb, with tall
    and wonderful spires,
Rich, hemmed thick all around with sailships and steamships—an
    island sixteen miles long, solid-founded,
Numberless crowded streets—high growths of iron, slender, strong,
    light, splendidly uprising toward clear skies;
Tides swift and ample, well-loved by me, toward sundown,
The flowing sea-currents, the little islands, the larger adjoining islands,
    the heights, the villas,
The countless masts, the white shore-steamers, the lighters, the ferry-
    boats, the black sea-steamers, well-model'd;
The down-town streets, the jobbers' houses of business—the houses
    of business of the ship-merchants, and money-brokers—the river-
    streets,
Immigrants arriving, fifteen or twenty thousand in a week,
The carts hauling goods—the manly race of drivers of horses—the
    brown-faced sailors,
The summer-air, the bright sun shining, and the sailing clouds aloft,
The winter snows, the sleigh-bells—the broken ice in the river, passing
    along, up or down, with the flood-tide or ebb-tide;
The mechanics of the city, the masters, well-formed, beautiful-faced,
    looking you straight in the eyes;
Trottoirs thronged—vehicles—Broadway—the women—the shops and
    shows,
The parades, processions, bugles playing, flags flying, drums beating;

---

1 specific and perfect] interlined in the light ink above deleted 'native and definite'.

3 that word up there,] interlined in the light ink between deleted 'the word Man-|nahatta,'.

4 that word] 'that' interlined in the light ink above deleted 'the'; at the same time, apparently, after 'word' was deleted 'Mannahatta' originally beginning the next line, its capital mended from a miniscule.

4 and] the original 'and' was deleted in black ink and then restored as an interlineation above a caret with a fine pen.

6 skies] sk written over cl.

7 Tides] originally 'The tides', the first word being deleted in the light ink and 'tides' capitalized by mending.

12 The river] T triple underscored.

16 Trottoirs] originally 'The trottoirs', the first word being deleted in the light ink and 'trottoirs' capitalized by mending.

16 thronged—] a following 'the' is deleted in the light ink.

16 Broadway—the women] originally, 'Broadway— | the cheerful and well-dress'd | crowds, the women', the deletion being made in the light ink.

A Million people,—manners | free and superb—open | voices,— hospitality,— | the most courageous | and friendly young men,
The free city! No slaves! | No owners of slaves!

[*leaf* 5]

20 The beautiful city! The city of hurried and sparkling waters The city | of spires and masts!

The proud and turbulent | city! The city nested | in bays! My city!

The city of such women | I am mad to be with | them—I will return | after death to be with | them!

The city of such young men, | I swear I cannot | live happy without | I often go talk, walk, | eat, drink, sleep, with | them!

18 A Million of people—] originally, 'Millions of people', the 'A' being prefixed above the line, the final *s* of 'Millions' and the following 'of' being deleted all in the regular ink. By a slip the capitalization of 'Million' was not reduced. The dash after 'people,' was added later in the light ink, as were the dashes after 'voices,' and 'hospitality,'.
18 superb—] interlined in the light ink above deleted 'rich,'.
20 The city of hurried . . . waters] interlined in the light ink with a guide line above a caret. By a slip no punctuation was added after 'waters'.
21 The proud] originally this continued the verse above, but a new verse was indicated by deleting the original 'The' and prefixing another in the margin, in the light ink. 'proud' is interlined in black ink with a fine pen above deleted 'free'.
22 them!] the exclamation mark was added in the same ink after a deleted comma.

[FOLDER 71. Twenty leaves of pink paper, including two of white wove. Leaves 1–3, 5–6, 9–10, 13–20 are on p1(b) paper from the same pack, and leaves 7–8 on p1(a) paper, that on which most of "Premonition" was written. Leaf 4 is pink paper of a different cutting, p2(a). The white wove paper of leaves 11–12 cannot be linked with other of the white paper. The original lower part of pink leaf 10 is pasted at the foot of white leaf 12, demonstrating that white leaves 11–12 are a later insertion. In the upper right margin the leaves are numbered (by Whitman?) as 1–20; but two earlier though incomplete series are also present. One of these series foliates leaves 7–13 at the head as 1–7. The other, in the lower left corner, numbers leaves 4–9 as 1–6, leaf 10 as 6½, leaves 11–12 as 15–16, leaves 13–14 as 7–8, leaf 15 as 14, and leaves 16–20 as 9–13. Leaves 2–3 are curiously headed 56a and 56b. Possibly this is intended to have something to do with a poem number, but since there are already pink-paper poems numbered 55 and 56, the numbers on the two leaves probably signify something else, the purport of which is uncertain. There are difficulties in the way of working out fully the meaning of the variant paper and of the early foliation. However, the paper study in the general introduction has made it evident that the white-paper leaves 12 and 13 must have been added to the

[*Cont. on page 197*]

A million people—manners free and superb—open voices—hospitality
   —the most courageous and friendly young men;
The free city! no slaves! no owners of slaves!
The beautiful city! the city of hurried and sparkling waters! the city
   of spires and masts!
The city nested in bays! my city!
The city of such women, I am mad to be with them! I will return after
   death to be with them!
The city of such young men, I swear I cannot live happy, without I
   often go talk, walk, eat, drink, sleep, with them!

[Cont. from page 196]

poem about two years after the last pink-paper leaf was inscribed; hence, in
the main, the question of the paper is not intimately associated with that of the
rejected foliation. Since p1(a) and p1(b) paper represent adjacent packs, the
only real interloper is leaf 4, which has the original title "Contact." It is hard
to be certain whether this represents the very first leaf inscribed, or whether it
is an independent poem brought late into the series. The latter may seem the
more probable, however. Of the two rejected trial foliations, it seems evident
that the longer series beginning with leaf 4 numbered as 1 is the original,
although it must be emphasized that no foliation was made at all until after
the white paper had been added in 1859. What the original order of inscription
was, therefore, we cannot know except that it is likely that the p1(a) paper
either directly preceded the p1(b), as in "Premonition," or directly followed
the last leaf to be inscribed on p1(b) paper. The original foliation proceeds
very well in order if we imagine the two white paper leaves placed at the end
of the manuscript except for the pink leaf 10 which was to be numbered $6\frac{1}{2}$.
This numbering can probably be explained as the result of the secting of the
leaf and the pasting of its lower portion at the foot of the second white leaf,
the upper part of the leaf then being moved back into the already numbered
sequence and thus perforce foliated as $6\frac{1}{2}$. Since this seems to be the only ex-
planation for the odd numbering, the other series of 1–7, which numbers the
part leaf normally, is almost certainly later. 1860, pp. 259–68; Camden, I,
213–22.]

[Leaf 1, pink paper ($8\frac{7}{16} \times 5\frac{1}{16}$), cluster of pinholes in center and one set in upper left corner. The poem number 36 was added later in a black ink, the poem itself being written in a dark ink.]

36—

Poem of Joys.

O to make a most jubilant poem!
O full of music! Full of manhood, | womanhood, infancy—Full |
    of common employments— | Full of grain and trees.
O for the voices of animals! | O for the swiftness and balance | of
    fishes!
O for the dropping of rain-drops | in a poem!
5 O for the sunshine and the | motion of waves in a poem!

O to be on the sea! the wind— | the wide waters around;
O to sail in a ship under full | sail at sea!

O the joy of my spirit! It is uncaged— | It darts like lightning,
It is not satisfied with this globe, or a | certain time—it will have
    thousands of | globes, and all time.—

[Leaves 2–3; same cutting of pink paper as leaf 1 and the same matching pin-holes. At the head of leaf 2 pencilled in Whitman's hand is '56a', and at the head of leaf 3 is '56b'. On leaf 2, in the left margin between lines 1 and 2 is a pencilled '5', the hand uncertain but probably Whitman's. The leaves are numbered 2–3 (by the annotator?) in the upper right corner.]

10 O the engineer's joys!
To go with a locomotive!
To hear the hiss of steam—the merry | shriek—the steam-whistle
    — | the laughing locomotive!
To push with resistless way, | and speed off in the distance.

O the horseman's and horsewoman's | joys!
15 The saddle—the gallop—the pressure | upon the seat—the soft
    gurgling | by the ears and hair.—

O the fireman's joys!
I hear the alarm at dead of | night—I hear bells—| shouts! I pass
    the | crowd—I run,
The sight of the flames maddens | me with pleasure.—

Poem of Joys.

1. O TO make a most jubilant poem!
    O full of music! Full of manhood, womanhood, infancy!
    O full of common employments! Full of grain and trees.

2. O for the voices of animals! O for the swiftness and balance of fishes!
    O for the dropping of rain-drops in a poem!
    O for the sunshine and motion of waves in a poem.

3. O to be on the sea! the wind, the wide waters around;
    O to sail in a ship under full sail at sea.

4. O the joy of my spirit! It is uncaged! It darts like lightning!
    It is not enough to have this globe, or a certain time—I will have thou-
        sands of globes, and all time.

5. O the engineer's joys!
    To go with a locomotive!
    To hear the hiss of steam—the merry shriek—the steam-whistle—the
        laughing locomotive!
    To push with resistless way, and speed off in the distance.

6. O the horseman's and horsewoman's joys!
    The saddle—the gallop—the pressure upon the seat—the cool gurgling
        by the ears and hair.

7. O the fireman's joys!
    I hear the alarm at dead of night,
    I hear bells—shouts!—I pass the crowd—I run!
    The sight of the flames maddens me with pleasure.

---

1 make] interlined in black ink above deleted 'write'.

2 trees.] a dash following the period has been deleted.

3 O for the voices] a paragraph sign in a lighter ink precedes this line to indicate the start of a new stanza.

3 animals] 'wild' preceding this has been deleted in the same ink.

10 O the engineer's joys!] an addition in the light ink.

11 To go] originally 'O to go', the 'O' being deleted and 'to' capitalized in the light ink.

12 To hear] interlined in the light ink above a caret and deleted 'O'.

13 To push] originally 'O to push', the 'O' being deleted and 'to' capitalized in the light ink.

15 soft] interlined in the same ink above a caret.

17 bells—] a preceding 'the' has been deleted first in pencil and then in black ink. A comma before the dash has been excised.

17 shouts] a preceding 'the' has been deleted first in pencil and then in black ink.

17 run,] an original exclamation mark has been smudged out and crossed through while wet, and the comma inserted.

[Written progressively smaller to crowd in at the foot of the page.]

    O the joy of the strong-brawned | fighter, towering in the arena, | conscious of power, thirsting to meet | his opponent!

[leaf 3]

20 O the joy of that vast elemental | sympathy which only the | human soul is capable | of generating and emitting | in steady and limitless floods!

    O the mother's joys!
The watching—the endurance—the | precious love—the anguish — | the patiently yielded life.—

    O the joy of increase, growth, | recuperation!
The joy of soothing and pacifying! | The joy of concord and harmony!

25 O to go back to the place where | I was born!
    O to hear the birds sing once | more! To ramble about | the house and barn, and over | the fields once more—and | along the lanes once more.—

[Leaf 4; pink paper originally numbered 1 (deleted) in the lower left corner. The cutting is different from any of the other pink leaves in this series, and though the leaf shares some pinholes, it has others, as at the top, which differ from those in leaves 1–3 but agree with the leaves that follow. At the head is the title 'Contact.' deleted in black ink. The first line, and especially the first letter, is written large as at the start of a major poem. Verse 31 was once crossed out by diagonal pencil strokes, but these have been erased, allowing the verse to stand.]

    O male and female!
    O the presence of women! | I swear | nothing is more exquisite | to me than the presence | of women;
    O for the girl, my mate! O for | perfect happiness with my mate!
30 O the young man as I pass! | O I am sick after the | friendship of him who | seems indifferent to me!
    O of men—of women, toward me as I | pass—The memory of | only one look—The boy | lingering and waiting.—

8. O the joy of the strong-brawned fighter, towering in the arena, in
perfect condition, conscious of power, thirsting to meet his op-
ponent.

9. O the joy of that vast elemental sympathy which only the human Soul
is capable of generating and emitting in steady and limitless floods.

10. O the mother's joys!
The watching—the endurance—the precious love—the anguish—the
patiently yielded life.

11. O the joy of increase, growth, recuperation,
The joy of soothing and pacifying—the joy of concord and harmony.

12. O to go back to the place where I was born!
O to hear the birds sing once more!
To ramble about the house and barn, and over the fields, once more,
And through the orchard and along the old lanes once more.

13. O male and female!
O the presence of women! (I swear, nothing is more exquisite to me
than the presence of women;)
O for the girl, my mate! O for happiness with my mate!
O the young man as I pass! O I am sick after the friendship of him
who, I fear, is indifferent to me.

14. O the streets of cities!
The flitting faces—the expressions, eyes, feet, costumes! O I cannot
tell how welcome they are to me;
O of men—of women toward me as I pass—The memory of only one
look—the boy lingering and waiting.

---

20 that] *at* mended over *e* in the same ink.
22 watching] the *i* inserted.
22 patiently] interlined in the light ink above
a caret.
26 about] 'by' was first written and crossed
out before 'about' was inscribed.
28 I swear] preceding this is 'As for me,' deleted in the light ink.

28 women;] the semi-colon inserted before a
smudged and crossed-out exclamation
mark.
31 toward me] interlined in the light ink
above a caret. Earlier, 'toward me' had
been interlined in pencil above a caret
after 'men'; finally, the pencil markings
were all deleted and the interlineation
made in ink.

[Leaves 5–8. Pink paper; the leaves are numbered in the lower left corner 2–5 (deleted except for the 5). At the head, leaves 7–8 are numbered 1–2. The pinholes seem to match in these four leaves. At the top left on leaf 7 is the deleted annotator's pencil figure '361'; and at top right above 'May' in verse 46 is Whitman's pencilled 'Fifth Month'. Beginning with leaf 7 the ink for the verses seems to be somewhat darker. There was a clear group, or stanza, break after verse 37 but none thereafter until the end of this section.]

[*leaf* 5]

O the streets of cities!

The flitting faces—the expressions, | eyes, feet, costumes! I | cannot tell how welcome they | are to me.—

O to have been brought up on | bays, lagoons, creeks, or | along the coast!

35 O to be employed there all my life!

O the briny and damp smell—the shore— | the salt weeds exposed | at low water!

O the work of fishermen—the | work of the eel-fisher | and clam-fisher!

O it is I!

I come with my clam-rake | and spade—I come with | my eel-spear;

40 Is the tide out? I join the | group of clam-diggers on | the flats,

[*leaf* 6]

I laugh and work with them— | I joke and sing at my | work, like a mettlesome | young man;

In winter I take my eel-basket | and eel-spear, and travel | out on foot on the ice— | I have a small axe to | cut holes in the ice,

Behold me, well-clothed, going | gaily, or returning in the | afternoon—my brood of | boys accompanying | me,

My brood of grown and part-grown boys, who love to | be with none so well as | they love to be with me— | by day to work with me, | and by night to sleep | with me;

45 Or another time, in warm weather, | out in a boat, to lift the | lobster-pots, where they are sunk with | heavy stones, (I know the buoys,)

[*leaf* 7]

O the sweetness of the May morning | upon the water, as I row, | just before sunrise, toward | the buoys!

15. O to have been brought up on bays, lagoons, creeks, or along the coast!
   O to continue and be employed there all my life!
     O the briny and damp smell—the shore—the salt weeds exposed at low water,
  The work of fishermen—the work of the eel-fisher and clam-fisher.

16. O it is I!
   I come with my clam-rake and spade! I come with my eel-spear;
   Is the tide out? I join the group of clam-diggers on the flats,
   I laugh and work with them—I joke at my work, like a mettlesome young man.

17. In winter I take my eel-basket and eel-spear and travel out on foot on the ice—I have a small axe to cut holes in the ice;
   Behold me, well-clothed, going gayly, or returning in the afternoon—my brood of tough boys accompanying me,
   My brood of grown and part-grown boys, who love to be with none else so well as they love to be with me,
   By day to work with me, and by night to sleep with me.

18. Or, another time, in warm weather, out in a boat, to lift the lobster-pots, where they are sunk with heavy stones, (I know the buoys;)
   O the sweetness of the Fifth Month morning upon the water, as I row, just before sunrise, toward the buoys;

---

36 and damp] 'damp' was interlined above a caret, perhaps in the same ink; at some later time 'and' was prefixed in pencil; and still later an ink guide line added down to the caret.

38 O it is I!] inserted later in a darker ink.

43 brood of boys] originally 'brood of half-grown boys'. First 'half' was deleted and 'grown and part-' interlined in black ink above a caret with a guide line. This was deleted in ink, and 'grown' excised later in pencil.

44 grown and part-grown] interlined above a caret in pencil and then traced over in black ink.

45 Or another time . . .] this verse is written in progressively smaller letters to crowd it in at the foot of the leaf.

I pull the wicker pots up slant-|ingly—the dark-green lobsters |
    are desperate with their | claws as I take them out— | I insert
    wooden pegs in | the joints of their pincers,

I go to all the places, one | after another, and then row | back to
    the shore,

There in a huge kettle of boiling | water the lobsters shall be |
    boiled till their color becomes | scarlet:

50 Or another time mackerel taking— | Voracious, mad for the
    hook, | near the surface, they seem | to fill the water for miles;

[*leaf* 8]

Or another time fishing for | rock-fish in Chesapeake | bay—I one
    of the brown-faced | crew;

Or another time trailing for | blue-fish off Paumanok, | I stand
    with braced body, | my left foot on the gunwale, | my swift
    right arm throwing | the coils of slender rope,

In sight around me the quick | veering and darting of fifty | skiffs,
    my companions.—

[*remainder of leaf 8, after a space. The last verse is written progressively
smaller to fit it on the leaf.*]

O boating on the rivers!

55 The voyage down the Niagara, | (the St. Lawrence,)—the superb
    | scenery—the steamers—the ships | sailing—the thousand
    islands—the occa-|sional timber-raft, and the raftsmen with
    | long-reaching sweep-oars—the little huts | on the rafts, and
    the stream of smoke | when they cook supper toward eve-
    ning.—

[Leaves 9 and 10. Both leaves pink paper, but leaf 10 is a part leaf measuring
$5\frac{5}{8}$ vertically. The cut-off lower part has been pasted to the foot of leaf 12.
Both share some (but not all) pinholes with leaves 7–8, and have others differ-
ing. The deleted leaf numbers 6 and $6\frac{1}{2}$ appear in the lower left corner, and
undeleted 3 and 4 at the head. The three sections are separated by spaces
from each other.]

[*leaf* 9]

O something pernicious and dread!

Something far away, from a puny and pious life!

O something escaped from the | anchorage! Something | driving
    free!

I pull the wicker pots up slantingly—the dark green lobsters are desperate with their claws, as I take them out—I insert wooden pegs in the joints of their pincers,
I go to all the places, one after another, and then row back to the shore,
There, in a huge kettle of boiling water, the lobsters shall be boiled till their color becomes scarlet.

19. Or, another time, mackerel-taking,
Voracious, mad for the hook, near the surface, they seem to fill the water for miles;
Or, another time, fishing for rock-fish in Chesapeake Bay—I one of the brown-faced crew;
Or, another time, trailing for blue-fish off Paumanok, I stand with braced body,
My left foot is on the gunwale—my right arm throws the coils of slender rope,
In sight around me the quick veering and darting of fifty skiffs, my companions.

20. O boating on the rivers!
The voyage down the Niagara, (the St. Lawrence,)—the superb scenery—the steamers,
The ships sailing—the Thousand Islands—the occasional timber-raft, and the raftsmen with long-reaching sweep-oars,
The little huts on the rafts, and the stream of smoke when they cook supper at evening.

21. O something pernicious and dread!
Something far away from a puny and pious life!
Something unproved! Something in a trance!
Something escaped from the anchorage, and driving free.

---

50 Voracious] *V* is triple underscored.
52 rope,] a dash was first written but then deleted and the comma inserted before it.
55 rafts,] a dash following the comma has been deleted.
55 when they cook] originally 'where they are cooking', the *re* of 'where' being mended in black ink to *n*, the *ing* of 'cooking' crossed out, and 'are' deleted in the same black ink.

55 toward] interlined in black ink above deleted 'at'.
56 pernicious] interlined in the light ink, with a guide line to a caret, above deleted 'wild'.
56 dread!] interlined in black ink and fine pen above deleted 'untamed!'
57 Something far. . . .] this verse interlined in the light ink above the deleted line 'Something as in a dream!', which originally continued the first verse.

O to work in mines, or forging | iron!
60 Foundry-casting—the Foundry | itself—the building—the rude
| high roof—the ample shadowed | space—the furnace—the
| hot liquid poured out | and running.—

O the joys of the soldier!
To feel the presence of a brave | general—to feel his sympathy—
| to behold his calmness—to be | warmed in the rays of his |
smile!

[*leaf* 10]

To go to battle! To hear | the bugles and drums!
To hear the artillery! To see | the glistening of the bayonets | and
musket-barrels in | the sun!
65 To see men fall and die and | not complain!
O to taste the savage taste of | blood!
To be so devilish! To gloat | so over the wounds and | deaths of
the enemy!

[Leaves 11 and 12. White wove paper ($8 \times 6\frac{1}{16}$), sharing some pinholes with
previous leaves but also having others different. Written in black ink with
a thick pen. On the blank lower part of leaf 12 is pasted a piece of pink paper
measuring 3 inches vertically and identifiable as the original lower part of
leaf 10. At the head the leaves are numbered in pencil 5–6, and in the lower
left corner, deleted, 15–16, the 16 on the pink-paper piece.]

[*leaf* 11]

O the whaleman's joys! O I voyage | the old voyage again!
I feel the ship's motion under—I feel the Atlantic breezes fanning
me.
70 I hear the cry again sent down from the | mast-head, *There she*
blows.
Again I spring in the rigging to look out | with the rest—We see
—we descend, | wild with excitement,
I leap in the lowered boat—we row | toward our prey where he
lies,
We approach stealthy and silent—I see | the mountainous mass,
lethargic, basking,
I see the harpooneer standing up—I | see the weapon dart from
his | vigorous arm;

22. O to work in mines, or forging iron!
Foundry casting—the foundry itself—the rude high roof—the ample and shadowed space,
The furnace—the hot liquid poured out and running.

23. O the joys of the soldier!
To feel the presence of a brave general! to feel his sympathy!
To behold his calmness! to be warmed in the rays of his smile!
To go to battle! to hear the bugles play, and the drums beat!
To hear the artillery! to see the glittering of the bayonets and musket-barrels in the sun!
To see men fall and die and not complain!
To taste the savage taste of blood! to be so devilish!
To gloat so over the wounds and deaths of the enemy.

24. O the whaleman's joys! O I cruise my old cruise again!
I feel the ship's motion under me—I feel the Atlantic breezes fanning me,
I hear the cry again sent down from the mast-head, *There she blows,*
Again I spring up the rigging, to look with the rest—We see—we descend, wild with excitement,
I leap in the lowered boat—We row toward our prey, where he lies,
We approach, stealthy and silent—I see the mountainous mass, lethargic, basking,
I see the harpooner standing up—I see the weapon dart from his vigorous arm;

---

60 the Foundry] *F* triple underscored.
66 O To taste] the 'O' is prefixed, and 'taste' is interlined above deleted 'feel', both in black ink and fine pen. The capital of original 'To' was inadvertently not reduced.
67 wounds and deaths] 'wounds' is interlined in pencil above deleted 'deaths'; and 'deaths' in pencil above deleted 'wounds'.
69 I feel . . . fanning me.] this verse crowded in later in the light ink. In 'motion' the

ti is heavily mended as if Whitman by a slip had first written 'moot', but the letters underneath are uncertain except for a final *t*. In 'Atlantic' the *A* is mended over some letter which may be an *a*.
73 the mountainous] a smudged out *h* and the beginning of a following letter was apparently written and wiped out before 'the' was inscribed.
74 harpooneer] originally 'harpooneersman', the *sman* being deleted in the same ink.

75 O swift, again far out in the ocean, | the wounded whale, settling,
running | to windward, tows me,
Again I see him rise to breathe— | we row close, again,
I see the lance driven through | his side, prest deep, turned | in
the wound,

[*leaf* 12]

Again we back off—I see him | settle again—the life is | leaving
him fast,
As he rises he spouts blood— | I see him swim in circles | narrower
and narrower, cutting | the water,
80 I see him die—he gives one | convulsive leap in the centre | of the
circle, and falls flat | and quiet in the bloody foam.

[*leaf* 12, *pink paste-on*]

O my old manhood, my joy!
My children and grandchildren— | My white hair and beard,
My largeness, calmness, majesty, | out of the long stretch of | my
life.—

[Leaves 13 and 14. Pink paper, the first numbered at the head as 7, the second
unnumbered; both with deleted lower left corner numberings as 7 and 8. A
space appears between the two poems.]

[*leaf* 13]

O the ripened joy of womanhood!
85 O perfect happiness | at last!
I am more than eighty years | of age—My hair too is | pure white
—I am the | most venerable mother,
How clear is my mind! How | all people draw nigh | to me!
What attractions are these beyond | any before? What bloom, |
more than the bloom of | youth?
What beauty is this that | descends upon me and | rises out of me?

[*below, on leaf* 13, *written progressively smaller to crowd it on the leaf*]
90 O the joy of my soul leaning in the | centre of itself—receiving
| identity from materials and loving | them—observing char-
acters, and | absorbing them,

75 again far out] after 'swift,' appear two
unreadable deleted letters (possibly 'on')

and then deleted 'the', with 'then' interlined above. This 'then' is crossed

O swift, again, now, far out in the ocean, the wounded whale, settling,
    running to windward, tows me,
Again I see him rise to breathe—We row close again,
I see a lance driven through his side, pressed deep, turned in the
    wound,
Again we back off—I see him settle again—the life is leaving him
    fast,
As he rises, he spouts blood—I see him swim in circles narrower and
    narrower, swiftly cutting the water—I see him die,
He gives one convulsive leap in the centre of the circle, and then falls
    flat and still in the bloody foam.

25. O the old manhood of me, my joy!
    My children and grand-children—my white hair and beard,
    My largeness, calmness, majesty, out of the long stretch of my life.

26. O the ripened joy of womanhood!
    O perfect happiness at last!
    I am more than eighty years of age—my hair, too, is pure white—I
        am the most venerable mother;
    How clear is my mind! how all people draw nigh to me!
    What attractions are these, beyond any before? what bloom, more than
        the bloom of youth?
    What beauty is this that descends upon me, and rises out of me?

27. O the joy of my Soul leaning poised on itself—receiving identity
    through materials, and loving them—observing characters, and
    absorbing them;

---

through and in pencil 'again' is written
in above a caret. 'far out' is interlined
in the light ink above deleted 'out there'.
75 ocean,] interlined in pencil above deleted
'sea,'.
75 settling] *i* mended over an *e*.
76 Again] interlined above deleted 'Then'
in a slightly lighter ink.
76 rise to breathe—] interlined in the same
ink above the first part of deleted 'appear
again—we | are nigh, and row'.
76 again,] interlined above and to the right
of 'close,'.
77 through his side,] interlined in a slightly
lighter ink above deleted 'into | him,'.
Preceding 'into' is a separately (and earlier) deleted 'deep'.

77 prest] written immediately after deleted
'pressed'.
77 turned] mending in the *ne* looks as if
Whitman had started to write *turning*
but had stopped before *g*.
79 he spouts] 'his' was written and deleted
before 'he'.
79 water] *te* heavily mended, possibly over
tt, but with some chance that the word
was first 'waves'. After 'water,' appears
deleted 'coming to a point,'.
80 flat] *t* heavily mended over some letter,
just possibly *d*.
85 happiness] before this appears deleted
'health and'.
86 My] *M* is triple underscored.
90 the joy of] interlined with a fine pen
above a caret.

[*leaf* 14]

O my soul, vibrated back to | me through them—through facts, sight, hearing, touch, | my phrenology, reason, | articulation, comparison, | memory, and the like,

O the real life of my senses| and flesh, transcending | my senses and flesh,

O my body done with ma-|terials—my sight done | with my material eyes,

O what was proved to me | this day that it is not | my material eyes that | finally see, nor my ma-|terial body that finally | loves, walks, laughs, | shouts, embraces, procreates.—

[Leaves 15–20. Pink paper with deleted numbering in left lower corner as 14 and then 9 through 13. Spaces separate the different sections.]

[*leaf* 15]

95 O the farmer's joys!

Ohioan's, Illinoisian's, Wiscon-|sinese', Kanadian's, Iowan's, | Kansian's, Missourian's, Or-|egonese' joys!

To rise at the peep of day and pass | forth nimbly to work,

To plough the land in the | fall for the winter-sown | crops,

To plough the land in the | spring for maize,

100 To train orchards—to graft | the trees—to gather apples | in the fall.

O the pleasure with trees!

The orchard—the forest—the oak, | the cedar, the pine, the pekan-|tree, the honey-locust, the black-walnut, | the cotton-wood, the magnolia.—

[*leaf* 16]

O death!

O the beautiful touch of | death, soothing and be-|numbing a few moments, | for reasons

105 O that of myself discharging | my excrementitious body to be | burned, or rendered to | powder, or buried,

My real body doubtless left | to me, in further spheres,

My voided, and discharged body nothing | more to me, return-ing | to the purifications and | offices of the earth.

O my Soul, vibrated back to me, from them—from facts, sight, hearing, touch, my phrenology, reason, articulation, comparison, memory, and the like;
O the real life of my senses and flesh, transcending my senses and flesh;
O my body, done with materials—my sight, done with my material eyes;
O what is proved to me this day, beyond cavil, that it is not my material eyes which finally see,
Nor my material body which finally loves, walks, laughs, shouts, embraces, procreates.

28. O the farmer's joys!
Ohioan's, Illinoisian's, Wisconsinese', Kanadian's, Iowan's, Kansian's, Missourian's, Oregonese' joys,
To rise at peep of day, and pass forth nimbly to work,
To plough land in the fall for winter-sown crops,
To plough land in the spring for maize,
To train orchards—to graft the trees—to gather apples in the fall.

29. O the pleasure with trees!
The orchard—the forest—the oak, cedar, pine, pekan-tree,
The honey-locust, black-walnut, cottonwood, and magnolia.

30. O Death!
O the beautiful touch of Death, soothing and benumbing a few moments, for reasons;
O that of myself, discharging my excrementitious body, to be burned, or rendered to powder, or buried,
My real body doubtless left to me for other spheres,
My voided body, nothing more to me, returning to the purifications, further offices, eternal uses of the earth.

---

94 embraces] *br* mended over some letter with a descender, possibly *p*.
96 Wisconsinese',] probably first 'Wiscon-|sin-ian's', the ending beginning the second line then being smudged out while wet and 'sinese' mended over it. Later, probably dissatisfied with its doubtful legibility, Whitman in a fine pen interlined 'sinese'.
97 the peep of day] interlined with a fine pen above deleted 'daylight'.
102 oak, the cedar,] dashes following the

commas after these two nouns have been deleted.
105 my] written with the fine pen over a caret above deleted 'its'.
105 body] originally interlined in pencil above a caret, both word and caret later traced over in black ink, and then deleted. With a fine pen above a caret and with a guide line, 'body' is once more then interlined.
107 voided, and] interlined with fine pen above a caret.

O to bathe in the swimming-|bath, or in a good place | along shore!

To splash the water! To walk | ankle deep! To race naked along | the shore!

[*leaf* 17]

110 O to realize space!

The plenteousness of all—that | there are no bounds,

To emerge and be of the | sky, the sun and moon, | and the clouds, as one | with them.—

O while I live to be the ruler of life—not a slave,

To meet life with superior | power!

115 No fumes—no ennui—no | complaints or scornful | criticisms.—

O me repellent and ugly!

O to these proud laws | of the air, the water and the ground, | proving my interior soul | is commander, and no ex-|terior law or thing is | commander.—

[*leaf* 18]

O to attract by more than attraction!

How it is I know not—yet | behold! the something which | obeys none of the rest,

120 It is offensive—Yet how it draws | with resistless magnetic | power.—

O the joy of suffering!

To struggle! To meet enemies | undaunted!

To be entirely alone in their | power! To find how | much one can stand!

To look strife, torture, bloodshed, | prison, poverty, death, | popular odium, face to | face!

125 To mount the scaffold! To advance | to the muzzles of guns with | perfect nonchalance!

To be indeed a God!

[*leaf* 19]

O the gleesome saunter over | fields and hill-sides!

The leaves and flowers of the | commonest weeds,

31. O to bathe in the swimming-bath, or in a good place along shore!
   To splash the water! to walk ankle-deep; to race naked along the shore.

32. O to realize space!
   The plenteousness of all—that there are no bounds;
   To emerge, and be of the sky—of the sun and moon, and the flying
      clouds, as one with them.

33. O, while I live, to be the ruler of life—not a slave,
   To meet life as a powerful conqueror,
   No fumes—no ennui—no more complaints or scornful criticisms.

34. O me repellent and ugly!
   O to these proud laws of the air, the water, and the ground, proving my
      interior Soul impregnable,
   And nothing exterior shall ever take command of me.

35. O to attract by more than attraction!
   How it is I know not—yet behold! the something which obeys none of
      the rest,
   It is offensive, never defensive—yet how magnetic it draws.

36. O the joy of suffering!
   To struggle against great odds! to meet enemies undaunted!
   To be entirely alone with them! to find how much I can stand!
   To look strife, torture, prison, popular odium, death, face to face!
   To mount the scaffold! to advance to the muzzles of guns with perfect
      nonchalance!
   To be indeed a God!

37. O the gleesome saunter over fields and hill-sides!
   The leaves and flowers of the commonest weeds—the moist fresh still-
      ness of the woods,

---

109 splash] after this appears deleted 'in'.
113 O while . . . slave,] this verse added later in the light ink.
114 To] originally 'O to', the first word being
   deleted and the second capitalized in
   the light ink.
117 to] interlined in blacker ink above a
   caret.
117 of the air, the water and] interlined in a
   blacker ink above deleted 'these sweets |

and riches of'.
117 Thing is] to the right of this line is a
   pencilled cross X.
119 know] *k* mended over some smudged-out
   letter.
119 behold!] the exclamation mark added
   with a fine pen after a deleted comma.
120 Yet] *Y* triple underscored.
120 power.—] a following exclamation mark
   is deleted.

The moist fresh stillness of | the woods—The exquisite | smell
of the earth, all | through the forenoon.

130 O love-branches! love-root! love-|apples!
O chaste and electric torrents! O | mad-sweet drops!

O the orator's joys!
To inflate the chest—to roll | the thunder of the voice | out
from the ribs and | throat,
To make the people rage, weep, hate, | desire, with yourself,
135 To lead America—To quell America | with a great tongue.—

[*leaf* 20]

O the joy of a manly selfhood!
Personality—To be strong in | your own measureless strength,
To be servile to none—to defer | to none—not to any tyrant |
known or unknown,
To walk with erect carriage, a | step spring and elastic,
140 To look with calm gaze or with | flashing eye,
To speak with full and sonorous | voice out of a broad chest,
To confront with your personality | all the other personalities
| of the earth.—

O to have my life henceforth | my poem of joys!
To dance, clap hands, | exult, shout, skip, leap, | roll on, float
on, | an athlete, full of | rich words! full of | joys!

131 torrents] interlined in the same ink above
deleted 'drops', which had a following
exclamation mark.

135 To quell] *T* triple underscored.
137 To] *T* mended from *t* in the same ink
and triple underscored.

[*Cont. on page 215*]

[FOLDER 73. Five leaves of pink paper; the same cluster of pinholes appears
in the center of all leaves, and a set in the left margin. Written in a dark,
almost black ink. The poem number 87 is mended over 86. Whitman numbered
the leaves in pencil 1–5 in the lower left corner. Leaf number 1 is placed after
a deleted '6,' and 2 is written over what is probably a '7.' 1860, pp. 406–7;
Camden, I, 287–88.]

The exquisite smell of the earth at day-break, and all through the fore-
noon.

38. O love-branches! love-root! love-apples!
    O chaste and electric torrents! O mad-sweet drops.

39. O the orator's joys!
    To inflate the chest—to roll the thunder of the voice out from the ribs
        and throat,
    To make the people rage, weep, hate, desire, with yourself,
    To lead America—to quell America with a great tongue.

40. O the joy of a manly self-hood!
    Personality—to be servile to none—to defer to none—not to any
        tyrant, known or unknown,
    To walk with erect carriage, a step springy and elastic,
    To look with calm gaze, or with a flashing eye,
    To speak with a full and sonorous voice, out of a broad chest,
    To confront with your personality all the other personalities of the
        earth.

41. O to have my life henceforth my poem of joys!
    To dance, clap hands, exult, shout, skip, leap, roll on, float on,
    An athlete—full of rich words—full of joys.

[Cont. from page 214]

144 hands,] after this, 'laugh,' ending the line
   is deleted in the light ink.
144 float on,] after this, 'dazzle | on,' is de-
   leted in the light ink.
144 rich] originally 'sparkling', then deleted.
   Above this and a caret appears in a
   blacker ink 'rich' followed by deleted

'strong'. Whether 'rich strong' was written at one time cannot be told, but the
crowding and the lack of a comma after
'rich' lead to the view that 'strong' was
the first revision, and that 'rich' was
added after 'strong' was deleted.

87—

France, the 18ᵗʰ Year | of These States.

A great year and place,
There and then that harsh, | discordant, natal scream | of Liberty
    rising, to | touch | These States close, and all humanity close.

I walked | the shores of my | Eastern Sea,
I heard over | the waves the little voice,
5 I saw the divine infant | where she woke, mournfully | wailing
    amid the roar | of cannon, curses, | shouts, crash of falling |
    buildings,

[*leaf 2*]

I was not so deadly | sick from the | blood running in the gutters
    — | nor from the single | corpses, nor those in | heaps, nor
    those borne | away in the tumbrils,
I was not desperate at the battues—I was not shocked | by the
    repeated | fusillades of the guns.

Pale and stern | what could I say to the | long-accrued retribution?
Could I wish humanity different?
10 Could I wish the people made of wood and stone?

1 A great year and place,] interlined in the light ink above deleted 'The great destiny,'. In the original, 'The' had its capital *T* enlarged by mending in the same ink. In the revision, 'A' was first interlined above original 'The'; later, in the light ink, 'great year and place,' was added.

2 that] interlined with a finer pen above deleted 'the'.

2 Liberty] originally 'liberty'. This was deleted and 'Freedom' interlined above it, this then being deleted and 'Liberty' written below the original in a slightly lighter ink.

2 to touch These States] originally, 'to | touch my race the closest,'. First 'my' was deleted and 'the' interlined. Then this was deleted, along with 'race' and following 'the', 'men | and women' was interlined. All the above seems to have been in the original ink, or one slightly darker. Then in pencil 'men and women' was crossed through and the three alternatives 'us', 'humanity' (above the line), and 'These

States' (below the line) interlined, 'us' and 'humanity' then being deleted in pencil. Finally, with a fine pen and slightly lighter ink, 'closest' was deleted, and immediately following it was added, 'close, and all humanity close.' Presumably when it was seen that pencil 'These States' was too far to the right to be brought down conveniently, it was crossed through with the same pen and ink and 'These States' interlined above a caret before 'close'.

3 I walked the shores] originally, 'walked trembling and excited | on the shores'. 'trembling . . . on' was deleted and 'distracted' interlined in a darker ink, this also being deleted.

3 my] original 'my' was deleted and 'the' interlined, this then being crossed out and 'my' added at the end of the line in a darker ink.

4 I heard . . . voices,] originally 'I heard the little voice over the waves,'. First 'afar there' was interlined in a fine pen and darker ink above a caret before 'over',

France,

The 18th Year of These States.

1. A GREAT year and place,
   A harsh, discordant, natal scream rising, to touch the mother's heart
   closer than any yet.

2. I walked the shores of my Eastern Sea,
   Heard over the waves the little voice,
   Saw the divine infant, where she woke, mournfully wailing, amid the
   roar of cannon, curses, shouts, crash of falling buildings,
   Was not so sick from the blood in the gutters running—nor from the
   single corpses, nor those in heaps, nor those borne away in the
   tumbrils,
   Was not so desperate at the battues of death—was not so shocked at the
   repeated fusillades of the guns.

3. Pale, silent, stern, what could I say to that long-accrued retribution?
   Could I wish humanity different?
   Could I wish the people made of wood and stone?
   Or that there be no justice in destiny or time?

---

but deleted in pencil. Finally, in the light ink 'the little voice' and the comma after 'waves' were deleted, and after 'waves' the addition made, 'the little voice,'.

5 curses] *r* mended over *s* in process of writing.

6 I was not so . . .] above this and heading leaf 2 appears the verse 'I did not despair so | much—I did not | weep so much,' deleted in the same ink by two vertical slanting lines joining horizontal lines, these last drawn with a fine pen.

6 so deadly] original 'so' was deleted but then restored by interlineation.

6 blood running] originally, 'running blood', the first word being deleted and written after 'blood' above a caret in the same or a slightly darker ink.

7 not desperate at the battues—I was] interlined in the same ink above a caret and guide lines. There is some possibility that 'desperate' was first interlined, and the rest added at a later time.

7 shocked] following 'so | much' deleted.

8–10 Pale and stern . . . wood and stone?] originally the stanza ended with 'fusillades of the guns.' and the next began 'O Liberty!'. This present three-line stanza was an addition, heavily revised, crowded in in the space between the two stanzas. First, Whitman proposed to end the previous stanza with an addition, and in pencil appended the concluding line 'O retribution!'. This was deleted in ink and 'I saw, I heard, I knew' interlined above it, this being deleted in turn. Then in the space to the right, he wrote 'Pale, trembling, distracted, | what could I say to the | due retribution?'. 'distracted,' was then deleted, and 'long-accrued' interlined above deleted 'due'. Apparently as a result of the deletion of 'distracted,' the comma after 'Pale' was crossed through and 'and' interlined above it. Later, in the light ink, 'trembling' was deleted and 'stern' interlined, and at the same time the two last verses beginning 'Could I . . .' were added. These had earlier been worked out, since they appear as a note at the very bottom of the leaf, written in the blackish ink and fine pen, and deleted in the light ink.

O Liberty! O mate for my | soul!

[*leaf* 3]

> I myself keep the blaze, | the bullet and the axe in reserve, | to fetch them out in time of need,
>
> I too, if I be long | represt, surely | rise at last slaughtering, and | extatic,
>
> I too would demand full arrears of | vengeance!

15 Hence I sign this salute | over the sea,

> And do not | deny that terrible red | birth and baptism,
>
> And remember the little | voice that I heard | wailing—and wait with perfect trust, | no matter how long,

[*leaf* 4]

> And from to-day, sad and | cogent, I maintain | the bequeathed cause, | as for all lands,
>
> And I maintain the unequalled glory of that year | and place, | in the name of all lands,

20 And I send these words | of mine to Paris, with my love,

> And I guess | some chansonniers there | will understand | them,
>
> For I guess | there is latent music yet in | France—floods of it,

11 O Liberty!] 'Freedom!' was interlined in the blackish ink above deleted 'Liberty!', then deleted in the light ink and 'Liberty!' restored above a caret.

11 soul!] preceding original 'stern' has been deleted.

12 I myself keep] originally, 'I too have'. First 'have' was crossed out and 'keep' interlined; later, in the light ink, 'myself' was interlined above deleted 'too'.

12 the bullet and the axe] interlined with a caret above the second word of deleted 'and | blood'. In the addition, 'sternly' after 'axe' has been deleted in the light ink.

12 reserve,] in the blackish ink and fine pen, 'back there,' was added but deleted with the same pen.

12 to fetch . . . need,] an addition in the light ink.

13 be] originally 'were', deleted and 'ever I be' interlined, the 'ever I' being deleted in the same black ink. A short stroke through 'be' in the light ink does not seem to represent a deletion.

13 represt] *t* mended over *sed* smudged out while wet. After this an original 'should' was deleted in black ink and 'will' inter-

lined, this also then being deleted.

13 at last] interlined in darker ink.

13 and extatic,] originally, 'and | mad, at last, for my | joyful extatic vengeance,'. First 'for my' was deleted and 'till I take' interlined, and 'due arrears of' interlined above a caret before 'vengeance'. Then everything after 'slaughtering' was lined through, and 'and | extatic,' interlined.

14 I too . . . vengeance!] this is a revising addition crowded in the space between stanzas. The first version of the addition read, 'By Earth—By the impassive rocks! I will | ['have' *immediately deleted*] take due arrears of | vengeance!', in this form after 'take' appearing deleted 'the' and the deleted start of some other word beginning with *b* or *l* (possibly 'lon'). The first sentence from 'By' to 'rocks!' was crossed through in the same ink. 'too' was interlined above deleted 'will', and 'know how to' in the fine pen above a caret placed before 'take'. Lastly, in the light ink 'know how to take due' was deleted and 'I too would demand full' interlined above a caret.

4. O Liberty! O mate for me!
   Here too keeps the blaze, the bullet and the axe, in reserve, to fetch
       them out in case of need,
   Here too, though long deprest, still is not destroyed,
   Here too could rise at last, murdering and extatic,
   Here too would demand full arrears of vengeance.

5. Hence I sign this salute over the sea,
   And I do not deny that terrible red birth and baptism,
   But remember the little voice that I heard wailing—and wait with
       perfect trust, no matter how long,
   And from to-day, sad and cogent, I maintain the bequeath'd cause, as
       for all lands,
   And I send these words to Paris, with my love,
   And I guess some chansonniers there will understand them,
   For I guess there is latent music yet in France—floods of it,

---

15 Hence] interlined with the fine pen above
a caret after deleted 'And now'. A short
horizontal line is drawn above this verse
to mark off, apparently, the start of a
stanza from the crowded revisions above.
15 this] interlined in the light ink above deleted 'my'.
16 And do not] originally, 'And henceforth
I do not', the two deletions seemingly
being made independently.
16 red] interlined with the fine pen above deleted 'new'.
16 baptism,] a following dash and 'nor | the
l' have been deleted before the next verse
was started.
17 And remember] an intervening original
'I' has been deleted.
17 and wait with perfect trust,] originally
'and I wait trustfully,', the 'I' being deleted and 'with perfect trust,' interlined
above deleted 'trustfully,' with a finer
pen.
17 no matter how long,] this appears to be an
addition made with a finer pen.
18 And from to-day,] a false start was made
with the single letter 'F', and then the
verse begun beneath this. 'from to-day'
is interlined in a slightly blacker ink above
deleted 'henceforth'.
18 maintain] after this an interlineation in
the finer pen, 'from this hour' has been
deleted.
19 And I maintain . . . lands,] this verse is an
addition crowded in with the blacker ink
and finer pen. The 'that' has been altered

from 'the' apparently in the course of writing. Following is the false start 'p' deleted
and then 'day' crowded in, this being
deleted and 'year' interlined above a caret.
At a later time, with a very fine pen, 'in
the name of all lands,' was crowded in,
the 'all' being interlined above a caret.
Before 'all' and heavily deleted are two
or three letters which just possibly may
be 'for'.
21 guess] interlined with fine pen above deleted 'think'. Before this change 'there
are' following 'think' had been deleted,
and 'who' before 'will'.
22 For I guess . . . floods of it,] the original
verse read, 'And I think there are | floods
of music in | France,'. As an alternative to
deleted 'there are', first 'I hear' was written above; then 'hear' was crossed through
and 'know of' added, 'of' being independently deleted. Then the whole remaining
interlineation was deleted and in the fine
pen above a caret placed before 'floods'
was interlined 'there are', and 'latent' interlined with a caret before 'music', and
'yet' after 'music'; what seems to be an
alternative, 'remaining' above 'yet' is deleted. At the start of the line 'For' was
interlined above deleted 'And'. Above deleted 'think' is 'think', deleted, and then
'guess'. Finally, in the light ink 'are floods
of' was crossed through and 'is' interlined,
the comma after 'France' being deleted
and '—floods of it,' appended to the verse.

I hear already the bustle of instruments— | They will soon be | drowning all that would | interrupt them,

[*leaf 5*]

O I think now The east wind brings a | triumphal and free | march—It reaches | hither.—It swells me | to joyful madness,

25 I will run transpose it | in words, to justify | it,

I will yet sing a song | for you, ma femme!

[FOLDER 74. Five leaves of pink paper of the same cutting, a cluster of pin-holes in the center and a few sets in the left margin. Written in a dark ink. The poem number 82 has been altered from 81. Above and to the left of the title is '(Leaf of)' in a lighter ink with a question mark above it, the words being deleted by a pen stroke. In the first verse the initial word 'Nations' is written very large. Whitman numbered the leaves 1–5 in pencil in the lower left corner. 1860, pp. 412–14; Camden, II, 144–46.]

82—

Unnamed Lands.

Nations ten thousand years | before These States, and many | times ten thousand years | before These States,

Garnered clusters of ages that | men and women like us | grew up and traveled their | course, and passed beyond,

What vast-built cities—What | orderly republics—What | pastoral tribes and nomads,

What histories, rulers, heroes, | perhaps transcending all | others,

5 What laws, customs, wealth, | arts, traditions,

What sort of marriage—What | costumes—What physiology and phrenology,

[*leaf 2*]

What of liberty and slavery | among them,

What they thought of death | and the soul,

Who were witty and wise— | Who beautiful and poetic— | Who brutish and undeveloped,

10 Not a mark, not a record | remains—And yet all | remains.—

1 many] interlined in black ink above deleted 'ten'.

2 clusters] *s* mended over some smudged-out letter.

2 traveled] interlined in black ink above deleted 'filled'.

2 course,] interlined in black ink above deleted 'time,'.

2 beyond,] interlined in black ink with a caret above deleted 'onward,'.

O I hear already the bustle of instruments—they will soon be drown-
    ing all that would interrupt them,
O I think the east wind brings a triumphal and free march,
It reaches hither—it swells me to joyful madness,
I will run transpose it in words, to justify it,
I will yet sing a song for you, ma femme.

---

23 already the bustle of instruments—] first written as, 'the instruments strike—'. With the fine pen 'already' was interlined above a caret after 'hear'. Then in pencil 'al-ready' was crossed through and above a caret 'touch of' interlined before 'instru-ments', 'touch' then being deleted and 'bustle' interlined above a caret. 'strike' is crossed through in pencil and a dash added above it. Finally, in the light ink 'already the' is placed before interlined pencil 'bustle of' and brought down by a guide line to the pencil caret.

23 would] appears to be an addition in a lighter ink at the end of the line.

24 O I think now The east wind brings a] the verse began originally, 'I hear over the sea | the'. This was deleted and in a finer pen interlined 'The east wind brings a'. Then in pencil 'O I think already' was interlined above a caret placed before 'The'; and finally in the light ink 'al-ready' was deleted and 'now' written above it, the pencil caret being traced over in ink. Failure to reduce the capitalization of 'The' was a slip.

24 joyful madness,] interlined with a finer pen above deleted 'join with it,'.

25 justify it,] the comma after 'it' was added and following original 'anew,' deleted.

26 ma femme] the *a* of 'ma' seems to be mended in the tail and there is a smudge. A short horizontal stroke connecting with the tail is probably also a smudge and not a hyphen.

Unnamed Lands.

1. NATIONS ten thousand years before These States, and many times ten
    thousand years before These States,
    Garnered clusters of ages, that men and women like us grew up and
        travelled their course, and passed on;
What vast-built cities—What orderly republics—What pastoral tribes
    and nomads,
What histories, rulers, heroes, perhaps transcending all others,
What laws, customs, wealth, arts, traditions,
What sort of marriage—What costumes—What physiology and phren-
    ology,
What of liberty and slavery among them—What they thought of death
    and the Soul,
Who were witty and wise—Who beautiful and poetic—Who brutish
    and undeveloped,
Not a mark, not a record remains—And yet all remains.

O I know that those men | and women were not for | nothing,
any more than | we are for nothing,
I know that they realized | themselves, and fulfilled | parts of the
world
And that they belong to the scheme | of the world every bit as |
much as we now belong to | it, and as all henceforth | will
belong to it.—

[*leaf 3*]

Afar they stand—Yet near | to me they stand,
15 Some with oval countenances, | learned and calm,
Some naked and savage— | Some like huge collections | of insects
Some in tents—herdsmen, | patriarchs, tribes, horsemen,
Some prowling through woods— | Some living peaceably on |
farms, laboring, reaping, | filling barns,
Some traversing | paved avenues, amid temples, | palaces, fac-
tories, books, | art, shows, courts, theatres, | wonderful monu-
ments.—

[*leaf 4*]

20 Are they gone? those | billions of men?
Those women of all | the old experience of | the earth?
Do their lives, cities, | arts, rest only in us?
Did they achieve nothing | for themselves?—

I believe of all the billions | of men and women | that filled the
unnamed | lands, every one | exists this hour, here | or else-
where, invisible to | us, in exact proportion | to what he or
she grew | from in life, and out of | what he or she did, felt, |
became, loved, sinned, in life.—

17 in] original 'in' was deleted and 'with' interlined, this being excised and 'in' restored in black ink above a caret.
19 traversing paved] originally, 'walking in
superb paved'. 'in superb' seems to have
been first deleted, perhaps in the same
ink; then in the black ink 'traversing' was
interlined above deleted 'walking'.

20 Are they gone? those] interlined in black
ink above original deleted 'But what of
the disappeared'. It is possible that the
last word, 'disappeared' was crossed out
at a different time.
21 Those] originally, 'What of the', the first
two words being crossed out and 'the'
altered to 'Those' in black ink.

2. O I know that those men and women were not for nothing, any more
    than we are for nothing,
  I know that they belong to the scheme of the world every bit as much
    as we now belong to it, and as all will henceforth belong to it.

3. Afar they stand—yet near to me they stand,
  Some with oval countenances, learned and calm,
  Some naked and savage—Some like huge collections of insects,
  Some in tents—herdsmen, patriarchs, tribes, horsemen,
  Some prowling through woods—Some living peaceably on farms,
    laboring, reaping, filling barns,
  Some traversing paved avenues, amid temples, palaces, factories, li-
    braries, shows, courts, theatres, wonderful monuments.

4. Are those billions of men really gone?
  Are those women of the old experience of the earth gone?
  Do their lives, cities, arts, rest only with us?
  Did they achieve nothing for good, for themselves?

5. I believe of all those billions of men and women that filled the un-
    named lands, every one exists this hour, here or elsewhere, invisible
    to us, in exact proportion to what he or she grew from in life, and
    out of what he or she did, felt, became, loved, sinned, in life.

---

21 all] before this was written, Whitman began 'th' [*query* the] but deleted it before
continuing with 'all'.
21 old] interlined in black ink above deleted
'past'.
22 Do] interlined in black ink above deleted
'Have they, and'.
22 rest only in us?] interlined in black ink
above deleted 'merely descended | to be
us?' in which 'be' had been interlined later above a caret.

23 Did] interlined above deleted 'Have'.
23 achieve] *d* concluding this word has been
crossed through.
23 for] original preceding 'beyond' has been
deleted.
24 filled the] before 'filled' an interlined
'have' written above a caret has been deleted. 'the' is interlined above deleted
'those'.
24 every] a following 'single' has been deleted, apparently in the light ink.

⟦ 223 ⟧

[*leaf* 5]

25 I believe that was not the | end of those nations, | or any person
  of them, | any more than this shall | be the end of me;
 Of their languages, phrenology, | government, coins, medals, |
  marriage, literature, products, | games, jurisprudence, wars,
  | manners, amativeness, crimes, | prisons, slaves, heroes, poets,
  | I suspect their results | curiously await me in the yet | unseen
  world, counterparts | of what accrued to them | in the seen
  world,
 I suspect I shall meet them | there,
 I suspect I shall there find | each old particular | of those un-
  named lands.—

25 end] preceding 'real' beginning the line
has been crossed through, perhaps in the
same ink.
26 curiously] interlined in black ink above a
caret.

26 world] *l* mended currently over half-
formed *d*.
28 old] interlined in black ink above deleted
'curious'.

[FOLDER 75. Two leaves of pink paper; a cluster of pinholes in the center
and a few sets in the left margin. Written in a dark ink. The poem number 56
has been altered from 55. 1860, pp. 414–15; Camden, II, 167.]

56—

Kosmos.

Who includes diversity, | and is nature,
Who is the amplitude of the | earth, and the coarseness | and sex-
  uality of the earth, and the | great charity of the earth, | and
  the equilibrium of | the earth,
Who has not looked forth from | the windows the eyes for | noth-
  ing—or whose brain | held audience of messengers | for
  nothing,
Who contains believers and dis-|believers—Who is the most |
  majestic lover,
5 Who holds duly his or her triune | proportion of realism, spir-
  |itualism, and of the esthetic, | or intellectual,
Who having considered the body, finds | all its organs and parts
  good,

6. I believe that was not the end of those nations, or any person of them,
    any more than this shall be the end of my nation, or of me;
 Of their languages, phrenology, government, coins, medals, marriage,
    literature, products, games, jurisprudence, wars, manners, amative-
    ness, crimes, prisons, slaves, heroes, poets, I suspect their results
    curiously await in the yet unseen world—counterparts of what
    accrued to them in the seen world,
 I suspect I shall meet them there,
 I suspect I shall there find each old particular of those unnamed lands.

Kosmos.

Who includes diversity, and is Nature,
Who is the amplitude of the earth, and the coarseness and sexuality of
    the earth, and the great charity of the earth, and the equilibrium
    also,
Who has not looked forth from the windows, the eyes, for nothing, or
    whose brain held audience with messengers for nothing;
Who contains believers and disbelievers—Who is the most majestic
    lover;
Who holds duly his or her triune proportion of realism, spiritualism,
    and of the æsthetic, or intellectual,
Who, having considered the body, finds all its organs and parts good;

---

1 diversity, and] originally, 'the diversity, |
of men, and', the 'the' then being deleted.
In pencil above a caret before 'men' was
interlined 'women and', later the *en* being
mended in ink to *an* and 'men' altered
by mending to 'man'. Finally, all between
'diversity' and 'and is' was deleted.

2 and sexuality] interlined in black ink
above a caret.
4 Who is] *W* triple underscored.
5 or her] interlined in pencil above a caret.
5 esthetic] initial *e* has been mended, apparently from an original *e*, but the letter
is now a mere blob and the intention cannot be determined.

[*leaf 2*]

7 Who out of the theory of the | earth, and of his or her | body,
    understands, by subtle analogies, the theory | of a live city, a
    poem, | and of the politics of These | States,
  Who believes not only in our globe | with its sun and moon, | but
    in other globes with their | suns and moons,
  Who, constructing the house | of himself or herself not | for a
    day but for all time, | sees races, eras, dates, | generations, the
    past, the | future, dwelling there | like space inseparable |
    together.—

[FOLDER 76. One leaf of pink paper; a cluster of pinholes in the center and
some in the left upper margin. Written in a blackish ink. The poem number
83 has been altered from 82. The original title was '*Looking-Glass.*', which was
deleted and in the light ink 'A hand-mirror.' placed above it. 1860, p. 415;
Camden, II, 30.]

83—

A Hand-Mirror.

Hold it up sternly—See this it | sends back—(Who is it? Is it |
    you?)
Outside fair costume—within, ashes | and filth,
No more a flashing eye—no more | a sonorous voice or springy
    | step,
Now some slave's eye, voice, hands, | step,
5 A drunkard's breath, unwholesome | eater's face, venerealee's
    flesh,
Lungs rotting away piecemeal, | stomach sour and cankerous,
Joints rheumatic, bowels clogged | with abomination,
Blood circulating dark and poisonous | streams,
Words babble, hearing and touch | callous,
10 No brain, no heart left—no mag-|netism of sex,
Such, from one look in this Looking-Glass | ere you go hence,
Such a result so soon—and from such a beginning!

Who, out of the theory of the earth, and of his or her body, understands by subtle analogies, the theory of a city, a poem, and of the
large politics of These States;
Who believes not only in our globe, with its sun and moon, but in
other globes, with their suns and moons;
Who, constructing the house of himself or herself, not for a day, but
for all time, sees races, eras, dates, generations,
The past, the future, dwelling there, like space, inseparable together.

---

7 Who] an original following comma seems
to have been smudged out while wet.

7 understands, by subtle analogies,] the
comma after 'understands' was added in
the light ink and 'by subtle analogies,' interlined above a caret. It is probable that
the second *a* in 'analogies' has been
mended from an *o*.

8 believes] interlined in black ink and fine
pen above deleted 'sees'.

8 in our] 'our' was first interlined, perhaps
in the same ink, above deleted 'this'; later, with the fine pen, 'in' was prefixed to
it.

8 in other] 'in' interlined with the fine pen.

A Hand-Mirror.

HOLD it up sternly! See this it sends back! (Who is it? Is it you?)
Outside fair costume—within, ashes and filth,
No more a flashing eye—no more a sonorous voice or springy step,
Now some slave's eye, voice, hands, step,
A drunkard's breath, unwholesome eater's face, venerealee's flesh,
Lungs rotting away piecemeal, stomach sour and cankerous,
Joints rheumatic, bowels clogged with abomination,
Blood circulating dark and poisonous streams,
Words babble, hearing and touch callous,
No brain, no heart left—no magnetism of sex;
Such, from one look in this looking-glass ere you go hence,
Such a result so soon—and from such a beginning!

---

1 back—] this dash seems to have through
its center a short, slightly curving stroke.
But whether this is a deleting stroke, or
whether the dash was written over a
comma rather high above the line, is uncertain.

1 (Who . . . you?)] crowded in later with a
fine pen.

2 costume] interlined in a darker ink above
deleted 'surface'.

10 brain,] a plural *s* has been deleted currently and the tail of the *n* mended over
it.

[FOLDER 77. One leaf of pink paper written in a dark, blackish ink. The poem number 53 has been altered from 52. The underlining of the title is perhaps later and with a fine pen. At the very bottom of the leaf, after some space, is a small squiggle, doubtless to indicate that the poem was complete. 1860, p. 417; Camden, I, 12–13.]

53—

Savantism.

Thither as I look I see | each result and glory | retracing itself, and nestling | close, always obligated,

Thither hours, months, years— | Thither trades, compacts, | establishments, even the | most minute,

Thither every-day life, speech, | utensils, politics, persons, | estates,

Thither we also, I with my | Says and Songs, trustful, | admirant,

5 As a father, to his father | going, takes his children | along with him.—

[FOLDER 78. Five leaves of pink paper. Only the first two leaves are of the same cutting; the remaining three each differ independently. All leaves have a cluster of pinholes in the center and one set at top left. All the verses are written in a dark ink, the title also being written large. The leaves are unnumbered.]

[*leaf* 1. The poem number 86 has been altered from 85. 1860, p. 418; Camden, III, 301.]

86—

Says.—

I say whatever tastes | sweet to the most perfect | person, that is finally right;

[*below, without spacing.* 1860, p. 418; Camden, III, 301.]

I say nourish great ideas, | (If I have said any thing | to the contrary, I hereby | retract it.)

[*below, without spacing.* Unpublished.]

I say of money, lands, costumes, | amours, friendships, diet, | furniture, learning, all | are to interplay with great ideas;

[*below, without spacing.* Unpublished.]

I say humanity's rights for-|ever, without compromise— | I henceforth refuse to | compromise,

1 finally] interlined in black ink above a caret.

Savantism.

THITHER, as I look, I see each result and glory retracing itself and
    nestling close, always obligated;
Thither hours, months, years—thither trades, compacts, establish-
    ments, even the most minute,
Thither every-day life, speech, utensils, politics, persons, estates,
Thither we also, I with my leaves and songs, trustful, admirant,
As a father, to his father going, takes his children along with him.

---

1 always obligated,] added later with a fine
pen.
5 As a] the original verse started thus. Then
these two words were deleted and in a
blacker ink 'as a' was added after 'admirant' in the line above and a guide line
drawn to bring them down to 'father', thus
combining the two verses. Finally, in pencil 'as a' is deleted, and 'As a' interlined
above the original.

Says.

1.

I SAY whatever tastes sweet to the most perfect person, that is finally
    right.

2.

I SAY nourish a great intellect, a great brain;
If I have said anything to the contrary, I hereby retract it.

[*below, without spacing, and carrying over to leaf 2.* 1860, p. 418; Camden, III, 301.]

5 I say that man cannot hold | property in man, [*end leaf* 1]

I say the least developed | person on earth is just | as important
    and sacred | to himself or herself, as | the most developed
    person | is to himself or herself,

[*leaf* 2; *below last verse above, without spacing.* Unpublished.]

I say no compact, marriage, | government, President, Legis-|lature,
    or what not, is to | be permitted to annul | rights,

[*below, without spacing. A deleted verse,* 'I say the word' . . . *marked around
and diagonally crossed out in pencil, with* 'tr' *in the left margin. This is re-
copied in pencil in a blank space at the foot of the leaf.*]

[*below, crowded in below the horizontal pencil line marking the lower limit of
the deleted verse. Written in black ink.* Unpublished.]

(I am not faithless to you, O dead! Nor faithless to | you, O
    unborn!)

[*below, without spacing.* 1860, p. 418; Camden, III, 301.]

I say that where liberty | draws not the blood out | of slavery,
    there slavery | draws the blood of liberty.—

[below, recopying in pencil of transposed verse. 1860 *ed. runs-on with verse
above.*]

10 I say the word of the good old cause | in These States, and re-
    sound it | hence over the world!

[*leaf* 3. The poem number 87 is altered from 86. Leaves 3–5 are written in
a blacker ink than leaves 1–2. On the verso of leaf 3, at the head, appears the
line 'And though I lie dead', written in blackish ink and with a fine pen. This
has been crossed through with a single stroke. 1860, p. 419; Camden, III, 301–
302.]

87—   Say.

I say the human shape | or face is so great, it | must never be made
    | ridiculous,

I say for ornaments nothing | outre can be allowed,

And that any thing is most | beautiful without ornament

And that exaggerations will | be sternly revenged in your own |
    physiology, and in others' | physiology also;

15 And I say that clean-shaped | children can | be jetted and con-
    ceived only | where natural forms prevail | in public;

And I say that genius need never | more be turned to romances,

For facts properly told, | how mean appear | all romances!

3.

I SAY man shall not hold property in man;

I say the least developed person on earth is just as important and sacred
to himself or herself, as the most developed person is to himself or
herself.

4.

I SAY where liberty draws not the blood out of slavery, there slavery
draws the blood out of liberty,

I say the word of the good old cause in These States, and resound it
hence over the world.

5.

I SAY the human shape or face is so great, it must never be made
ridiculous;

I say for ornaments nothing outre can be allowed,

And that anything is most beautiful without ornament,

And that exaggerations will be sternly revenged in your own physiology, and in other persons' physiology also;

And I say that clean-shaped children can be jetted and conceived only
where natural forms prevail in public, and the human face and
form are never caricatured;

And I say that genius need never more be turned to romances,

(For facts properly told, how mean appear all romances.)

---

10 resound] *re* added in black ink joined to
'sound' by tracing over *s* in ink. The deleted original verse had also read 'sound'.

11 I] mended over smudged-out original 'I'
in order to make a very large letter as
heading.

12 nothing] Whitman first wrote 'now' and
then immediately altered to 'nothing' by
writing *th* over *w* before continuing.

14 sternly] interlined in pencil above a caret.

15 children] before this 'and vigorous' has
been deleted in pencil.

16 genius] before this word Whitman later

placed a caret and interlined 'henceforth',
but then deleted it.

16 more] interlined in blacker ink above a
caret.

16 turned] interlined with a fine pen above
deleted 'demeaned'.

16 romances] *o* heavily mended over another
letter, perhaps an *a*.

17 For facts properly] originally, 'For if facts
are properly', the deletions being made in
a darker ink.

17 appear] a preceding 'will' has been deleted.

[*leaf* 4. The poem number 88 is altered from 87, the 87 having been currently altered from 86. 1860, p. 419; Camden, III, 302.]

88—

Say.—

I say the word of a land | fearing nothing—I will | have no other land,

I say discuss all and expose | all—I am for every | topic, openly,

20 I say there can be no sal-|vation for These States | without inno-vaters— | without free tongues, and | ears willing to hear the | tongues,

I say a glory of These | States shall be that | they respectfully listen | to propositions, reforms, | fresh views and doctrines, | from successions of men | and women, each age | with its own growth.—

[*leaf* 5. The poem number 89 is written to the left of deleted 88. The title 'Say', later than the change of poem number, was interlined in pencil above and to the right of deleted '*Thought*.' heading two verses which originally began the section but which have been deleted by a diagonal pencil and then an ink stroke down to a horizontal pencil line. The new title 'Say' was then traced over in ink. The semi-colon after 'circumstances' in the second deleted verse presumably indicates that the lines that follow beginning 'I have said many times' were written to continue without a break. 1860, p. 420; Camden, III, 302. For the rejected verses, see below at the end of the poem.]

89—

Say

I have said many times | that materials and the soul were great, | and that all depends on physique,—

Now I reverse | what I said, and affirm that | all depends on the | aesthetic or Intellectual,—and that | nothing is greater than beauty,

24 And I affirm now that the mind governs | —and that all depends on the mind.—

[*leaf* 5, *at head; deleted verses*. Unpublished.]

Thought.

O steadily cultivating strength | and serenity of mind,

Of the processes of the mind | arriving at last at such | a condition that it is | happy under any cir-|cumstances;

6.

I SAY the word of lands fearing nothing—I will have no other land;
I say discuss all and expose all—I am for every topic openly;
I say there can be no salvation for These States without innovators—
without free tongues, and ears willing to hear the tongues;
And I announce as a glory of These States, that they respectfully listen
to propositions, reforms, fresh views and doctrines, from successions
of men and women,
Each age with its own growth.

7.

I HAVE said many times that materials and the Soul are great, and that
all depends on physique;
Now I reverse what I said, and affirm that all depends on the æsthetic or
intellectual,
And that criticism is great—and that refinement is greatest of all;
And I affirm now that the mind governs—and that all depends on the
mind.

8.

WITH one man or woman—(no matter which one—I even pick out the
lowest,)
With him or her I now illustrate the whole law;
I say that every right, in politics or what-not, shall be eligible to that
one man or woman, on the same terms as any.

---

18 say] interlined above deleted 'repeat'.
21 a] interlined in blacker ink above deleted 'the'.
22 that materials and the soul were great, and] this is all an addition, crowded in and written in a different ink.
23 Now] this new verse originally continued the one above in mid-line. Whitman later wrote in a paragraph sign to indicate that a new verse was to be printed.
23 reverse] interlined in blacker ink above deleted 'retract'.
23 what I said,] interlined with a caret above deleted 'that,'.
23 aesthetic or Intellectual,] interlined, perhaps in the same ink, above deleted 'mind,'.
23 —and that nothing is greater than beauty,] added later with a fine pen after the interlineation ending with 'Intellectual,'.

This last addition revises the deleted verse, which originally followed, 'And I say now that | nothing is greater than | Beauty—'. Before this verse was deleted in favor of the addition, the 'now' was interlined above a caret and an original 'now' after 'And' was crossed out.
24 And I affirm now] this new verse originally continued the deleted verse ending in mid-line with 'Beauty—'. Whitman capitalized miniscule a in 'and' and placed a paragraph sign before it. 'I affirm now' is a later addition, written in black ink with a fine pen above a caret.
24 —and that all . . . mind.—] interlined in a different ink above deleted 'just as much as any thing governs.'. It would appear that 'thing' was independently deleted earlier than the other words.

[FOLDER 79. Two leaves of white wove unwatermarked paper ($6\frac{1}{4} \times 4$) in a conjugate fold, two sets of pinholes at the upper left corner. Written in the light ink. 1860, pp. 449–50; Camden, II, 271.]

[*leaf 1*]

Nearing Departure.

Though I have, as I laid | out, been warbling | happily,
Though I hear in the air, | resonant, the echoes I | charged myself
    to arouse,
Suddenly at the height and | close of my career, a | Cloud,
A dread beyond, of I know not | what, darkens over me.—

5 I shall go forth,
  I shall traverse The States— | But I cannot tell whither | or how
    long,
Perhaps soon, some day or night, | while I am singing, my | voice
    will suddenly cease.

Then all may amount to but this,
The glances of my eyes that swept | the daylight,

[*leaf 2*]

10 The unspeakable love I inter-|changed with women,
My joys in the open air—my | walks through the Manna-|hatta,
The continual good will I have | met—the curious attachment |
    of young men to me,
My reflections alone—The ab-|sorption into me from the | light,
    the landscape, | stars, animals, thunder, | rain and snow, in
    my | wanderings alone,
The words of my mouth, rude, | ignorant, arrogant—my | many
    faults and derelic-|tions,
15 The tracks which I leave over the | side-walks and fields,
May but arrive at this beginning | of me
This beginning of me—And yet it | is enough, O soul,
O soul, we have positively appeared— | That is enough.—

7 voice] *o* mended over the start of an *i*.   was originally, 'people', then deleted.
13 The] *T* mended from *t*.   14 arrogant—] a comma before the dash was
13 landscape,] following this to end the line   smudged out while wet.

To My Soul.

1. As nearing departure,
   As the time draws nigh, glooming from you,
   A cloud—a dread beyond, of I know not what, darkens me.

2. I shall go forth,
   I shall traverse The States—but I cannot tell whither or how long;
   Perhaps soon, some day or night while I am singing, my voice will
       suddenly cease.

3. O Soul!
   Then all may arrive to but this;
   The glances of my eyes, that swept the daylight,
   The unspeakable love I interchanged with women,
   My joys in the open air—my walks through the Mannahatta,
   The continual good will I have met—the curious attachment of young
       men to me,
   My reflections alone—the absorption into me from the landscape, stars,
       animals, thunder, rain, and snow, in my wanderings alone,
   The words of my mouth, rude, ignorant, arrogant—my many faults
       and derelictions,
   The light touches, on my lips, of the lips of my comrades, at parting,
   The tracks which I leave, upon the side-walks and fields,
   May but arrive at this beginning of me,
   This beginning of me—and yet it is enough, O Soul,
   O Soul, we have positively appeared—that is enough.

[FOLDER 80. Seven leaves of blue laid paper (average 6 × 3½), faintly ruled on verso; a cluster of pinholes in the center. In the course of the heavy revision given this poem, a number of slips were pasted on several leaves, but these have now been loosened and hinged only at the left in order to permit one to read the rejected lines. After all the paste-ons had been made, Whitman numbered the leaves in pencil in the upper right corner (except for leaves 6–7 at top center) with the foliation 75 to 81. Leaves 6–7 (pp. 80–81) are pasted together hinged in the left margin. That they are about ⅛ of an inch wider than leaves 1–5 perhaps indicates that leaves 1–5 were once so hinged but have been cut apart. On leaf 5, for example, a few letters are cut into by the present left margin. Pasted over the foot of leaf 4 (p. 78) is a piece of the same blue paper (slip number 1), the recto now faded gray. This slip measures 2¼ vertically. Leaf 6 was first covered by two paste-overs, the lower (number 2), measuring 3 inches, being first affixed, and the upper (number 3) measuring 3⅛ somewhat later. About $\frac{9}{16}$ of an inch below the top of slip number 3 was then affixed another revision slip (number 4), measuring $1\frac{5}{16}$. Later, along the top of this slip number 4, and completely obscuring it, was pasted on another slip number 6, measuring $3\frac{5}{16}$. The unobscured upper part of number 3 contains two verses of the final text in a blackish ink crowded in, and seemingly not the original beginning of the paste-over slip, but added later. Slip number 6 also contains final text, although part has been deleted. Below number 6 was earlier hinged a slip (number 5) measuring 1½, its text deleted in pencil. This slip completes the obscuring of the earlier slips number 2 and number 3. Leaf 7 (p. 81) was first revised by a large paste-over piece number 7 measuring 5⅛ and completely covering the original text. Over the upper part of slip number 7 was then pasted another slip (number 8), this time of white wove paper, 2½ × 4, cut from the top of a larger piece of w1(b) paper, its right margin folded over and pasted under, and extending out beyond the right margin of the blue leaf. It is clear that slip number 7 was affixed after leaves 6 and 7 had been hinged in the left margin, and—one would suppose—at a time later than the revisory slips on leaf 6. Leaf 3 has on its verso deleted verses in a different pen and ink; and leaf 5 deleted verses written in pencil. A pink-paper draft of verses 53–55 is found in folder 45. For the text of these rejected verses, see Appendix I below. Appendix II contains the lines rejected or revised on the original leaves and successive paste-on slips after the initial inscription. 1860, pp. 451–56; Camden, II, 286–90.]

[*leaf* 1]

103—

So Long!

To conclude—I announce what comes | after me,
The thought must be promulged | that all I know at | any time
    suffices for that | time only, not | subsequent time
I announce greater days, | orators, bards—and then depart.

So long!

1. To conclude—I announce what comes after me,
 The thought must be promulged, that all I know at any time suffices
  for that time only—not subsequent time;
 I announce greater offspring, orators, days, and then depart.

---

2 must be promulged,] interlined in the light ink above deleted 'rolls through me, filling | me full,'.

2 not subsequent time] the verse originally ended 'for that | time only,'. First Whitman added in pencil, 'and is not enough for the | subsequent,'. Then in black ink pencilled 'and is' was deleted, 'not', traced over, 'enough' deleted, 'for the subsequent' traced over, and 'time' added. Finally, in the same ink 'for the' was crossed out.

3 orators, bards—] interlined in the same ink, with a caret, above the lower-line portion of deleted 'songs, per-|sons—'.

I remember I said at the winter-close, | before my leaves sprang,
    that I | would become a candid and un-|loosed summer poet,
5 I said I would raise my voice | jocund and strong, with reference
    | to consummations.—

O when America does what was promised,
When each part is peopled with free | people,
When there is no city on earth to lead | my city, the city of young
    men, | the Mannahatta city—but when | the Mannahatta leads
    all the cities | of the earth,
When there are plentiful athletic poems, | Southern and North-
    ern,
10 When through These States walk a | hundred millions of superb
    | persons,
When all parts away for superb persons, | and contributes to
    them,
[*leaf 2*]
When fathers, firm, unconstrained, nonchal-|ant, open-eyed—
    When breeds of | the most perfect mothers denote | America,
Then to me ripeness and conclusion.

O not me, after all! Rest not with | me!
15 I seek a man better than I am, or | a woman better than I am,
I invite defiance, and to make myself | superseded,
All I have done I give to be trodden | underfoot, to be the soil of
    su-|perior poems.—

I have established nothing for good,
I have but established these things, | till things further onward
    shall | be prepared to be established,
20 And I am myself the preparer of | things farther onward.—

I have illuminated myself for your sake,
I have offered myself to every one—I | have journeyed with con-
    fident step,

---

4 at the winter-close, before my leaves sprang, that] this was the original reading, all deleted and 'when I began, singing, that' interlined. When this was crossed out, the original was restored by inter-lineation in black ink.

2. I remember I said to myself at the winter-close, before my leaves
   sprang at all, that I would become a candid and unloosed summer-
   poet,
   I said I would raise my voice jocund and strong, with reference to
   consummations.

3. When America does what was promised,
   When each part is peopled with free people,
   When there is no city on earth to lead my city, the city of young men,
   the Mannahatta city—But when the Mannahatta leads all the cities
   of the earth,
   When there are plentiful athletic bards, inland and seaboard,
   When through These States walk a hundred millions of superb
   persons,
   When the rest part away for superb persons, and contribute to them,
   When fathers, firm, unconstrained, open-eyed—When breeds of the
   most perfect mothers denote America,
   Then to me ripeness and conclusion.

4. Yet not me, after all—let none be content with me,
   I myself seek a man better than I am, or a woman better than I am,
   I invite defiance, and to make myself superseded,
   All I have done, I would cheerfully give to be trod under foot, if it
   might only be the soil of superior poems.

5. I have established nothing for good,
   I have but established these things, till things farther onward shall be
   prepared to be established,
   And I am myself the preparer of things farther onward.

6. I have pressed through in my own right,
   I have offered my style to every one—I have journeyed with confident
   step,

---

4 poet] first written 'poem', the *m* being
smudged out while wet and the *t* mended
over it, the comma added at the same
time. Between this verse and the next
is the original verse, deleted in the light
ink, 'I said I would not forget you or |
The States,'.
10 superb] before this, original 'the most'
has been deleted.
22 offered myself] originally, 'reached my
hand'. The order of revision is not quite

certain but seems to have been as follows.
First 'reached' was deleted, and 'offered'
interlined. Perhaps at this time 'myself'
was tried after interlined 'offered' but
deleted. Then 'hand' was crossed out and
'love' interlined. Finally, in pencil, 'love'
was deleted and 'hand' tried beneath the
line, only to be deleted. Thereupon, in
pencil, 'my' was crossed through and 'myself' interlined above a caret placed before
the succeeding word 'to'.

While my pleasure is yet at the full, | I whisper *So long*, and take the | young womans hand and | the young man's hand, for | the last time.—

Once more I enforce you to give play | to yourself, and not depend on me, | or on any one but yourself,

[*leaf 3*]

25 Once more I proclaim the whole of | America for each individual, | without exception.

As I have announced the true theory | of the youth, manhood, womanhood, | of These States, I adhere to it;

As I have announced myself on | immortality, the body, procreation, | hauteur, prudence—As I joined | the stern crowd that still confronts | the President with menacing weapons | —I adhere to all;

As I have announced each age for | itself, this moment I set the | example.—

I demand the edifices of the govern-|ment, to destroy them;

30 Room! Room! for new far-planning | draughtsmen and engineers! Clear that rubbish from the building-|spots and the paths!

So long!

I announce natural persons to arise;

I announce Justice triumphant;

35 I announce uncompromising liberty | and equality;

I announce the justification of candor | and the justification of pride;

I announce adhesiveness—I say it shall be limitless, unloosened,

I say you shall yet find the friend you was | looking for.—

[*leaf 4*]

I announce the continued union of | The States,

40 I announce splendors and majesties | to make all the previous poli-|tics of the earth insignificant.

---

23 take] originally 'pess', which was deleted and 'press' interlined, this being crossed out and 'take' substituted in a fine pen with guide line to a caret.

23 womans hand,] originally, 'woman on the lips'. An *s* has been added to 'woman' and 'hand,' interlined in black ink above deleted 'on the lips'. The lack of an apos-

While my pleasure is yet at the full, I whisper *So long,*
And take the young woman's hand, and the young man's hand, for the
last time.

7. Once more I enforce you to give play to yourself—and not depend on
me, or on any one but yourself,
Once more I proclaim the whole of America for each individual, without exception.

8. As I have announced the true theory of the youth, manhood, womanhood, of The States, I adhere to it;
As I have announced myself on immortality, the body, procreation,
hauteur, prudence,
As I joined the stern crowd that still confronts the President with menacing weapons—I adhere to all,
As I have announced each age for itself, this moment I set the example.

9. I demand the choicest edifices to destroy them;
Room! room! for new far-planning draughtsmen and engineers!
Clear that rubbish from the building-spots and the paths!

10. *So long!*
I announce natural persons to arise,
I announce justice triumphant,
I announce uncompromising liberty and equality,
I announce the justification of candor, and the justification of pride.

11. I announce that the identity of These States is a single identity only,
I announce the Union more and more compact,
I announce splendors and majesties to make all the previous politics
of the earth insignificant.

12. I announce adhesiveness—I say it shall be limitless, unloosened,
I say you shall yet find the friend you was looking for.

---

trophe was a slip.

23 man's hand,] the apostrophe and *s* have
been added to 'man', and 'hand,' interlined in black ink above deleted 'on the
lips,'.

30 Room! Room!] the second exclamation
mark seems to be a later addition in the
light ink.

37 adhesiveness—I say it shall be] interlined
in black ink with a caret and guide lines

above deleted 'a'.

37 unloosened,] the verse originally continued with another line, which has been deleted in consequence of the interlineation made in line 82. This line read, 'love
—and that whoever you are,'.

38 I . . . for.—] opening and closing parentheses to this verse have been crossed out.

39 I announce . . .] above this is deleted
verse '*So long!*'.

So long!

I announce a man or woman coming | —perhaps you are the one,

I announce a great individual, fluid | as nature, chaste, | affection-
ate, compassionate, fully armed.—

So long!

45 I announce a life that shall be | copious, vehement, spiritual,
bold.

And I announce an old age that shall | lightly and joyfully meet
its end.—

[*paste-over slip* #1]

O thicker and faster!

O crowding too close upon me!

I foresee too much—It means more | than I thought,

50 It appears to me I am dying.

Now throat sound your last!

Salute me—Salute the future once more! Peal the | old cry once
more! [*end slip* #1]

[*leaf* 5]

Screaming electric, the atmosphere using,

At random glancing, each as I notice absorbing,

55 Swiftly on, but a little while alighting,

Curious enveloped messages delivering,

---

41 *So long!*] this, the original reading, was deleted and then restored. From verses 41 to 46 in the left margin is a brace made up of short separate lines deleted by cross strokes.

43 nature, . . . armed.—] originally, 'nature, strong in life, fully | armed, compassion-ate as fate.—'. The alternative 'death' appears above 'fate'. First, 'strong in life, fully armed,' was deleted, 'chaste' inter-lined above 'fully' with a caret, and 'af-fectionate' with a caret after 'armed'. Next 'death' was deleted, and then 'as fate', a comma being added after 'compassionate' and the verse continued in the line be-low, 'altogether content.—' A pencil ques-tion mark was later placed before this line, and another above the word 'alto-gether', this word then being deleted in ink. Finally, 'content.—' was deleted, and 'fully armed.—' written above earlier ex-cised 'death'.

44 *So long!*] this, the original reading, was deleted and then restored.

45 be copious, vehement, . . . bold.] origi-nally, 'be fully | bold, copious, resolute, spiritual,' | . 'fully' was deleted and 'open' interlined, only to be deleted. 'bold' was crossed out and interlined again with a caret after 'spiritual,'. 'resolute' was de-leted, and 'vehement' interlined above a caret.

13. *So long!*
    I announce a man or woman coming—perhaps you are the one,
    I announce a great individual, fluid as Nature, chaste, affectionate,
        compassionate, fully armed.

14. *So long!*
    I announce a life that shall be copious, vehement, spiritual, bold,
    And I announce an old age that shall lightly and joyfully meet its
        translation.

15. O thicker and faster!
    O crowding too close upon me!
    I foresee too much—it means more than I thought,
    It appears to me I am dying.

16. Now throat, sound your last!
    Salute me—salute the future once more. Peal the old cry once more.

17. Screaming electric, the atmosphere using,
    At random glancing, each as I notice absorbing,
    Swiftly on, but a little while alighting,
    Curious enveloped messages delivering,

---

46 its end.—] first written merely as 'death'.
Interlined to the left was 'decease' with a
prefixed question mark, the word then
being excised. 'death' was then deleted
and 'its fate.—' written beneath, 'fate' then
being crossed out and 'end' placed beneath it, this last word preceded by a
deleted false start, probably a misshapen
e.

47 faster!] later, an addition was written in
(presumably as a contemplated revision
of verse 48), 'I am crowded too | close!',
but this was crossed out.

49 I foresee . . .] between this verse and the
next is the verse, deleted in light ink, 'A
strange something settles through | me—
it unties me and disjoints me,'.

50 appears] interlined in the light ink above
deleted 'seems'.

51 throat] preceding 'old' has been deleted.

52 —Salute the future] interlined with a fine
pen.

52 Peal] interlined above deleted 'Salute'.

52 old cry] originally 'future'. Preceding this,

'free' was added and deleted. 'future' was
excised and 'wild cry' interlined, 'wild'
being deleted and 'old' substituted in the
left margin.

53 the atmosphere using,] originally, 'through
the air swooping,'. Apparently 'air' was
first deleted and 'atmosphere' interlined;
then 'through' and 'swooping' were crossed
through and 'using' interlined above the
latter.

54 random glancing,] first written, 'once appearing,'. First, 'random' was interlined
in black ink above deleted 'once'; then,
later, in the light ink 'appearing' was
crossed through and 'glancing' interlined.
The comma after 'glancing' is taken from
the undeleted mark after 'appearing'.

54 notice absorbing,] first written as 'pass
saluting'. First 'pass' was deleted and 'notice' interlined in black ink; and then,
as an alternate, 'pass' rewritten below the
line. Both are present in the manuscript.
'absorbing,' was interlined in the light ink
above deleted 'saluting,'.

Sparkles hot, seed ethereal, down in the | dirt dropping,

Myself unknowing, my commission obey-|ing, to question it
never daring,

To the next age, to many ages, the growth | of the seed leaving,

60 To troops out of me rising,—they the | tasks I have set promulg-
ing,

To women certain whispers of myself | bequeathing—their affec-
tion me more | clearly explaining,

To young men my problems offering— | no dallier I—I the
muscle of | their brains trying;

So I pass—a little time vocal, | visible, contrary—afterward a |
melodious echo, passionately | bent for, undying,

The best of me then when no more | visible—For toward that | of
myself when no more visible | I was incessantly preparing.—

[*leaf 6*]

[*visible portion of paste-over slip #3; black ink, the verses perhaps written-in
later than those originally heading the slip.*]

65 What is there more that I lag and pause? | That I crouch extended
with unshut mouth?

Is there a single final farewell?

[*paste-over slip #6, blackish ink.*]

My songs cease—I abandon | them,

From behind the screen where | I lay hid I advance per-|sonally.—

This is no book,

70 Who touches this touches a man,

(Is it night? Are we here alone?)

It is I you hold, and who holds you,

I spring from the pages—decease | calls me forth.

---

58 Myself . . . my] these were the original
words, but they were deleted and 'Yourself' and 'your' interlined. Finally, the
original readings were restored by writing
'My' and 'my' over 'Your' and 'your'.

60 me] original 'me' deleted and 'you' interlined, then 'me' written over 'you' to
restore the original.

60 I] original 'I' deleted and 'you' interlined;
this then deleted apparently while wet
and 'I' restored.

64 For toward,] originally, 'For it is toward',
the middle words being crossed through.

64 I was] first written, 'I am'; the 'am' deleted and 'have been' interlined in black
ink over a caret. Finally 'have been' de-

Sparkles hot, seed ethereal, down in the dirt dropping,
Myself unknowing, my commission obeying, to question it never
daring,
To ages, and ages yet, the growth of the seed leaving,
To troops out of me rising—they the tasks I have set promulging,
To women certain whispers of myself bequeathing—their affection me
more clearly explaining,
To young men my problems offering—no dallier I—I the muscle of
their brains trying,
So I pass—a little time vocal, visible, contrary,
Afterward, a melodious echo, passionately bent for—death making me
undying,
The best of me then when no longer visible—for toward that I have
been incessantly preparing.

18. What is there more, that I lag and pause, and crouch extended with
unshut mouth?
Is there a single final farewell?

19. My songs cease—I abandon them,
From behind the screen where I hid, I advance personally.

20. This is no book
Who touches this, touches a man,
(Is it night? Are we here alone?)
It is I you hold, and who holds you,
I spring from the pages into your arms—decease calls me forth.

---

leted and 'was' written below the line in
pencil.

64 incessantly preparing.—] below a space for
the end of the stanza appears the deleted
verse, 'I foresee—I peal one loud cry of |
triumph,' in which by inadvertence 'triumph' was not crossed through. Below
this, crowded in at the foot of the leaf
written in pencil and deleted in ink, a
pencil question mark preceding it is the
line, 'With my own voice I announce myself', a second pencil question mark being
placed immediately above 'myself'.

65 That I crouch ,. . . month?] crowded in
between the lines as a later addition.

71–72 (Is it night . . . who hold you,] these

two verses were written in the light ink
and placed, for lack of other space, before
verse 67, 'My songs cease'. . . . , an asterisk against them in the margin and guide
lines bringing them down to their present
position, also marked by an asterisk. Since
the asterisks and guide lines are written
in the same light ink, it is clear that the
position of these two verses was never in
doubt, and that they were written down
only where there was a blank space. Their
composition clearly was after the final
paste-over number 5 had been affixed,
since the letters of the first line are partly
on paste-over number 5 and partly on
number 2.

[*leaf 7, white paper paste-over #8, light ink.*]

O how your fingers drowse me!

75 Your breath falls around me like | dew,

Your pulse lulls the tympans | of my ears,

I feel immerged from head to | foot,

Delicious—Enough.—

[*paste-over slip #7, unobscured lower portion beneath #8; blackish ink.*]

Enough, O deed impromptu and secret!

80 Enough, O gliding present! Enough, | O summed-up past!

Dear friend, whoever you are, here, | take this kiss—I give it es-|pecially to you,

Do not forget me—I feel like one | who has done his work, I progress on,

The unknown sphere, more real than I dreamed, | more direct, darts awakening rays | about me,

Remember my words—I love you— | I depart from materials

85 I am as one disembodied, trium-|phant, dead.—

79 Enough, O deed . . .] between this verse and the next was originally written the verse, 'Enough, O fastened and loosened contact!', but this was deleted in pencil.

82 I progress on,] this was the original reading, deleted and then restored by interlineation. A dash after preceding 'work' has been crossed through and a comma substituted.

83 The unknown sphere . . . rays about me,] this verse was crowded in as an addition in the black ink. The latter part read first, 'awakening rays around me and about me —I progress on.' First, 'around me and' was deleted in pencil; then in ink the first two words were crossed through, the dash after 'me' deleted and a comma substituted, and 'I progress on.' deleted (the restoration being made in the verse above).

Appendix I

[leaf 3 (paged 77), verso. Written in black ink and deleted by two vertical strokes. See verses 47–52.]

Yet, old throat, one loud | cadenza!

Now for your own sake,— | for the past, and for | the future

O old throat! what have you | been? What are you? What | will be?—

Come! | one cadenza for your | own sake, for the past, | and for the future!

5 O thicker and faster!

21. O how your fingers drowse me!
Your breath falls around me like dew—your pulse lulls the tympans
of my ears,
I feel immerged from head to foot,
Delicious—enough.

22. Enough, O deed impromptu and secret!
Enough, O gliding present! Enough, O summed-up past!

23. Dear friend, whoever you are, here, take this kiss,
I give it especially to you—Do not forget me,
I feel like one who has done his work—I progress on,
The unknown sphere, more real than I dreamed, more direct, darts
awakening rays about me—*So long!*
Remember my words—I love you—I depart from materials,
I am as one disembodied, triumphant, dead.

O crowding too close upon me!
I foresee too much—It means | more than I thought,—
A strange something settles | through me—it unties | me and dis-
joints me,
It seems to me I am dying.—

1 throat,] a comma was the original mark; this was deleted and followed by an ex-clamation mark, this being deleted and a comma added. Above 'Yet' is the deleted false start, 'O'.

1 one loud cadenza!] 'one loud' is interlined in the first line above deleted 'O yet | one'. A deleted 'a' appears in the second line above deleted 'one'. The final *a* of 'ca-denza' has been mended from some other letter(s), perhaps *as*. After 'cadenza' the exclamation mark is an addition, and the verse originally continued 'to show | what we are—now'. This continuation seems to have been broken off and was then crossed out.

3 have you] 'you' is interlined as an alter-native above undeleted 'we' and a ques-tion mark placed before it.

3 are you] 'you' interlined above deleted 'we' and a question mark placed before it.

3 will be?] the verse originally continued, '—I do not' before being broken off and deleted.

4 Come!] above this is the deleted false start 'I' and then, to the right, the deleted sec-ond false start, 'Have you'. After 'Come!' the line first continued, 'before we es-cape,', which has been deleted, 'escape' seemingly independently before the rest. In the line below, 'let us' is interlined in a lighter ink above and to the left of 'one', as a continuation of 'escape,' |.

7 thought,—] following this and ending the line is a deleted 'a', the false start of a continuation.

[leaf 5 (paged 79), verso. Pencil verses, only partly deleted. See verse 79.]
[*deleted with a diagonal stroke*]

O brief! O minute | of us two. O secret | and sudden

1 minute] added after 'secret | moment' had been crossed out.

[*below, after a space; crossed through with a horizontal stroke.*]

O us two only! secret | and sudden—impromptu | and secret! [*no revisions*]

[*below, after a space; lines not deleted. See verses 79–80.*]

1 Enough O contact | abrupt and secret
Enough O fastened and | loosened twain!
Enough O impromptu and gliding present!
Enough O summed-up past

1 Enough . . . secret] first written, 'Enough are the s[ ] moment'|. 'is' was interlined above 'are', and then eventually 'O contact'. The word before 'moment' is too heavily crossed out to be deciphered. It is fairly certain that it begins with s and ends with d. Possibly the word was 'sad', but there is rather too much space for this to be plausible. 'sweet' is a very faint possibility. The following 'moment' was independently deleted, very likely later. Beginning the second line of the verse is also a deleted 'moment'. Above 'abrupt' is deleted interlined 'impromptu'. 'secret' is interlined above deleted 'aching'.
2 Enough O fastened . . . twain!] Whitman began originally, 'Enough on wo[ ] winding and | unwinded arms!' 'O' was written over 'on'. 'winding' was changed, perhaps currently, to 'winded' by writing *ed* over *ing*, and then the word deleted in favor of 'fastened' interlined above it. 'unwinded'

was crossed through and 'unloosened' interlined, the first two letters *un* then being independently deleted. 'twain' was interlined above deleted 'arms'.
3 and gliding] interlined above a caret. The reading 'gliding' is confirmed by the later version, although in the present the descender is so small as to make the letter look something like a carelessly formed *s*. However, there is little doubt that *g* is right.
4 Enough O summed-up past] the verse read originally, 'I depart from materials'; then this was deleted and Whitman began again, 'Enough o past'. 'o' was altered to 'O', and a series of adjectives interlined above a caret after it. First was a word which may just possibly be 'exquisite' but has been so heavily deleted as to be uncertain. Before this is deleted 'acrid and'; and after it deleted 'acrid'. The final 'summed-up' follows this last.

[*below, after a space*]

I take the immeasurable | stride of

[*below, and to the right, written at a slight angle*]

The work is | done

[From folder 45. Written in blackish ink with a fine pen and deleted by vertical strokes in ink on the back of the pasted-on upper section of the second leaf. See verses 53–55.]

Screaming electric, through the air swooping,
At once appearing, each as I pass | saluting,
Swiftly on, but a little while | alight< >

1 Screaming electric . . .] above this verse are two crossed-out false starts, 'I am' and, below this, 'Passing quick, by the way stopping,'.

Appendix II.

(Deletions made after the original inscription)

[leaf 4 (p. 78); originally inscribed verses on the leaf under slip number 1. See verses 47–50.]

O thicker and faster!
O crowding too close upon me!
I foresee too much—it means more than | I thought—a strange
　　disjoining | settles through me—it seems to me I | am dying.—
You, old throat! one cadenza for me—what I | have been, am,
　　will be,
5 Then to pass, to escape.—

1 thicker] *er* added later.

2 O crowding too close] the original read, 'O coming too fast'. First 'crowding' was interlined with a caret above deleted 'coming', and then 'O' was deleted and 'Now' interlined, this then being crossed out and 'O' returned. 'close' is interlined above deleted 'fast'.

3 strange disjoining settles through] first written, 'strange loosening settles | through'. First 'loosening settles' was crossed out and 'separating' interlined, with 'disjoins' interlined in the next line above deleted 'through'. This was excised but again written in before being deleted once more. Then 'disjoining' was interlined ahead of deleted 'separating', and 'settles through' inscribed with a caret above 'me'.

4 You, old throat!] 'You' is interlined above deleted 'O'. The remaining lines, and those immediately above, are greatly obscured by water which an earlier owner seems to have applied in a vain attempt to loosen the paste-over. Above this verse, separated by horizontal deleting lines, is the crossed-out earlier version. This seems first to have read, 'Yes one wild cadenza, still to myself, | looking back, t[ ] with firm throat, | to pass, to escape.—'. First 'firm' was interlined after 'wild' above a caret, then deleted and 'loud' written before it, this then being crossed out. Then 't[ ] with firm throat' seems to have been deleted, and 'something firm' written beneath it, only to be deleted. 'Yes' was excised and the following word 'one' capitalized. Above was written 'O my firm throat! One'; but then 'firm' was deleted and 'old' placed before it; and after 'One' seems to have been written 'firm', then 'fair' traced over it. Finally, the whole verse was marked out.

4 cadenza] some illegible word is interlined and deleted before this.

[leaf 6 (p. 80). Undeleted original material on the basic leaf underneath paste-on slips number 2 and number 3. See verses 65–78.]

[*under slip #3*]

What Is there more, that I lag and | pause?
Is there a single final farewell?
The echoes and songs cease—I advance entered out of them—it
    is very | still,
Somebody's breath is close beside me— | Somebody's heart beats
    against the | tympans of my ears,
5 I feel fully repaid enfolded,—O this is | exquisite—O enough!

[*under slip #2*]

Dear friend, whoever you are, here, | take this kiss—I give it
    es-|pecially to you,
Do not forget me— | remember my words,
I love you—but I launch myself | from you—I depart from ma-
    terials,
9 I am as one disembodied, triumphant, dead.—

1 What] interlined above a caret, the capitalization of 'Is' being inadvertently retained.
1 there] after this, 'aught' has been deleted.
2 single] interlined in pencil above deleted 'dearer'.
3 and songs] interlined in pencil above deleted 'have'.
3 cease] interlined as an alternate above undeleted 'subsided'. The word was originally 'ceased', but the *d* has been crossed through.
3 I advance entered out of them—] interlined in pencil above a caret, probably later than the interlineation of 'ceased'.
5 fully repaid] interlined in pencil above earlier-ink-deleted 'myself'.
5 O this is exquisite—O enough!] originally

the verse ended after 'enfolded—' with 'O this is | exquisite! O brief!'. Deleted pencil 'enough' appears above 'is'. 'Exquisite! O brief !' is crossed out in pencil and 'enough!' then added. Then, below the line, 'exquisite—O' was added in pencil. Below this verse the stanza originally ended with the verse, 'I have withdrawn, and I withdraw'. This is crossed out in pencil.
7 forget me—] originally ending the line, 'I must depart—' has been crossed through in pencil.
8 —I depart from materials,] interlined in pencil above deleted 'and from all that live,'. The next verse, 'I am as one who has done with | materials,' is deleted in pencil.

[leaf 6 (p. 80). Verses written in black ink on slip number 2 on the lower part of the leaf. See verses 81–85. This revision was later itself covered over by slips number 5 and number 6.]

Dear friend, whoever you are, here, | take this kiss—I give it | espe-
    cially to you
Do not forget me—I must de-|part—

Remember my words—I progress | on——I expire | from ma-
terials,

4 I am as one disembodied,

2 depart—] following this is pencil-deleted 'I feel like one who | has done his work'.
3 I progress on] originally, 'I love | you, but I launch myself | off from you—'. This was deleted in ink. Above 'I love' was later interlined in pencil, 'I go', the word 'progress' then being written in ink above deleted 'go'. In the next line, above and to the left of 'off' was interlined a word in pencil, heavily deleted in ink. The reading is uncertain but is probably 'today'.

After this, following a space, is interlined in pencil 'farther on—', the 'farther' then deleted in pencil.
3 from materials] following is the deleted pencil words, 'for reasons,'.
4 disembodied,] the verse originally continued, 'tri-|umphant, dead.—'. This has been deleted in ink, except for the syllable 'tri-' ending the line, which was overlooked.

[slip number 3 pasted on the upper part of leaf 6. Verses 65–66, which seem to have been added later, were left unobscured when the other lines on this slip, written in black ink, were revised by slip number 4 and then by number 6. See verses 67–80, and the original verses given above.]

The echoes and songs cease— | I entirely abandon them—it
is | very still,
Somebody's breath falls like dew around me— | Somebody's
heart beats the tympans | of my ears,
I feel myself infolded from head to | foot—fully repaid,—
delicious,
O, this, this is enough!

5 Enough, O deed abrupt and secret!
Enough O fastened and loosened contact!
Enough O impromptu and gliding present!
Enough O summed-up past!

1 cease] before this is deleted 'entirely'.
1 entirely abandon them—] interlined above deleted 'advance out of them—'.
2 falls like dew around] interlined with a caret above deleted 'is close beside'.
3 —delicious,] added later than the interlineation in the verse below.

4 this, this is] interlined above a caret. Preceding this is deleted 'O it is exquisite!', in which 'this' had been interlined above independently deleted 'it', and 'delicious!' above 'exquisite!', the whole crossed through.
5 deed] interlined above deleted 'contact'.
6 contact] interlined above deleted 'twain'.

[paste-on slip number 4, leaf 6. Cancels verses 1–4 of slip number 3 given above. Written in black ink. See verses 67–78.]

1 My songs cease—I | abandon them—it is very still

Somebody's breath falls like dew | around me—Somebody's
pulse | beats the tympans of my ears,
I feel myself enfolded from head to | foot—fully repaid—
delicious,
O this, this is enough.—

1 My] interlined in pencil above deleted
'The echoes and'.
1 cease—I] after this Whitman seems to

have begun with the letter *a* (*for* abandon
[?]), then mended it to *e* and wrote 'entirely', this then being deleted.

[pencil-deleted lines at the foot of slip number 6 written, after a space, below
. . . 'desire | calls me forth'. Dark brown ink. See verse 73.]

Birth, life, the interview, the | quick separation,
2 Such, and my rounds for many | a year through The States.

2 The States] *T* mended from *t*.

[pencil-deleted lines on slip #5 below #6. Black ink. See verses 82–85.]

Do not forget me—I feel like | one who has done his work, | —
I progress on,
Remember my words—I love you— | I depart from materials,
3 I am as one disembodied, | triumphant, dead.—

3 depart] interlined above deleted 'expire'.

[Leaf 7, earliest lines on the original leaf beneath the paste-overs. See verses
82–85.]

[*the following written with a fine pen and independently deleted by diagonals
between horizontal lines above and below.*]

Dear friend, whoever you are, here! | take this kiss,—I give it
especially to you,
Do not forget me—I must depart— | I feel as one who has done
his work,
I love you—but I launch myself off | from you and from all that
live,
4 I am as one disembodied, triumphant, dead.

1 I give it . . . you,] crowded in, and very
likely an addition.
3 and] interlined above a caret after a deleted comma following 'you'. Just possibly
the remainder is an addition. Above 'from
all' is 'henceforth' deleted in pencil.

4 as one disembodied,] 'disembodied' is
written above deleted 'disentangled', with
a following undeleted comma. Preceding
this interlineation and apparently in a
different ink is deleted 'he who is' written
as an alternate above 'as me'.

[leaf 7 continued; below the preceding lines, written with a thicker pen and blacker ink. Deleted by diagonal strokes, which continue to the lines below, as well. Written later than the preceding lines. See verses 65–84.]

Is there aught more, that I lag | and pause?

Is there a dearer final farewell?

The echoes have subsided— | it is very still,

Somebody's breath is close beside | me—somebody's heart beats | at the tympans of my ears,

5 I feel myself enfolded—O this is ex-|quisite!—O us two only! | O brief!

All have withdrawn—and I withdraw!

Dear friend, whoever you are, here! | take this kiss—I give it especially | to you.

Do not forget me—I | must depart. | —remember me—

I love you—but I launch myself | from you, and from all that live,

10 I am as one who has done with materials,—

I am as one disembodied, triumphant, | dead.—

1 Is] before this, interlined deleted 'What'.

1 aught] interlined above deleted 'any thing'.

3 subsided] preceded by deleted 'altogether'.

4 Somebody's breath is] interlined above deleted 'I hear some one breathing'. In this interlineation, 'I hear' has been deleted after 'breath'.

4 somebody's heart . . . ears,] interlined above deleted 'I hear a beating heart,'.

5 O us two only!] added to the verse after the deletion of the verse below, 'O us two only! All else has fallen | behind, and left us,' which is followed by 'O brief!' (perhaps an addition) left undeleted, its exclamation point crossed out and then restored. In this deleted verse, 'fallen behind' is interlined above deleted '[ed] from', the bracketed word difficult to read but perhaps 'divided' but may be 'darted'.

6 have withdrawn—] before this is pencil-deleted 'the rest'. Following, the line originally continued, 'but | how can I withdraw?' First 'how can' was deleted and 'when should' interlined, in this the en of 'when' being a conjectural reconstruction under the heavy deleting stroke which excised the revision. After deleted 'when should' was then interlined 'must', which was later deleted in pencil and 'am' interlined, followed by the interlineation of 'to' in pencil above a caret before 'with-

draw'. When these pencil revisions were deleted in ink, at the end of the line 'and' was written above deleted 'but' to produce the present line, the query after 'with-draw' being mended to an exclamation.

8 I must depart] the verse originally read, 'Do not forget me—I must depart—I | feel like one who has done his | work'. Before 'depart' the 'must' was deleted in ink, and then 'depart' in pencil. Above, was interlined in pencil 'depart from materials'. This was deleted in pencil and the preceding original 'I', and above crowded in, 'I must depart—', brought down by a guide line to a caret. When this was subsequently deleted, 'depart from materials' was pencilled beneath the end of the line, but then deleted. In the second line of the verse, '—I' was prefixed in pencil to 'feel like'. Then in pencil all the original from 'feel' through 'work' was crossed out, as were the pencil additions or alternatives, 'planted I have [   ] finished my work,' in which 'I have' is an interlineation. Finally, in ink, 'must depart' was crowded in below the first line, and '—remember me—' below the second, this latter written over the deleted pencil 'my work,'.

9 launch myself] following 'off' is deleted.

10 I am . . . materials,] crowded in in pencil.

[paste-over #7 placed above the whole of basic leaf 7. The lines written in black ink. The following are the undeleted lines which have been obscured and cancelled by white paste-over #8. See verses 74–78.]

Somebody's hand thrills me,

Somebody's breath falls around me like dew— | —Somebody's
    pulse beats the | tympans of my ears;

I feel enfolded from head to foot— | —delicious,—enough.

1 hand thrills] interlined in pencil above 'fingers thrill'.

2 around me] interlined above a caret.

2 dew—] the dash is added in pencil above a caret in consequence of the pencil deletion of original 'around' after 'me'. Beginning the next line, 'me' has been deleted in pencil and then in ink.

3 —delicious] preceding this was originally, 'fully repaid', the first word deleted in pencil and then in ink, and the second in ink only.

3 —enough.] an addition in pencil, traced over in ink. Below is the verse, deleted first in pencil and then in ink, 'O this, this is enough!'.

[FOLDER 81. Two leaves of thick white laid paper, ruled (9⅞ × 7⅝), hinged together with glue in the left margin. A few pinholes appear in the upper and lower middle. The paper has been folded once horizontally and vertically. Written in black ink. In the upper left corner is Whitman's diagonally pencilled 'Long Primer | middling wide measure' with a line drawn beneath the note. On the verso of leaf 2, written in pencil in Whitman's hand along the length of the leaf, is 'The worship of God is, honoring his gifts | in other men, each according to his genius, & | loving the greatest men best. Those who ['enjo' *deleted*] | envy or calumniate great men, hate God | William Blake'. This has been crossed through with a single diagonal pencil stroke. The poem was first published in 1871 but is included in the Valentine papers and, on the evidence of the sales list, came from the Rome Brothers shop. Camden, II, 164–65.]

[*leaf* 1]

SPARKLES FROM THE WHEEL
By Walt Whitman

1.

Where the city's ceaseless crowd moves | on, the livelong day,
Withdrawn, I join a group of children | watching—I pause
    aside with them.

By the curb, toward the edge | of the flagging,
An old knife-grinder works at | his wheel, sharpening a great
    | knife;
5 Bending over, he carefully holds | it to the stone—By foot and
    | knee,

[1871 *Leaves of Grass*]

Sparkles from the Wheel.

1

Where the city's ceaseless crowd moves on, the live-long day,
Withdrawn, I join a group of children watching—I pause aside with them.
By the curb, toward the edge of the flagging,
A knife-grinder works at his wheel, sharpening a great knife;
Bending over, he carefully holds it to the stone—by foot and knee,
With measur'd tread, he turns rapidly—As he presses with light but firm
  hand,
Forth issue, then, in copious golden jets,
Sparkles from the wheel.

2

The scene, and all its belongings—how they seize and affect me!
The sad, sharp-chinn'd old man, with worn clothes, and broad shoulder-
  band of leather;
Myself, effusing and fluid—a phantom curiously floating—now here ab-
  sorb'd and arrested;
The group, (an unminded point, set in a vast surrounding;)
The attentive, quiet children—the loud, proud, restive base of the streets;
The low, hoarse purr of the whirling stone—the press'd blade,
Diffusing, dropping, sideways-darting, in tiny showers of gold,
Sparkles from the wheel.

---

1 on, the livelong day,] interlined in pencil above deleted 'up and down,'.
3 curb,] interlined in blacker ink above de-
leted 'curb-stone,'. Above this verse a pencil # indicates direction for a space.
5 By] *B* is triple underscored.

[leaf 2, numbered 2 in ink at head]

With measured tread he turns | rapidly—As he | presses with
    light but firm hand,
Forth issue, then, in copious, golden | jets,
Bright sparkles from the wheel.

2.

The scene, and all its belongings—how they | seize and affect
    me!
10 The sad, sharp-chinn'd old man, with | worn clothes, and broad
    shoulder-band | of leather;
Myself, effusing and fluid—a phantom | curiously floating—
    now here absorbed | and arrested;
The group—(an unminded point, set in a | vast surrounding;)
The attentive, quiet children—the loud, proud, | restive base
    of the streets,
The low, hoarse purr of the whirling stone—the | light-pressed
    blade,
15 Diffusing, dropping, sideways-darting, | in tiny showers of gold,
Bright sparkles from the wheel.

6 turns rapidly—] 'turns' is interlined in blacker ink above deleted 'whirls'. The dash after 'rapidly' is a later addition made presumably at the time that original following 'the wheel—' was deleted.

6 As] *A* is triple underscored.

6 presses with light but firm hand,] originally the verse ended 'presses the blade, to the stone,'. 'to the stone' seems to have been crossed through and 'lightly but firmly,' interlined in black ink above a caret and guide line but then deleted in the same ink. Later, with a fine pen, 'with light but firm hand,' was written below the line and brought by a guide line up after 'blade'. Finally, 'the blade' was deleted in pencil and the guide line altered in pencil to join 'presses' 'with light but firm hand,'.

7 copious] a preceding *g* has been smudged out while wet before 'copious' was written.

9 belongings] interlined above a heavily deleted word that is very likely 'sorrows'. A pencil # above this verse and the stanza-number 2 indicates a space.

9 seize] interlined with a fine pen above deleted 'arrest'.

14 the light-pressed blade,] before this is heavily deleted 'molten yellow'.

[FOLDER 82. One leaf of thick white laid paper ($9\frac{1}{16} \times 7\frac{7}{8}$), which has been folded once horizontally and vertically. Written in a black ink without following the rules. Clippings from a proof-sheet of this poem were incorporated into sec. 2 of "Passage to India." For the details, see *Modern Philology*, LI (1953), 102–17. The manuscript is a part of the Valentine folders and appears to have come also from the Rome Brothers shop.]

Fables.

By *Walt Whitman.*

Not you alone, O Truths of the world!
But Fables—the splendid fables!
The far-darting beams of the spirit!—the | unloos'd dreams!
The deep-diving fables—the mythical | bibles and legends;
5 The daring plots of the poets—the elder | and newer religions;
—O you temples fairer than lilies, pour'd | over by the rising
   sun!
O you fables, spurning the known, eluding | the hold of the
   known, mounting to | heaven!
You lofty and dazzling towers, pinnacled, | red as roses, burn-
   ish'd with gold!
Towers of fables immortal, fashion'd | from mortal dreams!
10 You too I welcome, and fully, the same as the rest;
You too with joy I sing.

1 Truths] *T* triple underscored.
6 —O] the dash is a later addition.
10 welcome, and fully,] the comma after 'welcome' was crossed out and 'and fully', interlined with a fine pen. Later, another comma was substituted. Before 'welcome' a pencil-interlined 'fully' has been partially erased.

[1871 *Leaves of Grass*]

2

³ Passage, O soul, to India!
Eclaircise the myths Asiatic—the primitive fables.

⁴ Not you alone, proud truths of the world!
Nor you alone, ye facts of modern science!
But myths and fables of eld—Asia's, Africa's fables!
The far-darting beams of the spirit!—the unloos'd dreams!
The deep diving bibles and legends;
The daring plots of the poets—the elder religions;
—O you temples fairer than lilies, pour'd over by the rising sun!
O you fables, spurning the known, eluding the hold of the known, mount-
   ing to heaven!
You lofty and dazzling towers, pinnacled, red as roses, burnish'd with gold!
Towers of fables immortal, fashion'd from mortal dreams!
You too I welcome, and fully, the same as the rest;
You too with joy I sing.

[Barrett Collection in separate case. One leaf of pink paper ($8\frac{7}{16} \times 5\frac{1}{8}$) identified as p1 (f) ; pinholes in the center. Written in a blackish ink. The corners of the paper have been trimmed by some owner for inlaying. The first two verses are written in a much larger hand than the rest. At the left margin the verso shows some sign of original gumming. These verses have been printed by Bucke, p. 26 and reprinted in Camden, III, 266.]

As of Forms.——

Their genesis, all genesis,
They lost, all lost—for | they include all.——

The earth and every thing in it,
The wave, the snake, the babe, the | landscape, the human head,
5 Things, faces, reminiscences, presences, | conditions, thoughts
—tally | and make definite a divine in-|distinct, spiritual
delight in | the Soul.——

Of the arts as music, poems, ar-|chitecture, outlines, and the rest,
| they are in their way to provoke | this delight out of the
soul,
They are to seek it where it waits— | for I see that it always
pa-|tiently waits.——

Have you sought the inkling?
Have you wandered after | the meanings of the | earth? You
need not wander;
10 Behold those forms.——

2 all.—] the period is added after a smudged-out comma.

5 tally] originally, '—Such tally', the 'Such' being deleted in a lighter ink.

5 and make definite] interlined in the lighter ink with a caret above deleted 'in the soul to'.

5 Soul] s mended to S in the lighter ink.

6 the rest] e of 'the' mended currently over some smudged-out letter with a descender, perhaps a y.

8 Have you sought the inkling?] crowded in in pencil. The sou of 'sought' is written over some other letters, not now to be distinguished. After 'sought' appears deleted 'after', with deleted 'for' interlined above it.

9 wandered after the] originally, 'wandered far after your | inkling of the', the deletions being made in pencil.

[Barrett Collection, in separate case. Two leaves of pink paper ($8\frac{1}{16}$ and $8\frac{3}{8}$ ×
$5\frac{1}{16}$ respectively); a large number of pinholes in the center. Written in a blackish ink. The corners of the leaves have been cut off diagonally in preparation
for inlaying. This trimming has destroyed the possibility of identifying the
cutting of the paper; moreover, it has been so extensive as to have excised a
poem number on leaf 1, provided such a number had been present. On leaf 2
the poem number '100' is written above deleted '99.' On the verso of leaf 2
(seemingly a quite separate poem) is a list of numbered titles, which should
have been continued on some other leaf. The poems, but not the titles, were
reprinted by Bucke, p. 26, and reprinted in Camden, III, 267.]

[*leaf* 1]

To an Exclusive.——

Your tongue here? Your feet | haunting The States?

But I also haunt The States, | their born defender—I, determined
    | brother of low persons | and rejected and wronged persons—
    | espouser of unhelped | women,
From this hour sleeping and | eating\ mainly that I | wake and be
    muscular | for their sakes,
4 Training myself in the gym-|nasium for their sakes, | and acquir-
    ing a terrible | voice for their sakes.—

2 States,] a following dash has been deleted.
2 their] interlined above deleted 'a'.
2 —I,] interlined above a caret, perhaps in
two operations since a second caret has
been partly smudged out.
2 and wronged] interlined above a caret.

[*leaf* 2, *recto*]

100

Rapacious! I take up your | challenge!
I fight, whether I win or | lose, and hereby pass | the feud to them
    that | succeed me;
And I charge the young men | that succeed me to train | themselves
    and acquire | terrible voices for disputes | of life and death—
    and | be ready to respond to | whatever needs response,
4 Training myself in the gym-|nasium for their sakes, | and acquir-
    South, when | the rapacious tongue | will not be heard, each
    | age in its own dialect,

[*leaf* 2, *verso*]

33 A Handful of Air
34 As of Eternity
35 As of the Truth

36 Poem of Joys
37 Walt Whitman's Illustration.
38 Walt Whitman's Laws
39 Walt Whitman's Caution
40 A Past Presidentiad, and one to come als<
41 Poemet,
42 Confession and Warning.
43 Leaf.
44 Leaf
45 Poemet
46 Longings for Home
47 Voices
48 Mediums
49 Beginners
50 Tests
51 Wander-Teachers
52 Buds
53 Savantism
54 Prairie Grass
55 Mouth-Songs
56 Kosmos
57 Mannahatta
58 Thought
59 Thought,
60 Thought
61 Thoughts
62 Thought,
63 Thoughts
64 Thoughts
65 Thought
66 Thought
67 Song of Things
68 Orators
69 Leaf
70 Leaf
71 Leaf
72 Leaf

Index of First Lines

[*Note:* This is a consolidated index of first lines from the manuscripts, the 1860 edition, and the 1892 edition as represented in the "Camden" text. The latter is added to assist identification when the traditional form of the line differs from that of either the manuscript or the 1860 text; this "Camden" text is printed in italic as a distinction and as a warning that the texts in this volume differ from it in their first lines. Small differences in wording between different texts have not called for duplication of first lines unless some difficulty in identification could be foreseen.]

PAGE

PAGE